... under the Constitution with Liberty and Justice for ALL

The TRUE accounting of why the US has fallen into the depths of financial and moral distress and what we need to do to right the country, financially, economically, and philosophically

by

Alex Hussein Ahmedinejahd

Dedication and Thanks

I dedicate this book to my beloved who means everything to me; for the love, support, and counsel and for the faith.

I also want to thank PC for being a great friend and for giving me a sanity check and being my sounding board.

I also want to thank BK for being the devil's advocate and providing me with an alternate view, misguided as it may be.

Last but not least to my parents: My father for his perseverance, moral courage, unyielding sense of honor and showing me through his example that honorable people can and do succeed and my mother for her unwavering faith, belief and trust in me and for her many wise counsel, history lessons, and strong value system.

Copyright

Table of Contents

Prelude

"I pledge allegiance to the flag of the United States of America for which it stands, one nation, **under the Constitution with liberty and Justice for all**." – The pledge of allegiance as it **should be** recited.

"But when a *long train of abuses* and usurpations, pursuing invariably the same Object evinces a *design to reduce them under absolute Despotism*, **it is their right, it is their duty, to throw off such Government,** *and to provide new Guards* for their future security." – The Declaration of Independence.

"For imposing **Taxes on us without our Consent**." – The Declaration of Independence.

"**Neither slavery nor involuntary servitude**, except as a punishment for crime whereof the party shall have been duly convicted, shall exist within the United States, or any place subject to their jurisdiction." – The 13th Amendment to the Constitution of the United States of America (ratified December 6, 1865).

"... *government of the people, by the people, for the people* ... ." – Gettysburg address by our 16th President Abraham Lincoln, Thursday, November 19, 1863.

"I have a dream that my four little children will one day live in a nation where they will not be judge by the color of their skin, but **by the content of their character**." – Dr. Martin Luther King, Wednesday, August 28, 1963 on the steps of the Lincoln Memorial in Washington, D.C.

Do you want to know why the world is a mess? It should be obvious that it is because of the collective action of the people living in our country. Regardless, having traveled all over the US, in my experience, I will say that the vast majority of Americans think that they are not responsible for the state of our country, but, ironically, believe that everyone else is. Rationally speaking, we all know that this cannot be, but what's worse is that most people don't really seem to care. Also, the reason why most people don't realize that they are partly responsible for the ills of our society is because most people have been lied to all their lives. So, when confronted with the truth, of course, people get upset, because they believe that the lie is the truth and the truth is the lie. So, it seems to me that most people are twisted up inside and greatly confused without even knowing that they're confused. These lies start with parents, then teachers, and eventually "friends" carry-on the lies. Then, as people "grow up," they don't get the truth at work either and finally, politicians of all stripes use people's ignorance to take advantage, jast so they can get elected/reelected. So, it's not surprising that most people remain ignorant and unaware. I know that what I've jast said is shocking and greatly upsetting to most people, but let me state that what I say in this book is not a message of hate or a blame game. However, it is a starting point; the start of truth telling and laying waste to lies and deceits.

The other important point to note is that in reality, all the liars – except for politicians – are likely **involuntarily** reinforcing the lies that have existed for decades, if not centuries, by continuing to repeat them without much thought. Having said this, the people who created the original lies probably did so to sustain their own selfish political advantage. With all the lies told to people, it is no wonder that very few, if any, people believe me and, in fact, can't believe me, because everything is filtered through a paradigm built on lies. However, the other more malicious and viral disease that exists in the minds of the vast majority of Americans is the fact that most people *want to* believe all the lies told to them, because the lies make them *feel better*. In contrast, the truth is sometimes hurtful. And, when people hear that they are the problem that is pushing our country into misery, poverty and moral decay, they become angry and hurt, because most people feel like they stand for good, and good people don't create misery, poverty and moral decay.

Another potentially surprising argument that I make is that what makes the US a great country (barely, for now) hasn't been the average American in many decades, if ever. In fact what makes the US great (and somewhat continues to allow the US to flourish) can be attributed to a relatively small handful of people like Abraham Lincoln, Thomas Alva Edison, Albert Einstein, Henry Ford, John Pierpont Morgan, John D. Rockefeller, Medgar Evers, Malcolm X, the heroes of World War 1, World War 2, and other wars, and other very select few individuals. In actuality, I strongly feel that the average American is a drag on the growth and development of the US. However, let me be perfectly clear, when I talk about an average American, I'm not talking about an individual's intelligence, social status, education, wealth, income level, or career position, but about people's ability to think and their philosophical underpinnings.

To fully understand why the average American is the problem, the rest of the book has to be read, but essentially it is because of what average Americans believe to be right versus wrong and how people act based on their beliefs. To put it simply, it is because of people's erroneous moral philosophy and misplaced value system, which then translates into unethical behavior. Here are some principles that many Americans believe in – some of the more controversial points to be precise – that make average Americans the involuntary destroyer of our country. Most Americans believe that:

1) Two wrongs do make a right,
2) Stealing is righteous,
3) Thinking is wrong and one shouldn't do it,
4) Rules and laws are always right and should be followed blindly,
5) It is justified to have slaves in society,
6) Equality is Justice, i.e., average Americans are largely strong believers in communism, and
7) Dictatorship is a perfectly valid form of government in the US.

Not surprisingly, most people think I'm crazy and profess to believe in exactly the opposite of these ghastly principles. Most people also contend that I could not possibly know what they do or don't believe in; that we are all individuals and believe in different principles; that I have no idea what America is about; and that I'm a ranting lunatic. Also, many people think that I'm an angry person; I'm not. I did not write this book with perpetual anger or hatred in my mind. Am I angry about having my money stolen from me by force? Yes, but I don't walk around hating and being angry at everyone and anyone all the time.

Regardless of people's opinion of me, I hope readers finish reading my book to find out why this country is headed for the precipice at the edge of the deepest abyss. However, despite what I want or don't want, though, I suspect that some of people are going to read on because they are curious to find out what a "lunatic" like me has to say and to get a good laugh or to watch a tragic train wreck. Much like watching a shooting, a freeway car wreck or some other morbid tragedy, which holds people's morbid attention – BTW, I hate rubberneckers. May be others will read on so that they can have a clever and witty conversation about how some people will publish anything to make a buck. Finally, some people will read on to satisfy their sado-masochistic curiosity, the same ones who knowingly or otherwise torture themselves everyday typically because of major insecurities. A very small number of people will read-on because of their genuine intellectual curiosity. It is this group that I hope to reach and convince of the validity of what I have asserted. It is my fervent hope that this group can create the engine of change for our country, perhaps inheriting the mantle of Justice last held by the civil rights heroes of the 1950s and 1960s.

However, the long-term end-objective of this book is far grander. My ultimate objective is to change the entire philosophical underpinning of this country, and, perhaps, the entire world someday. Actually, and more precisely, it is to take it back to the purest and most original form of Americanism, yes, Americanism. What I mean by this is very simple: Most US citizens don't know what it means to be an American. I know that this is a puzzling and confusing assertion, but let me say what being an American means before continuing my dissertation: What should make an American an American is their philosophy. This is unlike any other country in the world where what makes someone a part of a country is the color of their skin, genetic make-up, or religious belief or some combination thereof. To repeat, a true American is one who believes in true American morals and values and acts accordingly; so, this means an American isn't an American because of the color of their skin, religious belief, ancestral heritage, bloodline, or anything that is physically oriented or religiously rooted. This means that being an American means that one should believe in the American philosophy. However, most people have never learned, never been taught or have forgotten what it means to be American, know what constitutes the American philosophy, let alone believe in the American philosophy.

But this isn't the only point about being American that people don't know or weren't taught; however, more to the point, what people were taught is very wrong, distorted, confusing, self-contradictory, based on false or erroneous assumptions, and ultimately extremely harmful to our country. Therefore, if I'm right that people are operating under a very bad philosophical construct, it should not surprise anyone that the majority of Americans are the engine of destruction in this country. Compounding this problem is the fact that most people have never really bothered to review their philosophical underpinnings or haven't done so since their early adulthood. In fact, I will assert that a vast majority of people in this country don't even know what components make-up their morals and values other than the very obvious and in a very perfunctory fashion. In fact, I will guess that most people have never thought about these important issues, at least not in any great detail. And, even if they have, most people probably didn't come to any useful conclusions. This would not be a surprise to me, since most people not only don't seem to think, but also don't have the ability to even attempt to think. So, the main problem with this country is that there are very few true Americans left that know how to think. It is my intention to change that and to help re-create America, Americans and Americanism as it was meant to be.

One last administrative agenda, before we get to the main body of the text: Let us agree on a few basic assumptions. Please take a pen (not a pencil or an erasable pen) and put a check mark in the appropriate box:

1) A rose by any other name would still smell as sweet and look the same ( ).
2) Two wrongs don't make a right ( ).
3) Stealing is bad and immoral ( ).
4) Taking what doesn't belong to you is stealing ( ).
5) Accepting stolen goods is wrong and immoral ( ).
6) Using stolen money to do good is no good at all ( ).
7) In the eyes of the government, we are all equal and must be treated as such ( ).

Reference

Also, throughout this book I'm going to use words that are not in the English dictionary. These words are designed to either erase gender references or correct a confusing philosophical situation. I'm not going to go into the explanation of the second point, but the rest should be obvious.

I will use the following new words that I created throughout the book:

- I will substitute all references to he/she with the word **hesh**.
- I will substitute all references to him/her with the word **hem**.
- I will substitute all references to his/her/hers with the word **hes**.
- I will substitute all references to himself/herself with the word **hemself**.
- I will use a capital "J" when using the word Justice or Just.
- I will change the spelling of the diminutive "just," as in "hesh is just a retard," with the word **jast**, so as not to confuse it with the word Just as in Justice.
- I will make all references to and derivations of the words judaism and christianity with a small "j" and small "c."

- I will make all references to the jewish/christian god with a small "g."

Repetition is by design

Throughout this book, I repeat some points, concepts and arguments. This is by design. I want to reinforce certain concepts that I believe are very important and repeat them to make them memorable to the readers. Also, by making the same points in different contexts I believe that I am making it easier for the reader to not only understand the concepts better, but also to help apply them in new situations that I have not thought of or laid out in this book. I know reading the same things multiple times can be tedious, but I believe that there are many new concepts in this book that are so important that they have to be repeated, so please bear with me. Thank you for reading my book, and please have patience, but most of all I hope that my book helps to vastly improve everyone's life.

Introduction

At the heart of Americanism is individual rights, not "social rights"

As a country, when did we forget this? By the way, in case anyone is wondering or has any doubt, the transition from a country of individual rights to a country of so called "social rights" is undesirable, very, very undesirable. In fact, the transition to "social rights" from individual rights is the most evil public policy change that man has conjured, short of communism. At some point in the last 100 years, we went from a country of individual rights to a country of "social rights." At what exact point in time this occurred is unknown. Was it when labor unions started, was it when individual income taxes were introduced, was it when the great depression-era "social programs" came into existence, was it when the 1960s "social programs" came into being, or was it when the latest healthcare overhaul was passed? All I know is that we are no longer living in America, and we don't have many Americans left because Americanism is almost dead.

The funny thing is that if I ask people living in this country, "Is a large part of being American about individual rights?" At least in part, a large majority would say yes. Yet, in reality, most people don't practice what they profess to believe in. In fact, most people say they believe in individual freedoms and rights but practice and stand for socialism. In other words, most people don't practice what they profess to believe-in; this should make everyone wonder if people are hypocrites, liars, lazy, unintelligent, uneducated or totally confused. Mind you, this is not necessarily because people want to be bad or evil, but I believe it stems more from brainwashing, lack of real rational thinking or jast having given up. This goes to point #3 in the prelude: People don't think or don't want to think. This lack of real thinking is what is at the functional heart of what is destroying America and turning Americans into anything but being American.

The process of how thoughtless action contributes to the destruction of our society isn't that complicated: When people don't think they have to listen to others for direction and leadership because they can't come up with their own thoughts. Then when people listen to others, instead of thinking about what is truly being said and what it truly means, people go with what sounds good and more precisely focus on sound bites that sound good for the individual in the immediate future, because most people don't have the ability to see past the moment because they don't truly think.

To be more precise, if people don't think then the only action that they can pursue is to see what the *immediate* benefit or consequences are to taking or not taking certain actions and pursuing that which is best for them in the immediate future. This then *unknowingly* leads to some very bad long-term decisions. This kind of behavior leads to some devastating consequences over a lifetime; some very simple examples: Getting drunk, doing drugs, having unprotected sex, over spending on credit cards, borrowing too much money in general, cheating, taking things that don't belong to them, telling white lies, et cetera.

Now keeping these simple examples in mind, start thinking about some more difficult to understand examples, such as taxes, welfare, economic, monetary and fiscal policies, corporate and investment strategy, and social and cultural construct, and we find that the amount of harm that is perpetrated on Americans is quite staggering due to the vast majority of people's inability to think.

In this sense, one could argue that in order to have true individual rights, and a well-functioning society based on individual rights, the one key primary necessity that must exist in jast such a society is for the people of that society to *think, really, truly think*. Most importantly, one must not only think, but do so in a truly *rational* and *logical* manner, keeping in mind that *everything is black or white, logic is everything,* and *Justice – never equality – based on inalienable rights is the only fair principle when dealing with people in a society*. Finally, even if a society is headed down the wrong path, if people really think rationally, the wrong can and will be righted; it won't be easy, but it can be done. However, the longer a country waits to fix their problems, the more exponentially difficult it will be and the longer it will take to fix.

Taxes

The birth of new American slavery: Consequences of the current US tax code

Most people don't believe that they do and certainly don't say that they do, but believe it or not most people in our country believe in slavery. Not only that most people believe that stealing is a moral imperative; even a moral right. Again, people may not think so, but I am confident that most people do believe in slavery and also believe that stealing is a good thing.

Let's start with some facts that we can all agree with, please put a check mark inside the appropriate parentheses using an unalterable and inerasable pen.

- Vast majority of the money that the US government spends comes from taxes. Yes [ ] or no [ ]
- Vast majority of taxes come from individual income taxes. Yes [ ] or no [ ]

What is the definition of slavery: According to Dictionary.Com, one definition of slavery is *"Slavery, bondage, servitude refer to **involuntary subjection to another or others.**"*

Under this definition, I am a slave, because I make a lot more money than an average American, possibly as much as 10x the average. This makes me a slave because my tax bill is disproportionately higher than the vast majority of others, and I not only receive less benefit than most from the federal government, I am forced to pay these taxes no matter what, despite the fact that most of the money that I pay in taxes goes towards benefitting almost anyone other than me and mine. And, if I refuse to pay, I may as well be dead, because if I'm not turned into a pauper by the IRS, I'll be a convicted felon then turned into a pauper.

I can hear all of the protests, condescending remarks, haughty comments, and all of the rest of the careless remarks:

1) You're selfish;
2) You can afford to pay more;
3) It's your responsibility to pay more;
4) You didn't make the money by yourself, so you should share it with others; and

5) If you don't pay, you'll lose it anyway because the poor people will rise up against you and take it away from you anyway.

Let me dispense with #1 quickly: Yes, I am selfish, but not the way most people mean it, which is actually self-destructive; the difference is that I am *truly* selfish. And, I wish everyone else were truly selfish too. This, in conjunction with the ability to truly think, would actually solve most of the problems in our society.

The thing is, when people talk about being selfish, what they actually mean is selfish in the short-term, which is actually, in many instances, self-destructive in the long-term. For example, stealing is considered selfish by most, but I find this to be a very self-destructive behavior, not to mention stupid. Most people will say that taking something that doesn't belong to them is a selfish act, i.e., an act that benefits oneself at the expense of another. However, is stealing a truly selfish act? No, it isn't, particularly if one gets caught. However, it is still not a selfish act when one doesn't get caught, because the individual ends up putting a price on themselves. Whatever item they stole, they are saying that that is the price that they are worth or, at the least, part of what their life is worth.

This is so because the thief is willing to trade hes life or a part of it for the particular item that they stole. How is hesh willing to trade hes life? What if the thief breaks into a home and the owner of the home shoots and kills hem? The owner of the home has such a right (assuming the gun is correctly permitted and proper warning was given before the shot was fired) and will not be prosecuted. On may argue that the thief doesn't always get shot and they don't always get caught. True enough, which is why I said "... or, at the least, part of their life is worth." The reason for why it's only a part is based on simple probability. If there is a 1% chance that the thief will be killed in the act of a robbery then the price they are willing to risk is ∞ (the price of one's life) for whatever that they were going to steal. But even if the risk of death is 0%, the thief is still willing to risk going to jail. Also, I would argue that the price of 3-5 years in jail for someone making $15,000 year from welfare isn't much; however, the moral price cannot be measured. In fact, I would argue that the moral price may be higher than the monetary price of being in jail for 3-5 years. To illustrate the price of morality, we need to look no further than our own history and the number of people that died defending our morality. For example, during the Civil War some 500,000 Americans died defending what each thought was moral and Just. In addition, the financial cost of risking death in prison is also very high: Even if it is only 0.1% above that of a civilian, the thief is still risking $∞. So, this goes to show that what people commonly refer to as selfish is actually self-destructive.

The difference between truly selfish people and self-destructive people is the difference between white and black. Truly selfish people don't do things that are long-term, or otherwise, self-destructive, i.e., they don't trade more for less and they don't willingly incur long-term pain for short-term gain. So, how does this pertain to taxes? Very simple: It's my money. I should have total and absolute 100% control over my own money. Everyone should want to control 100% of their own money. Everyone should have the right to all of their money and have absolute control over it. But the wealthy segment of society doesn't, which brings me to point #2: I can afford to pay and pay more than most others.

Yes, I can. In the same vein, a healthy individual with two kidneys can afford to lose one of them too. So, according to the argument, "you can afford to pay more," it could be rationally argued that the next time someone needs a kidney transplant we should grab any healthy person with two kidneys that matches the patient's physiology and forcibly remove one of their kidneys for donation. I can hear all of the indignation: That's not the same thing, money isn't the same as kidneys, the two are incomparable, et cetera. I don't know why some people articulate these uncoordinated or disjointed thoughts, it puzzles me. I'm not suggesting anything like that, but for some reason people think I'm stupid and that I'm saying that kidneys are interchangeable with money. I don't get it. I think some people say these off-the-mark remarks as a knee-jerk reaction to buy some time until they can come up with a more cohesive argument that they can try to use to defeat my argument. If it isn't that, it doesn't say very many flattering things about the person's intellect who speaks these quizzically disjointed statements. Besides making these puzzling comments, most don't have a proper argument to defend their unjustifiable position, which is that first use of force is justifiable. Jast to make it clear, the example about the kidney transplant has nothing to do with saying that money and kidneys are equal in anyway. However, the principle behind the example is that the ability to do more should not be used as an excuse to use force or compel someone to actually do more, NO MATTER HOW JUSTIFIED THE CAUSE MAY BE in anyone's mind.

Think of it another way. Tiger Woods can also afford to never win another major golf tournament ever again, because – from a golfing point of view – his position in golf lore is already secured forever, and winning more tournaments could be viewed as selfish using the same argument that the rich can afford to pay more and if they don't, they are selfish. What about the case with billionaires? Why shouldn't we take Warren Buffet's $58 billion and take all but $100 million away from him and give it to 57,900 poor people and we'd create 57,900 less poor people. For that matter we could do the same with Bill Gates and all of the other billionaires and we'd have a lot less poor people in this country. Jast to make it all legitimate, we should pass a law that says all billionaires and millionaires must forfeit all but $100 million dollars of their assets and we'll call it the Poverty Remediation Tax. We may be able to help millions of people!

I hear people saying two things to my argument all the time: "That's different" and "that's an extreme." First, it isn't different. If stealing a $0.01 up to 35% of income above $350,000 or so is perfectly moral and legitimate, especially to serve a "worthy cause," then why isn't stealing anything above $100 million to solve the issue of poverty a moral and legitimate act? Second, the objection that most people express is to the word "steal," stealing," or "stolen" that I use to describe the act of assessing and collecting income tax by the government. Also, many clever people challenge my position by asking the following: "If you are such a strong supporter of the US Constitution then how could you object to the US government raising income taxes, since it is guaranteed by the Constitution? For one, the Constitution doesn't specify where congress can or cannot use the money that it raises. And, second, jast because something is the law, it doesn't mean that it is moral or right. Also, I find that frequently the clever arguments are made to distract from the main point.

Regardless, I want everyone to understand that stealing is stealing; there are no two ways about it and no way around it. Also, it doesn't matter whether people call it stealing, taxes or fluberguble. A rose is a rose is a rose is a rose is a rose. And, by any other name, a rose would still be a rose, smell jast as sweet and have jast as many thorns. Jast to be perfectly clear, I don't think it will be a surprise to anyone that the multi-billionaires would not want to have all but

$100 million taken from them against their will, no matter what legal – but doesn't mean moral – means are deployed against them.

Most importantly, *just because people vote on it, it doesn't make it moral or right, either.* Also, in the future, who would ever amass a fortune worth more than a $100 million dollars? Individuals would be pretty stupid to do so, knowing that anything above $100 million would not be theirs to keep. So, the Poverty Remediation Tax would work once and only once. However, more importantly, the long-term consequences of the Poverty Remediation Tax would be devastating to our future economic well-being. If you don't believe me, look at pre-Margaret Thatcher UK when the marginal tax rate was close to or around 90%.

Some have argued that many billionaires are giving away their billions, so what's the difference? The difference is that one is voluntary and the other is forced. One gives the opportunity for making a difference in people's lives to the individual that earned the money while the other forces such decisions into the hands of those that had nothing to do with the accumulation of the wealth. Clearly, forced extraction of wealth is not morally correct, yet most people believe that it is because the politicians are calling it a tax and use statements like "the rich can afford to pay more," "the rich aren't paying their fair share," "the rich didn't earn the money on their own," et cetera.

So, I believe that I have proven that most people not only believe in stealing as a moral imperative, but also believe that there is nothing wrong with receiving and spending stolen money. When individuals get their earned income tax credit or welfare checks or Medicaid or other tax benefits and they take it and use it, they are spending stolen money, whether they realize/know it or not. For 35%-50% of the people in this country that pay absolutely no income taxes, all of the benefits that they receive from these so called "social programs" are 100% stolen money. To me, this is despicable!

Also, who's to say someone can or cannot afford something? Let's say that I have $1 trillion in cash and I earn a $1 billion per year. Can I afford to pay $990 million in taxes? One would think so, but who's to say that strangers that had nothing to do with earning the money or for that matter the politicians should decide what I can or cannot afford to pay and what I can and cannot afford to do with my money? I can hear it now: It's a democratic process; the majority gets to decide; you'll lose it anyway; you didn't make the money by yourself, et cetera. Really? So, if everyone else decides to jump off the Brooklyn Bridge, and compelled others to do so, who would argue that the majority was right, and therefore everyone should jump off the bridge? When someone says something as perturbing as "You can afford to pay!" this is tantamount to saying that they have the right to compel others to spend their money in the way that *they think is right*. And, what they mean by that is **forced charity** whether others want to participate or not. In principle, this is no different than me coming into someone's home looking at the individual's spending habits and telling them where they should cut back their spending, so that I can redistribute their money to other people that I think deserve it more than they do. And, if the individual doesn't cooperate, they go to jail. How ridiculous is that?! No one in the world would agree to be subjected to such an extortion scheme. Yet, when the politicians call it taxes and justify it through "doing good," supported by so called democratic processes, people applaud it and support it whole-heartedly. Am I the only one in the world who thinks that this is insane?!

What's the difference between politicians, with the support of the majority, stealing from the wealthy to give to the poor and a mafia don stealing for a life time and redistributing the money in old age? I can hear the howls now, "that's not the same thing!", "how can you compare the two?!", "that's ridiculous!", "you're stupid!", et cetera.

Well let's examine it! One major difference, a mafia don typically preys on the poor and lower middle-class people and gives it back to the poor and lower middle-class people, the vast majority of Americans steal from the vast minority called the rich. A mafia don seriously hurts or kills people, if they don't pay. The majority of American would have no problems if the wealthy went to jail for not paying extortion money called "progressive taxes." A mafia don is the sole deciding factor as to who lives and who dies, who pays and how much. The majority of Americans decide who has to pay and how much and who lives or dies. A mafia don doesn't give a hoot about right and wrong or principles, neither do Americans that support so called "progressive taxes." Really, what is the difference? Legality? So, according to this logic slavery laws, Jim Crow laws and laws prohibiting women from voting should never have been overturned. From my perspective, jast because something has legal support, it doesn't make it moral. No one should have any problems with this fundamental principle: Legal doesn't always equal moral.

Some people have stated that the democratic process is what makes the so called "progressive taxes" moral, not jast legal. However, from a rational viewpoint, jast because the majority wants something, this doesn't make it right; it may make it legal, but not always right. As stated previously, right and wrong doesn't always coincide with legal and illegal (look at slavery laws, the Civil Rights movement, and the suffrage movement, among others). Right and wrong must be decided by principles that are CONSISTENT across ALL cases, and issues. Principles should be UNWAVERING and STEADFAST. Similarly, jast because the majority voted to do something, it doesn't make it moral. As previously stated and argued, jast because the majority votes to jump off the Brooklyn Bridge, this does not make the vote moral, legal, perhaps, but not moral. Another example: Jast because Americans vote to bring back segregation, it does not make segregation moral as a public policy. This comes back to thinking and responsibilities. So, let's talk about responsibilities, point #3.

So, what is anyone's responsibility to society? Is it my responsibility to help all of the poor people? Is it my responsibility to help all of the destitute and under-privileged? Why? Because my parents worked hard to provide for me and my future and I was "lucky" to be born to parents that did provide for me? Then that's my good luck for being born to good parents. Jast like it was good luck that super-models were born to their parents, high-performance professional athletes were born to their parents, genius creators and inventors were born to theirs, etc. But let me say this. My father went through more hell to be able to provide for his family than the vast majority of the people in this country could imagine or would be willing to bear to have what he has. On top of that, my mother invested wisely to ensure that our future was well protected. So, why should others benefit from my father and mother's hard work and wise decisions, why shouldn't I and my siblings be the sole beneficiary of my parents' efforts? The typical answer is that I got lucky and should share my good fortune with others. This *may* make a good argument if we had a fair taxation system and well-intentioned individuals were seeking charitable donations from me – I don't think it does – but regardless, we are not talking about charity, we're talking about government policy.

So, then one may ask what is my responsibility, for that matter, anyone's responsibility to society? My responsibility is to do the best that I can do to accumulate the wealth and use that wealth for my family and my benefit. That's it. I know many people are outraged, but keep reading keeping in mind that my argument is that the current so called "progressive tax" system is highly immoral. Be mindful that what is best for me and mine may include making private contributions to individuals outside of my family. I will elaborate more on this later in my book.

Again, the extent of my obligation to society is to accumulate wealth and spend it wisely. Does the economy care who spends the dollar, me or the person who is benefitting from stolen money? No. Does society as a whole benefit more or less if I spend my money or someone else spends it for me? Not really. Does it matter if it is invested by a single person or spent by thousands of people, if not millions? Yes, it does, because it's better if it is invested rather than spent. Does it make a moral difference, whether I spend the money or the person who benefitted from stolen money spends it? Yes, it does. Because of the moral factor, it is better that I spend the money than the person who received the stolen money. And, if we include the fact that bureaucracy will siphon off some of the money paid in taxes then it is absolutely better if I spend my money. Regardless, the most important reason for why I should spend my money is because it is moral, while receiving and spending stolen money is immoral whether the source of the ill-gotten gains is known or unknown.

One may argue: What if I don't spend it, then what? The short answer is that it doesn't matter whether I spend it or not, because the money doesn't go anywhere, it doesn't disappear into thin air and it doesn't take a permanent vacation. At worst, it stays in my bank account or I invest it. If it stays in the bank then the bank invests it. Either way, the money doesn't disappear it goes back into the economy. Putting the money back into the economy through investments is better for the country as a whole than giving it to charity, because it helps to build and strengthen the country as a whole.

As an aside, few people seem to understand that the gap between the rich and poor must continue to widen. It's because the rich have disposable income, which they invest to grow wealthier, while the poor cannot and do not invest. This is a natural part of capitalism and, not only explains the widening gap between the rich and the poor, but also clearly justifies it. More to the point, *this is the way it should be*; no, **this is the way it must be**. It is a sign of a healthy economy, even though many people can't/don't want to believe it.

If we allow the people who advocate for getting rid of the gap between the wealthy and the poor to realize their objectives by raising taxes on the rich to "help" the poor, not only will we bankrupt the country, we will create far greater numbers of the poor than we as a country can bear. And, in the process, we will lose more and more of our country's wealth and the wealthy will flee to another tax jurisdiction, if they can. This is one of the main reasons why the US government won't let the rich give up their US citizenship so easily. This policy is a clear sign that the government – by which I mean the majority of the people in the US – wants to continue enslaving the rich. If the US government were to allow freedom of movement for the wealthy, how many would choose to stay in the US as a US citizen, if they can find a more fair tax system? So, what's the solution? I believe that I can come up with a tax plan that would not only keep the wealthy in the US, but also attract more from all over the world, and help the US stay the wealthiest country in the world leaving the Chinese, Indians and all other challengers in the dust, while elevating the OVERALL standard of living for the vast majority of American citizens. Big promise, I know, but one that I'm confident that I can back up.

Point #4: I didn't make the money on my own, so I should give some back to society.

So, exactly who are we talking about when people say that I don't make my money on my own? Second, how did I not make the money on my own? For argument sake, let's say that I'm a small business owner that employs 10 people. Who are we talking about when people argue that I didn't make the money on my own? The employees? That's right. Without the employees, I can't make my money, but then no single employee is indispensable, and I pay my employees to help me make my money. Others have argued that I owe my teachers, but I would argue that they got paid too. So, who helped me without Just compensation that would justify forcibly taking money from me through so called "progressive taxes" to help the so called "society?" So, again, we come to the conclusion that the remark about responsibility (point #3) and giving back to society (point #4) is untenable and facetious.

As an adjunct to this point, a really smart person once said in such indignation, "but not all the rich made their own money; why should someone who got their wealth from their parents keep all of it?!" So, the implication is that this money should be forcibly taken away and given to those that did absolutely nothing to contribute to the accumulation of this wealth ... hmmmmm! Forgetting about the self-contradictory nature of the argument that people make for stealing inherited wealth through taxes, let's proceed as if the policy of stealing inherited wealth through taxes is proposed with good intent and figure out if it really makes sense or not.

When I argued that the people who are benefitting from the inheritance tax did absolutely nothing to contribute to the accumulation of the wealth, the argument I got back was, well the children did nothing either! This may be true, but the parents who earned it certainly derived happiness from their children, and this happiness likely contributed to the well-being of the earner, which then helped the person to make money and, more to the point, motivated them to make the money. But this point aside, the fact of the matter is that taxing the inheritance and giving it away to people who had nothing to do with the accumulation of wealth isn't Just, period! Furthermore, the inheritance isn't about allowing or disallowing the children to benefit – which strangers should have nothing to do with deciding anyway – but RESPECTING THE LAST WILL AND TESTAMENT OF THE ONE WHO ACCUMULATED THE WEALTH. If the self-made person wants to give away their money to charity, the charity does not get taxed 70%! So, why should the children get taxed 70%? I think it is highly immoral and despicable that total strangers are treated better than the children of the person who made the money. Moreover, the poor should not be the ones to decide, how much the children of the rich should or should not get, let alone such matters being put to a vote to begin with. The money made by the person, upon death, should be allowed to be distributed in whichever way the deceased saw fit to distribute it, 100% tax-free to everyone who benefits. This is only Just and, more importantly, the wealth-creator earned this right! This has some implications for family planning and Social Security which will be discussed separately.

So, this brings us to point #5, the last point: If you don't pay, you'll lose it anyway because the poor people will rise up against you and take it away from you anyway. That is one of the biggest misrepresentations of history that I've ever heard. Revolutions don't happen because people are poor; revolutions happen because there is injustice. So, if anything, the revolution should come from the rich, not the poor, because the injustice is being perpetrated on the rich not the poor. In fact, the poor are being heavily subsidized by the wealthy at the expense of the future welfare of us all. Think about it! The rich and wealthy pay more taxes as a percent of income (note that I did not say income and capital gains) and pay more in absolute amounts, but don't have anywhere near the benefits that the poor and the middle-class have. Isn't this involuntary servitude or slavery? How many benefits do the poor and the middle-class have that the higher income earners don't have: Medicaid, welfare, earned income tax credits, student loan deductions, food stamps, et cetera. And now, the greedy politicians and their poor and middle-class allies are trying to steal the last vestiges of equality in tax law from the wealthy: Interest deduction for mortgages. In fact, I'm hoping that this book helps to wake-up the moral consciousness of the country and imbue the wealthy with the moral imperative to unshackle themselves of the burden of modern slavery. Ayn Rand was right; this country needs to learn a lesson: All wealthy people should disappear from American society then let's see what happens to the country's economy!

Bottom-line: There is no justification for slavery and there is no reason to prejudice one group over another. However, the US government does this routinely. Apparently, the current justification for the modern tax law is that as long as the government treats one group identically then it is OK for the US government to tax different income levels differently. If that is truly the justification then we should have no problems bringing back slavery of African-Americans in the US. As long as we treat *all* African-Americans exactly the same way, i.e., as slaves, we should pass muster according to the logic used in defending the, so called, "progressive tax" system.

I would also note that if everyone were a billionaire – i.e., have one billion dollars of net assets – in this country, we'd all be in the poor house. I know most people are confused by this assertion: People routinely ask me, "how can that be?" It's economics. The only way that everyone can be billionaires is if all of the wealth created is taken from the billionaires and millionaires and doled out to the people that don't have a billion. How long do you think it will take before the billionaires and millionaires stop creating wealth and take their money and leave the country? The other way is to print the money and distribute it. If either were attempted, the country would go bankrupt well before we get to the point where everyone is a billionaire, which would send us all into the poor house. However, the rich would at least be able to leave the country. Therefore, the ones that would get hurt the most are the poor and the middle-class; how ironic!

The FAIR and JUST Tax Plan: There is a place for government and there is a place for individuals and individual rights

So, what is the solution? There are poor people, there are rich people, there is injustice, and there is the government. Most people's solution to this problem is to let the "government" take care of it. This shows the immense ignorance of the people in this country. To put it simply, there is no government in America. This is not to say that the function and institutions of government don't exist, but the concept of the people or individuals versus the government in America doesn't exist.   The *government is the people and the people are the government:* **Government of the people, by the people, for the people.** It seems that most people in America have forgotten this.

First, let us discuss what the role of "government" should be. Because, clearly, the current form of government is absolutely headed for insolvency, both financial and moral. This is absolutely clear now; we are headed for Greece's fate, regardless of the resolution to the debt limit that was debated and resolved in July and August 2011, the budget crisis that's brewing in 2012, and the future of so called "social programs." Also, most people are thinking that this latest financial/economic crisis was the creation of greed on Wall Street, but this is about as far from the truth as one can get. However, the reason why the politicians feed people these lies is because people want to blame someone and Wall Street is the most convenient target for the politicians to present to people as the cause. Meaning, that it sounds plausible – though it isn't – and they can get away with it, meaning it sacrifices the least number of votes. What people don't understand is that the real cause of the 2008-2010 financial crisis is the average American and *their greed*. By the way, this does include some people that work on Wall Street, but by no means the entire financial industry.

Anyway, getting back to the role of government in the US; the role of government in the US should be to facilitate the lives of ALL Americans, not to favor one individual or one group over another. And, the rights and privileges afforded to all Americans and the obligations mandated from all Americans by the US government should be IDENTICAL, excluding criminals. No ifs, no buts, no ands. In other words, based on Justice all Americans should be treated exactly the same way by our government – EXACTLY THE SAME WAY.

From a tax perspective, this means that each American should pay *exactly the same amount* every year (adjusted for inflation), regardless of income level *for exactly the same service* provided by the government. Insane, ridiculous, untenable, impractical, unfair, stupid, I've heard it all.

However, if we understand what the government is supposed to provide us, my tax plan won't strike you as a very whacky plan after all. So, what is it that the government should provide its citizens? In my opinion, jast three services:

- Self-defense;
- Infrastructure; and
- Education.

That's all that our government needs to provide us. Why jast these three services? Because these are the only three things that either the government can and does do well, or must provide so that it will ensure that all citizens have a chance or opportunity for financial success/gain/prosperity. Also, it upholds the premise that we all have the right to life, liberty and the **pursuit** of happiness.

Anyway, let me explain as to why my vision of the function of government is the right one. Let's start with self-defense. Self-defense would include the military, security agencies, court systems, domestic security (police force), prisons, and any other institutions that help directly protect our physical well-being. This is easy for all to understand, agree and support. This also happens to benefit everyone equally or pretty damned close.

Next: Infrastructure. This includes roads, bridges, tunnels, airports, shipping ports, fire houses, ambulatory functions, waste disposal, sewage, postal service and other public works, scientific/economic research and a bureau of information. Again, these are services that the government can be very good at or are relatively efficient at executing. There are points of debate about garbage collection and postal service, and ports and airports, but generally, not terribly controversial. Also, note that this also benefits ALL Americans, and pretty much equally as well.

Scientific/economic research is controversial, but I think very justifiable. There are certain functions private industry cannot do efficiently, but is absolutely necessary for the long-term prosperity of the country. For examples, fusion technology, space exploration, basic scientific research, et cetera. The decision for which specific projects get funding or not should not be left up to the individual voters, but to the president, congress, business leaders and the scientific community, but the total funding amount should be left in the hands of the voters.

The other concept that needs more attention or discussion is information. What do I mean by this? I mean literally information: What's a good product, what's not, which services are good, which ones are bad, which companies give consumers a fair deal, which play underhanded devious tricks, et cetera. Everyone benefits from this, not only when it comes to information on pharmaceutical products, credit cards and banking services, airlines, automobiles and other consumer products, but also educational information like how gasoline, electricity, food and other items are made, distributed and *priced*. Also, line by line explanation of how tax money is spent would be very helpful, too.

One may argue that private institutions such as Consumer Reports can provide such services. And, Consumer Reports does a fair and good job of evaluating a lot of products, but it can't do it all. This is where the government comes in. Perhaps the government should fund Consumer Reports, which should be more effective and remain more impartial than a government bureaucracy. More importantly, if this program does what it's supposed to do, consumer protection laws would be unnecessary. For example, Consumer Reports and JD Powers have done wonders for American car manufacturers, and have made it very difficult for car manufacturers to get away with inferior products. However, if the government were to be directly involved, it must have the same independence that the Supreme Court enjoys, and must be isolated from the lobbying that politicians are subject to. For purpose of this book, we designate the government organization to be called the Government Information Agency or the GIA.

Also, information provided by the GIA should include video recordings and transcripts of all contract negotiations between corporations and labor unions and the same for all meetings between politicians – including their staff – and lobbyists of any and all kinds. Recordings would include any meetings between politicians and all constituents as well, and between and among the politicians or their staff. Transcripts and video recordings should also be provided for all negotiations and meetings between political parties in congress and between congress and the white house. If Wall Street, businesses and other private institutions are to be more transparent and accountable, and, by force of law, guilty until proven innocent then I strongly believe that politics and politicians should be subject to the same harsh light of scrutiny. And, certainly, if any group in the US is to be subject to careful scrutiny, it should be the politicians and lobbyists. If politicians have nothing to hide then they shouldn't mind being monitored 24/7. Of course, the exception should be made for national security discussions. However, what constitutes national security and what doesn't should not be abused, and the final determination of what is and isn't subject to national security cover should not be left up to congress nor the white house. It should be determined by the Supreme Court. Any congressional or white house personnel abusing the national security cloak should be sent to jail for life or executed for treason against the American people.

Public education is somewhat controversial and debatable, but incredibly important. So, I will devote a separate section to this subject and intermingle some other issues such as welfare, Medicaid, health insurance and other "social programs" that the government is perpetuating or is trying to perpetuate. I will note that a strong educational system is not only vital to the long-term survival of the country, but it benefits everyone, which is why it actually is an infrastructure project; an infrastructure project for the mind. However, it is not a widely accepted concept, yet, so I'm segregating it for now.

Regardless, getting back to the tax plan, I believe that every American should pay the same dollar amount, because every American would benefit equally from self-defense, infrastructure and education. This is what is at the heart of my tax plan and why it would work: Every American should pay the same dollar amount because the service that is provided by our government is more or less equally applicable to all Americans and everyone benefits from these services fairly uniformly. So, every American should pay the same amount for those same services. Also, if there are people that don't want to pay even this low level of taxes then they should be thrown out of the country. Let them find a better deal than what they get in this country under my tax system, philosophical construct and economic program. My guess is that people will be fighting to get into our country, once again. And, this is the way it should be.

The last point that I will make, at the risk of seemingly beating a dead horse, is that the more "social programs" we perpetuate, the more we borrow from the future, when we will need the money to fix the vagaries of the economy's fluctuation. And, the more we try to stabilize the economic base through so called "social program," the slower our economic growth will actually be, the weaker our future, and the higher the pain we will have to endure in the future to fix our problems, when it becomes no longer possible for our economy to live on borrowed time, borrowed wealth and bullshit philosophical pretense called "social" Justice. Justice is Justice is Justice, there is no social, no capital, no whatever Justice. Social Justice is a term made up by socialists that want an excuse to steal from the wealthy to give handouts to the poor for free, so that they (socialists) can benefit. Some older folks probably still remember those days when people were ashamed of taking government handouts and money from charities. Look at the country now: The people that are getting government handouts are now DEMANDING their money, and DEMANDING that they get increases, and DEMANDING that their benefits expand. Where do these people think all this money is coming from? May be they think it's coming from Alice through the rabbit hole! How ridiculous has our society become?! What's even sadder is when told it is coming from their fellow Americans their reaction is typically, "So?! They can afford it!" How ridiculous is that!? And, how do they know whether someone can or cannot afford ever higher taxes!? How pathetic is it that they think stealing from other people is perfectly normal and justified?! May be that's "social" Justice: Stealing to do good – the contradiction should make everyone cringe and laugh at the same time! Perhaps we should award every mafia don the presidential Medal of Freedom for stealing great loads of money during their lives then giving it away before they die!

Because, at the end of the day, if people support the theft of money from the wealthy, these individuals should have no problems with the mafia stealing money, as long as they give it back before they die. You may argue that "that's different!" But, please try to understand that it's not the legal aspect of the argument that is being debated! It's the principle of the matter! And, it doesn't matter whether the issue was voted on or not.

Not to sound like a broken record, but I can't make this argument frequently enough. ***THERE ARE CERTAIN RIGHTS THAT SHOULD NEVER BE SUBJECT TO A VOTE, LIKE SLAVERY, OR WOMEN'S RIGHT TO VOTE, FIRST AMENDMENT RIGHTS, ET CETERA. YOUR RIGHT TO OWN YOUR PROPERTY IS ANOTHER RIGHT THAT SHOULD NEVER BE SUBJECT TO A VOTE; PROPERTY RIGHTS SHOULD BE AN INALIENABLE RIGHT TOO.*** You may argue that the government has the right to raise tax money, but does the government have the right to extort? If I don't pay my taxes, what happens? I go to jail. You may argue that I should go to jail, but why should I pay money for goods and services that I don't benefit from? Because, I can afford it? What does that have to do with it? Anyone with two healthy kidneys can afford to lose one of their kidneys, so should we vote on whether individuals should be forced to give up one of their kidneys if someone needs it and people voted for it? People have argued that that's different. Really?! Aren't both examples about the principle of what one owns, what is yours, what is mine and whether or not others have the right to decide what we do with our own assets and property? Again, never mind the legality; it's the principle, and only the principle that matters. I don't think that anyone will argue with the fact that slavery was immoral, but it was legal, so did it make it right because it was legal? What about women's right to vote? It was legal to ban women from voting, so should women have been given the right to vote? If one argues that poor people must be helped then anyone has the right to do so, but don't force me or others to do it against our will and don't help the poor with our money. If someone wants to help the poor with their money that's fine, but don't take my money by force to use it for what they *believe* to be a good cause. To drive the point home, I don't think anyone would argue that Nazi law confiscating jewish property was moral, despite the fact that it was legal in Germany.

The other point about charities is that under my tax plan, with all of the money that is not taken away from people in taxes, they have the right to donate all of that money to charities if they want to, which supports the goals that they want, while I will invest my money, which is what I want. In other words, under my tax plan, everyone will be able to live their life the way they want to and spend their money the way they want to without interference, without subjugation, and without extortion. This is a true society of individuals and individual rights.

I will discuss some of these issues and points in more detail in future chapters. All I'm doing here is giving you an outline and summary points. However, keep in mind the principles presented here, because they will repeat themselves throughout. The first of the detailed points that I will discuss is the point of inalienable property rights, which I think may be the most important of all the tax concepts underpinning this book.

Jast one *"practical"* solution to the FAIR and JUST tax plan

According to USGovernmentSpending.com the total spending for the fiscal year of 2011 for the US government was some $3.6 trillion (typically pre-2009, it was closer t0 $2.5-$3.0 trillion and pre-2002, it was under or close to $2.0 trillion) against our GDP of $15.3 trillion or 25% of GDP. Of this, according to USGovernmentSpending.com, defense spending was about $880 billion (~24% of total spending), Medicare/Medicaid was about $860 billion (~24% of total spending), Social Security was some $775 billion (~21% of total spending), welfare was approximately $475 billion (~13% of total spending), interest on federal debt was about $230 billion (~6% of total spending), education budget was about $115 billion (~3% of total spending), infrastructure was some $95 billion (~3% of spending), other spending was about $180 billion (~5% of total spending).

Again, based on information on USGovernmentSpending.com, the US government's intake of revenue for 2011 was about $2.3 trillion, creating a deficit of some $1.3 trillion. Of the revenue: Some $1.09 trillion (47% of total intake) from individual income taxes, roughly $0.82 trillion (36% of total) from Social Security and social insurance taxes, some $180 billion (8% of total) from corporate income taxes, jast about $130 billion (6% of total) from ad-valorem taxes and $83 billion (3% of tax collections) from other.

Obviously, under my tax plan, the following federal spending would be eliminated: ~$860 billion in Medicare/Medicaid, $775 billion in Social Security spending, $475 billion in welfare expenses, and at least half of the $180 billion in other costs. This means that the federal spending will be reduced to about $880 billion in defense spending, roughly $230 billion in interest expense, $115 billion in education, $95 billion in infrastructure and $90 billion in other or a total of some $1.41 trillion. This means that some $900 billion could be cut from tax collections every year, in particular from top tax bracket payers. However, for the sake of federal debt management, let's say we only return

$600 billion in tax collections, using the balance of $300 billion per year to reduce our massive $15.6 trillion in federal debt. By the way, at this rate, it would take the country some 50 years to pay off the federal debt.

In keeping with my thesis, if we eliminate corporate taxes, reducing the government's collections by $180 billion, we can only reduce tax collections by roughly $420 billion. However, as we close out the war in Iraq and Afghanistan, I believe we should be able to reduce the military budget by at least $350 billion enabling the lower tax collections to be increased to some $770 billion. However, under my tax plan we would dramatically increase both infrastructure and education spending, and my guess is that education spending would have to increase to about $350 billion and infrastructure to about $250 billion, a combined increase of about $390 billion. This reduces the tax savings to some $380 billion. For argument sake, we are going to assume that there are approximately 140 million tax payers.

To summarize, based on the calculations above, the total federal tax receipts must be some $1.66 trillion ($1.36 trillion on actual spending and $0.3 trillion on debt repayment), which means that based on 140 million taxpayers, the per capita tax collection has to be some $11,900 or so. Obviously, for someone making minimum wage of $7.25 per hour or $14,500 per year the tax burden of some $11,900 per year would be outrageous and unmanageable. So, what can we do?

Before anyone proposes a tax payment scheme, we should figure out who's paying what. According to The Tax Foundation in 2009, the top 25% of tax payers or some 34.5 million people paid some 87% of federal income taxes, but is accountable for only some 66% of all adjusted gross income (AGI). As an aside, here are some other interesting statistics according to Wiki.Answers for 2010 (The data is also summarized in Table 1 below):

- The average tax rate for all 138 million tax payers in 2009 was roughly 11.1%
- Top 1% of all tax payers number some 1.38 million people
- Top 1% of the taxpayers (income of at least ~$344K) account for about 16.9% of all AGI, but pay 36.7% of all personal income taxes at an average rate of some 24.0%

- Top 1%-5% of the taxpayers (income range from $155K to $344K)account for about 14.8% of all AGI, but pay ~22.0% of all personal income taxes at an average rate of some 16.4%
- Top 5%-10% of the taxpayers (income range from $112K to $155K) account for about 11.5% of all AGI, but pay ~11.8% of all personal income taxes at an average rate of some 11.4%
- Top 10%-25% of the taxpayers (income range from $66K to $112K)account for about 22.6% of all AGI, but pay only ~17.0% of all personal income taxes at an average rate of only some 8.2%
- The top 5% of all taxpayers account for 31.7% of all AGI, but pay 58.7% of all personal income taxes at an average rate of 20.5%
- The top 10% of all taxpayers account for 43.2% of all AGI, but pay 70.5% of all personal income taxes at an average rate of 18.1%
- The top 25% of all taxpayers account for 65.8% of all AGI, but pay 87.3% of all personal income taxes at an average rate of 14.7%

From here the numbers get outrageously ridiculous in the sense that the rest of the country pays extremely little, but where the complaints are the loudest. Here's the data. After looking at this no one in their right mind should be able to claim that the rich don't pay their fair share.

- Top 25%-50% of the taxpayers (income range from $32K to $66K)account for about 20.7% of all AGI, but pay only ~11.0% of all personal income taxes at an average rate of only some 5.6%
- Top 50% of all taxpayers account for 86.5% of all AGI, but pay 97.7% of all personal income taxes at an average rate of 12.5%
- The bottom 50% of the taxpayers (income of less than $32K)account for about 13.5% of all AGI, but pay only ~2.3% of all personal income taxes at an average rate of only some 1.9%

How could anyone look at these statistics and claim that the rich don't pay their fair share!? This is the ignorance and perhaps the willful blindness of the average American and the effect of lies that politicians tell.

So, if we pile up the numbers, it turns out that the bottom 75% of the taxpayers pay only 12.7% or some $110 billion. Under my tax plan, using the above 2009 data, we could easily afford to eliminate all income taxes for people who make below $66,000, assuming the extra $300 billion in federal deficit reduction payment is not collected. In addition, we could eliminate another $100 billion in Social Security taxes for the bottom 75% of tax payers and still afford to cut another ~$116 billion in taxes for people in the top 25% tax payers. On a per capita basis, the top 25% would pay some $3,400 less in taxes per taxpayer or a break in taxes of some 15.3% on average. As a reminder, don't forget that the top 25% of tax payers start at some $66,200.

Table 1. Breakdown of US Income Tax Collections in 2010

Tax Payers	# of Tax Payers (in Millions)	Income Range (in $000)	% Adj. Gross Inc.	% of Taxes Paid	Tax Rate
Top 1%	1.38	>$344	16.9%	36.7%	24.0%
Top 1%-5%	5.52	$155-$344	14.8%	22.0%	16.4%
Top 5%-10%	6.90	$112-$155	11.5%	11.8%	11.4%
Top 10%-25%	20.70	$66-$112	22.6%	16.8%	8.2%
Top 25%-50%	34.50	$32-$66	20.7%	10.5%	5.6%
Bottom 50%	69.00	<$32	13.5%	2.3%	1.9%
Top 5%	6.90	>$155	31.7%	58.7%	20.5%
Top 10%	13.80	>$112	43.2%	70.5%	18.1%
Top 25%	34.50	>$66	65.8%	87.3%	14.7%
Top 50%	69.00	>$32	86.5%	97.7%	12.5%
Bottom 50%	69.00	<$32	13.5%	2.3%	1.9%
Total	138.00		100.0%	100.0%	
Average					11.1%

Source: Wiki.Answers; data may not add due to rounding

In addition, if we can cut all of the other spending, we could allow almost another $90 billion in lower Social Security taxes to be collected from the top 25% of all tax payers. This would allow an average of another ~$2,600 per capita in lower Social Security taxes to the top 25% of all taxpayers. This means that all told some $6,000 per capita in tax breaks could be given to the top 25% of tax payers under my tax plan, while completely eliminating all income taxes and Social Security taxes for people who make anything less than roughly $66,200.

Now, if it were up to me, I'd tax everyone equally at about $11,900 per person; at the very least everyone should pay at least 10% of their income in taxes. However, I know that the liberals/socialists who don't get it will object to even everyone paying 10%, but we can make it palatable for most people. What if we made it so that people who made less than $66,200 pay no more than 10% of their adjusted gross income then gradually increase tax percentage in a linear rate until the top 1% pay no more than the lesser of 25% of their AGI or $1,000,000 in taxes depending on their tax bracket to pay for the government's

$1.61 trillion in spending for the three key federal government services and reduction in the federal deficit? We would also largely eliminate Social Security taxes as well.

However, as the debt is paid down the savings from interest expenses should go to the highest tax payers first – i.e., above $344K only. Also, as the economy grows, and unemployment is reduced, we ought to see steadily increasing tax revenues for the government. Again, the benefit of this excess should go to reduce the federal debt first then to reduce taxes to the wealthy next, since the wealthy pay a disproportionately higher amount of taxes.

Certainly, they'd still be many objections and logistics to overcome to institute my tax plan; however, if people were to think about it rationally, few if anyone would come to the conclusion that there is a better tax system. Certainly, my tax plan is far better for the vast majority of Americans than anything we have today.

However, regardless of the tax system employed, it is extremely unfair and unconscionable that upwards of 50% of employed people pay no income taxes, while the top-1% are **forced** to burden almost 37% of the income taxes collected, while only accounting for 17% of the adjusted gross income. If it ended there, it wouldn't be as insulting and exasperating; what makes it even worse is that the bottom-75% receive the majority of the benefits of government largess, while the top-1% receive almost no benefits! And then to add insult to injury the socialist/liberals talk about how the rich don't do their fair share! And the liberals/socialists do so with such venom and righteous indignation, it is laughable almost to the point of comical, not to mention highly offensive. Regardless, ultimately, what makes the liberal/socialist position so poisonous and dangerous for this country is that the weak minded and the thoughtless actually believe the liberal/socialist drivel and act on these malicious lies and incredulously irrational beliefs by voting for liberals/socialists. Therefore, it is critical that this cycle of smoke and mirror politics and ever increasing government largess and extortion be broken for the betterment of the entire country.

We should vote to see if we want to bring back blacks as slaves and how many slaves each non-black family will get

For that matter, why don't we put to the vote restrictions on first amendment rights, the 19th amendment (i.e., woman's right to vote), and the right of the president to suspend the Bill of Rights, anytime he wants. The reason why we don't, won't, and cannot is because the Supreme Court has repeatedly reinforced the inalienable nature of these rights. Therefore, these rights will never be allowed to be compromised in any way, shape or form – regardless of whether or not the outcome of the compromise would re-confirm these rights – and must be protected at all costs forever. Regardless of the sacrosanct nature of these rights, many people don't believe in inalienable rights, because if they do believe in inalienable rights and so called "progressive taxes" then they are being self-contradictory!

There are certain rights that should never be abridged, tested, violated, or otherwise taken away. These are what we call inalienable rights. Certainly the right to one's own life and freedom, the right to say what we want and when we want to (except for very specific carve outs like falsely yelling "Fire" in a theater), and the right to vote our leaders into office should all be inalienable rights. So, the notion of whether we should vote on whether to bring back slavery or not should not be even in the realm of possibilities or considerations. And, I know that the vast majority of people will agree as a matter of course.

Now extend this concept to property. If something is legally owned like a home, land, jewelry, investments, cars, furniture, et cetera, should the owner be allowed to keep it? No, I'm not crazy. I'm asking this question seriously. What about money? Should people be allowed to keep the money that they earned? Should people be allowed to do with it what they please? Yes, I'm asking these questions seriously. The problem is that most people believe that they should have control over their own assets – all of it – but in practice, particularly when it comes to other people's assets, people vote differently, which makes most people highly hypocritical.

How is it that issues of slavery, freedom of speech, right to vote and property rights are all inalienable rights but the right to one's own earnings and what one is allowed to do with it isn't an inalienable right? To clarify, why can't I do what I want to with the money that I've earned or accumulated? Most people believe that I do have that right, but I know that I don't. And, I know that I don't have the right to do with my money as I please, because most Americans have already voted to steal a lot of my money. I can hear the outrage, but people's voting records speak for themselves. And, people consistently vote to steal whether or not people think that is what they are doing or not. Here's how they do it: When people vote for politicians that promise to give poor more government benefits through so called "social programs," they are voting to steal my money through the government sanctioned extortion scheme called "progressive taxes." Let me remind you again why the current tax scheme is nothing but a government sanctioned extortion scheme.

What happens to me if I don't pay the full amount of the taxes that is supposedly rightfully due from me? I'm ruined, because I can't make the kind of money that I used to make before getting arrested for tax evasion. Also, I can be sent to jail, and I lose my property due to interest and penalties. This is why it's an extortion scheme, because if I don't pay the taxes that are forced on me, the government will ruin me. The vast majority of people are saying that that is the way it should be for people who avoid paying their fair share of taxes. I agree, but who says the current tax system is fair? Simply put, the tax system isn't fair because the majority forces the minority and dictates to them where we, the minority, should spend our money without any accrued benefits to us. Put it simply, the majority force us to pay for their benefits from our hard earned money. In other words, it's like me coming into your house and telling you how much to spend on what, making sure that a large part of what you spend goes to my benefit and only my benefit. Would you consider this to be fair? No one would think that that is fair, if it happened to them. Yet, that is exactly what most people are voting for when they vote for so called "social programs" paid through supposedly "progressive taxes." How despicable is that?!

The problem is that when the majority (the strong) is given the option of taking from the minority (the weak), it will almost always happen, especially when politicians provide justifying rhetoric and get elected by promising to steal more and more from the minority, and the majority is told that what they are voting for is not only moral, but imperative for the survival of the society. Throw on top of this distortion the belief that it is good to be charitable, money is evil, majority vote is the only fair way to settle disputes, capitalism is failing and communism is an ideal and the gullible and thoughtless masses have no choice but to vote for the extortion racket that is called "progressive taxes," even though there is nothing progressive about it. Jast look at what "social programs" have done to the country over the last 80 years! Jast in case you don't know the answer, we are on the slow path to self-destruction; we are quickly heading towards Greece's fate. People jast don't notice it because our economy has been growing, but I will point out two things: 1) We could have grown faster, and 2) look at the last Great Recession; we can't even spend our way out of it because we are taxed-out from all of the money that we had to borrow to support our past "social programs."

So, what is the solution to the current tax "policy?" We should no longer allow people to vote on taxes and federal or state "social spending." Nor should we allow politicians to game the system to get re-elected. In other words, the so called "progressive taxes" should be constitutionally banned. We need the US Supreme Court to rule that the current tax system is unconstitutional on the basis that it is selectively discriminatory, property rights are inalienable, and most importantly, that the current so called "progressive tax" system is forced indentured service or slavery. And, because ownership of property is an inalienable right, the US Supreme Court must rule that the dispensation of property, including money, should not be allowed to be voted on. In other words, people that contributed nothing to the creation of the income or the wealth should not dictate how any individual must spend the money that they earned or possess.

Therefore, the Supreme Court of the US must allow federal tax collection for only those items that benefit everyone equally. These items would include self-defense (including the military, court systems, jails, security agencies, state department, etc.), infrastructure (bridges, tunnel, roads, scientific R&D, consumer information, etc.), and education (the best kindergarten through post-doctoral programs). It would be even better, if the Supreme Court ruled that "social programs" are a form of an extortion racket or a shakedown. As an aside, please note that I strongly believe that the educational system is a core part of the country's future and that it should be considered an infrastructure; the only infrastructure that helps to develop minds. However, given that the vast majority of Americans don't see it that way, and I haven't fully explained myself yet, I will continue to leave it as a separate category.

In addition, the Supreme Court must make the ruling such that politicians can't game the system and find loop holes to pass new tax legislation that doesn't belong. For example, calling Medicaid, welfare, earned income tax credit, and Social Security, among others, a "social infrastructure" program that requires funding. One of the ways that the Supreme Court can ensure that the politicians don't game the system is by decreeing that each tax dollar that is collected must be for the benefit of the individual from whom the tax money is collected. Some may argue that some functions such as Medicaid expanded to cover everyone are for the benefit of each tax payer, but I'd argue need. Does someone with a full-time job need Medicaid? No, as long as the job provides health coverage, which most full time jobs do. So, Medicaid isn't and doesn't have to be for the benefit of each and every individual. The next litmus test would be privatization. Could the service be provided by a private institution or charity? Certainly, Medicaid could be turned into a private charity or function, but the military could not. The other test that must pass muster is that of self-provision. Meaning, can an individual pay for hes own military and infrastructure? The answer is yes, but it would be chaotic and too disorganized to be effective. However, an individual can pay for their own medical service or insurance, their own retirement, their own children's needs and other needs currently covered by so called "social programs." One could argue that individuals can provide for their own education, but, as stated previously, let me tackle this issue separately.

Therefore, the US Supreme Court should order the federal government to turn all of the so called "social programs" into privately run charities. Functions like Medicaid, Medicare, Social Security, welfare, food stamps and other supposed "social programs" should be turned into private charities, given that these programs are indeed charities. This is critically important.

The main concern in turning these so called "social programs" into private charities is that they will be starved of funding. However, given that they have to compete with all of the other charities, certainly, there is a high probability that these organizations would be made more efficient, which means that much of the reduction in funding could be offset by cost cuts. Regardless, the privatization of these institutions is of paramount importance. Also, if anyone is concerned about these organizations being starved of funding, they can donate the tax savings that they achieve under my plan to these various organizations. However, most importantly, everyone can pick and choose – or not choose at all – which charities to donate money to and how much based on what they believe is important and meaningful, instead of being blindly forced into supporting all these charities. This way **everyone can live the life that they want to**, exercising their moral judgment and philosophical prerogative the way they want to instead of being forced to abide by other people's judgments, objectives, desires and greed.

A particularly important tax issue that impacts Social Security is the care of our elderly in a privatized charity world. In conjunction, we have to consider inheritance issues and the independence of our elderly, which I discuss next.

Families should be allowed to support their own without tax consequences; this is vital to the long-term survivability and well-being of our country

Many have said that if we make Social Security a private charity program that many seniors will end up on the streets. I doubt that, but I do believe that it will cause many seniors a lot of pain, especially during economically difficult times. To devise a solution to this problem, we have to also think about the mentality of Americans toward seniors, which is absolutely appalling: Seniors are viewed similarly to obsolete technology, throw it out and go on to the next best technology or product. It's disgusting!

Yes, with technology, we ought to move on to the next best thing, no question. However, with seniors, even though we should move on to the next generation to actually do the work, we must keep our elders in positions of honor and counsel. Our elders have lived through many life experiences that are important to revisit, study, understand and learn from. However, this doesn't mean that they are in the best position to do the work, but it does mean that their perspective and experiences can be valuable and deserves respect. America needs to understand this, appreciate this, respect this and actually do something about this. But, most people are very condescending, disrespectful and patronizing to our elders and this makes our elders resent us and many seniors become hostile to the younger generations in return.

No one should be made to feel useless, because, in reality, virtually no one is useless. The young have the innocence, imagination and dreams; youths have the idealism, vitality and energy; adults are more thoughtful, have more knowledge and have better judgment, at least in theory; and the elderly have history, experience and perspective, again, at least in theory. The human being that can contain all of the characteristics of the young, youths, adults and the elderly will be a very valuable entity in society. The only ones that are capable of containing all four attributes are adults and the elderly, but the elderly lack the physical (and sometimes the mental) vigor to execute, so adults naturally become the pinnacle of value to our society. This doesn't mean that adults can be at their best without the perspectives and experiences of the elderly. Therefore, we conclude again that the elderly must be treated with dignity, respect and honor. But our society has reduced them to charity cases to be pitied and otherwise brushed aside. No wonder that AARP is not only one of the most active lobby groups in Washington DC, but wield a lot of power and use that power to protect the "rights" of the elderly, sometimes at the burden of the entire country. All this inter-generational hostility and confrontation are a waste of time, money and effort and must be stopped and changed.

One mitigating action that we can take to protect our elders when Social Security is turned into a private charity is to incentivize and allow Americans to protect and provide for their own. How is it that when we give money to strangers, we can deduct this from our taxes, but when we provide for our kin, we have to pay gift taxes then on top of that our kin have to pay income taxes above $12,000/year? How screwed up and twisted is that?! The government is telling us that we must care more for strangers than our own family! This obscenity should make everyone very angry!

The solution is very simple. We must allow Americans to financially take care of their parents without tax consequences, and without cumbersome requirements for allowing these financial arrangements, such as the requirement of living together in the same household. Regardless of living arrangements, an American should be allowed to take any amount of pretax dollars and send it directly to their parents' bank account without tax consequences to the individual. However, since the children are sending pretax dollars to their parents, the parents must be responsible for paying their own taxes. In addition, regardless of living arrangements, parents should be allowed into their children's medical insurance program. This will allow a lot more security for both the parents and our society. It will also emphasize the importance of family to the long-term health of our country. Most importantly, this should help stabilize the financial status of our elders and take away a lot of their fear in the new world of privatized Social Security and Medicare. This financial and medical benefit program should also be extended to grandparents, great-grand parents and as far up as one has living ancestors. And, it should extend as far down – as in children, grand-children, great grand-children, etc. – as possible as well.

What I mean by the last sentence is that parents, grandparents, great-grand parents, et cetera, should be allowed to give as much inheritance to their children, grandchildren, great-grandchildren, et cetera, as they please without any tax consequences to anyone. No inheritance taxes, no gift taxes, no income taxes, no extortion taxes of any amount. This is not only morally correct, but it reinforces the importance of family and family unit, yet again.

Many that I've discussed the problem of privatizing Social Security with argue that the children did absolutely nothing to deserve the money that their ancestors made, so they shouldn't be allowed to take the money for free, and besides, they don't need all that money to survive, so why should they keep it? Then let me ask a critically important question: Who deserves the money? The poor, the infirm, the disabled, the sick, any stranger that did less than nothing – if the children did nothing to deserve the money then strangers must have done less than nothing! Why do they deserve it?! Because they need it? So, again, if someone needs a kidney should we forcibly remove a kidney from the first healthy eligible donor with two kidneys because someone else needs one? Again, the principle and metaphor behind money and kidneys aren't whether money and kidneys can be used as substitutes, but it is about the principle of ownership. Meaning who has the right to one's own assets and who controls how it is used? Additionally, the point is that if I accumulate a billion dollars in net assets and I die at the ripe old age of 85, why do people want to dishonor my last will and testament? And, why is it nobler for me to give it away to strangers than to keep it in the family? Sacrifice? By definition, sacrifice means giving away more in return for less. Why would anyone do that? More importantly, why would anyone force others to make any sacrifices against their will? When sacrifices are made, by definition, value is destroyed and an evil is being perpetuated when value is wantonly destroyed. In addition, divvying up a billion dollars among millions has no real benefit, while concentrating it in one, two or even several children's control could do a lot of good in terms of creating wealth through investments. And, no money will be siphoned-off by the highly inefficient bureaucracy that is embodied in so called government run so called "social programs." Don't forget that every time a layer of bureaucracy is introduced between starting and end point, it costs money, and causes waste. This is not productive.

The point is that, currently, the money that I earn isn't really mine and mine to do as I please. It's an illusion that the politicians (with their socialist/liberal and poor allies) have created to make individuals feel like they own the wealth – when they really don't – with the intention of stealing the wealth from the individuals that earned it when they die. This way the politicians (again with their socialist/liberal and poor allies) can make people work hard to create the wealth, which they can then steal after the individuals die. The fact of the matter is that when a wealthy individual leaves the money to whomever (whether it is to his own children, charities or other institutions) and it happens, we are respecting the will of the person who created the wealth. However, when the IRS takes it away from them by force then the country is not only disrespecting the individual, but Americans are also committing an act of great immorality, perhaps the only immoral act in the world, stealing. Think about it carefully, the only act that is criminal or immoral is theft. Even murder is theft.

Anyway, let me repeat the question: Why should strangers that had nothing to do with earning the money not only be the determinant of how the created wealth is used, but also the beneficiary? Why shouldn't the ultimate determination of the use of the wealth be the sole prerogative of only the one who created the wealth? As a matter of fact, why should the dispensation of someone's wealth be subject to voting? Isn't this the principle that communists want to exercise? Think about it. When people agree to vote on how to use other people's money, they are advocating for stealing. It doesn't matter whether it is called taxes, stealing, coercion, blackmail, or gatewargkorim, the principle of stealing still applies: Taking something from someone against their will is stealing. And, the end use of the money is irrelevant, unless individuals believe that an initial act of immorality is justified, if the end action results in an act which they believe to be moral, i.e., the ends justify the means. If people believe this then they must believe that elderly mafia dons are good people who do good things.

The issue at hand is quite simple: Do we or do we not allow deception, theft and immorality as a way of life? Do we allow our country to be made-up of parasites or not? If we don't want to be a part of a parasitic society then, when it comes to family and family values, we, as a country, must allow every family to take care of their own in the manner that best fits their ideology. Period, full stop, the end. We cannot continue to allow the illusion that the wealth that one creates is one's own to do as one pleases when in fact that it is actually the furthest from the truth. We have to stop this lie and allow everyone the freedom to take care of themselves and theirs, and most importantly, for everyone to live their own philosophical beliefs, much like everyone has the right to believe in their own religion.

This is very American and the cornerstone of individual rights and, what I call, Americanism. This is particularly true given the fact that there is very little difference, if any, between philosophy and religion. In fact, the only significant difference is the deity factor. Both try to teach the way people should live based on a moral-value system that the philosophy or religion believes is the paramount truth and the "fountain" of all that is life. In the case of religion, it is a deity; while in the case of a philosophy, it is some fundamental/immovable/unwavering principle or principles.

This means that in our society, the judeo-christian philosophy/religion is the cornerstone of why and how our society functions and why the people "think" and behave the way they do. So, given that our society is extremely screwed up, what does that say about the judeo-christian philosophy/religion? I will answer the question first, but provide the explanation as to why it is so later on in the book. The answer to the question previously asked is that the *judeo-christian religion/philosophy is the root of all evil*, at least in western society.

Regardless, when it comes to taxes there are really only two questions that need to be asked and answered: 1) Who owns the money that was earned and is being taxed, and 2) does the money being collected for taxes directly accrue to the benefit of the one paying the taxes. If the answers aren't: 1) The person who earned it, and 2) Yes, then an injustice(s) exist and must be righted. In the case of inherited wealth, the only question that needs to be asked is: Was the wealth distributed according to the last will and testament of the one who created it? If the answer is anything but yes then, again, we have an unjust situation that must be corrected.

I've asserted that the poor don't rebel because they are poor, but because they have been treated with injustice, but where's the proof?

The classic example that people give for asserting that the poor rebel because of poverty is the Russian revolution. Many people are told and believe that the Russian peasants revolted because of their living conditions, which stemmed from poverty. However, the reality of the matter couldn't be further from the truth. The peasants didn't revolt against the Czar because they were poor, but because they were being treated unfairly or unjustly. They were forced into conscription to fight a war that, ultimately, meant nothing to them, their taxes were raised to fund the war, there was massive corruption at all levels of the government and poor people were treated worse than dirt by the bureaucracy, the government and the so called "nobility" – there was nothing noble about these people in many instances. But, it could be argued that the Russian revolution is far removed from our daily and current lives, and so it may be argued that it's not a good example. OK, how about Mohammed Wazizi? This is the hero that self-immolated in Tunisia that provided the spark for its revolution, which then served as the impetus for the revolution in Egypt, Libya, and now, Syria and brought about the movement called the Arab Spring.

The manipulators, e.g., liberal/socialist politicians that want to continue spending money by stealing from the wealthy will say that Mohammed was poor and revolted against his poverty, but, again, nothing could be further from the truth. According to investigations made by news agencies – which are not conservative – they concluded that Mohammed self-immolated to protest the corruption of the Tunisian government, not because he was poor.

The facts are as follows according to one investigative journalist's account of the historical incident. Mohammed made a living selling fruit. However, he did it illegally since Tunisian law required vendors to secure a government issued permit to do so, and he didn't have one since permits were very difficult to come by and costly – implication was that it required a lot of bribes. Using the lack of a permit as an excuse, a female government bureaucrat would come by and occasionally confiscate Mr. Wazizi's scale in the "name of the law." In reality, the female bureaucrat was looking for a bribe and was holding the scale as a bargaining chip, i.e., she was running an extortion racquet, similar to the protection racquets perpetuated on poor Italian immigrants in the early 20th century by the mafia in America. Apparently, she had done this to Mohammed several times in the past and was rewarded by him. There is another lesson to be learned about appeasement, but it is better left for another time.

Anyway, as the investigative journalist tells the story, and corroborated by friends and relatives, Mr. Wazizi had had enough. After repeated protests and official filings, he snapped having failed to get Justice from the government, so he decided to self-immolate to protest the injustice perpetrated on him. Had the government stepped in and imprisoned the woman for corruption and extortion, Mohammed would not have self-immolated, Tunisia would not have spontaneously risen up against the dictator, Egypt would not have exploded, Libya would also be business as usual, and Syria would not be at the brink of a potentially new era.

So, this is the evidence that the poor don't rebel because they are poor; they do so because of injustice, and the Mohammed Wazizi incident also demonstrates the power of the domino effect. For the betterment of our society, we must remember these lessons and apply them to our future. It is imperative that we do so quickly and effectively to restore the luster to our future.

The primary lesson to be learned is that injustice, whether perpetrated on the poor, the wealthy, a racial minority, people of certain sexual preference, religious sect, or other non-mainstream groups, will incite violence, if it is not correctly resolved with all due haste. Examples of injustice leading to revolutionary change are witnessed throughout human history, e.g., Tunisia, Egypt, Libya, 1960s America, Russia in 1917, and American Revolutionary war, among others. Ironically, correcting the injustice can also create violence (e.g., Greece, Ireland, Spain, Argentina, South Korea in 1998-1999), but typically, not a revolution.

When correcting for our immoral tax policies, protests will certainly ensue; however, we, as a country, must send a very clear and unequivocal message to the protestors: We are correcting for the decades of injustice, which was perpetrated on a minority group called the wealthy through the theft of their property from which the poor, unjustly, benefitted all these years. It should be noted that if full Justice is to be delivered to the wealthy, all of the people that benefitted from the theft of assets and property should refund the money that was extorted from the wealthy, plus interest. Is this not what the prosecutors are asking for as restitution in the Madoff case from those that benefitted from his mad scheme? Why should the victims – the wealthy – in the tax extortion scheme get any less?

In addition, if the poor do try and revolt and go on a rampage to steal from the wealthy to "protest" the correction of an injustice then they should all be arrested and thrown in jail for destruction of property, theft or attempted theft, vandalism, and probably assault and battery, among other criminal activities. This is only Just as no one has the right to object to the correction of an injustice. The would-be protesters should count their blessings that the extorted wealth is not being returned to the rightful owners at the would-be protesters' expense.

Regardless, it should be very self-evident that injustice is what causes revolt and rebellion, not poverty in and of itself. If poverty were the sole reason for revolt, they'd have been many more revolutions in a lot more countries over human history, given the number of countries that are very, very poor, even to the present day. However, this has not been the case. What more proof does one need?!

What happens to the economy if my tax plan is instituted? It will get a lot worse before it gets better, much better

I promise you that over the long-run my tax plan and the philosophical changes that I'd like to institute will greatly help the economy, the future of our country and our long-term competitive position versus the rest of the world, including China, Brazil, India, and other rising economies, not to mention western Europe and Japan. However, in the short-term, it will have both positive and negative impacts. The fact of the matter is that the negative impacts will be quite painful and more immediate. However, if we don't institute the changes that I'm fighting for, the end result will be even more painful and far longer lasting, not to mention out of our control to fix.

The biggest challenge in trying to correct our problems is going to be the insistent plea to be practical. However, the problem with being "practical" is that it makes the inevitable that much more painful and longer lasting. So, the question is, does our country have what it takes to fix what's wrong and take the pain for decades of mismanagement today or are we going to pass the problem down to our children, grandchildren and all of our future generations to suffer through? Mind you, the pain that our future generations will have to endure will be much worse than what we will have to go through today. Moreover, the pain may have to be imposed on our future generations unilaterally by an external force. Look at Greece; it is merely a shadow of what our children or grandchildren will face in the future, if we don't fix our problems today.

So, with that in mind, let me summarize what my tax plan entails. Reduce the tax bill for those that are currently paying a disproportionately high amount of taxes, have everyone pay at least 10% of their income as taxes, and budget the taxes so that the only functions of the government that gets covered is self-defense, infrastructure, education, and sustainable level of interest payment on the government debt. Eventually, the critical aspect is to make the tax bill basically the same amount for everyone. In addition to the ordinary income taxes, the US government could be allowed to collect surcharges from those that make a certain amount or more to cover for the principal on the portion of the debt that is deemed over the sustainable level of government debt. To compensate, these people that have to burden the additional amounts of revenue to the government should be given super-voting rights, i.e., more votes than other individuals that pay only the minimum amount of taxes, and the number of votes should be in proportion to the additional amount of taxes that they pay. This super-voting right should last only through the period of time that the US government collects surcharges to pay for the reduction in government debt to sustainable levels.

The sustainable level of debt should include the potential for $5 trillion in economic assistance that we can rely on to bailout the economy, when the economy experiences another paralysis due to massive systemic risk that will come in the future – not an if but a when. Should such a bailout be required the burden of the bailout should be borne by everyone equally.

Next, the government must privatize all "social programs." The other important factor is that the US Supreme Court must rule in favor of my tax plan, meaning that they must rule that congress and the president shall never again abridge the rights of people to outright own their own property, never again allow congress and president to favor one group over another, and restore equal rights – based on Justice – for every individual.

The end result of my tax plan is to eliminate the subsidies going to the poor, and commensurately reducing the tax bill for the wealthy. In so doing, money should eventually go back into the economy as investments and consumer spending, which should help lift corporate profits and employment, which then should create a virtuous cycle of growth and investments. This trickle-down effect will help the poor a lot better than most people expect. Also, the elderly will get money from their children to help both with living costs and medical expenses, but may force the consolidation of households.

Regardless, the layoffs from privatized "social programs" and elimination of subsidies to the poor and elderly will have a very negative effect in the short-run. But over the long-run, higher consumer spending ability, higher potential investment opportunities, lower government debt – particularly on-going ability of the government to act on behalf of the economy when it gets into trouble – will spur growth, lower unemployment faster, reduce inflation pressures, lower interest rates, and not only increase the long-term viability of the economy, but also strengthen its long-term viability. In the long-run, this will help the poor more than the rich due to a more robust economy. Even if the short-term pain is far greater than what I suppose, there is no question that the long-term results will be far superior to the direction we are headed today – it doesn't even begin to compare.

The key point that must be remembered is that fixing decades of mismanagement and misconduct will be very painful, by definition, and the deeper and longer the mismanagement and misconduct the more painful it will be and the longer it will take to fix the problems. Think of it this way. When someone gets infected in the leg – let's assume that there are no antibiotics – and it isn't taken care of quickly and correctly, at some point the patient is going to face a very difficult decision: Cut it off or die from the infection. The choice is difficult, but the leg has to be cutoff, and the longer the patient waits to make the right decision, the more of the leg the patient is likely to lose. And, after the leg is cut off, the patient's life will be very difficult in the near-term, but hesh will live on and, eventually, hesh could even restore almost 100% of hes life before the infection.

Put another way, think about a drug addict. The easy solution is to keep giving drugs to the addict to not only relieve the short-term pain, but also to keep the addict pacified. However, the better long-term solution is to rehabilitate the drug addict, first by taking away the drug addiction then educating the drug addict to a life away from drugs. This is a perfect analogy to the state of our country and economy. Politicians have been feeding drugs to the poor in the form of stolen money from the wealthier segment of our society for decades. To take this addiction away would, of course, be very painful in the short-term, but it must be taken away for the benefit of everyone concerned in the long-term. Similarly, the poor must be taught to free themselves of the immorality of benefitting from stolen goods, and find a better, more moral, beneficial and sustainable long-term lifestyle. If we don't, we cannot avoid the fate of Greece, whether in a decade, two decades or several decades from now.

This is the choice that we are facing today.   Because of decades of mismanagement and poor choices by the vast majority of Americans, we are in the position of needing to take some dramatic action to save ourselves, and go through more pain and suffering than we would otherwise have had to go through. And, what's worse, this could be our last chance to do right by our country's future – in any event one of the very last chances – so the question that needs to be asked is what is everyone prepared to do?   Are we, as a country, ready to live or are we going to kill our children and grandchildren and all of our future generations? Though it may be hard for Americans to believe, that is the choice that we are all facing today.

If we don't make that choice today then the pain will be forced on us, like it is being forced on and dictated to Greece by the other Euro-zone countries. Look how painful it is for Greece to right their ship! Do we want our children and grandchildren to suffer through what Greece is still suffering through since 2008 or is it better to bite the bullet today and finally take appropriate action to save our future? Keep in mind that the pain our children and grandchildren will face will be exponentially harsher, deeper and longer lasting than what we would face today, if we don't fix our problems today.

Also, if people are looking to blame someone for the position that we are in today, don't look at president George W. Bush, don't look at president William H. Clinton, don't look at president Barack H. Obama, don't look at any of the politicians going back to the beginning of the last century. Look in the mirror, look at your neighbors and look at your and your neighbors' family albums, for we (Americans as a group) for decades are the irresponsible ones that stole and continue wanting to steal from the rich thinking that it is a good policy for our country and the moral way to prosperity. Basically, the majority of Americans not only believe that a free lunch is possible and believe that it is a good thing, but also believe that stealing from the wealthy is moral!

The bottom-line is that if we want to avoid becoming the next Greece, we must fix our problems today, and the pain that we, as a country, have to endure to fix our problems is only the reflection of how decrepit our society has been over the last 80 years or so. Furthermore, the longer we wait, the less self-determination and flexibility we will have to fix our problems, and the bigger the pain we'll have to endure. Moreover, if we end up like Greece, the Great Depression is going to look like a vacation. Like I said, we have one last chance to fix our philosophy and, therefore, our economy. Keep in mind that the money we've borrowed (by some estimates well over $1 trillion) to fix our economy since 2008 is only an indication of how big our problem really is, and the fact that our country may not be able to afford it is reflective of how much we've borrowed from our future to pay for immediate problems over the last 80 years or so, basically since FDR was elected into office.

One last point: The real issue is Social Security. For those that are not yet in the program, it's easy. They don't pay into Social Security and they don't get paid Social Security. For those that have only been working a few years, this is part of the change they're going to have to accept; this is the "sacrifice" they have to make, to turn a phrase. It really comes down to the people who have paid into Social Security in a substantial way but haven't started collecting or are already retired and collecting. How does the country make these people whole? I would suggest that perhaps the only way to fix the issue is for the US government to calculate for every individual the net present value of the money paid into Social Security vs. the net present value of the money paid out to each person, and the after-tax difference should be paid to the individual as a tax-free US government bond. For any elderly or the wealthy that can make their ends meet without benefit of Social Security, we should appeal to their good nature to forgive any money owed. If we do this then the amount of money that we'd have to collect for taxes may have to temporarily increase to cover for the bonds that the government has to issue to cover for excess Social Security payments.

The reason why Social Security is such a difficult problem to solve is that it is essentially a Ponzi scheme. This is the one thing that the despicable Bernard

Madoff uttered that was shockingly close to the truth: When it comes to Social Security, the US government is running a Ponzi scheme, one that is doomed to collapse at some point in the future. Think about what a Ponzi scheme is: It's a fraudulent investment scheme that promises a certain return on the investors' money in the future, if they invest today. The returns are paid from money raised from others in the future under the same promise made to the earlier victims. Now, what is Social Security: It's the promise of future Social Security payments with interest to current tax payers, if they help to pay for Social Security payments today. Both the Ponzi scheme and Social Security are doomed to failure, because there aren't enough available funds in the future. In the case of a real Ponzi scheme, because the criminals run out of victims and in Social Security because there isn't enough tax money to support future payments that rise with inflation or the population growth slows down or even turns negative. The difference is that the government can either print money, which would lead to inflation or force increases in taxes, which would choke off the economy, while with a financial Ponzi scheme, at some point, there are no more victims to steal from.

So, the money paid today into the Social Security fund is paid out immediately to the current recipients of Social Security, while future Social Security payments are to come from future contributors. This creates a despicable chain of slavery-like dependence (or indentured servitude) that is not easily broken, but **must be broken** in order to return Justice to the country. There will be a lot of people that are displaced due to the change in Social Security, but this is the price that the so-called liberals and socialists are going to have to live with for their greed, short-sightedness and inability to think. **AGAIN, THE EXTENT OF THE PAIN THAT WE HAVE TO ENDURE TO FIX OUR CURRENT PROBLEMS IS ONLY INDICATIVE OF THE EXTENT OF THE DEPRAVITY THAT THE SO-CALLED LIBERALS AND SOCIALISTS HAVE FORCED ON THE COUNTRY OVER THE LAST 80 YEARS OR SO.**

If anyone truly wants to know how depraved so called "social programs" are, we jast have to look at the pain it WILL inflict on people in order to fix the problems caused by these so called "social programs;" that is the measure of how evil socialism is for any country. Look at Greece, Argentina, UK pre-Margaret Thatcher, Russia, China pre-Deng Xiaoping, the list is almost endless. To put it in another way that most people can understand, the payment the world had to pay for appeasing Adolf Hitler was the net number of people killed in the European theater of war, including all of the civilian deaths and deaths of brave Americans. If the politicians at the time had the temerity to control Hitler in 1932, 1935, 1936 or 1938 that I know of, we would have avoided those millions of deaths that needed to occur to remove the evil that he represented. Analogously, the price that we have to pay for fixing the socialist/liberal agenda of the last 80 years, can and will have to be measured by the pain that it will inflict on the financially weakest among us, which is very ironic. There is no avoiding it. If we postpone fixing our economy and tax system, it will be that much more painful and that much more devastating, mostly for those that the socialists/liberals wanted to help.

Regardless, if we don't take the responsibility to fix our economy and tax system on our watch then our future generations will suffer even worse agonies. Ultimately, if we wait until the whole system caves on our heads, we will no longer find that we have any control over the situation and the rest of the world will dictate the terms of our own survival. I guarantee that that will not be a pleasant experience; in fact, it will be unimaginably far worse than what we have to go through today. Ultimately, the responsibility of the depth and breadth of the agony that Americans have to suffer for correcting the unjust tax system must be borne by supporters of so-called liberal and socialist policies of the last 80 years. In this sense, many Americans will be paying for their own sins, but there are people like me who will suffer because I was dragged into the depths of hell against my will. Unfortunately, there is nothing I can do about that. If it were up to me, I'd make the so-called liberals and socialists pay for all of the pain and agony the rest of us suffered and will suffer in order to correct the problems the socialists and liberals created. This would only be fair. In fact, according to their philosophy, they should have no problems taking responsibility and paying for the dislocation and disenfranchisement, since they are helping the poor people, which, ironically, they created. However, identifying the people responsible for the pain and agony we have to suffer to correct the injustice due to the socialist/liberal agenda of the last 80 years or so would be very difficult. So, alas, I'm resigned to the fact that these so-called liberals and socialists will get away with stealing, creating pain and misery, and avoiding Justice. What can we do!? Anyway, regardless of who is responsible, we still must correct the injustices of the last 80 years. At the very least, we know which politicians stood for what, and we can start correcting the problem by sending all the socialist and liberal politicians home.

The good news is that what awaits us at the end of the rainbow, once we adjust to the new reality, will be a far better world than what we find ourselves in today. One of the benefits will be that the federal government debt will be far less than what it is today, giving the US government the flexibility to stimulate the economy in the future, when the economy takes another downward spin, which it will regardless of which tax policy we adopt. The difference will be that with the current tax policies, the downward spiral will get worse and worse, the impact, deeper and deeper and more and more difficult to work out of. At some point, we will not have the ability to work our way out of the economic problems and then we become Greece. With my tax plan, the opposite is way more likely to occur. The problems that we will likely face in the future will be easier to correct, recessions are likely to be shorter-lived, and difficult economic environments will be less frequent.

Next, because more and more money will be available to invest from reduced tax burdens, both at the individual and corporate levels, the economy will have more resilience, more opportunities, more innovation, higher growth, and lower unemployment, which then reinforces the virtual cycle of higher employment, more consumer spending and strengthening economy.

Overarching the financial changes will be the philosophical changes that I've spelled out here. This is what will ensure that the future will not be usurped – nor allowed to be usurped – by the liberals and socialists ever again, assuming people remember the philosophical framework that relies on Justice, and only Justice. This is not to say that individuals cannot or should not engage in compassion, charity, sympathy or empathy, nor does it prevent individuals from spending their money the way they want to in the form of charitable donations, gifts or rewards. However, it **does mean** that the **government cannot, must not, should not and will not engage in charitable activities**, because this means taking money from one group by force and giving it to another, which is theft at best and slavery at worst.

The compulsion of Justice and the moral and ethical imperative that this commands must be the only principle by which any government should be formed, represented, administered, adjudicated, and periodically revitalized.

Any other principle, no matter how noble any one person or the entire world may believe that that other principle may be, it cannot be a part of government ideology, because it is likely to introduces bias and favoritism or invite anarchy. The difference between individuals engaging in charitable work and the government forcing it on its citizens is the difference between voluntary and forced or coerced activity. One is Just and the other is immoral, one could be viewed as noble, while the other is despicable, one may be right, but the other is definitely wrong and while one may be righteous the other is absolutely evil.

I repeat, **IN THE SUSTAINABLE LONG-RUN, FOR ANY GOVERNMENT TO BE RIGHTEOUS IN THE EYES OF ITS CITIZENS JUSTICE IS THE ONLY PRINCIPLE THAT ANY GOVERNMENT MUST AND SHOULD UPHOLD IN GOVERNING ITS COUNTRY AND ITS PEOPLE**. All other sentiments and ideology must be abandoned. History is replete with examples of governments that did not uphold the principle of Justice to the detriment of its rulers and its people. I propose that we avoid becoming one of those abject lessons of history that will be taught to future generations by changing the way we think about government and allowing principles of Justice and only Justice to govern our society. Becoming Greece of 2010 and 2011 is not an option and certainly not a good idea; however, without a change in the way we govern, we will eventually become the next Greece; there will be no way to avoid it at the pace and direction that we are pursuing socialism.

One last point that must be made: Jast because Justice is the best public policy, it doesn't mean that it is perfect, and because it isn't perfect, it doesn't mean that it should be abandoned. My philosophy will not solve all problems for all people, and it will not prevent all future ills and problems of our society. Nevertheless, it is still the best philosophy for any society, because it guarantees individual freedom and allows everyone to live their lives the way they want to. Further, my philosophy eliminates forced subsidies and charities that exist today, which are indentured services imposed on the wealthier segment of our society by the majority.

What annoys me to no end is when people come up with examples of how my philosophy happens to not work in a very special and odd examples and use this as a reason to say my philosophy is wrong, flawed, errant, naïve, or irresponsible. However, people don't seem to realize that government policy is, by its nature, not like doing surgery with a laser. It's more like doing demolition work with a wrecking ball. Therefore, no matter how hard we try, humans will never come up with a perfect solution for all of our problems and solve everyone's idiosyncratic issues. Therefore, what we must focus on is the best policy – morally as well as financially – for the largest number of people in the long-term. In this regard, my philosophy meets this requirement, while socialism fails miserably.

Let me put it this way: If a person is ill and requires surgery, would you suggest that they not go to the hospital in case on the off-chance they contract staph infection? Of course not, but when people object to my philosophy by introducing highly idiosyncratic examples of why my philosophy may not work, they are suggesting that a person avoid going to the hospital because they may contract staph infection. Again, very, very short-sighted and illustrates how little people actually think.

I've been told that I'm heartless, but who is truly heartless?!

Who's more heartless: The one who wants to prolong the agony, torture and pain and continue to make it slowly, but surely worse and worse or the one who wants to end the bad situation despite the immediate pain and start clean with the right framework? Who's more heartless: The one who continues to give drugs to a drug addict, because it takes the edge off for the moment or the person who says no to the addict and tries to dry them out and eventually rehabilitate the drug addict? Who is more heartless: The one who wants to continue to enslave people and steal more and more of their productivity at any and all cost or the one who wants to free people of the bonds and shackles of slavery? What's worse is that most of the people that want to continue the enslavement and torture don't even know that that's what they stand for. And, when confronted with this fact, they deny that they are the purveyors and advocators of slavery, misery, poverty, decay and mass suicide through slow, long, drawn out and torturous death induced by the poison of forced charity – a prettier way of saying indentured servitude.

Contrast this to my position: I'm saying let's end this death spiral and enslavement before nothing can save us, and we all die a slow, torturous, painful and agonizing death. Sometimes it is better to cut off a finger, toe, limb or even part of an organ before it is too late than to allow death to take hold slowly. Again, look at what's happening in Greece. We are headed in that direction because of the people who bleed for the poor and decry the rich without understanding that taking from the rich is making the poor even poorer, while not realizing that helping the rich to prosper allows the poor to gain as well. This is something the socialists, communists and the liberals never understood despite the numerous lessons throughout history: Soviet Union, China pre-Deng Xiao Ping, Greece, Latin America pre-1990s, the UK pre-Margaret Thatcher, et cetera.

For us to save ourselves, everyone must realize and understand that we are all in the same boat. This means that if one of us is deliberately harmed, we are all harmed. However, jast because we are in the same boat, it doesn't mean that stealing from one to give to another is justified in anyway: one cannot create wealth when the first step towards the creation of wealth is to steal it. Look at the Soviet Union post the Russian revolution in 1917. It is beyond comprehension how so called intelligent people don't see this. How do these people not see that moral corruption, no matter for what end purpose, no matter for what good intention, no matter who it serves, no matter how many it may seem to serve, it will not make them right, nor Just, nor moral?!

During the Nuremberg trials in 1948, Ernst Janning (the head of the Ministry of Justice for the Nazis) was asked why he supported the Nazi regime, despite what he thought, despite his knowledge, despite his moral philosophy. As background information, please note that prior to the Nazis coming into power in Germany, Janning was considered to be a brilliant legal scholar, a beacon of hope in post-World War 1 Germany, and an inscrutable moral jurist. Getting back to the point, his answer to the question of why he supported the Nazis was that he thought a little moral corruption for the sake of the country would not matter, because he thought the intention was good for the country in the long-run and that the Nazis would be a passing phase, *"What difference does it make if a few political extremists lose their rights?! What difference does it make if a few racial minorities lose their rights?!"* He also stated that he did not realize that his little moral violations in the beginning would ultimately lead to the death of millions in both concentration camps and ultimately because of World War 2. In response, lead Justice Dan Haywood of the US, who presided over the part of the Nuremberg trials that involved Janning said, *"It came to that the first time you sentenced a man to death that you knew was innocent."*

I repeat, moral corruption, no matter for what end purpose, no matter for what good intentions, no matter whom it serves, it will not make anyone right, nor Just, nor moral. Moral corruption can only lead to death; death of individual rights, death of individuals and ultimately the death of society and country. When, as a society, did we forget the lessons of history? By doing so, we are at the door step of catastrophe for ourselves and our future generations, and we have utterly wasted the "sacrifices" of some of our moral ancestors and predecessors. And, the longer we willingly or otherwise choose to live with moral corruption, the more painful it will be to fix, the longer it will take to reverse and more of our future generations will be negatively affected. This is no mere speculation; this is a matter of fact; history tells us that it will be so.

I'm generally not a fan of John F. Kennedy, but one thing that he said has always left an indelible impression, "If not now, when, if not me, who?" The time is now, and the will must be ours before we become Greece.

So, who is truly heartless: The one who would continue to give drugs to the addict and subjugate the productive to the drug addict's desperation or the one who would stop it and try to rehabilitate the addict? Who is truly heartless: The one who is blinded by the plight of the poor and would steal from the wealthy to try to solve the problem of poverty or the one who would say there are ways to help the poor without stealing? Who is truly heartless: The one who would be immoral and act unethically to solve a problem or the one who would use Justice to address the issues and work towards a better life for everyone?

It has to be all or nothing, or else it won't work, i.e., a chain is only as strong as its weakest link

Many people that I've discussed my philosophy with have stated incorrectly – on multiple levels – that my philosophy on taxes is really nothing more than supply-side economics and that supply-side economics have failed. These people love to cite the 1980s Ronald Reagan era as the poster child for why supply-side economics is a failure. It is a very clever argument, but it is merely a very savvy distortion of the truth and holds no basis in truth.

First of all, my tax plan isn't merely a supply-side economics plan; it goes much further than that in that it incorporates philosophy, family planning, societal change, constitutional reform and rediscovery of Justice. Second, I'm proposing to permanently and radically reduce the size of government, which did not happen during the Reagan years. Third, from a financial point of view, my plan addresses the need for the federal debt to come down and come down fast, which again was not the case in the Reagan-era. This is where the people who criticize the 1980s, so called, supply-side economics plan have got it wrong. And, I'd hardly call the 1980s economic framework a true supply-side economics model anyway. During the 1980s, had congress turned the federal deficit into a federal surplus by cutting spending and maintained the surplus thereafter, while also cutting taxes, our economy would be in far better shape than we are today, and we would not be in such dire straits.

So, this means that what occurred in the 1980s isn't truly reflective of the power of supply-side economics. In fact, in my opinion, it was circumvented by socialists and liberals, who needed to get re-elected on the basis of promised additional spending. In pursuit of their misplaced priorities, the liberals and socialists forced increases in the federal debt at a record pace. According to the Office of Management and Budget (OMB; a White House office), during the Reagan era federal deficit grew by some $177 billion or 0.9% of the US GDP. This is by far the highest increase in terms of absolute dollars and as a percentage of the GDP since World War 2. "Social spending" increased by some $220 billion (a 70% increase), while defense spending grew $156 billion (a 117% increase).

As an aside, according to the OMB, since 1988 while defense spending grew by about $426 billion (including the two Iraq wars and the Afghanistan war) to $716 billion or by 147%, **"social spending" has grown by a staggering $1,940 billion to $2,473 billion or an increase of some 364%!!!** What's more, while defense spending is projected to go down to some $589 billion by 2017 or by about 18%, **"social spending" is projected to go up to $3,110 billion** or an increase of some 26%!!! Why isn't everyone in our country outraged?!

The conservatives during the Reagan-era do not escape criticism either. Following president Reagan's initiative against the "evil empire," the defense budget was also allowed to sharply increase by congress as previously outlined. Therefore, due to congressional conservatives' own priorities, they did not fight back the massive increases in federal debt due to "social spending" afraid of their own re-election and allowed the federal debt to balloon. This is why the 1980s turned out the way it did and why it seems to have left a legacy of mounting debt along with the fall of communism as the only real consequences. At least the fall of communism gave us a more robust global economy, and lower potential for global nuclear war. However, we traded the downfall of communism with the rise of global terrorism, so I can't necessarily say that this was a good outcome overall. We shall see how the war on terrorism progresses. Anyway, therefore, the 1980s is far from a good example of how supply-side economics really works. In fact, I'd go so far as to say that the 1980s had little, if anything to do with supply-side economics.

So, to summarize, it wasn't that supply-side economics failed, it is that politicians never gave supply-side economics a chance to work by deliberately loading up the government with more debt, which choked-off any potential economic benefits that supply-side economics would have provided. I strongly believe that this may have been a deliberate attempt by politicians to try and discredit supply-side economics, which threatened cozy spending arrangements. This way the politicians in general – and socialists and liberals specifically – can claim that capitalism is a failed experiment and supply-side economics doesn't work. It was a very clever ruse, and a ruse that hasn't been figured out by most people in this country.

So, cutting taxes alone in the 1980s was not enough. Without a more than commensurate cut in spending, the domestic economic agenda that Ronald Reagan tried to develop was wasted. This is the true lesson we need to take away from the 1980s: Without every component of a moral and rational plan in place, partial execution of a plan entails great risk and entertains high potential for failure.

Similarly, my tax plan will not work without ALL pieces coming together. These include: Supreme Court rulings, a reorganization of government functions, massive philosophical change and the complete decapitation of the socialist/liberal agenda. Furthermore, we have to remember that the great pain and agony – and it will be great – that we have to go through to fix the problems are the direct result of the failed socialist/liberal policies and agenda, which resulted in the gross mismanagement of the economy, taxes and finances of this country. However, without going through this torturous path, there is no way to fix the problems largely created by the irresponsible and short-sighted socialists and liberals that have mostly ruled the country since the Great Depression.

And, to not fix our problems and continue on the path set by the socialists and liberals would result in our country continuing to march down the path that Greece has blazed and becoming jast as bankrupt and morally decrepit. And, the resulting problems that we would have to face when the clock runs out would be exponentially far worse than the problems that we would have to face today in looking to correct past mistakes. In fact, it would be unthinkable and likely result in an economic catastrophe the likes of which the world has never seen before. Think about it: America, which is about 25% of the world's GDP that is in as much trouble as Greece is in since 2008. At least, with Greece, there are countries still remaining that could bail them out, but who would bail out the US? China?! No economy in the world could do so, not even a group of countries could do so. The end result is that the US would have to print so much money that it would bankrupt everyone and result in a global economic meltdown that would be far worse than what we saw even during the Great Depression. This is what the liberal/socialist agenda is forcing our country and the world's economy towards. Who would knowingly and voluntary embark down that path?

If you doubt what I say, jast take a look at Greece. Look at what they have gone through over the last 50-60 years. No one can deny that Greece had a very "progressive" socialist agenda, and look where it got them! At some point, all that the tax and "socially-spend" policies of the liberal/socialist agenda will buy our country is utter financial ruin for *everyone*. Ironically, the ones that this will hurt the most are the poor. Within our own history, look at the progression of socialism since the 1930s: Has socialism increased or decreased? And, are we better-off or worse-off? Who is hurting the most, the rich or the poor?

So, if we are to migrate to the right path, we have to make sure we do so with no reservations, with our eyes wide-open, with full knowledge of how we got here, who and what is to blame for the pain and agony, and what we need to do to fix it. But rest assured that if all of my policies outlined here are executed, the long-term results will be far more rewarding than will be imagined while we go through the dark days. And, the resulting healthy long-term foundation of our economy will be assured. Furthermore, we must resist the temptation for quick fixes and short-term solutions, while we are progressing through the various stages of change that we must go through to achieve success. Don't forget that the short-term fixes and Band-Aid solutions perpetuated by the socialist/liberal cadre, coupled with the inability of the general public to think beyond the tip of their nose, are what got us into economic and financial trouble to begin with.

I will also note, once again, that my plan will not eliminate poverty, will not and should not stop the widening gap between the wealthy and the poor, and will not stop the economy from going through cycles. However, what it will do is to lift up the overall living standard for **everyone**, including and mostly to the benefit of the poor, shorten the economic down-cycles, lower long-term sustainable unemployment, lower long-term sustainable interest rates, make our economy grow faster, innovate more, and attract more capital and financing, which then feeds the virtuous cycle. However, like all rational and moral long-term plans, we always have to be vigilant, we always have to have the confidence in our new path, and we must persevere and not give into short-term temptations. Think about our current economy as if it were a person hooked on crack. The near-term solution to the pain is to feed it more crack (socialist/liberal agenda and policies), but the real long-term solution is to take crack away from the addict and find a way to rehabilitate them. Similarly, for the economy, the only solution is to solve our problems based on Justice, long-term planning, true capitalism, education, investment and innovation/creativity, not based on short-term planning, a mountain of debt, moral corruption, stealing, forced charity and subsidies.

Therefore, for us to have a long-term successful economy, it must be the mission of every true American to forever forgo the liberal/socialist agenda that continues to bring slow but absolute ruin to our society. They have had over 80 years to help our country and have failed miserably. Now, it is time for true Americans to take back our country and return us to the right course to ensure the long-term health and viability not only of our economy, but also that of the rest of the world, which in turn benefits us.

Why do we need three layers of government, federal, state and local? Do people know how much waste that is?

Why do we need federal, state and local governments? This is so much unnecessary bureaucratic waste, it's unforgiveable! The amount of wasted money is staggering. Keeping track of all the nonsense in our current system is mind-boggling. Once my tax plan is instituted, we can get rid of a whole lot of bureaucracy and waste. We will no longer need 51 or more tax departments, we will no longer have to have 50 state police forces – perhaps unify them all under the FBI – we will no longer need 51 departments of education, we won't need all 51 welfare departments of any kind (Social Security, Medicare, Medicaid, etc.), we won't need 51 environmental protection agencies, we won't need federal, state and municipal judicial systems, we can get rid of all corporate tax attorneys and corporate tax accountants at both the federal and state levels, we won't have to collect so much in property taxes, we can get rid of all sales taxes, all state and local income taxes, and all other fees and charges levied by the state governments. Most of all, we can get rid of and unify a whole lot of laws so that we don't have to worry about what is and is not legal and how to go about enforcing and adjudicating laws in each state.

I'm sure if we all put our heads together, we can come up with a whole bunch of other cost savings ideas that we can implement to save consumers taxes that will then help to grow our economy and funnel more money into other causes that we, *as individuals*, cherish.

Also, what's with the Alcohol, Tobacco, and Firearms Department (ATF) that co-exists with the Drug Enforcement Agency (DEA) that co-exists with the Federal Bureau of Investigations (FBI), that co-exists with all of these other law enforcement groups? What a waste! Under my universal plan, the ATF and the DEA can be disbanded, all vice squads can be disbanded in federal, state and local law enforcement teams, and we can have a lot smaller bureaucracy, which saves tax payers a tremendous amount of money. At the federal level, we can disband the department of Agriculture, Commerce, Energy, Health and Human Services, Housing and Urban Development, and Labor. Department of Treasury can be significantly downsized, department of Homeland Security can be absorbed by the FBI under the department of Justice or absorbed by the department of Defense, the department of Interior and Transportation can be combined into the department of Infrastructure, and the department of Veterans Affairs should be absorbed into the department of Defense. So 15 federal departments will be reduced to 6 departments: Defense, Education, Infrastructure, Justice, State, and Treasury. Also, there are a ton of federal independent agencies and government corporations that can be eliminated, combined or downsized.

Also, I know that those of you that are federalist republicans are arguing that we as individuals have the choice of life-style and morality that we want to live by in our own state, but the point is that once we change the tax plan and government to my universal ideal then everyone has that option anyway. Remember, under my universal plan, everyone will have the right to do as they see fit with their lives, *as long as they don't interfere with other people's lives, their rights and don't steal.*

However, we may, and this is only speculation, we may still need a local government of some sorts. In actuality, these will be local representatives arguing on behalf of their local citizens' benefit, mostly dealing with local matters and interfacing with federal authorities as needed and necessary to achieve these objectives. Also, we're going to need local government at some level to run the local fire department, local police force, local ambulance services, and sanitation departments. However, even all of this can be made into federal functions, if we have to, so I'm not sure we'll need local governments, but I'll leave that up for debate.

"Uncle Warren" is one great investor, but he's also a great example of someone who has great influence that doesn't understand how bad he can be for society

Most people who know Warren Buffet are scratching their heads and going, "what?!" We all know that Warren Buffet, or as many people call him "Uncle Warren," is one of the wealthiest men alive outside of potentates, emirs, sultans, kings, dictator, emperors and the like. His wealth is estimated at some $50-$60 billion depending on the stock markets, and he accumulated this wealth from the bottom-up over the last 50 years or so after graduating from Columbia Business School in the 1960s. He accumulated his wealth by employing value investing techniques, and could be viewed as one of the pioneers of value investing. Regardless, there is no doubt that he is the most successful financial wizard of all time and exerts great influence on people from all walks of life not only on a financial basis, but also on a political and economic basis.

The problem is that Warren Buffet is no philosopher and not really an economist. So, his advice, particularly philosophical advice, should not be sought out let alone obeyed. Yet when he makes pronouncements of almost any nature, the world pays strict attention and gives it massive credibility and consideration, regardless of the validity of the argument. This should not be.

However, before I present my arguments, let me make it very clear that as an investor, I greatly value his opinion and respect him to the utmost.

Mr. Buffet argued that the US government should "stop coddling billionaires like himself and raise taxes on people like him," or something like it. Now most people listening to this would say something like, "see even Warren Buffet thinks that the rich should pay more taxes. So, let's raise the taxes on the rich and pay for government spending." I've already gone through the argument why this is not a good tax policy for our country, and I hope Warren Buffet retracts his statement. However, I do want to point out a few unspoken facts.

When Warren Buffet says things like taxes should be raised on billionaires and that the government should stop coddling people like him, he is suggesting – whether he realizes it or not – that the government should use force to take wealth away from billionaires regardless of whether they want to pay the extra taxes or not, and more to the point whether or not it is moral. Why? Because, he doesn't speak for all of the billionaires. I haven't taken a survey of all of the billionaires, but I'm guessing that there is a pretty big group of billionaires that think that they should not pay any more taxes than they already do. So, why should Buffet's opinion be the only one that matters? Because he's rich? What if another billionaire says Buffet is wrong? Shouldn't we listen to the other billionaire, because hesh is also rich? There's no reason why we should listen to Buffet on neither tax matters nor economic management of the country, because he's not an expert on either subject, and more so because he has sufficiently explained his position for us to know that it is not valid. Also, his reasoning for why billionaires should get taxed more is very deceptive and, therefore, highly misleading.

One of the most deceptive arguments that he makes is that in the 1950s and 1960s, the US had tax rates in the 50%-range and did very well on an economic basis, we had low unemployment, and, we, as a country, prospered. What he doesn't tell you or doesn't know is that the rest of the world was suffering and recovering from the devastation of World War 2 and that the US economy was about 90% of the world's GDP, post-World War 2. Because of this, there was only room for growth in our economy as all of the soldiers coming back needed houses, factories needed to convert back to manufacturing products for a normal economy from a war time stance, and there was pent-up demand for peace-time goods. Also, and more importantly, the rest of the world had no place to go to buy materials and merchandise to rebuild their economies other than the US. This meant that we had a very strong export-driven economy helped by the Marshall Plan – which was specifically designed to take advantage of our export capabilities. To top it all off, the US was one of the largest, if not the largest exporter of crude oil at that time.

By the 1950s, the US economy was still accountable for some 50% of the world's GDP and even by 1965, the US accounted for some 40% of the world's GDP; this versus some 20%-25% over the last decade. Clearly, while the world was in the process of rebuilding their economies, the US was a great beneficiary of this trend, which allowed overall tax rates to be in the 50%-range (top marginal tax rate of some 90%) with little to no consequences.

Next, Mr. Buffet's contention that he pays less tax than his secretary on a percentage basis is technically correct. However, this ignores three very key and critical points. The first is that on a strictly income only basis – excluding dividends, long-term capital gains and qualified interest – there is no way that his secretary pays more in income tax as a percentage of her income than he does. However, if he does pay less in income taxes than his secretary on a percentage basis then this means that Warren Buffet is paid less in wages, salary and ordinary income than his secretary. If this is true than it is only fair that he pays less in income taxes than his secretary. Second, regardless of whether or not dear uncle Buffet pays less in taxes than his secretary on a percentage basis, there is no question that Warren Buffet does more for the country than his secretary. He not only helps to create jobs, including his secretary's, but also helps to grow our economy by investing in it. It can be effectively argued that this is far more valuable than what he does or does not pay in taxes. In fact, I would argue that he shouldn't pay any taxes at all, because he is so good at investing money and promoting growth, he can do more with the taxes he pays by investing it than the government can do with it by spending it. Third, regardless of the tax rate, there is no question that Warrant Buffet pays way more in taxes than his secretary in total dollars. This means that people, including Warren Buffet, are using the word "taxes" deceptively and arguing that there is no difference in income taxes and capital gains taxes (including taxes on dividends). If this is what Warren Buffet and others are arguing then we should all be very, very afraid of our future.

What all this means is that Warren Buffet is either ignorant or lying, either way, we should not be listening to his advice on taxes and the economy. We should also stop mixing apples and oranges when talking about taxes and tax policies: We must separate income taxes from capital gains taxes (including taxes on dividends). In fact, if anything, to stimulate economic growth, we should lower our long-term capital-gains taxes even more than the current 15% rate. Equally importantly, everyone should pay at least 10% in income taxes. As previously mentioned to achieve truly fair tax policy, we need to eliminate all "social programs."

Most people are gasping, yet again, and thinking how stupid this is, how bad this is, how inhumane this is, how despicable this is, and how brutal this is. Even the people who have higher incomes are probably concerned that this will incite class warfare and would be opposed to it. However, think about this: In part, whether we want it to or not, taxes serve to provide incentives and disincentives. Therefore, if we tax something less, it typically encourages more of that something, while if we tax something more, it typically encourages less of that something. So, could it not be argued that to discourage poverty, we should tax lower incomes relatively more on a percentage basis, while if we want to encourage prosperity, we should tax higher incomes less? Think about it, if we get to keep more and more of our money as we get paid more and more, doesn't this have the effect of encouraging people to make more and more? This is a rhetorical question. There is a lot of evidence to prove my point. Think about it from your personal point of view: If the government taxed 99% of your income above $50,000 would you try to make more than $50,000 if you could? Personally, the answer is, "hell no!" For getting $1 for every $100 I earn above $50,000, I wouldn't lift a finger to make a penny over $50,000. It jast wouldn't be worth it. In fact, I propose that practically no one would make incomes above $50,000; not to mention the rampant – but justified – evasion of taxes. However, if the tax rate was 10% for every dollar earned over $50,000, the government would collect a hell of a lot in additional taxes. So what should the government do? This implies that we should eliminate minimum wages and have a progressive tax rate that is higher with lower income and lower with higher income.

Next, if Warren Buffet thinks that he is not taxed enough and the government should tax him more to reduce the deficit, he doesn't have to drag the rest of the billionaires with him against their will, i.e., he shouldn't goad the government into using force to expropriate wealth from others. That's instigating and condoning theft and is wrong, and he should know better! If he thinks that the reduction of government debt is that important, he can choose to take whatever he thinks should be taken away from him in additional taxes and use that money to buy government bonds and refuse to accept interest and principal on the bonds, and burn all of the bonds. Or, he could make a donation to the US Treasury, so that the government can use the money to pay down its debt.

Furthermore, if Buffet feels passionate about the cause then he can go around to all of the billionaires and ask them to do the same using logical and rational arguments as to why that is a good way to spend money, much like another billionaire who is going around asking other billionaires to donate half of their money to charity, and getting a good response.

Regardless, I don't think voluntary donations from billionaires or others will solve the government's deficit problem. But then again, asking for voluntary donations versus raising taxes on billionaires isn't really about solving the deficit problem; it's about fairness, Justice and eliminating force from government policy. This is something that Buffet is missing, whether deliberately or otherwise.

Therefore, I think it is despicable that someone of Warren Buffet's stature would encourage the government to use force to expropriate wealth without consideration for so many issues and in such a flippant manner; it's very disappointing to say the least. No one, and I mean absolutely no one, should condone the use of initial force, let alone actually using initial force, whether it is wielded by the government or private citizens. Furthermore, no one, absolutely no one, must be allowed to perpetuate theft – again, regardless of whether the theft is being perpetrated by the government under the guise of taxes, or it's a private citizen stealing from another – as a tool to solve any problems, no matter how noble the cause may seem in everyone's eyes.

For me personally, it is very disappointing that Warren Buffet would be so inconsiderate, careless, and, most of all, short-sighted and not a long-term thinker when it comes to government policy – worst yet, I just hope that he is not a liar or a manipulator. This is highly contradictory to his behavior when it comes to investing where he is the king of long-term rational thinking. More to the point, it is especially puzzling that he doesn't get it when it comes to thinking rationally and for the long-term with regards to taxes and the economy when he's made so much money by thinking rationally and for the long-term – when others could not and cannot – in the investment world; very, very disappointing indeed.

Lolo Jones: Poster-child for more than her sponsors; she proves socialism is not only unnecessary, but totally wrong

All these bleeding-heart and short-sighted socialists/liberals talk about how the poor don't have a chance and how the poor don't get a break and how the poor "need our help" – code and justification for socialists/liberals stating that they are going to steal more money from the wealthier segment of our society. Then they use these excuses to continue to steal and spend, steal and spend, and steal and spend everyone else's money. However, the liberals/socialists conveniently forget the fact that there are people who do get out of poverty and escape the "shackles" of perpetual "misfortune" and "bad luck," which the liberals/socialists would have everyone believe is impossible to escape from.

And, yes, there is no question that poor people are in a difficult financial position; however, given that there are a lot of people who escape the "bondage of poverty," there is no excuse valid or otherwise to continue to steal from the productive to give to the poor. Especially, if the poor that are being "helped" aren't helping themselves. If the poor that are supposedly being "helped" don't have the intelligence, ability, mindset, value system, morals, ethics, integrity, fortitude, mental strength, courage, vision, determination, or jast the will to escape poverty on their own then no matter how much money we give them they won't be able to escape their situation. In contrast, if a person has the intelligence, ability, mindset, value system, morals, ethics, integrity, fortitude, mental strength, courage, vision, determination, or the will to escape poverty then they won't need financial help. This is not to say that they couldn't use it or need it to speed-up their "escape" from poverty, but they don't **need** the financial charity to be successful.

Look at all of the recent African and Asian – Chinese, Indians, Koreans, Pakistanis, Vietnamese, et cetera – immigrants in the last 20-50 years that have succeeded without handouts, and then, look at how many other poor people have been receiving handouts for generations without a single family member successfully and legally escaping poverty. Why? What makes these two groups different? If, as I contend, the difference is their intelligence, ability, mindset, value system, morals, ethics, integrity, fortitude, mental strength, courage, vision, determination, or jast the will to financially succeed then no amount of money is going to help people buy the intelligence, ability, mindset, value system, morals, ethics, integrity, fortitude, mental strength, courage, vision, determination, or will to financially succeed.

There isn't room here to recount the stories of hundreds of thousands of people who have escaped poverty without financial handouts, but let me illustrate one story: That of Lolo Jones, the track and field champion that I hope will soon be Olympic champion in London. According to a story I saw on HBO Real Sports, Lolo grew up poor with three siblings, an absentee criminal father and an abused mother that had to work multiple jobs to make ends meet. Times got so bad that after her mother ran out of money and favors they ended up living in the basement of the local YMCA. Lolo constantly moved around attending EIGHT schools in EIGHT years. Lolo even had to steal to avoid starvation for her family – I'm not condoning theft of any kind, but illustrating how bad her life was.

Despite these deplorable circumstances, when she was told that the family had to move yet again to accommodate her mother's work situation, she put her foot down and decided to stay put in Des Moines, IA, so that she could go to the same high school for four straight years. During these years, she was shuffled from one family to another, ending up living with three of them throughout her high school years. Amazingly, during those four years, she worked extremely hard to earn a full athletic scholarship to Louisiana State University, graduated as an honor student and, despite her absolutely gorgeous physical beauty, and, therefore, many, many temptations, she remained a virgin, and at 29 is still a virgin.

Now, she is financially well-off and supports her mother, but what is most impressive about Lolo is that she is going for Olympic glory in track and field at the ripe old age of 29! There's more, her siblings are also supposedly successful with one brother being a chef that we know of. The Jones' siblings accomplished all this despite an absentee father who abused their mother, constant relocation, and living in squalor and poverty that sent them to the brink of starvation. Truly inspiring! Always, fly like the wind Lolo, especially in London!

Another story that I saw on the same HBO Real Sports episode is the story of Matt Long, the former New York City firefighter that literally was ran over by a bus in NYC. If anyone wants to know what it means to overcome almost impossible situations, they should watch this story as well. Before being crushed by the bus, Matt was not only a firefighter, but also a marathon runner. To make a long story short, he not only overcame his injuries (which constituted a detached pelvic bone, a fused thigh bone, a shortened right leg, among others) from which he should have not been able to walk let alone survive, but also through extremely hard work and dedication to rehabilitation, he became an Ironman Tri-athlete!

Both stories show that virtually nothing is insurmountable and that with hard work, dedication, vision, and strong will people can overcome their personal difficulties to succeed, no matter what goals they set for themselves. These stories also show that the path to success is not about giving or taking help from others, but starting with helping oneself. If a person doesn't have the internal fortitude to be successful then no matter how much help one receives it won't and can't make someone successful. On the other hand, if an individual does have the internal fortitude to be successful then anyone can achieve success. If these two examples don't illustrate and demonstrate to the reader that socialism is the most useless and counter-productive force in our society then our society is headed for an abyss from which we will never recover. I hope that that is not the case, and it isn't too late for our country.

Education

Education: The key to financial success and the only legitimate and Justified means to prevent an uprising of the poor

As stated before, people don't rebel because they are poor; they rebel because they are treated unfairly and unjustly. And, as proposed, there is NOTHING UNFAIR about my tax plan. On the contrary, my tax plan is *correcting an injustice*. Therefore, even without an extensive change in other areas, if and when the US tax code is changed to the way I've outlined, no one has the right to rebel or protest. This is not to say that people won't, but once the populace gets used to the idea they will have very little to protest about, because the logic is irrefutable. For example, look at the civil rights movements of the 1960s. How many people rose up against and disagreed with the civil rights movement? How many disagree with it now? Despite the Just nature of a particular act, if it means change from doing the "same-old, same-old" then regardless of the Just nature of the act there will be mass protest and objections against the Just change. So, when contemplating change, all we have to know are two things: 1) Is it rational and 2) is it Just (Just is moral and moral is Just, but moral and Just isn't always equal and equality is not always Just and Moral)?

So how is public education rational and Just? It is Just because it is the only consistent and viable path to financial success. Therefore, as a country, we must ensure that everyone has a chance at achieving financial success through education. In this regard, very few, if any, will disagree that the key to financial success in this country should be, is, and must remain education. With it and with the acquisition of skills – technological expertise, expertise of any kind, professional knowledge, scientific knowledge, and any other advanced knowledge – people tend to get financially wealthier. The more advanced the knowledge, the more difficult to acquire, and the better education that one obtains, the higher the probability that one becomes financially successful. And, with financial success, all other of life's necessities such as healthcare also becomes affordable and negates the need for reliance on charity. However, we note that higher education doesn't always guarantee financial success.

Regardless, if implemented, my educational policy will give anyone who has the desire, the brains, and the moral fortitude all of the available means to pursue their financial dreams through education. As an aside, this means that public education should be the highest caliber in the country, which is currently not the case. By making the best education available to any citizen who has the necessary ingredients, but not the means to attain this education, the country ensures that the poor can achieve financial success. In addition, the poor cannot make the excuse about how they never got the opportunity or how they never had a chance, and the politicians that use these pathetic excuses to extort money from the wealthier segment of our society will also run out of excuses.

This tactic of the politicians/poor to hold the wealthier people hostage is a dictatorship perpetrated on the minority by the majority; otherwise known as a "dictatorship of the masses." The promise to steal more and more money from the wealthy and transfer it to the poor has been a successful strategy of politicians for decades in democracies. Of course, the excuse is that the poor need help and the rich can afford to pay. However, we all have to come together to put a stop to this injustice perpetrated on those that have succeeded!

Also, as a relatively wealthy person, education is the one and only public program that I can and will support once the tax codes are revised to a Just standard. What is a Just tax system was described above. So, moving on, why should the wealthy support an education system in the US for everyone? Because it is not only the way to allow everyone equal access to the American dream, but also a way to maximize the country's technological potential, which is the key to future economic prosperity for *everyone*. When new products, technologies, processes, or other innovations are created, the country benefits as a whole. And, for an advanced economy like that of the US, the only way to stay at the top of the economic ladder is to continue to innovate. If we lose the war of technological innovation then we lose economic leadership. Therefore, education not only helps the poor, but also the country as a whole to stay on top of the economic ladder. Of course, this is good for everyone.

Anyway, a clever – clever doesn't mean smart – person once asked me then why not universal healthcare? Very good question. Simple answer. Because, if people have a great education, they can make money and buy their own insurance or get it through their job, but without education, they don't stand a chance at making good money and cannot get anything of substantial use, including healthcare. Therefore, once we, as a country, provide for every opportunity at a great education for everyone, what each individual does with it should be left up to them and what one gets out of it should also be left up to each individual. This then does not necessitate a national healthcare program. Therefore, beyond the *opportunity* at a great education, it is up to each individual to decide what they do and do not want to do with their education *and* their money. To be perfectly clear, the basic building block to financial security and access to other basics in life is education, what one does with it thereafter is all up to the individual. This is why a strong educational system must be supported by all, because it is the key fundamental building block to everything else, and, more importantly, the key to long-term prosperity for ALL. Simply put, if any individual wants healthcare benefits or medical benefits, they should make their own money to afford it, if they don't have the money, then they should get the education necessary to make the money to afford medical insurance.

Jast to be perfectly clear, the only "social program" that an American should support is access to the best education in the world. However, in my opinion, education is not a "social program," but an infrastructure program; infrastructure for the mind and for the economy as a whole.

Someone asked me about school meals too. I think at least breakfast and lunch should be provided to all students as long as they are not trouble makers and "can't afford to pay." What constitutes trouble makers should be left up to the school to decide. We will discuss more about this later, including the issue of teacher pay and the educational structure.

Also, with access to the best education in the world for "free," no one can claim that they never had a chance. If their family life doesn't afford them study time then they should study in the library, if they don't have a safe place to sleep and wash then the school should provide for boarding facilities. If they don't have the support of parents and family then they should stay at school 24/7. And, as long as the tax system is fair, I will support this educational system, including boarding facilities, school meals and supplies, including clothing, and healthcare.

Once this system is established, we should expect all students to do their best without worry and concern. Therefore, all people run out of excuses, and we can finally have the chance to break the cycle of excuses and poverty, poverty and excuses. This is why education is an investment in our future and more of an infrastructure program than a "social program."

Through education, we also not only give everyone the opportunity to better themselves, but also we can identify and develop exceptional talent in all areas of endeavor. This way, we don't waste any potential. As a society, to compete in this modern global economic stage, we must develop all "productive" potential and not let any productive talent go to waste. By providing this no holds barred educational system, we can identify and develop these talents, which is so crucial to our future.

However, the key to a successful educational system has to start with the teachers. This is imperative. We must ensure that we attract and maintain the best teachers in the world. Here's how I think it should be done.

Educational structure should start with the teachers and teacher pay must be increased dramatically as a starting point

Let's start by making the teaching profession one of the most – if not *the* most – desirable professions in the country. We must make teachers respected in our society as they will have control over our society's future through teaching and molding our children. But, how do we do this?

Even though money isn't the end all be all, it certainly holds a lot of sway in our society and attracts a lot of people, some good, and some bad. Regardless, to attract the best of the best, we must pay for this. So, let's make the starting salary for teachers $100,000 – adjusted for standard of living where the professional is teaching – with long-term potential of $333,333 per year or more, again, adjusting for standard of living. This implies an average raise of 3.5% per year for 35 years, which takes a 25-year old teacher to 60-years old. The increase in pay and the ultimate retirement package should be adjusted according to the objectives of the school with input from parents and alumni.

The next problem that we should address is how to measure the efficacy of teachers. The current standardized testing for students doesn't cut it as teachers are being forced to teach children how to pass tests and not teaching essential knowledge and skills. The problem is that measuring teaching success cannot be done in the short-term, i.e., through tests; it can only be done over a long time period based on the long-term success of the students. But how that is done must be determined by each locality and their constituents. Regardless, the first review of the teacher should not occur until five to seven years after they begin teaching and during that period, they should be on probation. Furthermore, no teacher should be allowed to fly solo until they've had at least two years of apprenticeship. However, for this tumultuous road these teachers should be paid the kind of salary that I mentioned in the previous paragraph.

Further, no teacher should be allowed tenure until and unless the children they taught become successful and nominations for tenure are received in overwhelming numbers from the teacher's students once they have graduated high school for more than 4 years. The problem comes with kindergarten through 5th or 6th grade. These children won't remember the influence of their teachers. Here, the nominations may have to come from other sources such as teachers in middle school or parents (my least favorite idea), but again, well after the students have moved on from elementary school. I don't have a clear idea for elementary school teacher reviews and tenure-ships, but I strongly believe that this is where communities can develop their own standards and methodology.

Over time, communities that have a successful education program will continue to produce more and more successful people and will separate themselves from other communities. Then communities that are not doing well can learn from those communities that are doing well. However, every community **MUST CONSTANTLY REVIEW THEIR PROGRAMS** and should not rest on their laurels.

The key is that everyone must be aware that there are no short cuts and that short cuts will end up hurting way more over the long run. Think about this: If a more rational education system were developed 50 years ago, by now we'd have a great educational system all across the country, but people 50 years ago decided to take short cuts. Following the lead of that generation, all generations that followed continued to take short cuts. So, now look what we're left with! I don't think that anyone wants future generations to look back and say we were also negligent. If we don't want to be viewed as selfish, lazy incompetents by future generations, we have to make sure to pay attention to the educational system and fix it today. This is the most important issue that we can deal with locally to ensure the long-term economic prosperity of our country.

The other educational priority is discipline in schools. We have to give schools and teachers real authority over the students and their behavior: None of this politically-correct liberal-agenda that has done absolutely nothing to improve discipline in schools. Corporal punishment must be brought back, but in addition, we should tie future education access and opportunity to discipline. Any child that is unruly and undisciplined should be subject to escalating discipline, culminating in military style regimen. If this fails to bring about change then the child should be expelled from the system with no opportunity at any further public education.

Of course, for those students with wealthy parents, expulsion from public education would not be a problem, because the parents will have money to send their children to private schools and that's OK. That's what private schools are for. However, if we get public education right, private schools will be less attractive relative to public school education, and therefore, less competitive and will actually limit access to top universities, which is the complete opposite of what we have today. Furthermore, private schools will become magnets for trouble makers, which will further degrade the quality of private education. This is the way it should be as education is the key to everyone's future. Therefore, US public education should be the best available anywhere in the world.

In addition to mainstream academic schooling, we should also develop strong honors and vocational education programs, but one which reviews children's progress annually and to some degree gives children and their parents a choice. What I mean by this is that once a child is selected to go to the honors program, it must not be written in stone that they will stay in the honors program, which means that grading has to be absolute. Similarly, jast because a child is in the mainstream program, this does not mean that they will stay there forever. Based on performance and the child's and the child's parents' desires, they should be moved to the honors program or to any one of the vocational programs as necessary. Also, children in the vocational programs should be monitored based on progress and given the option of going to one of the academic programs, if the child and the parents are willing to take that route.

For this to occur in a fair way, we must start thinking about people in a completely different way. Some of the specifics will be addressed in different chapters, but I will note one concept as an example of what needs to change in our thinking: A person who is the best at anything (we're talking about non-criminal activities for those clever detractors that want to discredit my arguments) and has maximized their potential is more honorable and successful than someone that is a mediocre performer in what we now refer to as a high prestige occupation (doctor, lawyer, judge, financial professional, engineer, et cetera). The change in how we look and measure people has to be vastly different than how we do it today. As an extreme example, think about it this way: The best and most talented male escort in Las Vegas or New York should be considered more of a success and more of an honorable person than an average skilled doctor that would have made a much better engineer. Much more on this subject will be addressed in later chapters.

We should also develop a culture that respects education, the educated, intelligent people, proficiency and, most importantly, the morally and ethically virtuous people that have integrity and strong value systems with a keen sense of honor and honesty. This may sound like it's obvious, but our society is very far from actually accomplishing this. Evidence of my contention: Look at the kinds of people that are achieving notoriety, fame and financial success, including self-promoters like the Kardashians and Paris Hilton, reality show stars like the mother of the octuplets, and morally corrupt ex-politicians like Eliot Spitzer. What does it say when our society rewards people like these and respect and admiration goes to actors, athletes, entertainers and certain film-makers that make a living distorting truth. Also, what does it say about our society, when adulterers are still capable of being moral leaders, which to me is absurd! Specifically, I'm talking about someone like Martin Luther King. Personally, I don't understand how someone like Martin Luther King, who is a documented adulterer, can command such respect and adoration. I hear the howling already. Accusations of bigot, racist, et cetera. I don't necessarily know for sure what most Americans think is moral, what constitutes morality and who should be moral leaders, but here's how I'm thinking about it: If someone wants to claim moral superiority and leadership then their actions, ALL OF THEIR ACTIONS, must be held up to the harsh light of moral scrutiny and pass muster on all major issues, including adultery. Otherwise, no matter what the supposed moral leader says – and, admittedly, someone like MLK has said **MANY GREAT THINGS** – we have to wonder, if the person is speaking these great words because the individual is truly great and wants to change the world or is saying great things to gain something, whether it is money, fame, or something else. Also note, that in our society, family values are deemed to be the cornerstone of our value system and the cornerstone to family values is marriage. So, what does that say about someone who commits adultery?

Regardless, let me set the record straight. I do believe that some of the words uttered by MLK were brilliant, inspiring, enlightening, rational, moral and Just, but I'm not sure I believe in the moral and ethical standing, integrity and values, and sense of honor and honesty of the deliverer. In my opinion, he contrasts starkly to someone like Malcolm X, whose earlier words were stupid, inflammatory, detrimental, irrational and unjust. However, when Malcolm X realized his mistakes and changed then he became a truly great man. Not necessarily jast because of what he said and truly believed in, but because he was a man who was willing to acknowledge his mistakes and make restitution, starting with an apology followed-up by action. Most of all, he was a man who's character, moral standing and conviction were unshakeable and pure. He was devoted to his wife and children, and truly meant to change the world for the better: HIS CHARACTER WAS UNASSAILABLE. This is much more than we can say about people like Martin Luther King, Mohandas Gandhi, Eliot Spitzer, Michael Vick, and others. I will have more to say on this later in the book.

This diversion isn't without intention. The simple truth of the matter is that teachers must be beyond reproach when it comes to their morals, values, ethics, integrity, and sense of honor and honesty. However, to ensure that this is the case, there is nothing wrong with putting hidden video cameras in every room, hallway, broom closet, bathroom and play area in the school and in the immediate environs. Furthermore, teachers and administrators who do violate the sanctity of their relationship with students should be subject to very harsh retribution, including the death penalty for teachers and administrators that molest, rape or sexually abuse children.

On the other hand, morons like the principal that fired the teacher for having a Facebook page with a picture of her with a glass of beer in her hands should be caned in public, stripped of hes career, and hes pension money should go to the teacher that was fired. If this example isn't one of the telling signs of why political correctness, superficial morality, and pretense aren't stupid beyond idiotic, and why we should stop being so insecure and overly sensitive, I don't know what will convince Americans. This episode is a consequence of our society's lack of truly rational morals and values and our great insecurities as a country and is very telling of how decrepit and distorted our society has become.

The bottom-line on this matter is that education is paramount to the long-term success of any society. However, it must be accomplished in a well-organized, thoughtful and rational manner, because if it is carelessly done then the educational system will become poison. Ultimately, whether the educational system is the long-term nutrient for our society or poison will depend on the way the people in the society think and what they believe in. And, therefore, the results of the educational system will be a strong litmus test for whether a society is healthy or rotting. There is no other issue that is more paramount than education, when it comes to the long-term survivability of a society. Not healthcare, not Social Security, not the economy, and not taxes; the only issue that may be more important than education is self-defense, because without it there is no independent and free society.

Who cares if we're 25th in math; we have the greatest group of minds in the world, for now

A lot has been made of our country's less than stellar results in worldwide standardized tests in math and science. For example, we are told in one television advertisement that we rank #25 in math and, in another, we are told that we rank 17th in math and science. These test results are based on the OECD's Programme for International Student Assessment (PISA), and the results are unalterable and verifiable facts that US students start out poorly and end up abysmally. Most people point to this data as proof positive indication that our education system is failing and that we must do something to raise the quality of our education. Moreover, many people strongly believe that given the amount of money per child that we spend on education versus some of the top ranking countries that we not only have a serious fundamental problem, but also no excuse to not be able to solve the problem.

However, compare the above statistics to the following: Between 1990 and 2011, out of a 194 Nobel Laureates in Physics, Chemistry, Physiology or Medicine, or Economic Sciences, 99 were Americans or about 51%. Between 1960 and 1989, 215 Nobel Laureates were crowned in the same four categories of which 81 were Americans or about 38%. What about this statistic shows that

American education is failing? Keep in mind that the US accounts for less than 5% of the global population.

Why does one statistic say that America's educational system is failing while another says that the American educational system is getting better? To solve this conundrum, we first have to figure out which of the two statistics are more important to our country. Then, to figure out whether this means that our education program is succeeding or not, we have to compare our educational system to those of some of the other countries' that are outscoring our children on the PISA tests. Finally, we then have to figure out what are educational system serves versus what those other countries' educational system serves.

As I discuss later in the book, it is my assertion that for our country to succeed long-term, we need to continue to innovate and develop new technologies to stay ahead of the rest of the world. For this to happen we need great minds to create these new innovations. To me this implies very strongly that the statistics concerning Nobel Laureates is far more important and significant than the PISA test results.

However, this does not necessarily mean that our education system is succeeding. But before we get to a definitive answer let's look at what some other countries are doing with their children: Let's take France and South Korea as examples. France separates their children at a very early age; too early to tell if they should be on an academic track or a vocational track. In my opinion, this discourages creativity and outside-the-box thinking, and grossly suppresses ambition. They are also punished for being different, standing out and being independent. Also, there is a strong elitist element to their educational system which allow the ones that went to the "right" schools to have more opportunity and flourish more than the ones that did not; a glass ceiling of sorts based on which school a person attended, if at all. The French system is about categorizing, separating, classifying and giving opportunities to only those that show promise at a very early age. The French system does not allow for self-discovery nor does it allow children to develop on their own time, and certainly not make their own choices.

The South Korean educational system is worse. In particular, it is about socialization of education. It is about bringing the entire group up the learning curve. Worse, the South Korean education system is not about learning, but about rote memorization. The ones that have the best memory get the best grades. Therefore, again, it is not about creativity, out-of-the-box thinking, learning or development. Also, like the French system, children are categorized and herded starting in middle school between an academic track and a vocational track. And, given that the ultimate objective of a South Korean student is to go to college, regardless of whether they belong in college or not, there is strong stigmatism to being in the vocational track. Furthermore, given that the competition to get into ANY college can be as high as 10-to-1, and without it there is little to no chance of financial success, the pressure on children to study and get good grades is enormous. To accomplish this, Children in 7th grade through 12th grade in South Korea attend school between 8AM and 3PM then they go to an "academy" where they get intense training in English, Math and other key subjects until 9PM or later; all based on rote memorization. That's not where it ends. The vast majority of South Korean middle-school and high school students go to these "academies" all day during weekends and vacations as well. Therefore, these kids have little to no time to themselves let alone the opportunity to develop their own talents or choosing their own paths. The South Korean system is about producing a very disciplined, homogenous, predictable, replicable and highest quality *average* work force possible.

Now let's compare the European and Asian educational systems to our educational system. There is no question that the average American student is of poor quality relative to the rest of the world, particularly compared to the average Asian student. However, look at what it allows our children to do. It allows them to develop their own talents and skills, most of the times at their own pace. It allows our children to explore their own strength and compensate for their weakness, and finally, our children mostly get to choose what they want to do and when and how to go about developing it. However, more importantly, our educational system mostly rewards creativity, innovation and encourages students to think outside-of-the box, excel and accelerate learning if and when a student wants to. Lastly, the ones that want to advance faster can do so independently of the rest of the class provided that they do it on their own time and those that excel on a broad basis can skip grades as necessary. In addition, children have time to themselves, which allows them to discover themselves, their talents and allows them the time to develop their talents.

As trivial as the advantages of the US educational system that I mentioned may seem, ultimately, it is what allows our country to be technological leaders and stay ahead of the rest of the world. From a simple statistical point of view, if we employ a distribution curve to graphically plot the ability of French, South Korean and American children I believe that what we'd see is that the South Korean plot would have a narrow base with a high peak, and an average score that is the highest among the three. The French plot would have a broader base than the South Korean plot with a slightly lower peak and a lower average score. The US plot would have the broadest base, the lowest peak and the lowest average score. However, the most important thing to note is that the US plot is likely to have a *very broad base with fat tails*. What this indicates is that the US plot would have more extremes, both good and bad. And this is what's important: The extreme right side of the plot is what makes our country great. It is likely that no other country has this broad base with these extremes. The far right extreme represents the very small group of people that invent, create, innovate and revitalize our country's economy.

What people in our country don't realize is that we can't have our cake and eat it too. Therefore, the risk in trying to push the average and the peak higher is that we will also lose the all-important extreme right-side of the normalized plot. For our country, losing the extreme right is tantamount to stagnation and slow decay. And, for a country like South Korea and Japan, the key to their future survival is the development of that extreme right.

Therefore, in the US, we need to worry less about what the average score of our children's PISA scores are and more about how to preserve the extreme right of our statistical plot, possibly even expanding it. This means that we have to continue to spend a lot of money on education, starting with hiring, maintaining and paying for the best teachers in the world. We also have to maintain smaller class sizes, provide more individual attention, continue to provide extracurricular activities like science clubs and sports, expand creative subjects such as music and art, and, most importantly, we must continue to allow our children to have freedom of choice, freedom of development, freedom of experimentation and freedom to expand their minds and grow.

This may sound like it's not much of a solution or much of a great plan, but what people neglect to understand is that what we have is such a fragile balance that even a minor change could make a big difference. The key to my plan isn't something very complex and is actually quite simple: Let our children largely figure out for themselves what it is that they are good at, interested in and want to pursue. This freedom will help the very minute percentage of our children that will eventually become innovators, revolutionaries and visionaries that keep our country on the leading edge of technology to find themselves and rise to the very top of the proverbial pyramid in their chosen profession.

Regardless of what we do for the rest of our children, we must preserve the aspect of freedom in our educational system for the very minute minority of our children that will keep us in the forefront of technological and innovative leadership. However, none of us are smart enough or have the skills to be able to discern which one of our children will grow to become the next great innovator that keeps our economy at the forefront of the technology curve. Therefore, we should not try. Not only should we not try, we should take the emphasis off of socialization and standardization of our educational system. The only achievement that socialization and standardization of education will achieve for our country is to eliminate the extreme right (by definition the extreme left as well) of our statistical plot making us economically no better than and likely worse off than countries like Japan that is in economic stagnation where it is likely to remain. Of course, the socialization and standardization of our educational system would raise our country's PISA scores, but this is likely to do very little for our long-term future. Again, it seems to me that people in this country are more worried about short-term gains and confused between short-term effects and long-term benefits.

Finally, I will note that France has a population of some 65 million and between 1960 and 2011 the French have won 15 Nobel prizes in physics, chemistry, physiology or Medicine, and economic sciences. France represents about 1% of the world's population and won some 4% of the Nobel prizes excluding Peace and Literature. South Korea has a population of about 49 million and has not won a single Nobel Prize. Japan has a population of over 127 million or about 2% of the world's population, and between 1960 and 2011 Japan has won 12 Nobel Prizes in the 4 scientific categories, representing about 3% of the Prizes.

The Economy

The only way for the US to stay on top economically is to constantly reinvent and innovate; this is the only way to truly help the poor in the long-term, too

Anyone who has studied history knows that countries that established dominance throughout history had a technological edge over its neighbors. When some cavemen figured out how to use stone weapons, they dominated over the ones that were using jast tree branches then the bronze-age started to dominate, which was overtaken by the iron age, which gave way to gunpowder and rifles, et cetera. Look at the Roman Empire. They not only developed roads, aquifers, and advanced military strategy and weapons, but also they figured out how to incorporate conquered territories to help them maintain control and dominion over the conquered. The Chinese developed numerous technologies and made countless scientific discoveries. The British developed technically superior ships and naval tactics to match then followed this up with the industrial revolution.

We've – the US that is – long made obsolete the industrial revolution and we are now marching down the path of technological development through advanced electricity-based technologies, customized medicines, and information-based businesses. However, this transformation was not easy and was fought all the way by unions, labor organizers, bleeding-heart liberals, socialists and self-serving politicians. If we had listened to these people, we'd be bankrupt trying to remain competitive in industries and businesses we have absolutely no business being part of like textiles, home electronics and appliances, commodity steel, ship-building, et cetera.

By the way, I'd like to note that all of the yelling and screaming that the unions did in the 1970s and 1980s about the millions of workers that were laid-off from uncompetitive industries suggesting that all of the layoffs and restructurings would cause a permanent decay of the middle-class was dead wrong, i.e., where are the millions that were supposed to be homeless? The data from the World Bank also indicates that I'm right: Until this last Great Recession, per capita GDP has been growing consistently at about 1.8% per year adjusted for inflation since 1970. So, either the union leadership was completely stupid, but pretended to know something to try and protect their own worthless jobs or they knew the future would actually work out for the better and were lying.

Either way, it is not a very flattering portrayal of union leadership and unions in general.

Let me give you a concrete example of how unions act as an anchor to the US economy. Did you know that the technology of high-speed toll-payment tags was invented in the 1970s? So, why did it not come to wide-spread use until the new millennium? Unions were afraid of toll-booth workers losing their jobs. How much money was wasted waiting in long toll lines?

However, despite these short-sighted objections, our economic edge over the last 30 years was painfully remade from an industrial base to a service-and-technology-based economy. Part of this transformation was possible, I would argue, because of all of the layoffs and restructurings that freed up the laborers necessary to allow the transformation of the economy to what it needed to be: A strong advanced economy based on information technology and service, as it should be. The US was not capable of competing with other nations in certain industries such as textiles, apparel, steel, autos, ship-building, light machinery, electronics (stereos, TVs, radios, home entertainment), cameras and films, office equipment, watches, and even computers for a while. And, in many of these areas, the US still cannot compete. It took massive transformations, bankruptcies and restructurings to get to where the country needs to be. However, there were some bright spots like Ford, which survived through the recent downturn through strong vision, leadership and planning to reinvent and reestablish a competitive auto business in the US. With the computer business, it took the will, vision, leadership and a strong new business model (in the case of Intel and Apple) to reestablish the dominance of the US in the computer business.

Anyway, our economy is now more or less set on the right path, but we cannot remain complacent like we were in the 1950s and 1960s. And, history tells us that we have to continually reinvent ourselves or we will be made obsolete by others – with glee and joy to boot. However, we can take a page from Intel's playbook to make sure that we can continue to reinvent ourselves. Since the 1970s the Japanese – as I understand it namely Fujitsu – tried to develop a microprocessor for personal computers. However, every time the Japanese thought they succeeded in bringing to market a competitive product to Intel's they discovered that they were already a generation or two behind and were already obsolete. After two decades of banging their head against the wall, the

Japanese finally gave up. This rare victory over the Japanese in the latter part of the 20th century was only made possible, because Intel continued and still continues to reinvent itself and make itself obsolete before another company gleefully does so.

Contrast this to the US auto industry in the 1970s and 1980s. In the 1970s, Detroit actually laughed at the European and Japanese imports. Laughed at them! Then in the 1980s, Detroit finally made a half-hearted effort to try and adapt itself to the new reality, but to no avail. Overtime, we know what happened between the ridiculously expensive labor structure forced on the industry by the unions, pathetic designs, and incompetent business strategy (due to mostly the high cost labor structure that the companies had to cope with) Detroit almost went the way of the Neanderthals. But what got the auto industry back?

Ford was the only one that succeeded the American way, so let's talk about it. Ford knew it was in trouble, so it borrowed all that it could by leveraging everything, including the blue oval, the symbol of Ford. This was done so that Ford could work through a massive transformation of the company and weather through massive spending in order to fix the company, particularly through the approaching Great Recession. Using this capital to reinvent the company, Alan Mullally pushed Ford to focus (excuse the pun) on, what else, the latest and greatest technology, quality and design. The strategy change that also revolutionized Ford was the global platform, instead of regional designs, which helped to reduce costs without sacrificing revenue potential. The Japanese, and to a lesser degree the Germans, proved that the same car could be successfully sold in Japan, Europe, Asia, and the Americas. In contrast, American car companies had different designs for all of these markets. Has anyone ever heard of or seen the Ford Granada? What about the Ford Cortina? How many are familiar with the Opel brand?

As an aside, prior to the arrival of Alan Mullally, one of the dumbest decisions I've ever seen a company make was when Ford discontinued the Taurus name. One of the smartest decisions that Alan Mullally made was to bring it back. As another aside, Alan's decision to sell Aston Martin, Volvo, and even Range Rover was the correct decision, but in my opinion, he went too far when he sold Jaguar. Ford needs a luxury segment and the Lincoln brand isn't cutting it. However, discontinuing the Mercury brand was very smart. Jaguar, with the right labor contract and technologies, could have been a great brand for Ford and become a leading luxury segment staple with several adjustments that Ford could have brought to bear, including the development of four-wheel drive options on its sedans, a line-up of SUVs, and compact luxury models. Lastly, the brand needs a makeover of its old man image. All of this could have been accomplished by Ford resulting in Jaguar reaching new heights.

Anyway, Ford has now reinvented itself using the greatest, latest and best technology around to manufacture cars, trucks and SUVs that people actually want and continues to reinvent itself. In addition, they have "right-sized" the company, which prevents the company from having a bloated cost structure and incurring waste through the hiring and firing rollercoaster ride that many companies have to endure.

This constant reinvention and creative-destruction must continue in every segment of the US economy for us to stay on top of the technology curve. Jast to make it completely clear, the reason for why it is so imperative for the US to continue pursuing new technology is because WE CANNOT COMPETE IN OLD TECHNOLOGY INDUSTRIES and more importantly *nor should we try to*. Reasons include: Inability to compete with lower labor costs, newer facilities, lower land costs, government subsidies, sometimes larger markets and lax regulations in other countries. Therefore, we must pursue that which is newer and constantly find ways to develop new technologies, and more importantly, stop giving these technologies away to other countries – admittedly, the US is better at finding ways to profit from our own inventions than we have been in our past, but we're still not taking full advantage of our creative edge.

Regardless, in addition to right-sizing our labor force, there are three other objectives that will be necessary for the US to continue maintaining our technological leadership: 1) The best educational system in the world; however, remember this, the educational system has a critically important feedback system: If we lose our competitive economic edge, we will lose our educational edge as well, 2) a flexible and well-educated labor force, which has to happen despite union and liberal/socialist politicians' interference, and 3) cheap and bountiful capital, commonly known as money.

Let me reinforce how the educational system fits into our future economic picture: It is vitally important for everyone to understand and know that education is the beginning and the end of the success of the US economy and that nothing can be substituted for education to guard the long-term success and survival of the US economy.

This means that those that don't, won't or can't get an education will be the most vulnerable in our society – and that's the way it should be. From a monetary and financial viewpoint, they will fall behind on an absolute and relative basis. Again, this is the way it should be; this is rational. Despite this logical and Just conclusion, if individuals want to cry over this fact and help those beleaguered people that don't have an education, anyone is free to spend their own money to help, but don't steal mine, advocate for stealing mine or vote to steal mine.

However, I would be prepared to voluntarily donate money to provide for a first class educational system for our country, and so should everyone else, because this is the only Just way to long-term prosperity FOR US ALL. The reason for this is that strong educational systems not only develop great people and a strong labor force, but it also develops the minds that will eventually go on to create the great technologies that we need to stay on top of the global economic ladder.

Second, if education is the long-term key to our country's success then a flexible and well-educated labor force is a must to continue to perpetuate our current economic advantage. This means that the continued training and education of the labor force as a whole is very important. And, most importantly, the labor force, again, as a whole, must be willing to accept disruptions in their economic life, because as technologies evolve and older technologies become obsolete, the laborer's skill level will also be made obsolete. However, this does not mean that these people should be abandoned or left to rot.

We, as a society, must allow for the retraining of these displaced workers. This does not mean that we should develop "social programs" funded by taxes to help displaced workers. Specifically, I propose that part of the compensation of workers must be in constant retraining and not in severance payments. In my opinion, one of the worst precedents that Jack Welch (formerly CEO of GE) established in the US economy was to justify short-term decisions, particularly when it comes to laying people off. From where I stand, he popularized the notion that when a company finds itself in trouble the first action it should execute is to eliminate jobs. Short-term this technique works, particularly for smaller companies that don't have deep pockets, but many labor studies have shown that in many instances these short-term moves are detrimental to the company in the long-run and costs more than keeping the displaced workers. To combat the expense of binge hirings and binge firings, severance payments have decreased dramatically, which makes the shock of separation even more painful and jarring. This short-term policy of terminating the temporary excess workers has a consequence to the long-term health of the economy, which isn't pleasant for any of us. This policy continues to drive a schism between management and the everyday workers (regardless of white or blue collar), it breeds suspicion, unproductive internal competition, back stabbing, paranoia, and, most of all, a lot of ass-kissing and brown-nosing. In combination with higher ups that respond to ass-kissing and brown-nosing, regardless of the person's ability, it focuses too much effort of our workers on how to survive politically versus increasing productivity and generating new ideas.

People wonder what harm there is in sugar-coating, white-lying, and being "gray." These behaviors lead to superficiality and pretense, subjective-based judgments, and obfuscation of issues. Taking advantage of this murkiness, the "politically astute" will manipulate issues with higher-ups that also believe in sugar-coating, white-lying and being "gray." This leads to ass-kissing and brown-nosing versus focus on solid performance measures and objectivity because in a "gray" world anything can be justified and nothing is determinable. This makes nothing wrong, justifies anything, and allows subjective judgment of higher-ups to become absolute without the need for proper reasoning. This destroys employee morale, takes time from productive activities and reduces revenue, while increasing costs. The net overall effect is that companies – including public corporations – suffer. Most Americans are saying, "so what?" Understand that without companies, there is no economy, without the economy there is no American-way of life. Whether people like it or not, we need healthy companies (including public corporations) to bolster the financial welfare of EVERY AMERICAN, particularly for the poor. However, in order to garner the cooperation and sympathy of the workers, the companies must take good care of their employees, not jast their shareholders. In the long-term, this is what will benefit shareholders too.

Therefore, each company must work toward providing a prosperous and stable life for all involved, including investors, employees, suppliers, consumers, and, ultimately, the country. Specifically, in regards to employees, one of the biggest priorities that must change with companies is actually putting action to the lip-service that workers are a company's most treasured asset. In addition to constant retraining and developing a system of self-technological obsolescence, i.e., constant innovation, owners must give employees two more incentives for the workers to be able to respond in a cooperative fashion with investors. First incentive is that ALL – I mean ALL – employees should share in the profit of the company and must have the same compensation structure as the CEO.

The first reason why having the same compensation structure for everyone in the company is so important in successfully adapting to the modern challenges of a global economy is that knowing and having the same compensation structure for all means that all are aware of what's at stake and what the effect of both success and failure truly means. This means that all are compensated accordingly and all sink or swim at the same time. This prevents all of the "us versus them" nonsense and shenanigans. It also makes it everyone's responsibility to improve, innovate, and invigorate. Put it simply, we all sink or swim together, which means that everyone is pulling in the same direction. That's teamwork. That's what we need.

Second, owners must give their employees both true responsibility, but also hold their employees truly accountable. The reason for this is that strategic contemplation and tactical machinations alone will not create a successful business. For most businesses, execution is perhaps more important than either strategy or tactics. And, when it comes to execution, it's like the weakest link in the chain: If one part of the company cannot deliver, whether from the factory floor or the executive suite then the execution gets messed-up and results in failure. This is not only why everyone should be on the same compensation structure, but this is also why every employee should be responsible for not only what they do, but also accountable for the results. The notion from the industrial revolution that workers are like machines (interchangeable and replaceable when worn out or obsolete) should be abandoned, just like the notion that labor unions are still useful in modern society.

The whole point is that we need a new paradigm for how we view relationships among investors, management, workers, suppliers and customers. The relationship among investors, management, workers and suppliers should be cooperative and collaborative and should be a seamless and integrated operation. This versus a contentious rivalry viewed with the idea that the revenue earned is subject to a zero sum game. I would contend that if any company has a collaborative and cooperative relationship with all of its stakeholders then the revenue pot is likely to not only be bigger, but also increase more rapidly overtime versus if a contentious and rancorous relationship continues.

Also, the relationship between companies and customers must also change. Instead of pretending that the company cares about the customers and that they provide customer service, they actually should care and provide real customer service. Also, instead of worrying about how much money the company can make from their customers, companies should start thinking about how to make them happier. In conjunction to this, companies should start learning how to rid itself of customers that are rude, obnoxious, and always looking for angles to take advantage of others, NO MATTER HOW PROFITABLE THESE PAINS IN THE ASS (PITA) CUSTOMERS ARE TO THE COMPANY. The reason is that this minority of customers are what costs the companies a disproportionate amount of their customer service expenses. These PITAs also upset the companies' customer service representatives who then become surly or uncaring and upset other customers in return, which then perpetuates the vicious cycle of companies versus customers. Also, these PITAs reinforce the belief for customer representatives that customers are abusive and out to get them and the company. This then makes customer representatives very defensive and overly sensitive, which then makes other customers more guarded and suspicious and ultimately more defensive, which results in more outbursts and anger at the customer service representatives (CSR), which perpetuates the negative cycle.

Therefore, it is better to get rid of the PITA customers to start off with. Let's take a credit card company (CCC) as an example. If the CCC got rid of all of the PITAs this should help to reduce the need for CSRs, which lowers costs, which helps to lower interest rates, which draws more customers, which increases profitability in the long-run. Contrast this to the CCC that takes the PITA customers. More expenses to hold and retrain CSRs as the turnover increases and marketing expenses increase as good customers leave for the more long-run focused CCC. This will force the CCC to either lower interest rates to bring back the good customers, which lowers profitability or raise interest rates to cover the excess costs incurred by the PITA customers. Either way, the CCC that retains and attracts PITA customers will eventually lose. This principle will work for all businesses large or small, for mass-market businesses or wholesale-oriented businesses. The subtle change in how the company is run between the mass market and the wholesale businesses should be easily adaptable by a smart management team.

One more consideration: Profitability of a customer cannot be measured by dollars and cents alone. It has to incorporate the non-direct-financial impact of the customer's activity with the company. This means that even financially low or lower profit customers can be very profitable to the company. The management also has to consider input from the customers; meaning, if the customer helps to improve the company's performance and profitability, the company should reward that customer, not jast take it as a free gift. This would open the company to additional input from customers, and trust me, there are a lot of suggestions that a customer can make to companies on how to improve its business.

In conjunction to this aspect of business, companies should also truly reward those employees that bring new successful technology and innovation to the company. If an idea increases profit by $10 million annually, the employee that came up with the idea should be financially rewarded instead of being given lip-service and a plaque, may be a promotion. How about $1 million bonus in the first year, $750,000 in the second year $500,000 in the third year, $250,000 in the fourth year and $0 from year five? How many more good ideas do you think the company can expect from employees?

It should be the same for scientists, researchers and developers. Those that create or develop products that make money for the company should share in the profit. The argument against this is that scientists, researchers and developers are paid to create these products. However, I would argue that when a corporation makes 100s of millions of dollars from the creation of a product, the salaries paid to scientists, researchers and developers are not enough and merely represent a token of gratitude and nothing else; more like a condescending pat on the back. This is not right. I strongly believe that should companies share part of the profit derived from the creation of a new product from research and development then not only will corporations see many more products, but also I believe that products will be developed faster. However, to insure long-term success, scientists, researchers and developers should also be held accountable on a long-term basis for developing products that are defective. Therefore, money from profit sharing should be withheld until a certain number of years pass and the product is sure to be safe.

This type of revision to our economic base is necessary since technology and creation of new products must be at the center of our economy for us to thrive in the long run. In addition, we must rethink and reengineer our labor relationships to create a flexible economy, including a flexible labor force that cooperates and collaborates with owners and investors instead of being combative and corrosive. Once we have this restructured labor force we can then move onto the core focus of what we really need to concentrate on, which is the development and growth of new technologies.

When we have a flexible and cooperative labor force with collaborative suppliers and rational customers, we can then work on innovation and technological advancement, which requires research, which requires capital, i.e., money, preferably, cheap money. To put into more simple terms, money is one of the three vital ingredients from a societal viewpoint that we need to continue our economic prosperity. This means that we have to keep the money in private hands, not the government's. In case it's been forgotten, let me remind everyone that central planning doesn't work; look at the economic history of the following countries: Soviet Union, China pre-1980, North Korea, and Cuba. Also, let me remind everyone that socialism and high taxes on the rich doesn't work either; look at the economic history of the following countries: Any Latin American country pre-1990s, UK pre-The Iron Lady, current day Greece, Spain, Portugal and Italy.

Continuing on: How does money in private hands work to create innovation? For the select few that have a degree in economics or business, this is the part that can be skipped, because it will be obvious. For others that don't know the relationship, I strongly recommend understanding this vital cause and effect relationship to understand why a smaller government, not a larger one, is the way to true long-term prosperity.

I think the vast majority of people understand that to innovate and develop new technology, research must be done. Also, to put these new technologies to the test, we need money to build prototypes, experimental modules and actually conduct the experiments and tests. Then we have to have money to build factories or facilities, build a distribution chain, do marketing and provide for working capital (this is the money needed to buy supplies, pay for rent, interest expenses, and other administrative and operational expenses, while waiting for products to be made, sold and revenue to start coming in). If the product is special and actually hits the market in a big way then the business owners have to have money to expand, develop new products, train new workers and educate and bring up to speed their supply and distribution chains. Business owners also have to provide for workers' healthcare, retirement and compensation, and provide a profit to investors, all of which takes money.

Quite a few people have asked me why it is that our country can't do all this by taking money away from the rich and having government workers use their judgment to make all the necessary decisions. Even though this may sound like it would work, history tells us that it will never work. If it did work socialism, central planning and communism should work too, but all have been miserable failures. The reason why government workers making economic decisions won't work for us is because, simply put, two heads are better than one. Also, most if not all the government workers aren't experts in any major or minor technological, medical or scientific fields. Let me repeat that THESE PEOPLE AREN'T EXPERTS IN ANY MAJOR OR MINOR TECHNOLOGICAL, MEDICAL OR SCIENTIFIC FIELDS. In addition, these government bureaucrats aren't putting their money where their mouth is and so their judgment could be motivated by a lot of issues that have nothing to do with the potential for success of any product (using this term broadly to include products and services). One of the biggest issues that could motivate the judgment of a bureaucrat is the fear of failure; more precisely, the fear of wasting a lot of tax dollars. This means they will go with the safest choice or the most defensible choice, not the best choice, which at times could be very high risk. Government panels aren't going to be any different either. Other than the fear of failure, there are a lot of other reasons why bureaucrats shouldn't be trusted to make decisions on behalf of the whole country.

So, why would private individuals be any different? First and foremost, individuals have to **put their money at risk**. Second, no individual would take the risk of investing in any business that they have no capacity to evaluate correctly. However, regardless of expertise, individuals will only select investments that they truly believe in and, by definition, will take responsibility for. The end result is that many of them will fail, but it only takes a handful of successes to create technological momentum. But most of all, with many individuals, many ideas get a shot, and even some of the craziest ideas could get to see the light of day, and some of them could actually become very profitable. Believe it or not, the personal computer was one of those crazy ideas that actually saw the light of day and flourished due to the passions of a very small handful of men. Even some of the more mundane ideas, when executed properly, can provide many benefits to society. What if I told you that I wanted to set up a sandwich shop in Manhattan, NY? You may think I was crazy, but what if I told you that this is exactly what happened to Cosi, which was founded in 1996? Even back then, no one thought that Cosi would be a success in New York City, the home of deli sandwich shops. In a bureaucratic system, something like Cosi would never see the light of day and hundreds, if not thousands of jobs would be lost.

So, the final question that needs to be answered is: How do technological advances keep the US on top? I think it's obvious, but let me explain. Think about how China makes money. What is the key to their economic prowess? Cheap labor – at least for now – but it's not cheap labor alone. It's also access to the level of technology appropriate for its work force and industrial development. In other words, China is where we were some 100 years ago. Now, given our standard of living and technological know-how, we shouldn't even try to compete with the likes of China for goods and products that they are capable of making, and making cheaper than we do. Let me put it another way, if a consumer in the US can buy the same TV for $500 versus $1,000, which would they buy? It doesn't matter whether or not it's made in China, for our economy it is better if we buy the $500 TV than the $1,000 TV. The buyer can then take the $500 in savings to buy something else like an Apple iPhone, which is largely American (at least the profit goes to an American company), or directly or indirectly invest in some other American businesses or the economy.

Don't forget that the Chinese have the same access to technology to make toys, sneakers, lower-end consumer electronics, textiles and other low technology products as any other country in the world. This means that given their lower labor costs, lower land prices, and lower supply costs for many items, they will be more profitable. Thus, for us to be able to compete with the Chinese on these lower technology items, we'd have to significantly lower our costs, which means lowering labor costs since supply costs and land costs can't change much and investors don't have to take less. However, if we do try to compete with the Chinese then our standard of living has to go down and we cannot support our technological development. Therefore, we must abandon our efforts to defend the indefensible and move on to industries where we have the ability to be the best. And, that which we do best is better and greater technological innovation. For the US, this is financial services, information technology, computer-oriented products and services, advanced electronics, higher-end pharmaceuticals, aeronautics, armaments, advanced automotives (ironically), specialty steel (ironically), entertainment (movies, music, sports, etc.), cultural products (fashion, fast food, life-style, etc.), natural gas-based chemicals business, oil and gas exploration, mining, technology-driven mass agriculture, cattle-farming, among others.

So, as we give up the low end of the technology spectrum and other industries and businesses where we are less productive, we must have something to replace it with. Obviously, what we can do to replace lower technology items is to develop higher end technology products and services. This is why we must continue to develop our technological capabilities. And, in order to stay as the leader among advanced economies, we must make our own technologies obsolete before some other country does it for us. A great example of the stupidity of resting on our laurels is well documented by the history of the automotive industry. Ironically, a great example of the comeback and restoration of leadership can also be seen with the automotive industry, specifically with Ford.

Due to this constant, dynamic and creative destruction process, we must have a flexible labor force to cope with the changes that need to take place in our country, but also to deal with other countries coming up the technology curve. Also, companies, in response to the evolutionary – sometimes revolutionary – process of the INEVITABLE technological march, must be prepared to continually make itself and its products obsolete, but also take care of its people and give them the opportunity to retrain and relearn.

Regardless, if we do try to compete on the lower technology areas – as the labor unions would have us do – then we must accept that we will be committing suicide very slowly and diverting precious resources away from areas that we should be more focused on.

However, let me remind everyone that all these changes need a lot of capital, a highly trained work force, strong educational system, great scientific and technological research, and great minds to put it all together, both on a financial and operational level. And, as lesser and lesser technologies become the domain of the "cheaper" economies, we should pass-on these lower technologies to these countries and take the labor force that are born from these disruptions and retrain them to support the latest and greatest technological developments.

Remember that we must have a strong educational system for long-run strength of our economy, a flexible labor force to maintain the dynamism of the present and the future, and access to cheap and bountiful capital to seed our future. This is the basic essence of the key plan for the future of America – by extension any industrialized or highly developed country. This is also one of the reasons why overtaxing the country, and in particular the wealthy is such poison. Don't forget the wealthy are the ones with the excess capital to invest. Taking money away from the wealthy can only result in a slow and agonizing decay for the country, like we are seeing today.

Now tell me that money is the root of all evil and the wealthy are the pariahs of society.

Labor Unions: The viral infection that continues to poison the American economy

I once asked the former president of the UAW what the responsibility and role of the labor union was in regards to the decline of Detroit. He promptly deflected the question by saying, "ask one of the CEOs of the big three." I responded by saying that I wasn't interested in what management did to destroy the US automotive industry, but what responsibility the labor unions had in the destruction of the US auto industry, in particular with regards to the high labor costs, including retirement funding, and layoff funding that the companies had to overcome versus their Japanese and European competitors. He refused to answer and kept on trying to deflect the issue. The howling I heard from pro-labor constituents in the meeting was predictable and ridiculous.

Regardless, based on the last three or four years, in my opinion, it's obvious that the former president of the UAW was either ignorant, blind or lying, whether it was through omission or deliberate planning. By now, he's probably dead, and I suspect he did not die a peaceful death, if he was an honest man.

So, why am I bringing this up? It goes to show that deception, intentional or otherwise, perpetrated by those with power in our society poses a stubborn threat to our well-being. It also goes to show that once a "truth" is established – in this case that labor unions are what made this country great – it doesn't take much to maintain this establishment view, regardless of reality and how this reality has transformed over time. The main reason for this unnecessary longevity for so called "historical truths" that have become false is simple, people don't think, and they only go by rules, established "truths," and what they are told is true. People have been told that labor unions fought for the workers against the robber-barons and struck a blow for Justice and prosperity. This is an absolute lie, but once people believed it, they assumed it was true forever. Think about this, as a baby whole milk is probably very good for us, as an adult drinking the quantities of whole milk proportionate to our body weight that a baby consumes is probably extremely bad for us. The same can be said about labor unions: Once, a long-time ago, labor unions may have been good for the economy, but sometime in the 1950s or 1960s, it became poisonous for the health of our country.

Having said this, I will say that historically the formation of labor unions were indeed good for the country, but not necessarily for the reasons why people think it was good for our country. Most people believe that labor unions were about raising the standard of living by taking-back some of the wealth that was stolen from the workers by the robber-barons. This is not only false, but also even if it were true it is not the main reason why labor unions were good for the country. Also, the rise in standard of living of American workers is not a bad thing, but it depends on how the standard of living was raised; jast ask the Greeks. Anyway, when it comes to the activities of the labor unions, the rise in the standard of living was only a happy coincidence and mostly temporary at that. However, more to the point, the way the labor unions went about trying to accomplish this rise in standard of living was atrociously devastating for the American economy and the average American in the long-run. So, the rise in the standard of living of Americans has virtually nothing to do with why labor unions were good for the country.

The primary reason why labor unions were once good for the country was because they represented Justice and fairness or more to the point the fight for Justice and fairness. However, since the early days, labor unions have turned into extortion machines, which is why they are not good for the country anymore and haven't been good for a very, very long time, may be since the 1930s or 1940s.

First, let us agree that if I can prove that labor unions are extortion machines then you agree that labor unions are bad for the country: Agree [ ] Disagree [ ].

My guess is that if you disagree, you are likely someone that runs labor unions, are a diehard union member (or know someone who is) or a Democrat. That's OK, but please keep an open mind while reading the rest of my book; I believe that honest people will change their minds about labor unions.

Anyway, let me talk about why I believe labor unions are extortion machines. What does a labor union do? The stated function of labor unions is to get a "fair" deal on compensation (including salary, benefits, retirement, and safety net) and to ensure safe work environments for their members from the company and industry that its members belong to. However, this is not what labor unions actually do. What the labor union representatives do is look for increases in compensation and benefits *regardless of the health and economic circumstances of the company, industry or the overall economy*. And, if the company and industry do not agree to these demands, the labor union representatives call for a strike that threatens the stability and profitability of the company, industry and sometimes the economy as a whole; however, the company cannot freely retaliate by firing the labor force and rehiring as necessary and needed. This is not fair and not balanced. This imbalance may be due to laws that prohibit companies from retaliating, and it should not be a surprise that labor unions are behind these laws that handcuff companies.

So, given the handcuffs that the companies are shackled with, the only recourse that is left to them is to pick the lesser of two evils. This means that companies have to do a risk-benefit analysis to choose the lesser of the two evils: Is it better to give into the demands of the labor union, which helps in the short-term, but hurts in the long-run or take the short-term loss and hold out for the right deal that will help in the long-run. Either way, the company takes a loss, but has to figure out which loss is less evil. This means that INVESTERS ARE PUT IN A NO WIN SITUATION. Also, rarely, if ever, do companies get concessions out of labor unions, and if they do get concessions, it is typically under very stressful economic situations for the companies, industry or the economy in general.

As an example, jast look at the automotive industry and the huge amount of extortion money extracted from the industry by the labor unions over the decades since the 1950s, and what it cost our country. Again, this is not to say that labor unions were the only piece of the puzzle that led to the decapitation of the US auto industry, but it is by far the largest piece, in my opinion. Management's reaction to the labor unions' antics is probably the second largest factor.

The thing of it is is that labor unions and the owners and managers of businesses need not and should not be at odds with each other and the pool of money that is to be divided does not have to be a zero sum game. Yes, in the short-run, it is a zero sum game: A dollar paid out to labor (this includes management) cannot be paid out to investors. However, in the long-run, the pool of money to be divided between labor and owners should grow, if the business is managed correctly and adapts correctly to the ever changing reality of the global economy. However, if the business is doomed anyway, then no amount of negotiation between labor and owner is going to change the fact that both groups are going to suffer horrific losses without dramatic effort from both. Especially in modern times when few, if any, businesses are insulated from the vagaries of the global economy, it is very critical that labor and owner form a strong cooperative relationship and both must work together to make more profit for all.

As previously stated, one change that must occur is to make sure that workers and management are paid the same way. This means that management has to negotiate with the owners as to what percentage of revenue will go towards the compensation of all of the workers, including, salary, benefits, insurance (this includes severance, training, and other disruption planning tools) and retirement for both so called management and so called labor. Once percentages have been decided then management should negotiate with labor to figure out how much management takes and how much labor takes. The alternative method would be to allow labor and management together to negotiate with owners a percentage of revenue that each would take. However, once the percentages have been decided, management and labor should leave it up to each other to decide how they would use this money to achieve the goals and objectives agreed to by all three (owners, management and labor) sides to uphold their respective end of the bargain, i.e., each group must decide for themselves, how to staff the jobs, how many to hire, how to train, how to retrain, how to plan for the future and generally leave it up to each group to decide how to best carry out their responsibilities. The underlying assumption is that management and labor must **decide together** what the goal and the objective of the company is and what each must do to achieve those goals and objectives; ***however, let each decide the best way to execute on those agreed upon objectives.***

Obviously, in either of the above compensation scenario, it is in the best interest of each group to minimize the amount of people they use to execute their side of the bargain and makes each very lean and highly productive. Also, in times of trouble, both labor and management will have to face the choice of how many to cut from where. In an ideal situation, they'd be no division between management and labor and they'd be one pool of money for all. However, given the historical context of labor relations, this may take some time to achieve.

The owners and labor should also agree to division of revenue above and beyond expectations and also what to do when revenue expectations fall short. The best strategy would be for all to take the minimum compensation to reduce costs and then take bonus from the excess profit generated. This pay scheme, which was in force on Wall Street before Congress messed it up, works very well, in general.

By the way, corporations were modeled after the military. What this means is that white-collar workers are like officers and blue-collar workers are like regular soldiers and non-commissioned officers. In fact, historically, large businesses were organized along the lines of military units, precisely because of the effectiveness of military organizations to carry out the orders of its leaders. However, in modern day armies try doing anything by dictating to the soldiers and not looking for their input and cooperation, and see how victorious such an army would be.

Anyway, regardless of the organization of companies, labor unions interfere with the process of cooperation and they continue to sell the concept of "us versus them." Otherwise, the union leadership has no job, no salary, no power and no prestige. Also, look at the history of labor unions. It's been a while since the labor unions were completely corrupted by the mob and controlled by them, but, nevertheless, suspicion of misdeeds continues and there is no question that the history of the labor unions is heavily tainted with corruption. The amount of money stolen – in the 10s if not 100s of billions of dollars – and misused is staggering, but the actual amount will never be known. And, more to the point, very deliberately swindled from union members and the public.

Remember that in almost all circumstances absolute power corrupts absolutely. This is but one reason why labor unions are poison and have the potential to be poison to society, but getting back to the main point, labor unions are poison because they prevent the cooperative work between labor and owners. However, as of the last economic crisis, labor unions did exhibit the kind of self-control that we have not seen in the past. Specifically, Ron Gettlefinger of the UAW is to be commended for doing the difficult job of convincing his constituents to accept cutting the ridiculously expensive UAW labor contracts and helping to turn the US auto business back to health.

However, the underlying temptation of taking more than labor should during better times still exists, unless everyone is put into the same boat. Second, the fact that labor union leaders still need to justify their existence and justify the continued collection of union dues makes them vulnerable to pushing for benefits and higher compensations that don't help the companies and industries in the long-run and therefore ultimately hurt the working ranks as well. Third, labor unions are still vulnerable to penetration from unsavory sectors of our society. Fourth, it continues to put a wedge between labor and owners by making everything "us versus them," and prevents both groups from developing a cooperative and productive relationship and ending the labor union's stranglehold on negotiating adversarial labor contracts. Fifth, the additional bureaucracy increases costs for everyone, and, therefore, the continued deception of labor unions being good for the country needs to be ended.

The bottom-line is that the time for labor unions has long come and gone. And, while labor unions were once good for the country, it is now a major barrier to the progress of this country. The one example that most people can relate to is the high speed toll-collection tags. As stated previously, the unions did not want to jeopardize union jobs from disappearing and the dues able to be collected from those members. So, the rest of us had to suffer some 20-years because of labor union greed and selfishness. Some people have said to me that it's worth it if it means that less people were thrown out of their jobs. I would argue that very few of those people would have become homeless and could have been retrained to do other jobs within a couple of years, not 20 years. So, the only explanation for the 20 year delay is that union leaders didn't want to lose their power or the money. The excuse to extend toll lines for 20 years: "We can use natural attrition such as retirements and people quitting to minimize the impact of the transition to toll collectors." The net impact of this largesse is to reduce the productivity of the rest of the country. And, in my opinion, the net financial effect was negative to the economy.

This is but one of many examples of labor unions distorting and interfering with the natural progression of technological and economic development. When this happens, the labor unions are poisoning our country and making us less competitive in the global economy. This weakening makes us more and more vulnerable to the economic attacks from our global competitors, which weakens our economic power and makes our people more vulnerable to disruptions. Don't forget, for the US, development of new technology and increased productivity (increase in revenue for the same cost or reduction in cost while generating the same revenue) are the two most important goals that we need to focus on to maintain our economic superiority. Labor unions heavily interfere with this process and create a hostile working environment by perpetuating the "us versus them" mentality that, in our modern global economy, is completely unnecessary and obsolete.

It is time for labor unions to go the way of the dodo birds and a new labor-owner paradigm to be developed; one that will accelerate our economic development and prosperity. Moreover, the childish thought that stealing from one constituent for the benefit of another is good must be abandoned. Along similar lines, one of the most critically erroneous and childish concepts that needs to be abandoned is that communism – and by extension socialism – is an ideal to be strived for. This is such nonsense that I can't even begin to express how exasperated I am when I hear this. I will elaborate on this in another chapter.

The reason for the current financial/economic crisis is because of the average American, and not because of Wall Street

First, let me make it perfectly clear about what I mean by an average American: It has nothing to do with race, sex, area of residence, income, wealth, social status, educational achievement, job, or any other superficial cue, but everything to do with the way people think and behave.

Forget even the financial crisis. All manner of ills that plague the US is the responsibility of the majority of the people living in this country. By now, if the reader doesn't understand why the average American is responsible for all these ills, let me be very specific. Let's start with the Great Recession.

What happened? But before we get to the explanation, let me ask a few questions first:

1) If I ask you to commit suicide for a million dollars would you? Yes [ ] or No [ ]
2) If I give you what you want, whose fault is it, if the end result of what you want isn't what you expected? My fault [ ] or Your fault [ ]
3) Think about your favorite sport that you like to play or watch, generally speaking, do you know the rules of that sport? Yes [ ] or No [ ]
4) If a rich person offered to flip a coin and asked you to bet your life savings and all or part of your future earnings on the outcome of the bet would you? Yes [ ] or No [ ]
5) If you live in a home or condo that you bought and for which you made a down payment of 5%-20%, who owns the home? You [ ] or the bank that you took out a mortgage with [ ]

Let me guess how the vast majority answered the above questions: The answer to the first question is NO. The answer to the second question is YOUR FAULT. The answer to the third question is YES. The answer to the fourth question is NO, and the answer to the fifth question is YOU. Now remember these answers because I will come back to these questions.

So, why am I telling you that the root cause of the Great Recession is the average American? Simply put it's because of the way the vast majority of Americans "think" or more likely don't think and the philosophy that they "believe in." By now most people know that the primary reason for the latest recession is largely due to the mortgage crisis, i.e., too many people borrowed too much money and over-extended themselves and when these people could not make repayments the housing market collapsed. The blame for this over-extension was put squarely on the shoulders of "greedy Wall Street people" who supposedly manipulated the mortgage and housing markets, forced the people to over-extend, manipulated the mortgage-backed securities markets and caused a ripple effect that collapsed the global economy.

The truth is that people who work on Wall Street don't directly talk to people who borrow money to finance their home purchases, so people on Wall Street could not have convinced home buyers to borrow more than they should. In fact, it can be said that if there were people that manipulated consumers to over extend, it would have been the real-estate and mortgage brokers. Ironically, these people are typically your average middle-class, middle-income people. Moreover, very surprisingly, these people, by and large, are relatively unsophisticated financial types who can only follow the edicts and goals set by their bosses or they own their businesses. However, the most important point to note is that whether or not the real estate and mortgage brokers enticed people to over extend, regardless, everyone should know the limits of their own financial ability and each individual must be solely responsible for planning for the inevitable downturn.   If people did not plan correctly and did not understand what they were getting into when they signed the mortgage documents then no one can be blamed for their financial troubles other than the home buyer and, most importantly, no one else should be made to bear the responsibility for the home buyer's mistakes or ignorance.

The first question I asked at the beginning of this chapter pertains to this issue. Would anyone commit suicide if someone offered a million dollars to do so? Of course not! So, why would anyone financially over extend themselves, because someone offers them more loans than they can handle? Short-term greed, of course (this is very different than long-term greed). Moreover, individuals should know their limits and plan for the worst. Therefore, the fact that some people were over-extended is nobody's fault but their own.

Furthermore, the job of Wall Street mortgage traders or bankers is to make money for their firm and themselves, not to figure out whether or not each individual can take on a certain financial burden or not. Please, keep this in mind when reading the rest of my dissertation. At the heart of the financial crisis was instruments called mortgage-backed securities. If anyone wants to understand why and how the financial crisis came about, they have to understand how these mortgage-backed securities or mortgage bonds work. The critical facet of these financial instruments that average Americans need to know is that they are designed to make the cost of mortgages as cheap as possible. How this happens is not really critical, but I will explain it anyway to paint a complete picture.

Here's how a mortgage bond works. When a bank lends money for someone to buy a home two events are triggered. First, the money the bank lends out has to be drawn from deposits gathered from where ever, and second, this money can be loaned once and only once by the individual bank, unless the seller of the property redeposits the money into the same bank that loaned the money to begin with. Therefore, the amount of money for loans will be heavily limited, i.e., limited by the amount of deposits available to the bank. Therefore, given that the pool of available money is restricted, as demand for mortgages grows the only option that the bank can employ to dampen demand is to raise interest rates. This is where mortgage bonds come into play. Mortgage bonds were created to increase the available pool of money to lend to consumers for additional mortgages. It was also designed to spread the risk of holding mortgages by allowing investors other than banks to hold mortgages. By increasing the pool of available funds for mortgages, it has the effect of making mortgage interests as low as possible, given that supply of money available to lend for mortgages is increased. The way it works is that the bank takes all of its mortgages and bundles it together and sells it to thousands of buyers, which spreads the risk and increases the amount of money available to make more mortgage loans. Let me give you a concrete example.

Let's say that a bank loaned out $100,000 increments to 10,000 consumers. If the bank held all of these mortgages on their books, all of the risk of holding these loans would remain with the bank. But, by packaging all of these loans into a single bond and selling it to hundreds of buyers, the risk is not only spread among these buyers, but also the bank gets back almost all of the $1 billion that it loaned out to consumers. The bank then takes the new money and loans it out to almost another 10,000 consumers for them to buy houses. Then the bank bundles the second round of mortgages into mortgage bonds and sells it to another group of buyers (some of these buyers could be the same buyers that bought into the first round of mortgage bonds). The bank continues to do this over and over again, which enables the bank to loan out roughly $10-$15 for every dollar they collect through deposits. There is a specific formula that determines what ratio the banks are allowed to "create" additional capital from the deposits they collect and this ratio is governed by essentially the Federal Reserve Bank.

The idea of mortgage bonds is simple and great, but the problem is that many investors bought these bonds based on faulty mortgage bond ratings due to rating agencies' incorrectly rating these bonds as very high quality bonds that had a very low potential for default. However, the bond ratings agencies were misguided by the mortgage investment bankers who proposed that the diversification of the portfolio would provide low default rates by definition; meaning, if there are a million mortgages in a portfolio the risk of so many defaults occurring to make investors lose money is low, especially if the bond investors buy a diversified portfolio of mortgage bonds, given that each bond itself is well diversified. However, the mortgage bankers were in turn deceived by the mortgage originators (the people who negotiate with the consumers to give the consumers the actual mortgage to buy homes) who were doing virtually no background checks, or credit analysis because their bosses were pressuring into producing better and better results, and in turn the mortgage originators' bosses were being pressured to deliver results by their CEO who was being pressured by investors in the bank to deliver ever growing profits. And, investors were being pressured by their constituents such as state pension funds, corporate retirement programs and individuals to turn ever growing and quicker profits. Note that the vast majority of people in state pension funds and corporate retirement programs are typically middle-income, middle-class people. Also, note that the vast majority of mortgage originators and their bosses are middle-class, middle-income people, too.

In addition, the federal government through the "Fair Housing Act" – another inane "social program" that ends up hurting our economy – was pushing banks to lend to lower income and less credit-worthy people and the easy-credit environment made it easy for banks to do so. To top it all off, some people lied or exaggerated on their mortgage applications, which were never checked, and many people stretched their budget to accommodate a larger house and therefore larger mortgages in the erroneous belief that housing prices would never come down. Further exacerbating the problem, many people were borrowing ever increasing amounts of money on their credit cards, taking out car loans and home equity loans or borrowing on other credit lines and taking financial risks that they shouldn't have.

Specifically, many people believed that not only would real estate prices continue to rise, but also do so at a pace that would far outstrip long-term inflation and population growth rates. Moreover, these people assumed that they would not only have their jobs forever, but that they would get raises that would make the mortgage look cheap over time. If these assumptions were true then buying over one's means and capacity could make sense, but it cannot be true. Therefore, when the economy started to weaken, more specifically, expectations for the economy weakened, everyone started to panic. This then caused a massive sell-off in everything and triggered a precipitous slow-down in consumer spending, which then caused companies to reduce production and staff, which exacerbated the problem even more. In a normal recession, the negative economic cycle wouldn't be a big deal, but when the economy is heavily over leveraged and there are multiple asset bubbles, there is no room for error as leverage magnifies both upside gain and downside losses.

Therefore, what started as a slow unwinding of investments – due to a fringe few that were fearful that the economy was on the brink of weakening – started to accelerate as economic news started to darken further. This created more fear and more selling, which then accelerated due to consumers starting to pull back on spending due to economic news and declining asset markets (stocks, bond, real estate and other major investment sectors). The accelerated selling then had an increasing and compounding negative effect on the economy, which caused more investors to sell and more consumers to curtail spending, which reinforced the negative cycle even more. Before anyone knew it, we were in the midst of the most serious economic downturn since the Great Recession.

And, to make matters worse, most people did not plan for a rainy day at all. In addition, almost everyone's pursuit of short-term profits and gain driven by their inability to think beyond the now makes it very difficult to fix serious economic downtowns, let alone avoid them. The bottom-line is that all of the events that transpired since about the middle of the last decade were the culmination of the many decades of decay in America's moral/value system, ethical behavior, and flaunting of integrity.

Think of it this way. The behavior of the majority of Americans over the last 8 decades or so is equivalent to well-tuned athletes eating fatty meats, cakes, pies, potato chips, pasta, ice cream, candy, chocolate and bread and butter in increasing amounts and with more frequency over their life time without doing any further physical activities. Sooner or later, the chicken is going to come home to roost. Chances are they get massive heart attacks or strokes, get inflicted with diabetes, get cancer of one type or another, or get some combination of the above, not to mention obesity, joint problems due to obesity, respiratory issues, and other medical issues. This is what most Americans have done to themselves on a financial basis, and, ironically, on a physical basis as well.

So, how can anyone blame jast the banks and Wall Street? All that the vast majority of hard workers at banks and Wall Street firms working in mortgage departments did was to fill the demand for ever more and cheaper mortgages. In other words, they gave Americans what they wanted, but it didn't work out the way Americans thought it would. This goes to question 2) in the beginning of this chapter.

There is no way, absolutely no way for the bankers and traders to push up the real estate market without the majority of Americans' eager involvement and participation. Is it true that some of these bankers and Wall Streeters did things that anyone would consider immoral? Absolutely, but if people blame the entire group for our ills then that's like saying that we should arrest all baseball players for using steroids and lying about it because people like Mark Maguire, Sammy Sosa, Barry Bonds and a select few others did so or arresting all money managers because Bernie Madoff ran a huge Ponzi scheme. The fact of the matter is that mortgage bankers and traders filled a need, America's insatiable appetite for cheap money to buy (more like gamble on) real estate. This is no different than liquor makers filling-in the demand for alcohol or gun manufacturers filling their constituents' demands or for pharmaceutical producers filling the demand for medicine. No one should condemn alcohol manufacturers for a drunk driver's carelessness or a gun manufacturer for murders and pharmaceutical producers for suicides, overdoses and abuses. At the end of the day, these industries are fulfilling a legitimate need for something that people want. Americans wanted cheaper and more plentiful mortgages, they got it! So, don't blame the mortgage bankers, originators, and traders for giving Americans what they want. And, by no means blame all the banks and Wall Street firms and their employees for our ills.

The next point goes to the third question at the beginning of this chapter. If people don't know what they're doing they should get educated, if they can't/don't then they shouldn't participate; it's that simple. If nothing else, everyone should know that if something sounds too good to be true then it probably is too good to be true. How is it that people know all of the rules pertaining to their favorite sport, but when it comes down to their money, they use the excuse that they didn't know the consequences? That defies common sense! If that were true then all that these people are saying is that to them playing sports the right way is more important than managing their money! Really, I don't think that this is what these people want to say! However, if that is true then all that they are saying is that they have truly distorted values or are plainly very stupid or irresponsible or both. Either way, when it comes to one's money, everyone should absolutely know what they are doing with it. In reality, the excuse that people were duped can only be interpreted in three ways: 1) People don't care about their money, 2) they are very stupid about their money, or 3) they were very greedy and blinded by that greed. Whichever is correct people should pay for their carelessness, stupidity or greed. Also, when people risk everything and bet all that they have on a single outcome, some are going to get very rich, but some are going to lose everything. So, when something bad does happen people must take responsibility for their decisions and actions instead of looking for someone else to blame and trying to get compensated for one's mistake by blaming others and taking their money.

In other words, one shouldn't gamble all of their life savings (and more to the point, other people's money) on one bet, but yet many were willing to do jast that when it came to so called "home ownership." Why would anyone do that?! Then they have the temerity to blame someone else for their troubles! That is incredibly shameful! These people directly contributed to the downward spiral of the entire country's economy and they claim innocents! I'm sorry, but I have no sympathy for people like that; and they can only blame themselves for their suffering. But the problem is that they are dragging the rest of us with them, and that's the real problem.

So, the real problem is people's greed, specifically, very short-term greed. People saw real estate prices going up endlessly in the short-term and decided that they wanted a piece of the get-rich-quick scheme. Then when they failed to get what they wanted, they turned around and blamed others and used that as an excuse to steal from wealthier people. NO ONE CAN HAVE THEIR CAKE AND EAT IT TOO. How do people STILL not know this? It is extremely incredulous to me that so many Americans still don't know this.

The relationship between people's philosophy and the current financial/economic crisis is that the end result of people's short-sighted actions and greed is driven by their irrational philosophical system. Yet people insist on continuing this path to murder/suicide. Whether they realize it or not, most Americans want to continue to steal money from the wealthy so they can escape the consequences of their actions. But the only real cure to their problem is, unfortunately, their bankruptcy. In other words, they must be held accountable for their actions.

Even people that did not overextend and didn't gamble on the real estate markets and therefore are claiming to be a victim aren't listening. All average and normal Americans are still very much responsible for the state of the country, if at least one of the following applies to the average and normal American: 1) Voted for either a Democrat or a Republican,2) taken out a mortgage with less than 2 years of reserves (100% of the money needed to live 2-years without working), 3) maxed out credit cards, 4) have a debt to income ratio greater than 25%, excluding the mortgage, 5) made a particular investment because everyone else was, 6) believe that the rich can afford to pay more and should pay more in taxes, 7) believe in government sponsored "social programs," and 8) generally believe in or said things that are outlined in the chapter titled, "Rules and laws: The destroyers of minds and therefore societies."

If someone thinks that they were not directly involved in causing the financial crisis, it is most likely because most of them didn't have the opportunity to do so, got lucky and got out before everything blew up, by some other fortune were able to avoid the catastrophe or were about to or were planning to when everything collapsed. Or, put another way: They got lucky. If not lucky then the individual was poor, was a student, was in jail, spending money in other ways, or somehow could not participate, but wishing they could have when real estate valuations were rapidly rising. The fact of the matter is that almost everyone in the US, other than children are directly responsible for the financial crisis, and it really does not necessarily have to do with anything that they did or didn't do. It has everything to do with what people think and believe in and how they act.

Finally, there are a very, very small handful of people that truly think and acted prudently that were still hurt by the Great Recession. To these people, my heart goes out to them, and I hope that they have a quick recovery to better financial standing. Good luck.

Anyway, the reason why virtually everyone in America is responsible for the Great Recession is simple: The vast majority of people make it possible for others to behave badly, because the vast majority approve of what everyone thinks and believes in. Some may argue that they don't believe in gambling on the real estate market and didn't do so themselves, but there is no escaping the fact they believe in the same things that the "bad" people do such as: Getting something for nothing (the rich should pay more in taxes), the lottery mentality (wow, I want to sue someone and make millions or I deserve to win the lottery or I should get more government benefits), "social programs," that they own the home that they live in despite the fact that they have a mortgage, white lies, political correctness, religion, short-term results over long-term prosperity, equality without Justice, and many other ridiculous things. Therefore, the society that we live in will act according to these beliefs as a whole. The only difference between the person that believes that they are not responsible and the "bad" person is that the person who believes that they did nothing wrong manifests symptoms differently that's all. Otherwise, the ones that feel that they are not responsible for the current financial crisis are virtually the same as the "bad" people and therefore all largely and equally responsible. Most people don't like this conclusion and will deny it, but few, if any, can avoid it. If people think that they are "normal" then the evidence is inescapable.

To make it into a concrete example, so that everyone can understand it, think of it this way: Most people are no different than someone watching a crime happening and doing nothing about it, or do something careless without thinking, which causes harm to others then either deny that they did it or deny responsibility for it, or say it wasn't their fault because they didn't mean it like a drunk driver causing an accident. Meaning, the vast majority of people are enablers, thoughtless, ignorant, stupid, lazy or careless. Regardless, the vast majority of people help to set up an environment that makes it possible for others to behave badly and get away with it or try to.

Bottom-line is that most people think they do, but they don't believe in Justice – real Justice – they don't focus on long-term consequences, they don't believe in absolutes and don't think in terms of black and white, they believe in free lunches and would rather look for them than work harder for what they want, they talk about morality and family values but either have no idea what those things really are, believe in the wrong things, or follow what everyone else believes in because it's easy. This is why most people in this country are responsible for what is happening in this country, and until people learn – really learn – we will never be able to escape the quagmire that we ALL find ourselves in today. The basics of what people must learn aren't difficult: 1) To think, 2) know what morals, values, ethics, integrity, honor and honesty really are and 3) learn the right morals and values, exercise the correct ethics and integrity, and always espouse and act on honor and honesty. It sounds simple, doesn't it? Let me assure everyone that it is actually very difficult, and it will take a long time to learn and behave accordingly.

If you really want Wall Street games to stop, separate the businesses the way they should be: Insiders versus outsiders

As I said before, there were many things that went wrong in the last several years, but Wall Street as a whole is not to blame. This doesn't mean that Wall Street doesn't have its own set of problems, but the underlying issues aren't what the politicians are telling you they are. The issues plaguing Wall Street are largely unrelated to the economic crisis. The real issue in Wall Street is that there are inherent conflicts of interests among the various business units that Wall Street operates and these conflicts of interests will always be manipulated by the managements of these firms to try and raise profits.

One of the biggest conflicts of interests that surfaced after the internet bubble burst in 2001 was the conflict of interest between investment bankers and research analysts. The practice of paying analysts from investment banking revenue necessitated analysts to not only kowtow to investment bankers' demands for favorable ratings to make it easier for the bankers to get banking fees, but also manipulating ratings to send managements not so subtle messages when managements did not award bankers with banking fees. Then in the current financial crisis, Goldman Sachs was penalized for advising clients to buy certain mortgage bonds that their own traders were selling and that Goldman Sachs' capital markets group thought was toxic.

Regardless of whether these accusations are true or not, or can be defended, the fact of the matter is is that these conflicts continue to exist and will not go away. After the 2001 financial crisis, Congress put into place many laws and the SEC put into place many regulations to try and keep research independent. Did it work? Hell no! I continue to hear stories from friends in the business that say that the underlying issue hasn't disappeared and, though the pressure is more subtle, the reality of the matter is that the pressure still exists more than ever. Pretty much everyone I've spoken to on this issue says that conflicts of interest in Wall Street firms are alive and well, but they'll never openly say it. Furthermore, these same people tell me that no one will ever be able to prove that these conflicts exist and would be crucified for trying. Lastly, these same people tell me that all Congress and the SEC managed to achieve is to increase costs for Wall Street firms, but actually have little effect on the underlying issues.

The solution seems simple: Remove the conflict of interest! One would think this was obvious. But this means that research, sales and trading will have to be separated from investment banking activities, and proprietary trading should be separated from the client servicing side, among other changes, which would make the banks and investment banks much smaller than they are today. However, the thought behind the solution – which is to eliminate the conflict of interest – is correct, nevertheless. So, how do we do this without making the separation ugly for bank managements and investors? The solution is that we should permit ALL businesses in the financial sector or dealing with financial matters to be organized between insiders and outsiders. Here's how I would organize the groups:

Insiders: Investment banking, business and corporate lending, accountants, corporate insurance, and management and financial consultants into one organization.

Outsiders: Sales, sales trading, research, retail banking, and retail insurance into another organization.

In this model, they'd be little need for Capital Markets function. The key question is where do we put asset management, and proprietary trading? I believe that asset management should remain an independent function, but it could be grouped with the outsiders. Proprietary trading is trickier. I think proprietary trading ought to be organized into independent entities as well, meaning they become another form of asset management or incorporated into asset management. Of course, the problem with incorporating proprietary trading into asset management is that risk goes up for investors in asset management businesses. Proprietary trading could be placed into the "Outsiders" group, if all else fails, but this would make the risk of this asset group go up more than necessary given all of its other businesses and would not be recommended.

Even though my plan makes all the sense in the world, and once established will be looked upon as a no-brainer solution, people are going to endlessly debate whether it is practical or not. I'll refer you to the chapter where I discuss practical versus ideal.

The reason why my plan works is simple: Conflicts of interests are reduced to the utter minimum level, costs are lowered due to less administrative burdens, and most importantly, "too big to fail" concerns are removed. Managements of banks will argue that this cannot be done because the businesses are very intertwined, but that cannot be true if Chinese Walls are really strong and in place. They'll also argue that the Chinese Walls are really working, and they'll force their analysts to trudge up to Congress and testify to that effect despite the reality. They'll also argue that sales, trading and research cannot support itself as an independent function. Then does that mean that they are being subsidized by investment banking revenues today? Doesn't that go against what Congress and the SEC is trying to accomplish?

If it is true that sales, trading and research is incapable of supporting itself then it either means that there is too much competition or that the market doesn't need the service. Regardless, once independent the markets will figure it out and right size that business sector, as it should.

One last issue: Note that the capital markets side of the business for public corporations still requires the distribution of stocks and bonds. Therefore, even if the business is split between insiders and outsiders, even without the investment bankers compromising the integrity of analyst ratings, corporate officers will be tempted to do so and give their capital markets business to the firm whose analyst has a favorable rating.

To prevent this from happening, I would suggest that regulations be promulgated that mandate public corporations to distribute its capital markets business according to the proportionate 3-year average volume of stocks or bonds traded by the analyst and hes firm of the public corporation. Alternatively, the capital markets business should be distributed according to how accurately an analyst has predicted a public corporations' earnings (or cash flow or EBITDA, whichever is the most relevant) estimates or target price over a three year period.

The way investment banking, financial consultants, asset managers, and sales, trading and research get paid should be changed

I have no arguments as to how much these people get paid; judging by the stress, hours and amount of travel that is required of these people, they deserve every penny that they get. So, that's not what I want to discuss. What I want to discuss is the way that these folks get paid.

For investment bankers, they should get paid like their auditors, meaning that every company that needs/uses investment banking services should pay a retainer to one or two investment banks and contract investment banks for a period of time. In addition, if the company does a capital markets transaction, e.g., issue stocks and bonds, investment bankers should get some fixed percentage of the proceeds. However, if the investment bank is involved in advising M&A transactions, the payout amount should not be changed, but the timing of the payment should be changed and subject to adjustments for the investment banker that is on the acquisition side. For the seller's investment banker a straight percentage of the proceeds should suffice. Specifically, for the buyer's investment banker, I'd look to the way that the CEO is paid. Once the merger closes, the buyer's investment banker should get paid according to the CEO's payout schedule. After the merger closes and for the next three years thereafter, the payment to the buyer's investment banker should be split 25%, 35%, and 40%, subject to how successful the CEO was achieving hes targeted financial objectives, but not all of them. So for example, if the CEO's and hes senior executives' compensation varies by how much and how quickly synergies are achieved then the bankers' pay should partly follow that formula. Also, EPS or cash flow metrics should be considered as well as successful access to the capital markets. The reason for this type of payout structure is that it largely eliminates the greed factor for investment bankers, who try to close a deal at any price so that they can get their fees, regardless of whether or not the deal is good for their client. Now, one may argue that all bankers would prefer to be on the selling side, but if a banker only has selling clients then they will eventually lose all of their clients. For all consultants too, their pay should also be partly based on a retainer and partly tied to the success of their advice. In addition, consultants should be hired by only outside board members and insider investors, which eliminate the desire for CEOs to manipulate consultants to justify their actions and for the consultants to give what the client wants, regardless of whether or not the advice is sound.

For sales, sales trading and research, the vast majority of their pay should and will come directly or indirectly from their clients, which are money, asset and investment management firms. For research, sales and sales trading personnel, pay ought to be based on a per unit (i.e., $0.05/share) of securities bought and sold, and research, sales and trading should split it three ways with all three being responsible and accountable for revenue generation.

For asset managers, I have no direct issues with how they get paid, but the tax system is what I believe that needs to be changed. If we are to truly get asset managers to focus on the long-term then we should establish a tax structure that supports long-term investments. In particular, I'd look to tax capital gains that were achieved in the first year at 100%, unless the sale occurred due to liquidation requests by their clients, at which point the client will pay 100% capital gains tax. Any capital gains that were realized in year 2 should be taxed at 80% and any capital gains realized in year 3 should be taxed at 50%. However, any capital gains realized after a 3 year holding period should not be taxed at all. For dividends and interest payments, the tax schedule should also match that of the capital gains schedule, but with the caveat that any amount below the average savings rate would be tax free. In the specific case of dividends, if the dividends are reinvested into the stock of the company that issued the dividend then the dividends would be taxed according to how long the original investment was held.

Let me give an example. Let's say that the average savings rate is 1%, and an investor bought $8,000 of one stock and gets $400 in cash dividends per year (or a 5% yield) or $100/quarter. Under my tax program, the investor would be entitled to receive $20/quarter in the first year tax-free with the balance of the money ($80/quarter) put into a reserve account. At the end of year 1, the investor would get a lump sum distribution of an additional $64 from the $320 that was put into escrow during the year. In year two, the investor would be entitled to $20/quarter plus $16/quarter more as capital gains tax is burdened at 80%, and again, the remainder or $64/quarter would be placed into a reserve account. At the end of year 2, the investor would get a lump sum distribution of an additional $192 from the $512 remaining from the year 1 and year 2 escrow accounts. In year three, the investor would get $20/quarter plus an additional $40/quarter more as capital gains tax is burdened at 50%, and again the remainder of the $40/quarter would be added to the escrow account. At the end of the third year, the investor would get a lump sum payment of $480, which should be the remaining amount in the escrow account. Then in year 4 and beyond, the investor would get 100% of the dividend paid to the investor every quarter and the escrow account for that stock would be terminated. Although this may be more cumbersome than collecting the tax immediately, for the sake of creating long-term investments, I believe it is the only fair tax policy.

I know that this tax structure will be strongly opposed by money managers because their payout gets delayed and because the vast majority has no ability to figure out how to make money over a three-year period. But then this would force these people to be replaced by those that are better at figuring out long-term consequences. Regardless, portfolio managers have the ability to track how much money they've earned, given their performance, so the process should still be very transparent.

This tax structure may also get heavily criticized by the elderly who may rely on dividend and interest income to live. For retired folks (beyond the age of 65), I think it would be a good idea, if they were given all dividend and interest income tax-free, but still assessed capital gains tax. Also, in the case of a documented illness or medical emergency, I believe that it would be prudent to allow families to pull money from all sources to take care of their loved ones after their insurance money runs out to cover for the medical bills that would accumulate. So, under such extreme circumstances, I believe that capital gains, dividend and interest income taxes ought to be suspended to pay for the medical expenses or other emergencies.

If you want to stop "too big to fail," have a variable reserve structure and charge fees for taking risk, it ain't rocket science

The resolution to "too big to fail" (TBTF) isn't rocket science. TBTF is driven by one thing: Risk. Whether it's systemic risk (i.e., system-wide or economy-wide risk) or idiosyncratic risk (i.e., specific or unique risk) if the risk overtakes the mitigation measures then the whole banking system will fail. Systemic risk is the more evil of the two. And, the only way that any country can work out of a systemic failure is for the government to step in to *begin* the healing process, but not to actually heal the economy. What I mean by this is that the government can only kick-start the road to recovery, but only the private sector can effectuate the full recovery. Therefore, to insure that the government has enough money when the time comes, we should charge banks fees to cover the government's bailout package. These fees should be paid by the banks that take the risks based on the transactions that they engage in and the size of their balance sheet devoted to riskier transactions. This fee should be collected regardless of whether or not the transaction is hedged, because if a systemic risk is triggered then hedging riskier transactions will be ineffective. The critical example can be seen from the latest financial/economic crisis. All of he hedged transactions on mortgages did nothing to stop the financial meltdown, because the ones that were ultimately insuring the transactions could not hedge out their risks. Ultimately, someone has to hold the risk, and if there is a systemic meltdown then these ultimate risk-takers cannot stop the tide of the financial meltdown. Therefore, by collecting these fees, when the time comes for the federal government to act, they won't have to burden the average tax payers as much, if at all. Also, by building this reserve, the risk of a systemic risk manifesting itself will also be reduced, which is exactly the outcome that we want.

The other risk is idiosyncratic or unique risk. This happens when one bank does something very stupid and ends up in financial bankruptcy, but other banks didn't take the same risk, so they are initially unscathed. However, if the bankrupt bank is big enough and intricately connected to other financial institutions then it could trigger a cascading effect that puts other financial institutions at risk. To mitigate this type of risk, the banks' reserve requirements should increase as the banks get larger and as they engage in more and more risky transactions. So, if all that the bank does is collect retail deposits and invest in US federal government bonds then their reserve requirements should be minimal, may be 0.25%. However, if the bank engages in consumer and mortgage lending then perhaps the current reserve requirements of between 6%-8% is enough unless the bank becomes so large that it could take down the whole system if the bank goes bankrupt. In such a situation, the reserve requirements should be 5x-10x or 40%-60%. Most banks could not be profitable if the reserve requirements are this high, and that is exactly the point: Initially banks could never become that big, which makes them impossible to be TBTF. Overtime, if the bank and their investors desire taking more risk then they could set aside bank profits into a reserve account to mitigate for the potential risk of a bankruptcy. Tax laws would have to be changed to accommodate reserve accounts, which I think is prudent.

I acknowledge the fact that the outline of my plan is easy to state, but the execution of the plan will be the challenge, i.e., the devil will be in the details. Nevertheless, I strongly believe that my plan is the best way that I've heard of to mitigate the issue of TBTF for banks and financial institutions.

Speculators and speculation are the American way and aren't the major cause for high prices and anyone who solely blames speculators and speculation for high prices are either ignorant or retarded and don't know anything about economics

Let me start off with a quote that is words to live by in the commodities world: "There is no better cure for high prices than high prices and there is no better cure for low prices than low prices."

It's not that complicated: When demand increases relative to supply, prices go up. How complicated is that?! Those that solely blame speculators for high prices will say that I'm saying the same thing, except for the fact that speculators are artificially driving up the demand that causes the price of commodities to go up. Sounds good, doesn't it? Well, it's wrong!

Let's cut to the chase: Speculators aren't responsible for high prices all by themselves, not by a longshot; however, it is true that s*peculators magnify the impact, both ways*, i.e., they help high prices go higher and low prices go lower. For now, I'm going to concentrate on the high-side only. The way speculators magnify price moves is by taking advantage of an *already* tight supply/demand situation: They do so by buying on the margin to magnify the tightness. This means that for speculators to be in a position to even attempt to magnify price moves, the fundamental market had to have taken itself to a tight supply/demand situation all by itself without the help of speculators. Let me give you a high level example.

On a rough basis, the global demand for oil is about 80 million barrels per day (MMBBLS/Day). At $100 per barrel (BBL), this has a market value of some $8 billion per day or about $3 trillion per year. Let's say that all of the world's oil producers combined have the ability to pump out 92 million barrels per day or, put it another way, the world has about 12 million barrels of excess capacity or about 15% room for error. So, if speculators buy 5 MMBBLS/Day for a year straight, market price of oil will go up, but would it be a dramatic price move? For now, let's ignore the fact that 5 MMBBLS/Day at even $50/BBL is $250 million per day or about $91 billion per year. The reason why this would not move the market in a big way is that the remaining excess capacity is still 7 MMBBLS/Day, which means that the world could still eliminate the export capacity of Iran (~2.52 MMBBLS/Day), Venezuela (~1.87 MMBBLS/Day), Angola (1.85 MMBBLS/Day) and Azerbaijan (0.65 MMBBLS/Day) and not have a disruption in global supply. This means that no one would be particularly worried about disruptions in global oil supply, so prices wouldn't move up in any dramatic fashion.

Therefore, after the speculators stop buying after one year, the excess capacity goes back up to 12 million barrels per day, which is more than enough to make-up for any future shortfalls that may have been caused by speculators buying and storing oil. Lastly, if speculators can't make any money, they will have to dump their stock of oil at or below their purchase price, which likely pushes down prices below fundamental levels.

Now, let's contrast this with today's situation, where the global excess supply for oil is only about 1.5-2.0 MMBBLS/Day. This represents only about 1.9%-2.5% of global demand. In this situation, if speculators bought 500,000 BBLS/Day at $100/BBL ($50 million/day or some $18 billion per year) this would make the excess supply capacity even tighter by 25%-33%. Therefore, even a minor disruption or concern for such an event would drive prices up higher very, very quickly giving speculators a very handsome profit. However, keep in mind that in order for speculators to even have a chance at this type of profit, the fundamental supply/demand picture has to be very tight to begin with. So, two questions: 1) Is that the end of it; we have high prices forever and we have to live with it? And, 2) whose fault is it that the world got itself into such a tight bind?

Let me answer the 2nd question first. The reason for the tight fundamentals is because the increase in demand has far outstripped the world's ability to meet that demand. This has caused oil prices to catapult from a mean-reverting price of about $20/BBL to their current levels. So, how did we get to such a demand level? First and foremost, the US consumes about 19-21 MMBBLS/Day, depending on the year and the state of our economy, or about a quarter of the world's oil supply when America accounts for less than 5% of the world's population. This means that we are ridiculously and outrageously thirsty for oil.

Let's compare some numbers on an annual basis (data for 2010; provided by the CIA):

Table 2. Crude Oil Demand of the Top 20 Global Consumers

Rank	Country	MM BBLS/Day	MM BBLS/Year	Population (MM)	Per Person/Year
1	The US	19.150	6,990	313.8	22.3
2	China	9.400	3,431	1,343.2	2.6
3	Japan	4.452	1,625	127.4	12.8
4	India	3.182	1,161	1,205.1	1.0
5	Saudi Arabia	2.643	965	26.5	36.4
6	Germany	2.495	911	81.3	11.2
7	Canada	2.209	806	34.3	23.5
8	Russia	2.199	803	138.1	5.8
9	South Korea	2.195	801	48.9	16.4
10	Mexico	2.073	757	115.0	6.6
11	Brazil	2.029	741	205.7	3.6

12	France	1.861	679	65.6	10.4
13	Iran	1.845	673	78.9	8.5
14	The UK	1.622	592	63.0	9.4
15	Italy	1.528	558	61.3	9.1
16	Spain	1.441	526	47.0	11.2
17	Indonesia	1.292	472	248.2	1.9
18	Singapore	1.080	394	5.4	73.0
19	Netherlands	1.009	368	16.7	22.1
20	Taiwan	1.002	366	23.1	15.8

Source: CIA

As you can see, the US consumes more oil than the next three countries combined, which represents some 35%-40% of the world's population. Counting only the industrialized nations on this list, the US consumes more oil than Japan, Germany, Canada, South Korea, France, The UK, Italy, Spain, and Taiwan combined. On a per capita basis, Saudi Arabia, Canada, and Singapore are the only countries that have heavier consumption than we do. However, Saudi Arabia generates all or almost all of its electricity with oil –about 1 MMBBLS/Day during the summer – whereas the US hardly generates any with oil, and Saudi Arabia and Singapore are very hot all year round, which requires air conditioning all year round. The Netherlands, Saudi Arabia, and Singapore also have a lot of export industries (e.g., chemicals, petro-chemical, refining, rubber processing, et cetera.) that rely on oil for feedstock or fuel and Singapore has many oil trading businesses that skew its data.

So, the relevant comparisons would be with Canada, Japan, Germany, France, The UK, and Italy. However, Canada is essentially the same as the US, just as bad, and can be lumped into the same bucket as the US from an economic perspective. So, moving on with the discussion, the reason for our propensity for high consumption of oil stems from several reasons: 1) We drive everywhere, almost unnecessarily (by far the biggest culprit to our oil consumption), 2) we love to throw everything away versus recycling, and 3) we consume a lot of everything, including anything made of, with, on or in plastics. If we were to use public transportation just once a week when going to work, we'd save almost a million barrels a day, on average. This alone would increase the global excess supply potential by 50%! Then, if we recycle more plastics and use less of it, including plastic bags, we could increase the reserve production capacity even more.

The other major reason for the tight supply/demand fundamentals is due to rapid demand increase from countries like China, India, Brazil, and Russia, and the Middle-East overall. For example from 2000 to 2010, China's oil consumption grew from ~4.8 MMBBLS/Day to ~9.4 MMBBLS/Day (a compound annual growth rate (CAGR) of ~7.0%), and India's oil demand grew from ~2.1 MMBBLS/Day to ~3.2 MMBBLS/Day (CAGR of ~3.9%). On a global basis, demand for oil has grown by some ~10 MMBBLS/Day. This represents a net increase in demand of about 13.3% or a CAGR of some 1.3%/year. Therefore, we can conclude that almost 6 MMBBLS/Day of global demand increase is accounted for by jast two countries: China and India. This rapid growth in jast two countries has had a dramatic effect on global fundamentals, which caused fundamentals to tighten relatively quickly.

Seeing this tightening unfold, speculators correctly assumed that prices would go up, and all that they did was to do what any other American would do and that is to buy low in the hopes of selling high. This is no different than a retail shop owner cashing in on a trendy item by ordering more than their usual inventory level and charging premium prices as the popularity of an item soars. Or, baseball card collectors buying cards of promising rookie players and holding onto the cards with expectations that the value of the cards will rise or for that matter any collector buying something that shows promise.

Simply put, speculators are pursuing the time-honored American tradition of putting their money where their brain is. This is no different than any successful American in the past – and hopefully into the future – that identified an opportunity and risked their money to realize their vision. How is this un-American and why is it being punished? Jast because of high prices? So, are speculators going to be rewarded, when they help to drive prices lower?

The reason why politicians have to find at least one scapegoat is because America is angry at high prices without knowing that we, as a whole, are at least partly responsible for these high prices. And, the politicians need to placate people so they can get re-elected, even though politicians themselves aren't to blame either for high prices. As stated before, we drive everywhere, and we do so in relatively big gasoline guzzlers such as SUVs or 8-cylinder vehicles or both. Although I can't figure it out, my rough calculation is that if we got rid of all SUVs and 8-cylinder vehicles for family use, turbo-charged every family-vehicle engine, and we manufactured vehicles that can't go over 65 MPH, we'd increase average mileage by at least 10% and would likely save at least 2 million barrels of oil equivalent per day in gasoline consumption. Our current consumption of gasoline is about 36 million barrels of oil equivalent per day.

So, then why did politicians pick speculators and speculation to blame for high oil and gasoline prices, knowing full well that high oil and gasoline prices aren't solely, directly, nor largely the speculators' fault? First, politicians are moral cowards. If they started telling the truth, they fear that they will lose their jobs, and this would be largely, and sadly, true. Sadly, because it shows how vain, insecure, self-destructive and pretentious average Americans really are. Second, the politicians can get away with it, because speculators are a very small group of people, even in New York City. Third, it makes for good sound bites. Fourth, it's a simple and seemingly plausible argument – "supply/demand fundamentals are tight because speculators are buying and driving up prices!" And, fifth, it deflects blame from countries with which America has delicate diplomatic relationships such as China and India.

Nevertheless, we, as a country, really need a reality check. The only good outcome from this whole situation is that some of us get to see how decrepit and morally corrupt our country has become. Remember, we are always going to pick people for political office that are most like us as a whole or on average. So, if the politicians are this slimy, it can't say anything complimentary about Americans as a whole.

At the end of the sixth paragraph of this chapter, I asked two main questions. I think I've amply beaten the dead horse in answering the second of the two questions. However, the first question, which I believe is the more interesting question was, "Is that the end of it; we have high prices forever and we have to live with it?" The simple answer is no, and we should see prices go down to about $60-70 per barrel on average over time, *if* we leave markets to their own devices. The long answer, as you can imagine is very, very complicated. However, I will attempt to explain.

Here are some facts and historical perspectives that we need to start with and understand:

- By all estimation, the cheapest cost to produce oil is less than $5/BBL, and it is oil produced from Saudi Arabia.

- The most expensive source of oil is thought to be shale oil in North America, which currently costs about $60/BBL to produce all-in, including a fair return to investors.

- The North American shale oil reserves are thought to be as large, if not larger than Saudi Arabia's oil reserves or about 250 billion barrels of recoverable oil.

- In the past, when OPEC felt threatened by alternative sources of oil, it choked them off by increasing production, which pushed down prices making it uneconomic for alternative sources of oil to be developed.

- Because OPEC is having a difficult time meeting increasing demand, it can no longer control the oil market like it did in the past.

- At $100/BBL, every producer in the world that has an all-in marginal cost of $100/BBL or less is strongly incented to drill and produce oil, if there is assurance that $100/BBL oil will last for a very, very long time.

- To develop any new oil field, it takes anywhere between 5 and 10 years without interference.

- Also, infrastructure around oil fields has to be developed, and methods of taking the oil to markets also have to be built, e.g., gathering lines, pumping stations, pipelines, ports, and ships.

- New refineries have to be built or old ones reconfigured to be able to take the new sources of oil, which tend to be "heavier" than traditional sources – yes, oil is not all the same.

- Environmentalists and politicians have interfered and continue to meddle with natural economic developments that have distorted markets and prices.

- Producers, particularly OPEC, do not want prices to go up so much as to choke off economic growth, because that kills demand, sometimes permanently.

- Many OPEC producers are not in any rush to develop new fields as they are enjoying $100+/BBL oil, and also because many of them lack opportunities, capital or technology or some combination thereof to do so, e.g., Venezuela, and Iran.

What this all boils down to is that the key to lower oil prices is more supply in the near-term (next 10-20 years) and in the long-run not jast more supply but better demand-side management as well (more use of public transportation, better gas mileage on vehicles, etc.). This means that if we continue to have

$100+/BBL oil and the markets are left to do what they do best, new sources of oil like the North American (NA) shale oil will be developed and taken to market. And, given that it can be produced at $60/BBL or less all-in, the producers will see excess returns of $40/BBL or more. This means that NA shale oil producers are very eager to develop and produce oil; however, the environmentalists, and the politicians kowtowing to them for all the wrong reasons, continue to interfere and block progress. I am told that the potential for NA shale oil is well north of 10 MMBBLS/Day and could be as much as 20 MMBBLS/Day. This means that even at 10 MMBBLS/Day, we would largely be free of oil imports, and at 20 MMBBLS/Day, we would be exporting some 7-9 MMBBLS/Day.

However, before getting too exuberant, we need to take into consideration several other factors, including what would happen to prices if NA shale oil fields were to actually push production up to 10 MMBBLS/Day. By the time production reaches this level, I would guess that excess global oil supply would be in the range of 5-7 MMBBLS/Day, which means prices would drop very, very rapidly. And, since the marginal production (the most expensive production that is actually being used) is most likely to be NA shale oil only 3-5 MMBBLS/Day out of the 10 MMBBLS/Day would actually be bought and used. This means that some 5-7 MMBBLS/Day would be unnecessary and would either be temporarily shut-in or completely plugged and abandoned. However, until this is achieved, price of oil would plummet to the cash cost of the marginal production, which I am told is about $30/BBL for NA shale oil. However, once NA shale oil production is reduced to 3-5 MMBBLS/Day from 10 MMBBLS/Day, prices would jump up to about the all-in price of the marginal production or about $60/BBL. Then, as global demand increases it will reduce the excess supply potential and price of oil will once again rise above $60/BBL then $80/BBL and may once again top $100/BBL. As prices start to climb, NA shale oil production will be increased to meet demand, which will then eventually push prices back towards $60/BBL, but if the producers overreact, as they tend to do, prices will once again dip below $60/BBL, at least, temporarily. This pattern should repeat over and over again, assuming little to no interference from OPEC, the US government (backed by the environmentalist), and other major externalities, such as the development of a completely new mode of transportation or transportation fuel. Thus, if the pattern holds then we should see oil prices mean-revert around $50-$70/BBL with low end pricing of $30-$40/BBL and high end pricing of $90-$100/BBL.

Finally, I will note that high oil and gasoline prices have helped Americans to involuntarily help the environment by reducing use of their cars, building and buying more fuel efficient cars, and generally by conserving more. Therefore, high prices aren't always bad, particularly in the long-run, because it helps to change people's behavior in a good way; yet another reason why markets should be left alone to work its magic without interference from politicians and environmentalists.

So, going back to the quote in the beginning of the chapter – "There is no better cure for high prices than high prices, and there is no better cure for low prices than low prices" – it tells us that the current state of high oil prices cannot last forever. As prices remain high, it incentivizes companies to increase production to take advantage of high prices, which eventually forces prices to come down. In contrast, in low price environments, producers will hold back on developing new production or even shut-in existing production until prices rebound to levels where the producer can receive a fair return. However, all this is contingent upon politicians and the environmentalists getting out of the way and letting markets work their magic. This is why the postponement of the Keystone pipeline was such an ironic development. After all of the whining and moaning about high oil prices, the politicians decide to shut-down one of the cornerstones to cheaper oil prices that we (Americans) can control.

Regardless, getting back to speculators and speculation, I strongly believe that speculators and speculation must not, should not and cannot be muzzled, because it is not only un-American (perhaps even unconstitutional), but also because speculators serve a vital function in helping to intensify market signals, which sends clearer messages to everyone so that we can all act accordingly. Also, speculators and speculation works both ways, meaning, when prices fall speculators can further attenuate prices by short selling oil. However, yet again, I note that either function – intensification or attenuation – cannot be served by speculators without market fundamentals largely dragging the entire market to a point where speculation is made possible.

So, the next time a politician blames speculators and speculation for high oil prices, challenge them to a debate and see how they do. I'm sure their comments will be comical and despicable at the same time. In any case, we should vote out of office any politician that points a finger at speculators for high prices, because they are: 1) Ignorant, 2) liars, or 3) underhandedly self-serving or 4) some combination thereof.

Wall Street Pay?! What about actor pay and athlete pay?! Why aren't people getting upset about that?!

Why is it that people get so worked up about Wall Street and corporate pay when top athletes and actors also get paid ridiculous sums of money, but create little value? Part of the reason why is because people worship actors and athletes and can identify with them and admire them and want to be them. But, when it comes to "Wall Streeters," and corporate titans ordinary people have little to no idea as to what the "Wall Streeters" do and how they create value, and with corporate leaders they look at stats like CEO-pay-to-lowest-paid and get angry about the difference between rich and the poor. All that the vast majority of people know is that they are told that "Wall Streeters" are cheats and greedy scum and corporate titans are all cheats, greedy scum, *and liars*.

However, all that this smear campaign is designed to do is to make it easier for politicians to justify taxing the rich even more. The politicians make it *sound like* the wealthy are stealing money – even though the politicians know that the wealthy aren't doing the stealing – and the politicians justify the real stealing through taxes by saying that the rich are scum bags and the "people" deserve to have their stolen money taken back by force. What utter boloney! The real liars and cheaters are the politicians, not the "Wall Streeters" and the corporate executives. If the rich were stealing then they should be arrested and thrown in jail. But the politicians can't do that because the super-vast majority of the rich aren't stealing, and throwing all of the rich people in jail would cut tax revenues by 40% or more, which would be unacceptable, so the politicians play on average people's resentment of the wealthy to justify stealing from the rich through so called "progressive taxes."

People rail at the fact that "Wall Streeters" and corporate titans get paid 6, 7, 8 and sometimes 9-digit compensations and wonder what they did to deserve it?! How could someone be *allowed* to take that kind of money home? I believe that a lot of people view this type of compensation as if they view the lottery or as if shady backroom deals came into play: "These people got lucky or must have cheated to get what they got or both." I think this type of resentment breeds the lottery mentality in this country: "If they can do something shady and get paid for it, why shouldn't I get a slice of that pie?" This is one of the main reasons why the politicians should stop lying and exaggerating about what's going on about pay in this country. There is always a consequence to one's actions and a reaction to that action. Simply put, unintended consequences are a bitch!

Anyway, getting back to Wall Street and corporate pay, if a waittes – another mash up from combining waiter and waitress – does a good job, they get 15% of the pretax bill as tip. In a fancy restaurant the tip could be as high as 20%-30% of the pretax bill. Yet, when an investment banker, trader, sales person or analyst get paid 5%-10% or even 20% of what they made for the company in revenue, people go nuts, because it happens to be 6-8 digits and sometimes 9. If a trader makes $100 million for the bank, how much should the trader get paid? If the trader were a waittes, they would get anywhere between $15 and $30 million. So, is it a crime to pay the trader $20 million? Now, an uneducated, simple waittes would get paid $15 million for doing much less than the trader who not only had to make the savvy trades, but to be able to do that had to study their butt off, put in long hours as a grunt, and had to go through a long internship process. This versus a waittes that, in most cases, only needs to know what the specials are, how to use a calculator to figure out the tax and add up the bill. So, who's getting overpaid? My point is that if a waittes gets a 15% tip then giving bankers, traders, sales people and analysts 10%-30% is not out of line or scale. It doesn't matter what the actual amount turns out to be. However, as a matter of fact, most of these folks don't even get paid 10%, which is unfair.

To reinforce the view, look at it from an athletic franchise or movie studios' viewpoint. I hear that Lebron James and Kobe Bryan are very good players. How much are they worth to their respective NBA teams? What are Natalie Portman, Meryl Streep, Angelina Jolie, Reese Witherspoon, Sandra Bullock, Russell Crowe, Tom Hanks, Brad Pitt, George Clooney, Tom Cruise, and Johnny Depp worth to a movie? This is no different than a star trader, banker, sales person or analyst making a difference for the financial firm that they work for or a talented CEO, COO, CFO or other senior officers working for a non-financial corporation. So, why shouldn't these people get the star compensation?

Also, how much should the top executives at a corporation get paid, if the market cap of the company that they are running goes up by $1 billion? Shouldn't the team get paid between $100 and $300 million? So, why do people freak out when the CEO gets paid $50-$100 million? Yet people don't think twice about paying top athletes 8-9 figures for an athletic contract. I think paying athletes $10 million is more of an affront than a great CEO, COO or CFO getting paid $100 million or more. I think fans should demand that owners of athletic franchises lower athlete pay, while lowering admissions to match the lower pay for athletes!

All too often, Americans confuse political savvy with intelligence

Be leery of top officers in financial institutions. The cream of the financial firms typically doesn't stay at the financial firms, because they have the ability to leave and establish their own business and make a lot more money. This means that the best of the best don't usually become leaders of financial firms. So who does? Typically, the ones that advance are the ones that have better than average intelligence – but most people that work in these firms on the revenue-side are above average intelligence – are well-liked and personable, but most importantly, very politically astute. Notice, I didn't say that the person is/was good at what they do/did; they jast have to be competent at what they do, i.e., moderately better than the middle of the pack. Perhaps this is part of the reason that the US went through the latest Great Recession, because leadership at financial institutions are highly lack luster overall.

This is why thinking is important. Instead of picking people that are not only smart and know how to think, most boards pick people that are politically astute. The screwed up point is that most boards don't even know that this is what they are doing! Jast because the person talks well and knows how to please everyone, they *APPEAR* to be smart and qualified. On the other hand, really smart and qualified people don't please everyone and don't always talk well. The problem is that for the vast majority of people, they can't tell the difference between truly smart and political savvy. Or mistake point-blank bluntness and clear communications with arrogance, cockiness or even stupidity.

Here's how the political game works – this is the same with politicians. First thing that the political players do is they try to charm you and make you like them on a personal level. The second thing is they try to find out what you like and dislike. If there is an overlap with your likes, they'll hone in on that and get you to believe that they are the same way without necessarily saying so. If you ask them about something you are opposed to, but they have a difference of opinion, they'll talk a lot without saying much and make you think that they agree with you without ever saying so. And, they'll rely on their charm and personality to win you over. Another tactic that these people use is what I call "crediting" others. What this means is that politically astute people will try to find things to agree with or points that they can credit as being intelligent – regardless of whether it is or isn't – regardless of whether or not they agree with the entire argument or the main point of the argument that the other person is presenting. They'll also try changing subjects on you in mid-answer – in particular, they'll try to steer you to a subject that you like talking about or hearing about – if they seem to be either losing you or the argument. This is how the game is played. By the time the conversation or meeting is over, they'll make you feel like that they are your best friend, when nothing could be further from the truth.

The other deception is demeanor. The politically correct people work on societal rules that spell out who is supposed to be intelligent. Some of these idiotic notions include the idea that those people who speak softly and don't get emotional are smarter and, more importantly, more credible and stable. Therefore, what do most politically correct people and politically savvy people do to try to impress: They speak softly and don't show any emotion. The other problem is that most people can't tell the difference between passionate and raving lunatic. The reason most people can't do it is because most people are extremely insecure, highly short sighted, don't know how to think, know only how to obey rules, lack passion and lack observational skills. Also, the perception that soft spoken and "emotionless" delivery is a mark of intelligence and poise has gone from social norm to becoming a solid fact and so most people don't feel the need to think about it, only abide by it – another reason why most people can get out of their own way.

The last observation I'll point out is that politically savvy people will never attack or confront anyone directly or through a frontal assault. Most politically savvy people will use others or use indirect methods to attack and discredit others. Therefore, many times, the victims will never know that they are or were the target of an attack until it is too late. So, if you hear gossip from someone about another keep your guards up, you may be a target of manipulation by the gossip monger who has a hidden political agenda.

Rules and the Law

We should reduce the number of laws and no need to distinguish from civil and criminal law

If you think about it any laws and regulations that we have comes down to three things: 1) The violation of people's rights, 2) setting the order of whose right takes priority, and 3) the punishment for initiating the violation of another person's rights. Even more specifically, I say that there is only **ONE** law that is necessary: **Do not steal**! Another way the law could be written is: **Do not violate the rights of others**. If we think about it carefully, the two pretty much uphold the same principle. Think about any crime, it can be seen that there are very few, if any exceptions to the two proposed laws:

- If something is stolen then the thief is violating the right of the victim to own their property.
- If someone commits a murder, the murderer is not only stealing the right of the victim to determine the course of hes own life, but also to own it.
- If someone rapes another, the rapist is stealing the victim's right of consent and control over their own body.
- If a company pollutes then they are taking the right to a clean environment away from us or harming our health, which reduces our life span, which is theft of our future life.
- If the government takes money through taxes from the wealthy to "help" the poor, that's theft, no matter whether it was voted on or not by the majority.
- Any kind of fraud is theft.
- Blackmail is the theft of one's privacy and money unless it is blackmail of someone that has committed something illegal, in which case, it is the theft of the right of the country's Justice system to prosecute the crime and theft.
- If someone commits vigilantism, they are not only stealing the right of the criminal to a fair trial, which is a violation of the criminal's rights, but also if they make a mistake then they are killing an innocent person, which is a violation of the right to someone's own life.
- If someone causes another person to get addicted to drugs, they are stealing the addicted person's future, which is a violation of the right to determine one's own future. If the violator then sells the addict into slavery or prostitution then they are stealing the right of self-determination.

- If a government censors that is a violation of free speech or the government is stealing the right of an individual to self-expression.

No matter what violation can be conjured up, you'll find that it will come down to stealing a right from someone or some organization.

The reason why I don't agree with civil laws versus criminal laws is because it comes down to a debate about intensity. This debate is irrelevant. It's still a violation or theft of a right.

The reason why I don't agree with morality-based laws like gambling or prostitution is that it is a theft of the right of the individual to self-determination. Furthermore, it is subjugating the right of self-determination to majority vote, i.e., giving people the right to vote on what any individual should and should not do with their life. Who among us would agree to this? The more troubling aspect of such laws is that it is subjugating certain rights to a vote that should never be subjugated to a vote in the first place. For example, regardless of the outcome, should we vote on women's right to vote? If the vote favors abolishing the right of women to vote by two-thirds majority, should we take away women's right to vote? What if the margin was 100%? What if the vote passed by only one vote? Should such fundamental rights ever be made a subject of a vote? The result doesn't matter; women's right to vote should never again be put into question in any way, shape, or form. What about constitutionally guaranteed rights, like the right to bear arms? What about drug and alcohol laws? Have drug laws prevented deaths or increased deaths? At the very least, drug laws have added a layer of additional criminal activity that doesn't need to be there and huge resources are wasted policing such activities.

I digress, but I will address some of these issues in other chapters. The main point being that all laws and regulations can be reduced to one of two: 1) Do not steal or 2) do not violate the rights of others. Then the only issue that is left to be determined is the penalty – which I believe should be greater than the crime – and determining which rights supersede other rights. Unfortunately, I think the penalty should be left up to majority vote, but the importance of rights, i.e., that which supersedes the other, should not be subject to a vote, but subject to absolute rational scrutiny.

Fundamentally, the issue of which right supersedes the other should be determined by who violated someone else's rights first. Whoever is the first to violate someone else's rights should be the one that is prosecuted. If someone drinks and drives and gets home safe and doesn't cause any danger to other drivers, pedestrians or property, why should that person be prosecuted? Most people will say that an intoxicated driver increases the probability of causing harm to others. However, I will contend that this is assumption of guilt before proving it, and there are many people whose alcohol tolerance is higher than most and, in fact, so much higher that these people are likely to have better reflexes and decision making abilities than certain sober drivers, say someone in their 80s or 90s, may be even in their 60s or 70s. So, should our country take away driving privileges of older people? The counter argument is that someone growing old cannot be helped, but one doesn't have to drink, if they know that they have to drive. True enough, but then this means taking away the right to self-determination. Yes, but one would argue that if it potentially prevents accidents then it would be worth it. So, what is being proposed is that taking the right of self-determination away from an individual is not a big deal. Really, then how about this? Why don't we throw all school bullies into jail, since the probability of these bullies turning into gangsters or otherwise future criminals is higher than an average student? Isn't it worth it, if we can prevent a future crime, including possibly murder? This is how our society gets into trouble; it routinely thinks that the violation of people's rights should be supported. In free speech, we don't do this and don't need to do this, yet in other issues, we see no harm in abridging people's rights. This is how it starts. This is always how it starts: Look at Nazi Germany, imperialist Japan, Soviet Russia, et cetera.

Specifically, in the case of drunk driving, we don't have to prosecute for intoxication. We can prosecute for the result of drunk driving: If a drunk driver kills someone, they should be prosecuted and convicted for first degree murder and all of their assets should be taken from them and given to the family who lost their kin. If a drunk driver injures someone, they should be prosecuted under attempted premeditated murder, and they should be made to not only compensate for the medical expenses, but also made to compensate for the loss of quality of life for the rest of the victim's life – I know, it will be extremely difficult to determine how much to pay for what loss and how to even determine the loss. If a drunk driver causes property damage then they should be made to compensate for the damage to property and any inconvenience that was suffered. Let's see how many people drink and drive, if we have these laws.

The real reason for many civil laws and penalties, e.g., traffic laws, is that municipalities and states need more money to spend, so they use "preventive" laws, e.g., traffic violations, as another way to levy taxes. Their excuse is, "don't violate the laws then you won't have to pay the additional taxes." My retort to that is, don't spend so much money, and the municipality won't need additional "tax" dollars. Don't forget, two wrongs don't make a right. Also, remember, if the country were truly serious about stopping people from speeding, they could easily force the manufacturer of cars made for the US markets from going over 65, 70, or 75 miles per hour. This way they don't have to spend all that money buying high speed police cruisers or hire police to monitor the freeways, highways, parkways, turnpikes and motorways for speeders. However, it is interesting to me that no government has ever proposed such a restriction, if safety is truly at the heart of speeding laws.

The punishment has to be greater than the crime otherwise, it isn't a deterrent

This is not rocket science nor is it a new thesis. If someone steals $25,000 and they go to jail for 2-5 years that's about right in terms of time served and money stolen. What if the thief was executed for stealing? How many would steal? The flip-side of the argument is that thieves would arm themselves to the teeth and try to fight their way out of being arrested. This is true, but there'd be a lot fewer people who'd try to steal to begin with.

More importantly, laws and rules have to be more fair to start off with, in order for the punishment to be harsher than the crime. Meaning absolute fairness and Justice must exist in not jast the law, but the execution of the law, whatever the law maybe, whether the law applies to someone or not.

Bottom-line is that punishment is not a deterrent unless it is harsher than the crime. Perhaps execution for stealing is too much, but what about loss of all assets for the wealthy, regardless of whether or not they have family and children, but no jail time. What about 2-year solitary confinement for the poor person then forced labor or charity work for 5-years without pay? How about castration for rapists and child molesters? What about life-time of torture for murderers or loss of limbs? Some say cruel, I say harsh. Some say unjust, and I say for whom?

What is the price that we all pay for continued and high rate of crime? What about crimes that beget more crimes? Who pays? Yes, ultimately, we all do. Yet most people are willing to continue to support criminals and criminal behavior. When are we going to change for the better as a society? When loved ones get killed in a mugging? When one's daughter or mother gets raped? Isn't it too late by then? Regret will do no good if something like that happens. Don't forget, most rapists, muggers and thieves are repeat offenders. Also, don't forget that the price of any crime is more than the crime itself. It breaks the bond of trust among people, makes people fearful, suspicious, and therefore makes them guarded and even hostile towards each other. How do we extract payment for these violations? For the indirect consequences of the crime, which leaves a mark on others that was not part of the original crime, how do we get Just compensation?

Punishment has to be a deterrent not a payment or a deal. Therefore, the only way to deter and account for the unseen indirect effects on society is to make the punishment far greater than the crime. By definition, that is the only way to deter.

Finally, the excess of the punishment cannot be slightly greater than the crime. It must be overwhelmingly greater than the crime. Look at how many people are willing to go to a casino and gamble. Everyone knows that casinos were not built on winners and that the odds are against the players, but look how many people still gamble! This tells me that the punishment has to be far worse than the crime for it to be a true deterrent or criminals will look upon their criminal activity as jast another gamble, and that won't deter anyone.

As an adjunct to what I'm proposing in this chapter, I will note that I am assuming that the Justice system is not only fair, but also is mistake free. Currently, this is not the case; we know that there are many prisoners that are not guilty of the crimes that they committed. Therefore, massive priority must be given to insuring that our Justice system is not only fair, but also mistake free as possible. This would include the wide-spread use of DNA testing where such tests would produce conclusive results. Of all the actions that we need to take as a country in regards to the Justice system, I believe that there is nothing more important than insuring that our Justice system is mistake free, perhaps even more important than making sure that it is fair.

People don't want to think, and they want rules because it's easier than thinking

Most people have been slammed for trying to think from when they were young. This unrelenting attack on one's natural senses and inherent ability is not necessarily an accident and the objective of these unrelenting attacks is to pound these natural senses and inherent ability into oblivion for many reasons. Most of it has to do with conformity and society's obsession over being "normal." This obsession with normalcy has to do with social strength and governance. If everyone thinks the same way, it's easier to govern and rule.

Of course, the problem is that in the long-run a society made-up of individuals that know how to think is better for the society, but in the short-run it causes all kinds of problems. Imagine everyone in an early human society thinking different things and, most importantly, acting differently. Imagine the chaos?! This is where concepts like religion come into play. Religion is controlled by the head of the religion and a select group of people around the leader, typically a male. And, given that the rules of religion are rarely, if ever, straight forward and never rational, it always requires an interpreter of the supposed divinity's intent and meaning. Therefore, by focusing these powers of interpretation into a handful of people, it makes those people very important, revered, and respected. This then makes it very easy for the powers to be to command and control, since they are the only ones that are allowed to divine the intent of the supposed divinity. Also, for this central governing authority to persist, this meant that most people have to be discouraged from thinking and coming up with different views. However, to make it easier for people to follow the leadership the powers that be set up rules for people to obey instead of encouraging people to think. In the beginning, these rules may have come with explanations, but over time, people likely began to conclude that there are too many rules to remember and remembering the reasons for these rules is largely unnecessary. Therefore, people started blindly obeying rules and forgetting the reasons for these rules to exist in the first place. This is the only conclusion that can be derived given people's current behavior.

Of course, the problem with following rules without thinking and knowing the reasoning behind the rules is that rules can and do become obsolete and, in many instances, completely stupid. Let's take statutory rape, for example. In this day and age, discrimination between male and female sexuality is absurd and charging a sixteen year old boy for statutory rape of a sixteen year old girl when consensual sex is involved is absolutely ridiculous. On the other hand, if the sex was not consensual then statutory rape be damned, prosecute under adult rape laws. Even if the male was over 18 and his consenting sexual partner is under 18, as long as there is intent by the girl to have sex with the man and this can be shown by the defense, I don't think sex with a minor should be enforced, more so for boys and girls 16 and older.

Obviously, there are certain ages for boys and girls where they should be protected, for example, a 12 year old should not be having sex under any circumstances. But when is it old enough for girls and boys to start engaging in sex? Most children become sexually aware – like adults – at around 11-13 years old. But is this early enough for the child to engage in sexual behavior? I think a vast majority of Americans will say no. However, certainly, by 16-18, most people will say that boys are certainly ready and girls may be ready, but not their own daughters (hypocrites!). It is more so exasperating, since girls tend to be more mature than boys at 16-18. Regardless, what is and is not an appropriate age to have sex comes down to maturity. This is a whole other subject, which I cover in a different section of this book.

Nevertheless, people have gotten used to obeying rules without thinking, because mankind has been doing this for millenniums. But, in this day and age, I think it is imperative that we learn how to think and question every law and rule that we've ever known, because for the most part, rules destroy and numb minds. Also, many of the rules and laws that exist today are very obsolete and unnecessary in an advanced, information-based society. But most importantly, rules-and-laws-based society will only help in morally corrupting the society as new and innovative technologies, products, services and ideas are born.

Think about the internet and child pornography. There was no need for so much debate or confusion, if we thought through the issues carefully. The rules and laws that we have today say we can't allow child pornography. But then when naked pictures of "children" were posted and graphic art of adults having sex with minors were strewn all over the internet, we had to go through multiple legal battles to outlaw even REPRESENTATIONS OF CHILD PORNOGRAPHY, and we had to make up new rules and regulations to disallow this. To most people that know how to think, this should have been obvious, but in a rules-and-laws-based society, we had no choice but to go through this crazy and largely unnecessary process to revise the law.

As a society, if we want to truly be strong, we have to raise citizens that know how to think, and we have to not only teach people how to think, but also teach them what basis we must use to think. Meaning, we have to teach people the basic paradigms and principles that we need to base our thinking on. The problem that we confront today isn't teaching people how to think – although this will be a tremendously difficult task in and of itself – but agreeing on what basic paradigms and principles we should use to base our thinking on. This is exactly what I want to contribute to society: The principles and paradigms or simply the philosophy that we should base our thinking on going forward. And, I strongly believe that my philosophy is not only rational, but also will be ultimately acceptable to everyone that is intelligent and reasonable all across the world.

In the long-term, there is no better society and social structure than having a citizenry that knows how to truly think and people living in a society that has very few rules and laws, but a strong philosophical underpinning. If and when we get there, I will know that we have a truly rational and Just society for the first time in mankind's history. Ultimately, this will be the manifestation of my objective.

Rules and laws: The destroyers of minds and therefore societies

One of the most serious consequences for not thinking and blindly obeying rules and laws is that, over time, we end up with very stupid, unfair and absurd rules and laws. So, what's the solution? Education is one priority that we, as a society, need to do differently. The second is that we need to hold parents at least partly accountable for their children's behavior, particularly the younger they are. Third, we should eliminate the vast majority of civil laws and convert everything to criminal laws. So, if someone is drunk and kills an innocent bystander with their car, they should be prosecuted under murder laws, not involuntary or voluntary manslaughter laws. In other words, treat people with the assumed maturity that they think they have, hold them accountable for their presumed maturity, and assume people are innocent until proven guilty. Certainly, make recommendations such as speed limits, stop signs, curve speeds, etc., but there is no reason to enforce these under civil penalties. Actually, there is one reason, as a disguised tax. That is the only reason to justify traffic laws.

Regardless of their age, people that are mature are going to act mature and those that are not are going to pretend they are mature. In many cases telling the difference is difficult, but there are clues:

- Those that blindly obey rules and advocate such behavior are those that don't think and therefore are immature;
- Those that always "see" the positive or always "see" the negative;
- Those that sugar-coat everything that comes out of their mouth;
- Those that blindly mask their emotions;
- Those that blindly obey and advocate for such behavior on the excuse that that is the only way to survive;
- Those that believe in shortcuts to life or think that they can find shortcuts to life;
- Those that deliberately speak in soft tones no matter what the circumstances dictate are also people that are pretending to be mature adults;
- Those that compromise for the sake of reaching a settlement are also immature and short-sighted people, but these people are also very dangerous people;
- Those that utter some of the following phrases with anything but ridicule:
  - "logic isn't everything,"
  - "money is the root of all evil,"
  - "everything is relative," or similarly "nothing is black and white,"
  - "everyone is equal," this is different than "everyone is **born** equal,"
  - "one should be humble,"
  - "don't be emotional,"
  - "don't generalize,"
  - "majority rule is always right and the only fair governance,"
  - "capitalism is dead" or similarly "capitalism doesn't work,"
  - "in the long-term we're all dead,"
  - constant "yes but,"

- "that's different,"
- "do as I say, not as I do,"
- "children should be seen not heard,"
- "animals are people too,"
- "who's going to know,"
- "you can trust me," or similarly, "I won't tell anyone, I promise,"
- "we're all special,"
- "if it weren't for you then I could have _____,"
- "oh, yeah, that's what I meant;"

- Those that become very defensive when criticism is lobbed towards them, especially those that don't show their insecurity, but go around subtly sabotaging those that criticized them, i.e., sneaks;
- Those that are politically correct;
- People who think humility is a virtue;
- People who are humble;
- Those that dream of and believe in equality for all;
- Those that are pretentious, and, worse, know how to hide it well;
- Those that are superficial, and, worse, know how to hide it well;
- Those that believe in and tell white lies;
- Gossip mongers;
- People who denigrate others jast because they can, and particularly those that enjoy doing so;
- "Sneaks;"
- People who measure superiority based on wealth, income, social status, or other superficial clues;
- Those that rebel for the sake of it, e.g., anti-establishment activists;
- People who substitute experience for judgment, future potential, intelligence and success;
- Those that blame others for their problems, ills and misfortunes;
- Those that avoid responsibility and deflect accountability;
- Those that compromise principles for convenience;
- Those that stab others in the back;
- Those that think about what others did to them without thinking about what they did to others;
- People who don't know how to distinguish between cause and effect nor understand it;

- Those that can' tell the difference between knowledge and intelligence, and vice-a-versa;
- Those that substitute knowledge for intelligence and vice-a-versa;
- People who want the government to take care of all grievances, justified or not;
- People who don't answer direct questions with direct answers;
- Those who only know how to criticize, but have no ideas of their own;
- People who don't have opinions, particularly on some important basic principles.

And, those that believe in these people as wise are not only immeasurably dumb and foolish, but those that have power and money to boot are extremely dangerous, particularly because they can force others to follow or perish; and many rich and powerful people abuse their resources and power.

Now, let me give you some great examples of obsolete laws, one of which is jaywalking. As I understand it, it came about because of cars. In the earlier days of cars, people were not tuned into the speed with which these machines could approach an individual. So, many, while crossing the streets, were run over. So, jaywalking rules were made, so that drivers would be less surprised with people crossing in the middle of the road and pedestrians would cross only at designated locations. However, as many would attest to today, especially it seems in New York City, jaywalking laws are pretty stupid in these modern times.

Prostitution laws are equally stupid. In general "morality" laws are very stupid, because it assumes that people are not capable of making their own decisions – note I did not say wise decisions. While this is true of many, it is far from true for all Americans. Take drug laws. People who don't want "dangerous" drugs to be legalized argue two main points: 1) To them it isn't about what the drugs do to the users, but what the users *could or may* do to others like mugging people or stealing from them or killing people due to driving while under the influence, and 2) these people don't want others to perceive that legalization of drugs equals condoning the use of them.

What people forget is that drug users will do what they do whether there is a legal barrier or not. So, point 1) is really not all that relevant, but 2) is an interesting question. It assumes that people are stupid and will assume that legalization of drugs will allow many to experiment and get trapped into becoming a habitual user. This worries people because it could turn a lot of people into useless bums and help to greatly reduce our society's integrity. My point is simply this: If people are stupid enough to get addicted to drugs and fall into disarray then they deserve it. And, if children are not taught well enough, parents can't earn their children's trust and parents can't monitor their children carefully enough (directly or indirectly) then it is no fault but the parents' fault. Regardless, we should all be responsible in monitoring and informing children so that the least amount of damage is done to them.

So, again, what is the solution? Don't make any morality laws. Let people make their own decisions and choices, but hold them to the consequences of their own actions. Don't worry about preventing something. The best prevention is having a society of mature, responsible and thinking citizens. So, let's focus on creating a society that can think for itself in a mature and responsible manner based on the correct philosophy. Creating laws and rules for every problem, every issue, every situation is very counterproductive, unfair, a waste of time, overly costly (rules and laws have to be administer, enforced and adjudicated), and creates more largesse, which in turn creates more irresponsible people, which then requires more rules and laws, et cetera, et cetera.

Traffic laws are a classic example of the ineffective application of laws and reinforce the belief that people don't have to think

Most people don't know how to separate being moral, responsible and right versus obeying and following laws, rules and regulations. So, most people think to themselves and tell others, "jast obey the laws, rules, and regulations to the letter and you won't get into trouble". But this doesn't mean that someone *is* being responsible or *is* right and moral. On the flip side, if people knew that if they killed someone by speeding and that they'd be prosecuted under murder laws and even subject to execution I know that not many people would speed. Similarly few people, if any, would park in front of hydrants, if they knew that the consequence of parking there would be to have their car confiscated in case of a fire or if the firefighters needed to gain access to a hydrant and someone's car blocked access that the owner of the car would have to be liable for part of the loss due to the fire.

Regardless, at the very least, if we are going to enforce traffic laws, let's do so with safety in mind, not tax revenues. For example, if someone slows down as they approach a stop sign or a red light, but they don't stop, and there isn't a car or a person anywhere near the driver, and the driver saw and knew this, why should the driver get a ticket for not stopping? The reason is because the municipality wants/needs an excuse to tax the driver – really that is the only reason – because there was nothing unsafe about what that driver did. But how many times has a municipal court or a police officer ignored the violation under such circumstances? Try never, unless the driver is a knock-down drop-dead gorgeous man or woman and the police officer happens to be a heterosexual of the opposite sex or the driver has "influence" in high places. So, why can we never get a break? Because, police officers are taught – even brainwashed – to not only apply the law, no matter what, but also they are fooled into believing that it is about law and order and nothing to do with tax revenue when in reality, the only priority that really matters is the almighty tax dollar. Municipal judges are no better because they need the money to get paid. On the other side, how many times do municipal police officers abuse their power and run red lights or speed or violate other traffic laws? Personally, I see it almost every time I see a moving police vehicle. It's ridiculous!

Getting back to the stop sign law, the problem with enforcing this law with safety in mind is the subjectivity of what speed is too high to be safe under the particular circumstances of each incident. Meaning, if the motorist slows to 5 mph approaching a stop sign, but doesn't stop, is that enough of a reduction in speed to be safe? What about 10 mph? What about 15 mph? The solution to this is reaction time and braking distances. Obviously at below 5 mph, almost anyone can stop their car on a dime, in case there is another car coming from another direction. But at 15 mph, it is unlikely that anyone can stop their car quickly enough to avoid an accident. Also, if a driver is 18, that driver is much more likely to have quicker reflexes than if the driver is 75. I think this difference should be taken into consideration post alleged violation. At least do a reflex test post alleged violation, if such laws are to be maintained at all. If the driver can demonstrate that they can stop at the speed they were traveling to avoid an accident then they should be freed, if not, then they should get a ticket, which has to cover for their testing. As for speeding, the only way to measure speeding violation is after an accident. However, people should be given some latitude. Certainly, one could argue for stopping people for exceeding the speed limit and giving them warnings, but no tickets and no points should be given, if speeding rules are to be enforced at all. Speeding should be taken into account at the trial for the accident. So, if the driver was frequently cited, but hadn't had an accident for more than double the time of a normal driver, the driver probably should not be given the maximum penalty. On the other hand, if the driver got into frequent accidents, and given repeated warnings especially due to speed then the driver should be given the maximum penalty, because this takes into account the "maturity" level, competence, and pattern of intent of the driver.

What I mean by this is that there are people who know when speeding is OK and when it is not. When speeding is safe and when it is not. If these people get into an accident for the first time after 25 years of driving that was probably an innocent accident, unless it kills someone then they should be prosecuted under murder laws, if gross violations of safety standards can be shown. On the other hand, if the violator speeds a lot and gets into frequent accidents then this is highly likely a good indication that the person is very "immature" and doesn't know their limits and abilities. Clearly, someone like this should not be allowed to drive regardless of how old they are or are not; whether they speed or not.

Regardless, again, the problem is enforcement and the perceived subjectivity of the rules. So, given that the current rules are unfair owing to the fact that it caters to the lowest common denominator and my relative rules would be perceived as subjective and random, regardless of the facts, this leads me to the only conclusion that a rational person can conclude. Traffic laws should be abolished, but if a driver hits someone and it can be proven that the driver is at fault and was going over the recommended speed limit, the driver should be arrested and tried for assault with a deadly weapon, and if they kill someone they should be arrested under murder charges. If the driver was not traveling over the speed limit, but it can be shown that it was the driver's fault anyway then the driver should be arrested and tried for assault, while if they kill a person, they should be arrested for involuntary manslaughter. However, if it is not their fault then they should be released.

Drinking and driving laws are also idiotic. Given my background and upbringing, I should not be subject to a universal anti-drinking and driving law. The counter-argument is that all citizens should be treated alike, i.e., the government should not discriminate. Also, the adjudication of differing standards for differing people would be a nightmare and costly or so goes the argument. Again, this is where advance citizenry comes into play. If I cause an accident then I should be tested for my blood alcohol level. Then a test should be administered to see if this level of intoxication truly impaired my judgment or if other factors influenced the accident. Then the adjudication of the accident should proceed accordingly.

In combination with other changes to our laws, overtime, I strongly believe that my progressive law-making will save more lives, but more importantly, it should create a citizenry that is overall more mature, responsible and accountable. The key is to focus on the big picture and not the minutia of the moment. We, as a society, have focused too much on the minutia and the irrelevant and have fostered a culture of laziness or more likely people who only want to obey rules (or "obeyers"). In contrast, we need people to think and be responsible and accountable; TRULY responsible and accountable. We do not have anything to lose, if we pursue my suggested changes. The biggest problem with current laws is that we forget why these laws were made and what the origins were for causing certain laws to be made. This has not only made us lazy, as a society, but also made us blind: We don't know when the law is obsolete, like jay walking laws and prostitution laws.

Prostitution and marriage are the different sides of the same coin; and prostitution should be legalized

Prostitution is the oldest profession in the world, or so people say, but nevertheless illegal in most parts of the world. Before we go on, let it be known that I've never hired a gigolo or a prostitute, and I wouldn't in the future. But I strongly support the legalization of prostitution. By now, the argument for why prostitution should be legalized should be familiar, but I think it's worth reinforcing.

I don't know for sure why prostitution was made illegal, but given the rhetoric about family values surrounding prostitution, destruction of morality, deep history of illegality, global universality and strong emotional reaction, particularly from religious fanatics, my guess is that it has to do with societal expansion and preservation of order. Here's my theory on why prostitution is almost a universally banned profession.

Imagine a primitive society in which males were allowed to spend a night with any woman. How many unplanned pregnancies would occur? And if multiple women were sexually active with multiple men, how would the society know who any child's father was and how would the pregnant woman survive, let alone her child? The society would descend into chaos. Children, if born at all, would die unless the "society," as a whole, took the responsibility to take care of the child. However, not many societies, if any, would be equipped to do so, or more importantly, would want to do so.

This is probably why marriage was invented, so that a single man can be made responsible for one woman and their offspring. This way there would be responsibility, accountability, and structure in the society. This would ensure that not only would children survive, but have a family structure that would anchor the child's future. Father would provide and mother would nurture. By having this stable family structure as the foundation of any society, it allows for a far more orderly and predictably growing society. I think this is how the concept of family values as the corner stone of society was born. Also note that the concept of marriage and anti-prostitution are almost universal in all societies.

Now, under my thesis, if sex was allowed only with marriage, so that there could be responsibilities and accountabilities then prostitution could not be allowed. Also, since the orderly expansion of the society was a paramount objective in most societies, if prostitution was allowed and the society ended up with a bunch of unwanted pregnancies that would destroy the family structure and the society. So, prostitution was directly counter to the objectives of a prosperous and orderly expanding-society. Therefore, it could not be allowed.

Now, wind the clock forward by some 15,000 years, how relevant or antiquated are anti-prostitution laws? Does a woman need a man to survive or thrive in the current world? Can women not plan their pregnancies now, at least to a large degree? Certainly, women have the ability to not get pregnant forever, if they choose not to. Most importantly, the vast majority of women can identify their child's father, if the need arise. And, if an absolute connection must be made, a DNA test can be performed.

I don't know for sure, if my thesis is 100% correct, but I'm sure that the origins of marriage and anti-prostitution laws are tied together and are along the lines that I've outlined. If I'm close to being right, and I strongly suspect that I am, then one can see how absurd anti-prostitution laws are in the light of modern societies.

Bottom-line is that I strongly believe that women should be given the right to do with their bodies what they want. As a matter of fact, I strongly believe that all people should be allowed to do as they will with their own bodies. This includes abortions and suicides. Let it be known now and forever more that I am opposed to abortion for my family, but my personal view should not be imposed on others and, therefore, all should have the freedom to choose what they believe is the right action for themselves and their family.

Remember that in my world, individual rights reign supreme, each has the right to choose one's own destiny, and everyone is given the freedom to exercise their philosophy, as long as it doesn't interfere with other people's right to exercise theirs. I strongly believe that this should be the rational end to a civilize society. Therefore, all so called "morality laws" are offensive and unnecessary in the society that I propose. This would also have the added benefit of reducing administrative costs due to enforcement and adjudication of these nonsensical and obsolete laws, thereby further reducing the need for taxes.

If prostitution is to be maintained as illegal then most politicians, a lot of investment bankers, securities research analysts, and consultants, and many women, and some men ought to be arrested and thrown in jail

Some people are probably laughing, while some others are wondering what I'm talking about. Let me take a very obvious example that a lot of people can relate to or can understand. Let's take the issue of gold-diggers (of which there are both the male and female types). As an aside, there is a good reason why most gold-diggers in the world are women. It is because most of the wealth is held and, most importantly, generated and controlled by men, at least for now. Unless most of the wealth is held, generated and controlled by women, it is unlikely that we would have more male gold-diggers than female. Anyway, getting back to the main point: What is the difference between female prostitutes and female gold-diggers or male gigolos and male gold-diggers? I would contend that the prostitutes and gigolos are far more honorable, particularly if they deliver good value and service the needs of their customers well. Most gold-diggers use deception and trickery to get money under the illusion and cover of love, while prostitutes and gigolos pretty much provide obvious exchanges of service for money. So there's no question that gold-diggers have more sinister motives and are more evil, so if we are to make prostitution illegal then, proportionately, we should look to impose the death penalty on gold-diggers, since gold-diggers are that much more sinister and evil.

What about some more gray areas like investment banking and consulting? Most people that are in the business of either investment banking or consulting will not need for me to explain myself and are probably quietly laughing under their breadth. In theory, consultants and investment bankers are supposed to provide unbiased and independent advice so that their clients can make the best decisions to provide the best service to their stakeholders. However, in reality, both investment bankers and consultants look for ways to maximize their fees in the near-term, usually irrespective of the effects to their clients. In particular, some investment bankers will try to get the company to do capital markets issues or M&A activity that may or may not be in the best interest of the company, while some consultants will try to provide advice based on what the CEO wants to hear. This is pretty close to what gold-diggers do. But, instead of selling sex, they sell their honor, integrity, morals and values for money. I think this is worse than selling sexual service for money, far worse. Therefore, in many ways, I believe that a truly professional, hard-working, high-quality gigolo or escort that provides impeccable service is far more respectable and admirable than the vast majority of investment bankers and consultants. So given that many investment bankers and consultants are collecting fees under false pretenses shouldn't we arrest them for fraud?

Regardless, there are many forms of prostitution in this society and some are more vial and repugnant than apparent, yet the most obvious forms, but more honorable, are the ones that are punished, vilified and considered dishonorable. We have gone mad, as a society, and have a lot to learn. By the way, prostitution is not a matter of perspective.

Suicide should not be illegal, particularly for terminally ill people

The argument comes down to who should be allowed to control one's own destiny or fate. If I ask anyone this question point blank, pretty much everyone says that they should be the one in control of their own fate and destiny. So then, when it comes to determining the end of one's own life, why is it that our society does not allow each of us to make up our own mind as to when and how to end it? Again, I strongly believe that the ban on suicide has to do with societal formation and judeo/christian religious doctrine. If people got it in their heads that it was better to die than live a tortured life, say as slaves, indentured servants and the like, or even as peasants that toiled and labored jast to survive, what would that do to a society?

Again, anti-suicide laws have nothing to do with the value and importance of life or with right versus wrong. It has to do with the health and wealth of a society and judeo/christian doctrine that says that it is its god who gave people their life, so it's only its god that should have the right to take it; and its god is the only one that should be allowed to determine when and how it should be taken. My guess is that the prohibition on suicides was also advantageous for slave owners and the upper echelon of societies that had dominion over the lives of other people and controlled their fate. Therefore, I'm sure that the powers to be had no objection to judeo/christian religious doctrine preaching that suicide is a sin. This leads me to believe that leadership in judeo/christian-based societies likely chose to codify anti-suicide doctrines into law with the backing of the religious establishment, which made for a very happy partnership. However, as societies moved beyond slavery, indentured servitude and other direct forms of human ownership and involuntary domination anti-suicide laws have become absurd. This means that the only reason left to enforce anti-suicide laws is due to judeo/christian religious doctrine. This then begets the question: Is our country determining laws based on judeo/christian doctrine, and, if so, what does this say about our rights to philosophical – including religious – freedom?

What makes me the angriest about anti-suicide laws is that there isn't even an exception for people dying of terminal illnesses – Oregon being the only state that allows assisted suicides. There is no reason for people to be denied a peaceful end to their life under such conditions. Again, it is because of religious zeal among believers of judeo/christian doctrine that such laws still remain unnecessarily in place and continues to make this antiquated law an abomination and blight on our humanity. This is one of the easiest injustices to correct, if people would jast think rationally, and a strong reminder of why thinking is so important and how little we – as a country and society – actually think.

By the way, those people that are using the excuse, "but a drug may come out tomorrow to cure the illness," to thinly veil their religiously-based objection for suicide or assisted-suicide should keep the following in mind: Even if a drug was created tomorrow for the particular illness plaguing an individual, it would take several YEARS for it to be put to clinical trials, and the person would most likely be dead well before then. Not only that, but in my opinion, most people are at least smart enough to have thought of these considerations before deciding to take their own lives.

To all of the pseudo-intellectuals that try to argue that one's own life should not be within one's own control, I say this: These pseudo-intellectuals are justifying slavery. How? If one's life is not within one's control for such a crucial decision then why not take other decisions about one's life away from people such as getting married, giving birth, getting an education, buying real estate? Since these matters are far less important than the question of one's own life or death, pseudo-intellectuals should have no problem taking these decisions away from the individual. If "society" has the right to take the decision to die away from people, certainly "society" should have the right to take other less important decisions away from people too. So, if this happens then what decisions are left to make for the individual? Isn't that slavery?

The vast majority of people are self-contradictory, mostly because they've been taught very confusing and inconsistent doctrines, which forces people to support the ban on suicides without even knowing why. However, some people are "lost" because they abide by the judeo/christian doctrine – which won't allow the faithful to support slavery nor suicide – despite may be something in the back of their minds telling them that suicides should not be outlawed. Therefore, people try to separate the two issues in their minds, and argue for why they oppose suicides using indoctrinated thoughts that are irrational and inconsistent. However, in reality, there is no rational reason why suicides should not be allowed, particularly for terminally ill patients. And, therefore, this is one law that must be changed for our society to become not only more rational, but also more humane and dignified.

Age of consent should depend on maturity, but in no event less than 21, and any deemed adult that proves otherwise should be permanently relegated to child status

The drinking age in most of America is 21, yet the voting age is 18. I don't know about most of America, but I think the responsibility to vote is more important than allowing someone to drink alcohol. Therefore, if anything, the voting age should be 21 and the drinking age should be 18. However, the argument for making the drinking age 21 is that people need the maturity to know when to stop drinking and not only avoid causing accidents that endanger other people's lives, but also know when to stop drinking to prevent harm to themselves and those around them. This is interesting. This strongly implies that an 18 year old is more than capable of executing their civic duty, but unfit to determine when to stop drinking. In turn, this suggests that voting requires less maturity, education, experience and judgment than knowing when to stop drinking. Personally, I don't think this is the case nor should it be so. I strongly believe that it requires exponentially more maturity, education, experience and judgment to vote in any election than to know when to stop drinking. Therefore, it is highly illogical that the voting age is 18, while the drinking age is 21.

Actually the history of this insanity was instituted through the 26th Amendment to the Constitution that passed in 1971. It was due to the fact that 18-20 year old males were being sent off to fight the Vietnam War but were not allowed to vote to influence the politicians that were sending them to war. The common slogan at the time was, "old enough to fight, old enough to vote." At the time – March 1971 – the Senate passed the 26th Amendment by 94-0 and the House of Representatives passed the 26th Amendment by a vote of 401-19. Then the states ratified the 26th Amendment within four months and it was signed by president Nixon in July 1971. The states ratified the 26th Amendment in the shortest time of any Amendments to the Constitution.

Regardless of this historical context and the reason for the passage of the 26th Amendment, it makes absolutely no sense that the voting age is 18, while the drinking age is 21. In addition, it makes no sense that people are given the label of an adult at 18, but cannot drink at that age. By definition, if one is an adult then this should mean that one is capable of making informed and mature decisions, including when to stop drinking. Therefore, "adults" should be allowed to drink.

In my opinion, to make sense of all this discombobulation, we need to lower the drinking age to 18, if we are to even have a drinking age at all. However, the most important issue isn't whether the voting age is 18 and the drinking age is 21 or whether or not it should be the other way around. The more important issue is how do we define who is and who is not mature enough to be an adult, and what, if any, restrictions do we apply to adults and by what age. If we could somehow truly test everyone for their level of maturity and judgment, we wouldn't have to worry about this issue. However, there is no test that we could employ to look into the brains of people to determine their level of maturity. Therefore, our society presumes and labors under the assumption that we must automatically grant adult status to individuals by date certain. More importantly, we assume that overnight – literally – people are mature enough to earn the label of adult at the age that we, as a society, decide that a child becomes an adult, regardless of whether they do or don't deserve to be treated as an adult. However, this is a mistake that has caused many detrimental results to our society; a mistake that can and should be fixed.

Ideally, I propose that as people prove themselves worthy of being an adult, they should be granted certain privileges and, in contrast, as people prove themselves unworthy of being an adult then privileges granted to them as adults should be taken away. For example, should someone that is deemed an adult cause an accident that destroys property after drinking and driving, not only should the deemed adult be prosecuted for the offense of destroying other people's property, but also, the deemed adult should have their privileges of adulthood taken away for a number of months or years. Therefore, this person should no longer be able to drive, drink, vote, gamble, marry, have children, or go to adult entertainment venues of any kind, including R-rated movies and bars during their probationary period and should generally be treated as a child by our society and made to attend adult education classes. Then once the individual completes their probation period, their adult privileges should be restored. However, we should institute a three strikes and you're out policy: If a deemed adult commits an offense that revokes their adult privileges more than three times, this deemed adult should be permanently relegated to being a child or an immature adult. However, when adjudicating an individual's qualifications to be an adult, we must take into consideration that individual's abilities such as tolerance for alcohol and other factors that may have bearing on their case. And, I do understand that the devil is in the details and that execution will be difficult, but I do not believe impossible.

Also, to institute my policy, we must rid ourselves of civil laws such as traffic laws, DWI laws, anti-drug laws, anti-prostitution laws and other petty-crime and so called "morality" laws. In addition, before a person becomes an adult, no one should be allowed to put any monetary value to their child's life for purposes of commercial contracts such as for movies, commercials, record deals, etc. And, anti-child labor laws must be strictly enforced until the child is capable of making their own critical decisions of self-determination. This point is not really all that different than what our current system provides for to protect the welfare of our children. However, it is important to reinforce the message that children must be protected.

The critical decision that needs to be made is at what age do we allow a person to become an adult. And, should we adjudicate adulthood according to the activity that is in question. For example, do we allow our children to drive at 15, start sexual activity at 16, gamble at 18, and drink at 20 or do we say one size fits all, i.e., at 20 years, 364 days, 23 hours, 59 minutes and 59 seconds a person is a child, but exactly one second later the child becomes an adult? Personally, I strongly believe that the former is a much more sensible plan than the latter.

If it were left up to me, each individual would be put on probation starting at 16 when most people are granted the privilege of driving, assuming that they pass their driving test. Then, periodically thereafter, additional adult privileges would be granted until all adult privileges are granted by 21; however, individuals would not be granted full adult status until 23. At any time between 16 and 23, if the individual displays "immature" behavior, all adult privileges granted up to that point will be revoked and the probation period would be lengthened by at least 2 years.

Also, to obtain full adult status, each individual must be tested for their knowledge of certain issues, facts about certain products such as tobacco, alcohol, drugs, and any addictions in general, including gambling, understanding of the US Constitution and all of the attendant Amendments, American history and societal courtesies, especially when drinking, smoking, driving or conversing in public.

However, I would grant exceptions to the above mentioned timeline for becoming an adult, if the parents of the child deem it appropriate for their child to experience certain privileges earlier as the parents see fit. Some privileges that could be accelerated at the discretion of the child's parents would include driving privileges, limited drinking privileges (under strict supervision of the child's parents), and age of consent for sexual activity with proper sex education provided by professionals and contraception provided by parents. However, irresponsible decisions by either the parents or the child must be appropriately punished. And, any parent who is on probation, were on probation or had their adult status revoked shall not be allowed to exercise the right to accelerate any privileges for any of their child.

Finally, once a child obtains full adult status, they should be free to choose, whichever profession they want and to use whatever product, including alcohol, tobacco, and drugs that they want to. However, if any behavior leads to the violation of other people's rights, the individual must be punished for the violation, but not the contributing factor to the violation. For example, if an automobile driver gets high on cocaine and kills a pedestrian, the driver should be prosecuted and convicted of first degree murder and punished accordingly, but not for the use of cocaine.

I strongly believe that my policy is the most Just and fair policy in adjudicating adulthood that we can devise that most closely coincides with our Constitutions' guarantee of individual rights while protecting society from the ills of irresponsible people and irresponsible behavior. And, again, I would seek a Constitutional Amendment to codify the process that I've outlined on how America should govern the transition from being a child to becoming a full adult.

Why the call for equality when it comes to tax laws, but inequality when it comes to traffic laws?

First of all, I'm advocating for Justice, not equality, in both situations, and this should be more than enough of a reason. Second, remember, I don't want any traffic laws, only recommendations and perhaps warnings. However, I did suggest that if we are going to have traffic laws that these laws must take into consideration each individual's ability to effectively and safely navigate roads. In contrast, I'm advocating for a flat tax amount for everyone regardless of their ability to "afford" such a tax. So, some of you are wondering, "how's that consistent, Just and fair?!"

The unifying principles in both situations are Justice, and individual rights and freedoms. It's Just that we pay the same amount of money for the same services that we receive from the government. In the same vein, it is Just that we are treated according to our abilities by the government (actually society) when it is forcing a rule, law or regulation on us. So, when it comes to taxes, we should get equal services for equal payment. This is no different than everyone paying the same price for the same product. However, when it comes to what the society is trying to force us to do, our individual abilities must be taken into consideration for it to be Just and fair. This is no different than athletic competitions or races, school admissions, getting a job, winning an award, or even to some degree getting paid. The concept is that in the case of taxes, it is about what anyone gives and takes on a monetary basis, but in the case of traffic laws, it is about one's ability or lack thereof, i.e., can a person be a safe driver and perform within the bounds of their own ability, which has nothing to do with the exchange of goods or services for money. Also, in the case of taxes, it is about who owns the money that a person earns, the one who earned it or someone else, and who has the right to use the money that an individual earns, the person who earned it or someone else. In the case of traffic laws, it is about whether an individual knows themselves or not and how well they conduct themselves according to their abilities.

One may argue, why isn't taxes according to abilities too? Meaning, if one can pay more, why shouldn't they pay more. First of all, to enforce such a law where the government takes more and provides less services for the wealthy, it has to collect the tax through the use of force, and no government should have to force their citizens to do anything – don't forget that in our country there is no government vs. its people, we are the government. This means that the liberals and socialists with their poor allies are forcing the wealthy to pay for their largesse. Also, if one were to argue this point, then it would be the same as arguing for people to pay for products at a store according to how much money each individual makes. And, that would be extremely unfair and unjust.

Also, if one thinks about it carefully that's pretty close to communism. In other words, if everything was priced according to a percentage of income then everyone would be incentivized not to work. Let's take an example. Let's say there are two people, A and B. A makes $100,000 per year and B makes $20,000 per year. Further, let's say that room and board costs 10% of one's income. This means that the person making $100,000 per year – person A – would have to pay $10,000 per year for room and board, while the person making $20,000 per year would pay $2,000 for the same room and board. Why would anyone strive to make more money? Also, this means that virtually no one will have money left over to invest, and, therefore, the economy would crater. Moreover, overtime, our economy will run out of everything; think about it. Imagine what would happen to the economy, if we started to run out of goods, materials and products! No one should pay more for the same service that everyone else receives; never! But what's worse is that the current tax system forces the rich to not only pay more, but also receive less in return from the government! That's ridiculous!

So, what this all mean is that when it comes to products and services, where a monetary exchange is involved, each individual must get the same product and service for the same money. However, when it comes to a unilateral directive – a one-way street – then ability must come into play. Ability should also come into play for competitions – including competitive admissions – awards, honors, jobs, contracts, etc. Also, when it comes to taxes, we must all be mindful of whose money we are collecting and who has the right to spend that money.

This isn't rocket science, but certain people, like politicians, socialists and liberals, try to make it murkier than it really is, because it is to their advantage to keep the issues muddied. However, the reality of the matter is is that Justice should be based on what exactly one is adjudicating, and we all have to remember that equality isn't always fair, but Justice must always be applied equally. So, for admissions to top universities, equal access would not be fair, or access based on how much you can pay is also unfair. However, when it comes to purchasing goods or services, equal payment for the same goods and services must apply and is fair.

Another example of equality and Justice can be seen in competitions. One cannot and must not give out gold medals to everyone and even though this is not equal, it is Just and fair. Another interesting example involves pay. As a society, we should never have a situation in which qualifications other than one's ability and contribution to the company determine one's pay. So, one's gender, race, religious affiliation, sexual preference, physical appearance, and other measures that do not impact one's ability should not be used in determining one's pay. However, in reality, we have all witnessed political savvy, good looks, or plain-old brown-nosing get people what they want.

Lastly, it is about individual freedoms and rights. When it comes to traffic laws, it is about the judgment and ability of any individual to determine whether or not hesh can do something safely or not. When it comes to taxes, it's about how much control an individual has over hes own money and who gets to spend it: The person who earned it, or someone else who had nothing to do with making the money. In both cases, it's about the individual's choice, freedom, and decision, and maximizing those rights; it shouldn't be about the government's or other people's judgment or directive imposed on any individual.

Always remember, when trying to determine that which is right or wrong, good or bad, or moral or immoral look at the root basis of the cause-and-effect relationship. If it is a material relationship then equality must apply, but if it is non-material then we need to think about what abilities, skills, and criteria for judgment lies at the very basic level of the endeavor and adjudicate and determine right, good and moral based on those very basic deciding factors.

A simple generalization of how I think about these issues could be summed-up this way: Equality when it comes to individual rights, ability when it comes to competition or so called societal privileges.

Personal and Family

If I ask you: "Who are you?" Your answer will be wrong!

Most people believe that they know who they are, but in reality – based on discussions with hundreds of people all over the world – my experience tells me that most people really don't know who they are. If I ask people the question, "Who are you?" I know that most people will talk about where they were born, grew up and went to school, what they do for a living, what they like to do with their friends, their hobbies, their favorite sports to play and to watch, their likes and dislikes, favorite color, food, places, movies, books, and people, their dreams, hopes, passions and desires, past and current relationships, political, social, religious and historical leanings, their (perceived) sense of humor and other mundane things. However, this is not who an individual is. So, most people are wondering what else people would talk about when they're asked who they are.

The key question to ask is why people have the hopes and dreams that they do, why they like certain things, what really drives people to engage in certain activities, favor certain movies, books, foods, et cetera, have specific friends and make the decisions that they do. Basically, we must ask, *what makes people individuals, what makes them tick?* Besides the things mentioned above, some people will talk about whether or not genetics or the environment or some combination of these two things determines who people are. But all throughout, the vast majority would likely miss the most central point of the question, *who are they?* Not how an individual got to be where they are, not what they do, not what they are, but *who are they*? What makes *the person be them*?

Let me end the suspense: There are really only six characteristics that make someone who they are. Those six attributes are: MORALS, VALUES, ETHICS, INTEGRITY, HONOR and HONESTY. Let's start with the basics: The definitions:

- MORALS: That which is right and wrong.
- VALUES: That which one ascribes importance to and ascribes value to.
- ETHICS: The physical manifestation of one's morals and values.
- INTEGRITY: The philosophical consistency and mental preservation of one's morals, values, and ethics.
- HONESTY: This is self-explanatory.

- HONOR: The physical manifestation of one's integrity under all circumstances and situations.

HONOR also has some other implications: The knowledge that one has the highest morals, values, ethics, integrity and sense of honesty and that one will do anything to uphold these core distinctions. Also, the pride of actually doing what one says, saying what one thinks, thinking what one believes and believing in the highest standard of morals, values, ethics, integrity and sense of honesty. But, most importantly, knowing when one is wrong and changing oneself accordingly. This last character trait of honor may be the most important.

However, after careful consideration, honor could be defined as a sub-item to ethics or integrity and honesty as a sub-item of ethics or morals. Nevertheless, I believe honor and honesty are special because so few people have them, let alone exercise them. Also, I believe honor and honesty to be very special attributes, which need to be highlighted and perpetuated.

Anyway, what defines any individual can be summed up by articulating these six attributes about oneself; what I call the Six Pillars of humans or jast The Six Pillars: Morals, values, ethics, integrity, honor and honesty. There is nothing more fundamental and basic than the Six Pillars to who anyone is. The rest of it is trivial – important in forging relationships, but still, nevertheless, trivial.

Therefore, why anyone behaves the way they do is because they're acting on what they believe is right and wrong (morals) and how they believe they should act on their morals (ethics). People covet and buy products that they want, which is driven by what they believe has value to them (values). And, people become angry when others imply that they did something bad (integrity), regardless of whether they did or didn't. People have pride in themselves, because they act for the **true** benefit of themselves and guard their own Six Pillars, as well as protecting the Six Pillars of others (honor). And, people try to portray themselves without cover, deceit or pretense (honesty). There is nothing more fundamental to who anyone is than their Six Pillars. So, the next time someone asks you who you are, you should talk about your Morals, Ethics, sense of Honor and Honesty, and your Integrity and Values. However, if you are listening to another person describing themselves, you won't know whether that person is truly who they say they are until time passes. This is what makes judging and understanding people so difficult – the necessity for the passage of time.

Anyway, the question that then looms in the air that must be answered is what are the right morals, values, ethics, and integrity? When is defending one's honor or the honor of others the right thing to do? Is there ever a time to lie?

I will answer these questions in other chapters and describe what I believe is the right set of rules and regulations that we should have in this country, and answer how the Six Pillars translates into anyone's lives and the future of our country.

It may seem like choosing your life-long mate is rocket science, and virtually none of you know how to do it, but really it ain't that difficult

Most people get married because they feel it's time and end up marrying the one that they happen to be dating at the time. Most people can't see this and wouldn't quite put it as bluntly as I've said it, but this is the reality. Also, when both women and men are asked, "what do you want in your boyfriend/husband or girlfriend/wife?" the answer is almost a carbon copy of each other.

For women, they want someone who makes them laugh, pays attention to them, someone who's got their head screwed on tight (code for makes a lot of money), loyal, fun, decisive, determined, hardworking and is a strong leader, good looking is a bonus, but certainly athletic, i.e., not fat, honest, charming, romantic, generous, sensitive and kind, have interest in similar activities and issues, neat, but not a freak, clean, but not compulsive, a man's man, but also likes to spend time with their girlfriend/wife, and likes children and animals. Also, in an honest and vulnerable moment (may be slightly drunk), women will also say they want a man who knows their way around a woman's body, i.e., someone who knows how to pleasure her.

For men, they want someone who is pretty, has a beautiful, sexy body and isn't going to gain weight after having children, someone who takes care of their physical appearance, but not obsessive, someone who's a "slut" in bed, but a princess in public, stands by her man, fun, knows how to talk to her man, isn't clingy and knows when and how to give her man some space, smart, but not too smart, personable, but not slutty or ditsy, engaging, but not overly chatty, clean, but not compulsive, someone with a good sense of humor and laughs at all his jokes, enjoys the same activities, and has a respectable education/career/job. In a moment of carelessness, he may confide that he wants a woman that can pamper and take care of him, like cooking, cleaning, and doing the laundry.

However, if one boils it down to the essence, it's not too complicated. Women want security, but it isn't necessarily financial, it could be psychological, as long as the finance isn't a big issue. For men, they want a woman that will stand-by her man. All the rest of it is somewhat extraneous. But there is at least one other characteristic that seems to be a truism: In most successful long-term relationships, the man typically loves the woman more than the other way around. I would suggest that this makes the man way less likely to look around and check out his options, which is what binds him to her more securely. And, for her, she is less likely to gamble on other men, if she knows the one she has is devoted to her.

However, in reality, the real core to a successful long-term relationship has nothing or almost nothing to do with any of the above, perhaps with the exception of the truism about most successful relationships starting with the man loving the woman more. Successful long-term relationships have to be based on the most basic of human traits. Couples have to have basic human traits in common for the marriage to work long-term, because the rest of it is superficial, learnable, adaptable, or trivial.

So, men need to stop paying attention to women's looks because all women grow old and wrinkly and no man can have it all, particularly given the fact that all men are going to grow old and wrinkly too. So, men should concentrate on characteristics that matter to both the man and the woman, because looks are fleeting and always will be. Most everything else that is superficial is fleeting or can be learned as well.

Women need to stop selling/leading with their looks/sexuality, because if they do happen to get a man with their looks/sexuality then they are capturing a man whose priority is obviously superficial. This means that when the man gets bored of the woman's looks/sexuality, he's going to move on, because that is his priority. So, it shouldn't surprise anyone when people hear stories about successful middle-aged men getting "trophy wives." Or, when a woman gets dumped because she gained some weight or gravity starts to exert its influence.

The reason why most people have such focus on superficial and trivial triggers is because they don't know any better, which makes them insecure, so they focus on what is observable in an attempt to latch on to something that they see, know, and can easily compare and control for. Also, innately, both men and women equate good looks, money, education, high-brow family background and success with being a good person, better mate, and more qualified I general, but these superficial characteristics aren't really highly correlated to being a good person. In fact, according to my casual observation, I'd say that in many instances, they are inversely correlated.

I'll make one last observation about relationships, even though I hate to say it: Men are going to have to drive the change. Rightly or wrongly, for good or for bad, for better or for worse, the vast majority of women follow their men, whether they want to acknowledge it or not, whether they think they do or not. To some degree, women *want to* follow their man. They want a strong leader that listens to them and considers their point of view and incorporate it before making decisions. I guess it is difficult to overcome evolution.

This means that men have to stop focusing on women's outward appearance then women will stop obsessing over their looks and body. This is not to say that we shouldn't all be focused on our health, but one's health doesn't necessarily have to correlate to one's looks or appearance.

This means that both men and women must focus on their Six Pillars and everyone should look for someone with the closet carbon-copy of their own Six Pillars (of course, excluding any and all incestuous relationships). The problem is that if an individual has screwed-up Six Pillars, then it will lead to wrong decisions. As an example, if a person puts aesthetic appearance as the most important quality in their value system then they are going to look for the prettiest or most handsome woman or man that they can find. This does absolutely nothing for them in choosing the right mate. And, when their chosen one ages, they are "stuck" with an unsatisfactory choice, which leads to unnecessary problems such as resentments, fights, and, eventually, affairs and separation. Ultimately, divorce becomes the only rational choice.

Anyone looking for a wife or a husband must first determine why they want to marry and what they want from marriage, keeping in mind that one's marriage should last 50 or more years (it is hoped). Therefore, if all one wants is good sex and fun then the individual really ought to reconsider their decision to get married. This person is far better off remaining single and changing out their boyfriend or girlfriend as needed and desired. On the other hand, if it is about having children then the person has to make sure that their partner/spouse, views the world the same way – has the same Six Pillars – so that they can deliver a consistent and strong message to their children. Also, it will not hurt that they are going to have a strong "meeting of the minds" in the decisions that need to be made throughout their lives. Obviously, if the couple agrees on a whole lot of issues, it makes for a far better and easier long-term relationship. This is how one creates strong family values, which then gets passed-down generation after generation after generation. Regardless, even with a very close match in Six Pillars, don't forget that to have a successful relationship, both people must still work very hard to actually achieve it.

Next, the natural inclination will be to ask, "what are the correct Six Pillars?" This is a natural question, but this is something that I will discuss in another chapter. The key point to take from this chapter is that when choosing a mate, if an individual wants a happy, long-term relationship, each must focus on the other's Six Pillars. Also, when looking for the person that best fits with one's own Six Pillars, keep in mind that any individual will be hard pressed to find someone that has even 90% common ground, let alone 100%. The threshold that everyone needs to decide is at what percentage point they will be happy to stay with their chosen mate, when confronted with someone in the future that they *know* is 100% in-line with their own Six Pillars. Or, what subcomponents of the Six Pillars must they absolutely have to have and in what form to be happy? If one can correctly determine this threshold and meet someone that fulfills these criteria or threshold, then they are very likely to have a happy long-term relationship, even if they meet the perfect person sometime in the future. I looked for and married someone that is 90% similar, in my opinion, and I have been extremely happily married for a long time. This doesn't mean that we didn't work hard to make the marriage continue to work, but being able to have faith in the knowledge that one chose well, certainly makes it much easier to get over the rough spots.

As an addendum, one should apply the same thinking in choosing friends. However, since the purpose of having friends isn't to procreate, and one doesn't have to see their friends constantly, one may argue that the threshold is lower. I'd argue that the threshold may be lower, but this means that the lower threshold should put more distance between friends versus husband and wife. Additionally, one's best friends should have the most similar Six Pillars, while acquaintances have the least similar Six Pillars. Also, consider that there are certain characteristics in the Six Pillars that one should not live without when it comes to choosing their close friends. For each individual, the criteria may be slightly different, but I'd urge everyone to consider several characteristics as being non-negotiable: 1) Honesty, 2) earned loyalty, 3) responsibility and accountability, 4) strong coincidence of morals, 5) strong ethics, 6) strong integrity, and 7) honor. Notice I did not include values. As friends, people don't have to value the same things. So, while one close friend may sleep with a different man every month, another may choose to have only long-term relationships. One may argue that this isn't a question of values, but of morals, but what morals are we talking about? Remember, in my thinking everyone has the right to do as they please with their body. So, questions of being a slut don't enter the equation. One friend may think of herself as a free spirit that needs to encounter different men to know which one suits her best, while the other may choose to stay with one person to explore the full potential of a relationship before moving on. Neither choice is necessarily right or wrong. However, through their individual and independent process, one friend may learn all she needs to about men in order to have a strong long-lasting relationship with the one, while the other may learn what she needs to about herself in order to have a strong long-lasting relationship with the one.

In actuality, I would argue that the essence and objective of one friend's behavior is to identify a man to take care of her and love her for who she is, while the other is looking for a relationship where she can play a more controlling role. In other words, while one friend is looking for a mate that suits her well, the other friend is looking for the mate that she suits well. Since this is not a book on relationships, I'll let you contemplate what I mean by the last thought and move on.

If you are a Blue Tiger (or Maltese Tiger), acting like you are a normal tiger will make it impossible for you to find another Blue Tiger, and brings into question whether or not you really are a Blue Tiger

Huh? Look, whether it is a spouse that one is looking for, a girlfriend or boyfriend, or a straight forward friend, if a person is as special and rare as a Blue Tiger (otherwise known as a Maltese Tiger), acting like a normal tiger isn't going to get that person any closer to their goal of finding another Blue Tiger to mate with, have relations with or jast have fun with. If an individual is as rare in their thinking and their behavior as a Blue Tiger is among the various tiger families then in order to attract another Blue Tiger, they had better think and act like a true Blue Tiger and advertise as loud and as often as they can that they are a Blue Tiger. It is going to be hard enough for anyone as rare as a Blue Tiger to find another rare Blue Tiger among so many common species, acting like they are not a rare Blue Tiger isn't going to help the matter. Also, if by chance a rare Blue Tiger that is pretending to be something else happens to meet another rare Blue Tiger how will the other Blue Tiger know that the first one is indeed a Blue Tiger, or pretending to be one?

Now, if one is a rare Blue Tiger, but pretends to be a normal tiger, is that Blue Tiger really a Blue Tiger? And, why should another proud and spectacular Blue Tiger have anything to want to do with the one that is ashamed of being a Blue Tiger? It doesn't matter if the Blue Tiger ends up attracting another rare species of cat like the White Lon (literally bright white, not an albino) of South Africa or the equally rare Golden Tabby Tiger (very faint beige coloring – almost white – with very light brown stripes) of India, unless the rare cat is actually a White Lion or a Golden Tabby Tiger, it's useless to attract those species to it.

So, if you are a Blue Tiger, be proud, be loud and be on the prowl! And, make sure you successfully attract a spectacular, bodacious, and fantastic Blue Tiger. It will be worth it; it was for me. Yes, I found my Blue Tiger and married the love of my life. And, after so many years, we're still crazy in love!

It's no coincidence that the divorce rate is jast under 50%

Now that we know why people choose who they choose to marry versus what it actually takes to have a successful long-term marriage, it shouldn't surprise anyone that the divorce rate is roughly 50%, because people are essentially randomly choosing their partners, the divorce rate ought to be about that. This is perfectly in-line with a normal distribution curve, which is symbolic of pure chance and random occurrences. In other words, if people were choosing carefully and well, the divorce rate should be well less than 50%. This would also suggest that two-thirds of the people are probably somewhat happily married to somewhat unhappily married, about 12% are very unhappily married, 12% are very happily married, 4.5% are extremely unhappy, 4.5% are extremely happy, and 0.5% are about to kill each other and another 0.5% are in heaven. This would be a normal distribution curve. Meaning, amongst any group of friends, any individual should find that about 50% of their friends that have been married about 7-10 years should be divorced or don't seem happy in their marriages, and 50% seem happy to very happy in their marriages. The next hurdle is people that have been married some 15-25 years. This is when we find that a lot of people get divorced too and where mid-life crises start to play a role and trophy wives come into the picture. However, if people get past the 25th-year anniversary, it seems that marriages go all the way.

Modern statistics contrast starkly with data prior to the 1950s when the divorce rate was well under 50%. Again, the reason why the divorce rate is about 50% today is that most marriages are a random occurrence, so naturally the marriage is or isn't going to work: A 50%/50% outcome. But, there are a few exceptions. These people actually know what they were getting into, why and with whom. These are the people that make the divorce rate, jast slightly under 50%.

So, why was the divorce rate so much lower in the past? Contrary to what the older generation tells us and what politicians are trying to sell us, it has nothing to do with the moral decay of the younger generation. If one looks at divorce statistics, it started to climb in the latter part of the 1960s and really started to accelerate in the 1970s. What changed is that women started to demand and got economic independence from their husbands. This made it far easier for women to seek a divorce from unhappy marriages. It isn't rocket science.

So, my guess is that the divorce rate will not change much from the 50% level until people start understanding their own Six Pillars, i.e., what about their Six Pillars are good and bad, and start fixing that which is bad, then identifying those individuals that match their Six Pillars and start marrying based on the closest match. In other words, over the long-run, it is unlikely that the divorce rate will go up much from 50%, but there is a chance that it will slowly get reduced overtime, if my philosophy takes hold. That would be one true indication and victory for the development of a Just and rational society. The sole exception would be if one side or the other's financial independence was taken away from them then this would also lead to a drop in the divorce rate.

If you are humble then you are either stupid or a liar, which one would you like to be?

Most people are thinking that of all the things that I've said, this has to take the cake for being outrageous. Believe me, I've heard it all. We've all been told throughout our lives that humility is good that we should be humble that people with humility are viewed with favor by society. But who among us have asked why humility is good? Before we get there, let us start with the definition of humility, so that we have no confusion. So, according to Dictionary.com, two definitions of humble are: "Having a feeling of insignificance, inferiority, subservience, etc." or "low in rank, importance, status, quality, etc." Again, according to Dictionary.com, as a verb it is defined as: "To lower in condition, importance, or dignity; abase."

Now, let us think about these definitions. What about these qualities are admirable or desirable in any human being? Why would or should anyone *feel* insignificant, inferior or subservient? This means that even though they aren't, they *feel* that they are. How stupid does an individual have to be to not know how they stand compared to others? And, if they do know, why would they misrepresent their position? At the very best, one could say that the person is intensely dull and has very little observational skills. Not a very attractive quality is it?

So, whichever way one dices it, slices it, fricassees it, humble means that the person is lying or stupid, and at best totally unobservant. So, again, from an objective viewpoint, I would say that none of these qualities are good traits in a human. So, why are we told that being humble is good? Unless our ancestors were completely daft, I believe that "being" humble is one of those norms and morays that everyone is taught to obey, but the reason for which no one remembers anymore. And, given that being humble isn't a good characteristic, I can only surmise that there has to be other reasons for why we are told to be humble; even forced to be humble by society. However, there is one aspect of this rule that is very interesting: It is that it is almost universal, at least in North America, Europe and Asia. I believe that this means that the rule had to have been invented a very, very long time ago, before humans migrated to different parts of the world, or it was independently and coincidentally created in different societies as a response to some universal human situation or circumstance.

Since it is unlikely that the rule was made up during the time of the African migration of humans to other continents – don't ask me to explain why I think this – I have to believe that it has more to do with the base nature of people than something cultural or normative in one particular society. If we think about it from this perspective, the rest of what I have to say will make a lot more sense.

The chances are that people all over the world figured out – independently of each other – that people who debase themselves appear less threatening and therefore get a better reception from those that have power than those that know who they are and advertise it. Also, by faking their inferiority to others or making others seem relatively superior, humble people make other people feel much better about themselves and become more trusted and better received by the people who have sway and power over people's lives. This is still very true today. Therefore, to make it easier for people to be accepted by others and make their "political path" easier to navigate, "wise" people all over the world came up with the idea of humility, i.e., manipulating to get ahead. This shouldn't surprise anyone since manipulation of all kind has existed for millenniums all over the world. Jast look at history books from all different countries, everyone can read how political games, intrigues and manipulations to get ahead in life and build fortunes large and small were very common throughout.

So, in today's society not much has changed: It is better for someone to be perceived as a non-threating, but useful entity versus someone who poses a challenge to the higher ups. Obviously, in our society, this mean that stroking the ego of one's superiors is beneficial to one's career and even stroking the ego of co-workers and subordinates help as well. Therefore, many of the accomplished political types know how to hide their true abilities and strengths until the time comes when it needs to be fully displayed to achieve one's objectives. Therefore, in order to get ahead, we must be perceived as not only being smart, but also an ally and supporter of the "boss." So, to succeed, we should try to make it look like good ideas are flowing from one's "superiors" instead of going around telling them what's right and what's wrong, what works and doesn't and what's good and what's bad. As sad as this may be, I think we all know that this is true and works to the benefit of one's career almost every time.

However, I think that the very rare few that are truly honorable, honest and morally and ethically upstanding will puke at the thought of "kissing-ass" and being humble, I know, I do. However, because the deception of humility works on the vast majority of people for the vast majority of times, I believe it has become a universal "virtue" that is strongly encouraged.

On the opposite side, it takes an exceptional person of strong moral character and honor to be immune to these tactics of deception, and to not succumb to the temptation of manipulation by others. But for this very special person, the world becomes that much more challenging and difficult to navigate and a price may have to be paid for their strong character. And, this price could mean their career. I know; I've suffered for it.

So, which kind of world should we strive for? The fact is that I know the vast majority of people talk a good game, but act very differently. People do this because they are supposed to espouse strong moral character, but it's easier to take the "low road," so most people don't put into practice what they verbally espouse – this is what I would call a lack of integrity and honor. However, what people don't realize is that they are helping to corrupt the moral character of our country as a whole. Many people have commented, "If I can get ahead and better provide for me and mine, why should I care?" When people help to condone, facilitate, and perpetuate evil and immorality, the society as a whole starts and continues to decay. This means that we go down the proverbial "slippery slope." So, when bad things happen to people – because people's moral character compels them to take advantage of others – who can people blame, other than themselves?

This is where individual's obligation to society comes into focus. Try to remember that everything has a price and a consequence: What one does affects others who then act out, which affects even more people then eventually all this comes back and the cycle starts again. However, most people don't have the ability, knowledge, foresight or training to make the connection between their behavior and what happens to them, so they keep on going down the road to perdition without even realizing that they're doing so. Here's how I know that most people don't have the ability, knowledge, foresight or training to make the connection between their behavior and what happens to them. Let me give you a very simple but highly illustrative example. How many times does an irresponsible driver do something stupid that causes others to take evasive action? Then when the driver that had to evade the irresponsible action honks to let the irresponsible driver know that hesh put their life in danger instead of getting an apology by way of a hand wave, they get the finger! Does this situation or something like this sound familiar? What's worse, many people ignore most situations like this and have stopped honking at people who endanger others on the road. Furthermore, I know that most people say to themselves, it's not worth going through the hassle of a confrontation, and may be getting the other "crazy" person angry at them, because that "crazy" person may do something worse like shooting them. The problem is that by not honking and making a protest "good" people are condoning bad people's bad behavior. Therefore, when each of us neglects to make legitimate protests, the only thing that we can expect is for the irresponsible person to continue their bad behavior, because they get away with it over and over again. I'm sure that many of people are saying to themselves that it isn't their problem; let the other victim deal with it. But, what happens if the first incident happened to me, and I didn't do anything about it, and the second victim is you, and in the process you, or worse yet, your beloved husband or wife or one of your children dies? This is but one responsibility that we have to each other in a well-functioning society: No matter how slight or minor the injustice, we must speak out on behalf of each other.

However, some people believe that one person cannot do much, so why bother. These people believe that the "crazy" person isn't going to change their behavior because one person honks at them! But, if every time the "crazy" person did something bad, they always got honked at, would the bad person change their behavior? What if they were always reported to the police? What if everyone responded by doing the same thing to them, i.e., people respond to them with road rage? Ultimately, what if they were rammed every time that they did something bad?

My argument is no different than asking what one person's vote is worth. And, like voting, one vote may not mean much, but a million votes make a big difference, and to get a million votes it has to start with one.

By the way, in case someone is wondering, which one in the example – the victim or the crazy driver – is the person that doesn't have the ability, foresight, knowledge or training to know and understand how one's behavior affects themselves in the long-run, the answer is both of them. So, don't forget that there is no free lunch, no short-cuts that work in the long-run, no easy money, no reward without hard work, no escaping from consequences and no true win without fair competition. Finally, remember that humility is either a lie or stupidity and the worst of all character traits, because it is posed as something virtuous when it is actually and realistically ultimately very evil.

The fact is that people are very, very ugly, regardless of how beautiful they are; and, so, many beautiful people are like shit painted in gold

Of course, when I say that people are ugly, I'm talking about what's between their ears. In particular, I'm talking about their Six Pillars. And, as I've said before, the worth of a person has nothing to do with what they are and what they do, but who they are, and who they are can only be defined by their Six Pillars. Let me review the conclusion of the chapter regarding humility: We are taught to be humble not because it is a good trait for us to possess, but because others respond well to the superficial and pretentious cue. But that is not where the argument ends. The question has to be why others respond well to humility when it is a deliberate lie. Very simply put, it is because the vast majority of people are very insecure and feel better/good about themselves when others present themselves as inferior, making the listener appear better than they really are. To put it simply and plainly, they're being made a fool of and they don't even know it, and more to the point, they like being made a fool of in the short-term because it makes them feel good. This is very, very sad!

So, what does that say about those that feel good when they see people be humble? What does this say about the people who feel better when someone of accomplishment lowers themselves, so that on a relative basis they "look" or "feel" better? What does it say about most people when someone who is more accomplished than they are can make the individual feel better about themselves by lying about who they are and what they've accomplished? What does it say about the people that don't know what's happening and feel better about themselves when others act humble in front of them? How insecure, unintelligent and mixed-up does someone have to be to be taken in by humility and think about it as being a good trait? It is very sad that our country has come to this.

This is the world that we live in where white lies (no different than plain lies), superficiality and pretense get a person farther than hard-work, truth and reality. This is the distorted screwed-up world we live in, and it is plainly because most people and our ancestors made it that way, whether they wanted to make it that way or not. The reason why this is the fault of average Americans is because most people still respond positively to these screwed up cues not even knowing that they are being manipulated, intentionally or otherwise. More troublesome than that most people not only condone such bad behavior, but also encouraging it, many times unknowingly or unwittingly.

Think of it this way, a movie studio is going to make movies that they think will make money, not make movies that they think are philosophically correct, but can't make any money on, i.e., they will make movies that they think that people will pay to see. Most people will say that this is smart. Well, in a way that's what people are doing when they are being humble; they are giving others what they want, so that they can get what they want from others in return. The difference is that when a movie studio makes a movie and people pay for it, the movie studios are giving people a relatively fair deal. When people are humble, they're taking advantage of others and their myopia. It's really no different than flattery, brown-nosing and ass-kissing, except it's a lot less obvious and a lot more sinister, because humble people are fooling others into giving them more than what the other person was prepared to give or they earned by pretending to be pious and virtuous.

Think about it carefully. Let's say that there are two people that have the same exact skills and track record in whatever field of endeavor that they are in and both of them are exemplary at what they do. Additionally, let's say that they are both morally, and ethically very similar, if that were even possible. However, if one is humble and the other doesn't even know what it means to be humble, my bet is that most who meet both within a very short timeframe will respect the humble person more, think that the humble one was better at what they do, and would be more likely to favor the humble person's friendship, advice or expertise. Moreover, most people would be more likely to recommend the humble person to their associates and other friends for whatever the humble person's expertise is or to become friends with. Most people would do this because humble people make others "feel" comfortable about their own position, humble people make others "feel" like they are smarter than they really are, humble people make others "feel" like they are treating others as an equal, and, generally, humble people make others "feel" good. Notice that it's all about the individual's "feelings," and not about truth and reality. In reality, people are not smarter for being in the presence of a humble person, and their physical and mental health doesn't change one iota. Despite these idiotic "feelings," the vast majority of Americans prefer humble people over honest people that tell the unvarnished truth as they know it. However, the exact opposite should be true. We should all strive to not only tell the unvarnished truth, but also seek out and listen to people who strive to only tell the unvarnished truth. And, we should always prefer to be in the presence of someone who has the right perspective and whose compass always points north. We should always prefer to be in the presence of someone who doesn't change their story or view as situations may dictate.

The problem is that when people accept anything that is false, they open the door to corruption and injustice, which are what destroys morality. At first, it is innocent: A false compliment, a fake praise, an empty reward. Then a small "distortion" starts collecting momentum and becomes bigger and bigger, messier and messier, and less and less manageable. Then corruption begets more corruption, which in turn begets more lies, which then turns into more corruption. Specifically, how this translates to being humble is that when a person lies about themselves and in the process makes others around them feel better, they have to maintain this false sense of security for the other person that they put on a show for in greater and greater ways. This then causes sequentially more corruption. But when the circle breaks, all hell breaks loose: Disappointment leads to anger, which leads to more unraveling of the truth, which then leads to more disappointment, which leads to more anger, and so on and so forth.

This cycle of white lies holds true when it comes to humility because a lot of people know that if they appear humble then that will make it easier for them to win over others and, more importantly, control the other person. So, regardless of what they actually believe in they will try to appear humble, but when you press them, their teeth will show, because they are not really humble. On the other hand, those that are really humble are fools who get used by people that aren't necessarily scrupulous, but because the humble person doesn't really know the full extent of their worth, they don't ever realize that they're being taken advantage of. So, I repeat, if a person is humble then they are either stupid or a liar. Either way, no one should want to be humble or even appear to be humble. Whether it's humility or another white lie, any masking of the truth cannot benefit anyone other than for the immediate moment, if that.

Does anyone still like humble people or humility?! Don't forget that a lie is a lie is a lie is a lie is a lie; remember this and it will save people a lot of grief over a long-period of time.

For beautiful people, of whom I am not one, it is even easier. Our society has become so superficial and pretentious that physical beauty alone commands respect and earnings power: Look at Paris Hilton, the Kardashians, etc. By the way, good for them, but, if you look at the way most beautiful people behave, it is appalling, and this is why, in my opinion, they are like shit painted in gold. This is not to say that my thesis applies to Paris Hilton or the Kardashians, but I'm generalizing.

Few people would not agree that the Spirit of Ecstasy is absolutely a beautiful work of art. This is the statue that sits on top of the radiator grill on all Rolls Royce cars. Now imagine that it is made into a life size statue in solid gold. That would be amazingly beautiful. However, would anyone be able to tell if it was made with shit and spray painted in gold jast by looking at it? Very few people, if any, would be able to tell the difference. This is what most beautiful people exploit; so, instead of working on what really matters they focus on their outward appearance because it is much easier and has greater impact on the vast majority of Americans. And, why shouldn't they? Most Americans make it so easy for beautiful people to get away with whatever it is that the beautiful person wants to get away with that there really aren't any reasons for physically beautiful people to change their behavior. Not only that, since beautiful people get a lot of what they want out of life without making as much effort as the rest of us, they don't have any reasons to change anything. It's only rational that the status quo remains.

If people want to change the cycle of superficiality and pretense, it can only come from a grassroots movement of honest individuals. If people don't then everyone will have to live with the consequences. And, the consequences aren't pretty; look at where we are as a society today. And, if anyone thinks that they cannot be an agent of change then they are mistaken. But, it will not be easy to be an agent of change, I promise. But, we need to change everything that is not real and not rational, not jast for our sake, but more importantly for the sake of our future generations.

White lies are the cornerstone for the destruction of a child's mind

It may not seem so, but "white" lies are every bit as bad as "black" lies. Many people think that I'm crazy for saying this, but it is particularly bad when used on children. For example, take the case of Santa Claus – the ultimate white lie with the ultimate bad impact. To a child of 6, 7 or 8 or so, it comes down to whether the child can trust the parent or not. So, instead of achieving the parents' objective of protecting the child's innocence, they shatter it. Repeated lying continues to reinforce the child's belief that hes parents are not trustworthy and over time, particularly starting in the child's teenage years, the child loses complete confidence in hes parents, specifically their advice and guidance.

So, teenagers turn to the only people they believe they can trust for advice and counsel when they can no longer trust their parents: Their friends. And, we all know how good the advice and counsel from their friends are. It's like the blind leading the blind! This is what many Americans are doing to their children. What does this say about people who believe in and tell white lies? I think it says that they are immature and don't have the ability to think beyond the tip of their nose. Yet, many of the "smartest" people I know believe in and tell white lies! Personally, I will never tell white lies to children, mine or to other's. The damage that white lies do to children's minds is quite astounding and shocking. Jast take a look at how many people still remember the day that they found out that Santa Clause was not real.

Now, let's take an example of white-lying to adults. If your friend is totally into someone and asks you, "so, what do you think about hem?" Let's say that you either know or have a strong feeling that hesh is jast not a good person or is not the right fit for your friend. What do you tell your friend? Keep in mind that your friend is totally enamored. To spare your friend's feelings, do you tell a white lie or do you tell the truth? Keep in mind that telling the truth doesn't have to be blunt. It can be done without belittling, malice, disrespect, condescension, or sarcasm.

Some have said to me that knowing is different than thinking (or guessing) that the person is bad or not a good match for one's friend, and this is largely true. Therefore, one would say that if one knew something then one would say something, but it's the guessing/thinking/intuition part that makes it less than straight-forward. Agreed. I've had the same situation happen to me. In all cases, I told the truth. In one situation, the person didn't talk to me for 2-3 years, but then we became close and since then my friend always asks me about relationships. In the other case, we stayed friends and the two got married. Thereafter, I ignored my better judgment and became friends with both; BIG MISTAKE. After 15 years or so and 2 kids later, my friend caught hem cheating with someone in their marital bed! In retrospect, I probably should have been more forceful. And, yes, sometimes even telling the truth doesn't work nor help prevent a disaster. However, it does build trust and my friends trust me and believe in me.

As outlined, never trust those that advocate for and tell white lies. They are dangerous and irresponsible, regardless of their intentions. These people don't think or think very short-term. This may be why the saying, "the road to hell is paved with good intentions" was born. Simple truth: Never trust those that think short-term. Evidence of such people: They utter such nonsense like, "we're all dead in the long-run," "no one can predict the future," "go for the sure thing," "what you have in front of you is certain, everything else is fantasy," "bird in hand is better than two in the bush," et cetera.

You cannot make anyone else happy until you are happy, so focus on your happiness, but be aware of what you focus on and what you desire

ADVISORY: I hesitated to write this chapter as it may confuse people, but I thought it important enough to add. Please be advised that this chapter is in regards to personal happiness and interaction among people that already know each other.

There is no question that an unhappy person cannot make someone else happy, but it is equally true that no one can be happy by making others unhappy, because retribution is hell. Therefore, the most important factor to bear in mind is that one must generate one's own happiness from within. No one should rely on others, depend on others or take from others to find their happiness. This is not to say that people can't help each other or work together to find happiness, but one cannot find happiness through one way relationships.

To find true happiness one must first understand who they are: What does one stand for, believe in, and value, what is one comfortable thinking, saying, and doing, and what will one represent, defend and protect, i.e., what is one's Six Pillars. Through this self-discovery process we must analyze and understand whether or not we like who we are. If we like what we find out about ourselves then we can find happiness through believing in ourselves and living our life according to who we are, but if we don't then we must change what we don't like. The next thing that we must evaluate is whether or not who we are imposes or burdens others, more importantly, we must make sure who we are does not violate other people's rights. If who we are does burden others then we must change those things that are the source of burden to others. Some may be thinking what if these things that burden others are what make one happy? Simple, you are a bitch/asshole, so change. The reason why imposing on others can't lead to happiness is because it causes others to hate people who are "selfish." And, eventually, the "selfish" person will have no friends, which means that there will be no people left to impose on other than strangers who can only be impose on once. So, the selfish person ends-up with no friends, no one to take advantage of and frustration and unhappiness builds because there's no one to take advantage of. So, why not change that which is causing frustration and unhappiness?

On the other hand, if something external is truly the cause of one's unhappiness, get rid of that external agitation. However, even the supposedly external source of one's frustration and agitation may actually be internal. This may be because one values giving blind love, loyalty or friendship which causes this external agitation to exist in one's life. And, since blind love, loyalty or friendship is unjust, the cause of frustration and agitation may be internally generated.

Some people have asked me, "what if I'm unhappy because I got 'restructured?'" Great question! You still have the ability to retrain, find a new job, do a new business, or go in a completely new direction. It is difficult to be "restructured," but you are the source of your own success or failure in the vast majority of situations, so if you can't find an answer to your problem, it's probably because you're looking in the wrong place. In my experience, most people look everywhere else, but inside of themselves when looking for the source that which makes them unhappy, frustrated or angry. My advice, look inside of you first, it may save you a lot of time, energy and effort.

Philosophy

Why is philosophy so important, particularly a black and white philosophy?

Without philosophy, particularly a black and white philosophy, nothing is wrong, and everything can be right. Therefore, simply put, no one can know what is right and what is wrong. This is bad because we can never come to a conclusion, and, therefore, we can never resolve problems. Perhaps more importantly, we can never achieve peace, whether it's among constituents in a state, a country or our entire world. The reason for this divisiveness is because no one can be right and no one can be wrong. This means that everyone will advocate for what they believe is right, accuse everyone else of being wrong and fight for what they believe in, never resolving important issues.

By the way, there is a contradiction in the argument I made above: No one can argue for something, if they don't believe in anything. And, if one does believe in something then that's a philosophy, especially when it applies to something that is applicable to the way people live and interact with others. So, what we need is not jast a philosophy (philosophy includes religion) but what we need is an objective philosophy based on reason, Justice and, more importantly, universal rights and individual freedoms.

The right philosophy will be outlined in later chapters, but, for now, everyone needs to know that whether we are aware of it or not, we all have our own philosophical construct. It may not be the right construct, it may not be a smart construct, and it may not be a construct that improves our lives, but we all have a philosophy. Furthermore, it is most likely based on the judeo/christian philosophical construct. And, therein lays the problem, the self-contradictory nature of the philosophy that is judaism/christianity.

So, one of the core problems with the vast majority of Americans' philosophy is that it doesn't make sense, but people don't even know it or realize it. For example, how many opinions from how many people does one get when anyone asks what the will of the judeo/christian god is? My experience tells me that anyone seriously asking this question will practically get a different answer for every time a question about the judeo/christian god's will is asked. This tells me that for anyone that is trying to listen to these varied opinions will end-up becoming very confused and learn absolutely nothing! Perhaps less than nothing! The only goal that the search for the judeo/christian god's will will succeed in accomplishing is confusing people, causing people to give up and stop thinking. Therefore, the key to having a good philosophy is to have one that is rational, universal, that improves people's lives and of those that they love and care about, and most of all helps individuals become better human beings. This may seem hard to accomplish, but I strongly believe that I have jast such a philosophy, which I present in this book.

The burden of change should be borne by the least well educated, not the best educated, and the living standard of the least skilled should decline relative to the most skilled, which argues for the liberalization of immigration

Most people think I'm crazy and off my rockers, because I'm suggesting that the least financially capable bare the most burden of the macro-economic global rollercoaster ride. Yes, that's exactly right. The logic isn't that complicated.

If we hold education to be the paramount achievement towards the success of a person's financial well-being then the one that has the best education (best technological skills, if you would) should be the safest and the furthest away from financial danger. Therefore, if we are to have a social net for unemployment – which I'm opposed to – then the ones with the best education should be given the highest benefits, while the ones with the worst level of education should be given the least or even no benefits. Most people are already rolling their eyes and saying that's what the current system does, in effect. This may be partially true, but the ones that have a high school only diploma and work as plumbers get their maximum allotted $405/week, jast like a doctorate degree holder in nuclear engineering. This isn't right. The plumber should get well less than that and the doctorate degree holder should get close to 100% of hes average 3-year compensation, at least for a few months anyway.

In addition, if we were to even have some sort of unemployment benefits then we should require that an individual cannot qualify for any benefits unless they graduate high school with at least a B-average. Not a B-minus average, but a solid B-average or 85 out of 100. But, even at this level, the benefit should be limited to no more than 20% of the individual's previous 3-year average annual compensation. A college graduate should get at most 70% of their base compensation, while master and doctorate degree holders would get no more than 90% of their base salary. However, even within the college and graduate school pools, there has to be a gradation of compensation with community college graduates qualifying for no more than 35% of their annual compensation, while graduates of top-25 universities and colleges would qualify for the full 70%. Also, grades should come into play as well, but not majors.

Many people will be aghast at what I'm proposing; however, if we, as a society, value education as the path to success then it only makes rational sense for our society to provide more for those that graduate from top universities versus those that only achieve a high school education. Those that object to my plan do so not because it doesn't makes sense and doesn't give priority to that which we believe has value as a society, but because of their sympathies for the poor people's plight. However, they forget the hypocrisy of their position, if they agree that education should be the only dominantly main path to financial success in our country. No if, buts or ands.

Some people ask me about the unfortunate few whose circumstances did not permit them to study in high school, despite their desires to do so. First of all that's jast an excuse a vast majority of the time, and second, even if it were true, all that the socialists/liberals are trying to do is to use that as an excuse to *force* wealthy people to take responsibility for taking care of the poor. Therefore, the argument that some people don't have the time or the circumstances to study in high school (or any school) is nothing but an excuse designed to guilt people into allowing politicians, socialists and liberals to steal more money from the wealthy. If an individual is claiming that the opportunity to study was not afforded to them because of their circumstances then I have to ask, how did the Chinese and Koreans send their children to Ivy League schools, while living out of a car? And now the Indians, Pakistanis, Vietnamese, Africans and other immigrant families are also sending their children to top universities and colleges. How is this possible in one generation? I know of cases where Chinese and Korean immigrants that lived out of cars that are now millionaires with children that are doctors, lawyers, engineers, traders, bankers or have successful careers in many fields of endeavor. If the environment is such a problem, how did the Chinese and Korean immigrants succeed in such a short time frame while living in squalor?

If someone wants to claim that the environment is what's forcing certain segments of our society to not be able to get a proper education then they have to answer how the Asian immigrants got it done and continue to get it done. If on the other hand, some people say that the Asians have strong foundations in education and value it then they can only blame the perpetually poor families for not supporting education for their children as the root cause of their perpetual "misfortune," not poverty itself. If people believe that some of these unfortunates don't have the ability then no one else but the individual that lacks the motivation, foresight, talent or intelligence can be blamed for their circumstance. If as some believe that the parents or guardians were abusive, again, the burden for correcting the situation cannot be placed at the feet of the wealthier and more fortunate strangers that had nothing to do with creating the poor person's situation. No matter what one argues, it will come down to the family supporting or not supporting the value of education, and whether or not the family and the individual believe that education is the only main way to a successful financial future. Therefore, bemoaning the unfortunate is nothing but the cry of sorrow, but then to take that anguish and use it as a weapon to steal from the people that have put in the effort and the toil to be successful is despicable!

The fact of the matter is that there is no reason why the poor and the unfortunate cannot get out of their situation with hard work, determination, a good education and vision. I admit, sometimes that's not enough, but if poor people have the commitment to hard work, determination, a good education and vision and they pass it down to their future generations, at some point, at some time, their future generations will get out of poverty. This means that even if it isn't the current generation that financially succeeds if they focus on education and commit to it then someday their children, their grandchildren or some future generation will succeed financially. This is the only way the poor should break the bonds of poverty, period. All other ways are fraught with risk or are immoral. Therefore, whatever avenues are pursued the responsibility for the consequences should lie with the person taking the risk or the opportunity. Regardless, whatever method is chosen by the individual to try and break the bonds of poverty, the one act that is unforgivable is the act of stealing from another or condoning theft using the beleaguered situation of the poor as an excuse.

This means that if the poor can't/won't escape the bondage of poverty then they have to be the one who bears the responsibility for it or ask for donations and charity to get through it. This also means that if they are willing to stay with the inertia of their situation of poverty then they will be stuck with the most basic of labors in a society that must continue to evolve technologically to survive. This means that if a poor person isn't willing to put in the time and effort to get out of their situation then they will be stuck with the lowest skilled jobs, which also typically means the lowest paid jobs. This is the way it should be, must be and is supremely Just.

Many people rail at the thought of the poor being at risk. However, there is logic and consequence to the philosophy that I've outlined regarding who in our society should bare the most risk of economic upheaval. As our society evolves and the technology advances the most basic of jobs and the lowest skilled jobs will become relatively more and more primitive compared to the advancing technology. Therefore, the relative pay difference should grow with the ever increasing technology gap. This means that the poor will and must get relatively poorer as the skill required to do their job becomes more and more basic relative to the advancing technology. The consequence of this divergent skill gap and the effect on pay is that the less skilled and unskilled laborers will get relatively poorer to the more skilled and productive workers in any society.

And, this is the way it should be, because the key to the long-term survival of the US is to ensure that we continue to dominate on the technological front and continually reinvent ourselves. To help us preserve and perpetuate this advantage, we should allow more liberalization of immigration. Specifically, we should allow students that excel in their field of study to remain in the US with a green card, if they get a job in the field of their studies. This should be particularly true of scientists, engineers, doctors, nurses, and other skilled professionals that this country has a short supply of. This is so much better than training all these people and sending them back to their country to compete with us! What's even more galling is that a lot of these bright, young people WANT to stay in the US, but we kick them out! This is ridiculous!

In addition, if there are wealthy folks outside the US that are willing to invest in the US – assuming that they are not terrorists or criminals – we should allow them into the US with a green card. Hold on, I know there are rules in place to allow something like this to occur already, but, from what I know the current rules are too restrictive.

Finally, we should import skilled laborers as needed, for example, machinery workers, drilling technicians, skilled miners, among others. Some would argue that we should retrain people out of work, and, I would agree, but these people have to be willing to be retrained and be good at their new profession. If they can't cut it then they should be substituted with imported laborers that can do it better. This will help our country stay more competitive and make it easier to stay in the forefront of technological development.

Also, if we lack people to do the "dirtiest" jobs in our society then we should import unskilled laborers as well to keep costs down for the general public. Personally, I frequently hear managements of companies complain about the lack of labor, particularly, skilled labor in our country. Also, I hear many complaints from employers who say that Americans don't want to do this or that and so they have no choice but to use illegal immigrants or close down their business. The fact of the matter is that most Americans are too comfortable and too unaware of reality. It's time we all woke up to the reality of the global economy. This means that a lot of people will be heaved into turmoil, but remember, when correcting for past mistakes, the road to success will be initially painful and there's nothing that can be done or should be done to avoid the initial burst of pain.

As an aside, let me make one thought perfectly clear: Jast because the lowest skilled jobs become relatively lower on the technology spectrum, it does not mean that the importance of these jobs necessarily diminish. Take for example garbage collection. This is one of the most basic jobs in any society and requires very little technology or skill. Nevertheless, the importance of garbage collection cannot be understated for the proper functioning of any society. Therefore, garbage collection is a vital and important part of a well-functioning society. However, this does not give the garbage collectors the right to use the importance of their jobs to hold the rest of society hostage and demand more money than the job function is worth, which is typically what happens when unions get involved. That's called extortion, and it's a criminal offense that should be prosecuted; yet, it is rewarded in our country.

Family values, why is it important and what does it mean?

Many people talk about family values, but when I ask people what is it and why is it important, inevitably most people talk about the family unit being the nuclei of society and that it sets the foundation of any well-functioning and cohesive society. That's great; however, how many people can tell me why it is the nuclei of society and why it sets the foundation of society? Very few, if any that I've asked this question to have given me anything that resembles a good answer.

Family values are that which each family believes is valuable to them. But it also encompasses that which each family believes is right versus wrong, the right way to conduct oneself, and the right way to preserve these morals, values and ethics. However, given that it is too difficult to constantly express these things, it is reduced to family values. Moreover, the reason why parents always say that you should always look after your siblings and bond together is because the people that have the most common "family values" to you are and will continue to be your siblings, in general, by definition. Ergo to survive in a brutal and harsh world having people around you that believe in the same family values as you do will be to your advantage. Think about it, if you can surround yourself with you, a lot of you, then you would be very powerful. You wouldn't even have to command these people, they'd think, do and speak exactly the same way that you do, which means that you'd have great power to sway the destiny of the world, especially if there were billions of you. Remind you of any movie, may be one starring a tall, cute brunette with sunglasses and a black trench coat?

Anyway, the definition of family values isn't too difficult to figure out. Now imagine if we all had the same "family values." We'd all act in unison making it easier for the leadership. Think 1950s America. Our society in the 1950s had harmony and uniformity because the country homogeneously believed in the same or very similar morals, values, ethics and integrity. Since then, society has been morally "disintegrating," because families have started to diverge and believe in different philosophies. Also, many of the philosophical concepts that Americans believed in in the 1950s proved to be false such as: That America stood for absolute good and did no wrong, that we always fought for good, that whites were superior to all other races, that separate but equal was good for the country, that jews killed the son of the judeo-christian god, that Muslims are evil, that all religions other than christianity is not only an invention of man, but pathetically childish and stupid, that cowboys and the cavalry were always good and Indians were always bad, et cetera.

The concept of family values unifying and bringing harmony is true for not just America and Americans, but for all of the rest of the world as well. Therefore, what this means is that in order to have world peace, we must all believe in the same Six Pillars. The problem and the issue is that every nation, sub-division, ethnic group and religious sect believes they are the only ones that know the "truth," that they are the only ones that know what is really right versus wrong, what should be held in importance or disregarded, how one should conduct oneself to be a good person, and what the best way to preserve these "family values" is. And, each group, for centuries, has tried to force others to believe in what they believe, which has been the root cause of many wars – along with differing economic agendas. However, this will never work, as the "truth" that most of these groups believe in is not only subjective, but also based on their version of a deity, the existence of which can never be proven. So, how do we achieve world peace? The vast majority of people don't even think it Is possible with this many divergent views of the world and the reason for its existence; however, I think it is definitely possible to have a unified view of the world and a rational and Just global Six Pillars that will bring about world peace.

The solution to this seeming quagmire is to perpetuate a rationally-based, objective philosophy that doesn't rely on proving the existence of a deity, and, most of all, that will prove to be economically the most beneficial to all mankind. If we can create such a philosophy, then I believe that we can achieve world peace. And, the starting point has to be the family unit.

Therefore, in order to bring about world peace, we must all believe in the same "family values." It isn't that complicated. For that to happen, again, a philosophical construct that is rational, objective, transparent, Just and economically prosperous for all mankind and that which transcends all divisiveness has to be created. I hope that my philosophy is all that and someday will be the basis for a unifying philosophical construct that brings universal peace. Regardless, the formula for world peace isn't difficult in theory, but in practice there has to be one more component: Each country must vote to agree to these principles. That's the tricky part.

Communism is not ideal; it's a grossly unjust and childish thought (not even a philosophy)

Think about this: If everyone in the US were billionaires, we'd all be very poor. If the US government were to print $300 quadrillion (that's $300 followed by 15 zeros or 17 zeros in total) and give out $1 billion to each individual in the US, we'd all be poor very quickly. And, this is the only way that we could all be billionaires. It is IMPOSSIBLE TO DO IT ANY OTHER WAY. The primary reason why it could not be done any other way is that the US economy is worth no more than $15 trillion or so.

What about in athletic events? Should everyone get the gold medal? What about at school, should everyone be given an A? This is communism. How would we all feel if we worked hard in school to get an A-average then find out that the laziest and most depraved students was also given all As? Imagine what this would do to student morale. Who would study? More to the point: No one would need to study. And, therefore, no one would learn! If this happens our economy would not develop nor grow. This is communism. Therefore, even if communism could be realized in its purest and idealistic form, ALL of us should resoundingly REJECT COMMUNISM!

People who believe in communism in this country are often confused by the notion that "all men are created equal." This is absolutely true, but it doesn't mean that all of us *are* equal. No one would argue that Hitler is equal to Sir Winston or that Osama Bin Laden was equal to general McChrystal. But were these men all born equal? Yes. However, like anything in nature, as the person grows they develop into individuals and as individuals they become different people. Differences in people make them naturally unequal, and this cannot be changed nor must efforts be made to try and change it.

However, communist ideology not only ignores the natural differences in people, but also aims to reward everyone the same way regardless of the person's ability, educational accomplishments, intelligence and, most importantly, their Six Pillars. This is the perversion of communism: That it would seek to throw Justice out the window, throw right and wrong into a conflagration, and make a joke of good and bad.

Communism makes it impossible for hard-working, educated and intelligent people that should get ahead from doing so, and if they do find a way to succeed their success is taken away and given to others that did absolutely nothing to create this incremental success. So, no one in communist societies is incented to work to create incremental wealth. This means that eventually everyone looks to do less not more because what any individual gets is the same whether or not they do more or less. This leads to lower and lower production and smaller and smaller distributions. Furthermore, imagine if such a society had a growing population to boot! So, it is no wonder that communist countries always have shortages and lines for everything. And, it shouldn't shock anyone to learn that North Korea had lost (i.e., they died) at least 2 million people due to famine caused by shortages over the last two decades; this from a population of less than 28 million to begin with.

Also, if a small group of people had the absolute power to tell everyone else how much each individual can spend on their basic items (like food, clothing and housing), but also had the right to look into everyone's bank account and tell them how much they will take from each individual's bank account and distribute to others, there isn't a person dead or alive in the US that would agree to that. However, again, this is what every communist country in the last almost 100 years has done to its citizens. Understanding what communism really means, I refuse to believe that there is a single human being left anywhere in the world that would still support communist ideology.

Now, some people have argued that reality is different than idealism and that the so called communist countries in history were not true communist countries but another form of dictatorships. Yes, certainly historically communist countries have been dictatorships and current remaining communist countries (e.g., China, Cuba and North Korea) are still dictatorships. But what most people don't realize is that communism can only be implemented in a dictatorial society, because the basis of communism is theft. Certainly, to the extent that a communist society has to achieve real equal wealth, the government has no choice: It must do it by force, i.e., literally at gun point. This means that any communist government must forcefully steal wealth from the rich to give to the poor. So, the argument that such societies as Cuba and North Korea are not true communist countries is a fallacy when it comes to the economic system.

Regardless, my point is that even if *the* ideal communist society could be established with a wave of a magic wand, it would not be a society that any one of us would want to live in. At least not the ones in our society that are honest and morally upstanding.

But let's imagine such a place, and further, let's assume that everyone is a billionaire. Many people have commented how wonderful such a society would be. OK, so let's say that such a society existed. Is that it? Is that the end to the development of this society? Does everyone live happily ever after? If anyone thinks that that would be the case, they are very foolish and most likely not very good at thinking beyond the tip of their nose.

Think about what happens next in such a "utopian" society. Let's take two different models. The first is a capitalist society (remember that everyone in this imaginary world is a billionaire). What happens next? Overtime, people will spend their money differently, but regardless the price of everything must rise dramatically. Initially, we'd all be able to afford big expensive houses, brilliant jewelry, multiple expensive cars, art works, and no one would have to work. What happens to the price of housing, jewelry, cars, and other desired items? Competition for it would be so keen that prices would go through the roof. Add to this the fact that no one would need to work, they'd be no production and output, which then makes prices for everything go through the roof even higher and faster. Imagine a society in which we'd have to spend a million dollars to buy a loaf of bread. As the society develops a billion dollars would start to look like pittance. Meaning that hyperinflation would destroy our economy much like it did Germany's in the 1920s. Anyway, hyper-inflation means that whoever can hold assets over a longer time period would be better off than ones who hold cash. In addition, overtime, people would spend money in different ways, which means that the smart or the unscrupulous would take money from the dumb and the naïve.

Overtime, in a capitalist society, after much painful disruption of the economy and our society, wealth would be redistributed assuming that the government wouldn't interfere. As some become poorer, these people would look for a job to make ends meet, while the wealthier would hire and expand their business, and we'd go back to a more typical capitalist society with one caveat; we'd be like Brazil of the 1970s. Of course, I'm grossly abbreviating the sequence of events, but my outline hits the highlights.

The second scenario assumes that the government will interfere to control hyper-inflation and periodically rebalance wealth. Still, initially, no one would work given that prices would be under strict control and a billion dollars would go a very, very long way. However, this means that no one would work anymore, so no one would create the goods that we'd all need and no incremental wealth would be created. More to the point, if we are all wealthy and prices for all goods and services are low and controlled by the government,

no one would want to or need to work. This means that the government would have to **force people to work** in order to produce even the most fundamental goods that a society would need to survive, such as food, clothing, shelter and medicine. Thinking about which jobs would get assigned to whom would lead to many headaches, in and of itself, but let's say that we are all honest people and so we all go back to doing the same jobs that we did before becoming instant billionaires. Even so, no one would *actually* do the work that is required of us; we wouldn't have to. Regardless, whatever the scenario that one can come up with there is no question that the end result would be massive shortages in any communist country. Therefore, to compensate, the society would have no choice but to develop a black market for anything and everything that is essential to society, mostly food items. Due to black market activity, without government interference, prices for even the most basic items would shoot through the roof, especially drugs, because this could literally be a matter of life and death. Other essential items like food and clothing would have to escalate dramatically too.

And, to achieve true equality, the government would have to equalize housing which means that everyone must live in mansions or slums. Of course the government would build slums, because it is the cheapest option and the quickest, so all of the big mansions and houses would have to be confiscated and torn down. But then how does the government compensate the people whose houses have been confiscated. For now, let's jast brush this issue under the carpet and continue on with the analysis.

So, what good would it do to have a billion dollars and no place to spend it? Yes, for sure, some people would participate in the black market, but items purchased in the black market would be extremely expensive and a billion dollars wouldn't last very long. Therefore, presumably, people either spend all of their money in the black market and end up poor again or they'd be a billionaire without anything to purchase and they'd be de facto poor.

Also, because the government would have to force people to do the job that they did before, no one would be productive. Shortages would alleviate some because they'd be at least some production, but the black market would still have to exist to fulfill all of the demand; however, black market prices would not be dramatically high, but probably 2x-10x or more depending on the item and abundance in the main economy. Regardless, for the government to maintain fairness and increase the main stream supply, they'd have to shut-down black market activity, which means shortages will continue. So, even though prices are low – because they're controlled by the government – they'd be virtually no supply and luxury items would be non-existent for sale given that even staples are in short supply. Again, this means that people would have a billion dollars, but no place to spend it. So, again, people remain de facto poor, because their standard of living would be meager or they'd have to risk getting punished for participating in the black markets. Even so, people are unlikely to be able to get all of the staples that they need let alone any luxury items. Either way, again, they'd end up poor. So, no matter how people try to structure a communist society, it cannot help anyone outside of the elite few and it will never be an ideal society.

By the way, if a former citizen of the Soviet Union were asked, what life in the old Soviet Union was like, I am confident that my description of a dictatorial communist government that controlled prices with long lines and shortages for everything and an active black market would be spot on. I know this to be true because I have already asked and seen documentaries directly and indirectly detailing the lives of people in the former Soviet Union.

In my opinion, despite the obvious stupidity of communism, it has persisted as an ideal society in people's mind, because people don't know how to think; in particular, beyond the immediate future. So, given that people were never taught how to think, it doesn't surprise me that many people hold communism as an ideal. If I were to look at this from a conspiracy theory point of view, I'd say that elements of society that want to steal money from the wealthy perpetuate the lie that communism is good for everyone. This makes it easier for them to put into place laws that permit the expropriation of money from the wealthy by force through the government.

Let me give another example of how people "think" and, from this example, it should be apparent why people don't know how to think, and, more importantly, why people get/are confused. I think many of us have seen movies where settlers from earth go to another planet like Mars and breath the ambient air as if we do on earth much to the settlers' surprise. We all can imagine something like this. However, when people pursue communism and think it is possible, it is no different than pursuing the settlement of Jupiter assuming that the surface is temperate and atmosphere full of oxygen and benign. Then when challenged about their assumptions, answering, "how do you know that it isn't; you can't prove otherwise?" The difference between really thinking and being creatively imaginative is this: Knowing that settling Jupiter is a fantastic fictional storyline vs. believing that it's real. Too many people "think" if it can be imagined, it can be achieved. And, in many cases, great achievements do start with great imagination. However, the difference between someone who really thinks and one who doesn't know how to is that a person who really knows how to think knows the difference between that which is truly achievable, even though it is not reality today, and something that can only remain in people's imagination.

Practical versus the ideal: They are one in the same. And, logic IS everything

A lot of very smart people have said to me the following statement: "Your ideas, thoughts, and propositions are representative of the ideal and rational, but not practical. And, logic isn't everything!" They say this as if they are so enlightened, despite the fact that I said something very smart, they are able to shed additional illumination, which is so brilliant and insightful that it negates all my ideas. Two things: 1) Let's see how illuminated their argument really is, and 2) pretty much everyone I talk to recognizes that the theories that I espouse are unique, that it is the first time they are hearing it – at least the way I argue and support my beliefs – and, most importantly, that it all makes sense and is rational. In contrast, I haven't heard anything new from anyone since my sophomore year in college – that may be a bit of an exaggeration, but not by far – and suffice it to say, that I have not seen the inside of a classroom in many years.

Nevertheless, let me start with the argument that logic isn't everything. Even when people say stupid things like, "don't generalize," "everything is relative," and "logic isn't everything," they are using logic to express that which they believe is illogical. Also, upon even a cursory examination, one should realize that all three of these statements are self-contradictory: When one says "don't generalize" that is a generalization, when one says "everything is relative" the statement is an absolute, and when one says "logic isn't everything" the statement itself is a logic-based statement. Also, try communicating anything without using logic. In fact, try living without logic and let's see how far people get in life.

The reality is that as babies, we immediately start to learn through our senses then as we grow older we begin to learn to talk, then we start to form rational thoughts in our minds: "Mama" is the one that feeds us and takes care of us, "milk" is the thing that quenches our thirst and feeds our hunger, "cookies" make us full and taste good, etc. From then on, we are taught everything using logic. We communicate back using logic, we develop our logical thinking and the world starts to make more sense, at least for a while, before it gets taken away from us later.

As an adult, when we talk to others, we use the tools of logic to convey our thoughts and to interpret communication from others. When we learn, we are taught using logical principles and if it "doesn't make sense to us" we are re-taught through logical reasoning or logical explanations. When we try to figure out how to solve a problem, we do so using reasoning, when we encounter situations, we ask why? When we try to make a decision, we choose among the best options available to us, which is rational. Regardless of what we want to think or believe, we can't escape it: LOGIC IS EVERYTHING. However, this doesn't mean that we all operate under the same assumptions or principles, but the logic applied to one's actions or speech based on the assumptions or principles we believe in doesn't change. What changes from person to person are the assumptions and principles.

So, if logic is everything then why would anyone pursue that which is not ideal? By definition, the ideal is that which is **rationally or logically the best** whether it's a thought, a principle or an action. Then, by definition, all else is inferior, and it should not be pursued. Actually, what I've discovered is that when someone says something isn't practical, they typically mean that it's difficult to achieve, particularly in the short-term. But, all would agree that the ideal would be the right goal to achieve.

So, let me provide some examples. Before slaves were freed people debated whether or not blacks could take care of themselves, they debated the integration of blacks into a white society, they debated the effect of the economic disruption, and, most of all, people didn't even think that there was a problem with prejudice against blacks and many concluded that though setting blacks free from slavery was the right (read "ideal") thing to do, it was impractical and therefore should not be done. Therefore, would keeping blacks enslaved be the right policy back in 1863 because it was impractical? Who among us would even argue or express these doubts today other than an extremely small number of racists, bigots and ignoramuses?

If one has the courage to face the truth and realize that which is ideal and work towards it then one will realize that overtime matters of practicality will seem not only a distant memory, but also turn out to be a laughable excuse to not pursue the right course of action for whatever retarded reason was thought up at the time. By pursuing the ideal, we will save ourselves a lot of time and grief over the long-run. When making decisions, if people opt for the "practical" or "optimal," but not the ideal then they are opting to choose that which may solve the problem today, but something that which will make the problem not only much larger in the long-run, but also far more difficult to solve in the future. Therefore, no matter how big of an issue or problem that one is dealing with, we must always strive to find the ideal solution and pursue it, no matter how daunting of a task one may think it is today.

I note that the US budget problems have spiraled out of control precisely because congress and the president for generations have been looking for the practical solution as opposed to the ideal or the right solution. If these issues were nipped in the bud 40-50 years ago, we wouldn't have anything like what we have today to deal with. But, instead, we are at the brink of insolvency and struggling to avoid the fate of Greece. Imagine if our parents and grandparents had the courage to implement the ideal course of action 40-50 years ago. Imagine what our country would look like today. Imagine how much wealthier, stronger, and brighter-our future would be today!

Never say "practical" or "optimal" is better than the ideal and always pursue that which is ideal, because, at the end of the day, that which is ideal is also optimal and practical. And, over the long-run, it will be the cheaper, better, smarter, and healthier choice, by far.

Death by millions of cuts: America is doing this to itself, which is fine, but the problem is they're doing it to me, which I can't accept

The problem with the lottery mentality and the theft of private property through taxes is that Americans are ultimately harming themselves. If that's where it ends, who cares?! The problem is that the vast majority of average Americans are harming me and others who know how to live a better life.

When the lottery mentality pervades and is rewarded then people turn more and more to such opportunities instead of working hard for what they want. For example, what would have happened if the famous McDonald's "hot coffee case" was thrown out of court and the elderly woman and her lawyers were fined for bringing a frivolous lawsuit to court? I wonder how many would be looking for similar "opportunities." As an aside, part of the reason for our high medical costs is because irresponsible people keep bringing frivolous lawsuits against doctors and hospitals and wasting a lot of money, which raises the cost of medical expenses for us all.

One may think that a little poison (e.g., payments that corporations have to pay for frivolous lawsuits) spread among millions would hardly have any effect, and this would be true. So, someone may think, "what if I sue and get away with $3 million; it hardly hurts anyone, but is a great benefit to me, it costs me virtually nothing and my lawyer makes a living." Well what if a 100,000 people get away with it? If we multiply $3 million by 100,000 then that's $300 billion, and if you multiply it by 1,000,000 then that's $3 trillion. So, how trivial is it now? How much "poison" are we being forced to swallow? That's what the lottery mentally is forcing America and Americans to absorb. Too many Americans are looking for that free lunch and looking for ways to gain something for very little effort. So, we all become suspicious of each other and become very guarded and defensive and spend a lot of time and money "protecting" ourselves. This is a lot of both time and money wasted. But, this is what many Americans are doing to our society.

The same can be said for the tax system. People may think it isn't a big deal because the rich can afford it, in their minds, but how much is enough? Look what happened to the UK when the marginal tax rate was close to 100% during the 1960s and 1970s. The UK was headed for an economic disaster. All of the state subsidies and support for the poor almost ruined the country. It took the steel hand of the Iron Lady to bring the UK from the brink of economic disaster, and despite the dire predictions for the UK economy, taking away the subsidies and reducing the marginal tax rate to well below 50% did wonders for their economy. Similar conclusions can be drawn from Latin American economies, China, India and other formerly highly socialized economies. It is extremely puzzling to me that Americans can't learn these lessons. This indicates to me that we, as a whole, must be very stupid and short-sighted, since we continue to miss lessons taught us by other countries. How screwed-up does our country have to get before we learn? It seems like America needs to die, before it can figure out that we don't want to. This is what we are asking for, if we support the current tax and fiscal policy of the US government – don't forget, the US government is the people of this country: *for the people, by the people, of the people*.

What people have to understand is that every decision that they make may not be significant, but if a lot of individuals make the same decision then it carries a lot of power and greatly influences everyone in the country. This is the idea behind why everyone must vote. One vote makes little to no difference, but when a million, 10 million or 100 million votes come together, it make a very, very big difference. If one person steals one penny, even from a bum on the street, it has no effect, but if one steals 100 million pennies that's a $1 million, if one steals 100 billion pennies that's $1 billion. All of a sudden, it makes a difference. A little poison spread around a lot of people wouldn't even be noticed, but if one spreads a little poison a million times, all of a sudden a lot of people become sick. This is the consequences of Americans' voting record: Death by slow poisoning.

Americans have been compromising their principles in small quantities for a very long time. However, when we, as a country, do this over and over again small principle compromises become very, very big. A 1% increase in marginal tax rate for the rich doesn't seem much, but a 1% increase 10 times is a 10% increase. Now it makes a big difference.

The reason why my tax plan is fair isn't jast because it's the right course of action to pursue morally. It is also the right public policy because it gives our country a lot of flexibility. If our national debt were lower by $10 trillion (from over $15.6 trillion to over $5.6 trillion); how concerned would any of us be about spending $1 trillion to fix the economy? For that matter, how likely would it have been for our economy to be in trouble in the first place had my tax plan been in place starting 40 or 50 years ago? And, if we did get into trouble, how quickly could we have recovered from the current economic trouble? We will never know for sure, but it is true that with $10 trillion less in government debt, we'd have had a lot more flexibility to work out of the economic trouble that we find ourselves in today. However, American's way of thinking, acting and voting over the last century or so has put our country on the road to bankruptcy, and every time we face a financial crisis, it is becoming that much harder to work our way out of trouble.

Americans have to realize how much has been stolen from our future economic health. Look at the current situation. We have stolen so much from the future that even a moderate down turn in economic activity is hurting us greatly and the debt forced on the wealthier – the wealthy are the only ones who can get our economy out of trouble – is so massive that a second economic blow in the near future (within the next 20 years) would be devastating and possibly irrecoverable. In fact, continuation on the current path can only make us become the next Greece. This is what average Americans are doing to our country. Instead of asking whether the rich can afford to pay more taxes, everyone in this country should ask if they can live with the rich paying more taxes. I assure everyone that average Americans can **LEAST AFFORD** for the rich to pay more taxes.

Ultimately, low taxes for everyone, helps everyone, because low taxes also help lift investments, which reduces unemployment. And, low unemployment not only makes our economy stronger and reduces the possibility of running into trouble, but also helps to reduce the intensity of the trouble. Also, low national debt helps everyone too, not only because it reduces the debt service, but also because it helps the economy to recover faster, given that we will have reserve debt capacity to help bail out the country.

And, ultimately, this is what low taxes and privatization of "social programs" will do for our country. No matter what our tax system looks like, the economy will go through ebbs and flows. When the economy ebbs, America is going to want both the people who can help revive the economy – i.e., the wealthy – and the government to have excess financial capacity, as much excess financial capacity as possible. This spare capacity is what gets thrown into the fight for the recovery of the economy. If we have huge excess capacity, even a moderately strong depression can be worked out of by deploying this excess financial capacity, mostly through investments. But, if the excess spare capacity is small, like we have today, the recovery will either never happen without massive reduction in debt – i.e., default by the US government, which is the last thing we want and exactly what Greece is going through now – or cause very high inflation to occur due to the US government having to print massive quantities of money to pay down the debt. In either case, the recovery will be extremely slow and very, very painful. Under such a situation, ironically, the ones who will suffer the most are the very people that the socialist and liberals are trying to help by stealing from the rich. Ultimately, I wish that the only ones that get hurt are the people responsible for our current tax system; however, this is not going to be the case, and everyone will suffer for the foolish acts, short-sighted view and immature thoughts of average Americans, and particularly the socialists and liberals.

What Americans must understand is that when they steal from the rich to try and help the poor on an ongoing basis, i.e., through welfare, Medicaid, earned income tax credit, childcare support, and other subsidies and so called "social programs," they are taking away from the ability of the wealthy to drive the economic recovery when, not if, the economy gets into trouble. Our economy is such that when it is humming the poor need a lot less help relative to when the economy is declining, so when the country gives the poor a constant stream of stolen money through so called "social programs," we are actually hurting the poor in more ways than one. The reason for this is simple. When people vote to steal what they perceive the wealthy can afford to give to the poor today, voters are taking away the excess capacity from the rich which the rich could use to help the economy as a whole in troubled times such as we face today in 2012. Also, when people vote to continue to pile on the subsidies, they are inadvertently or otherwise voting to increase the government debt. This is not a whimsical guess; look at how big the federal deficit has grown relative to the country's GDP since the end of the Vietnam War. This happens, because the politicians don't want to increase taxes, and get a lot of the wealthy people pissed off, because a lot of the campaign money comes from the wealthy. Also, politicians have been educated (barely) enough to know that high taxes on the wealthy is bad for the economy and have to balance this against getting votes from the poor.

What is scary is the fact that we probably only have one more chance left. If we don't fix our tax system and our economy this time around, my guess is that when the next Great Recession comes, perhaps in the next 30-40 years, we will not recover from the next one and will become the next Argentina or Greece.

Your existence is meaningless, didn't you know that?

A vast majority of Americans at one point or another in their lives have wondered what the meaning of life is and how they fit in. The vast majority of

Americans will have concluded one of two things: 1) Their life is in the hands of the judeo/christian god and it is it who will determine their place in life and after life, or 2) there is no meaning to life and they will live accordingly. As for me, since I don't believe in any religious deity, I'm guessing that the readers believe I fall under #2. That would be dead wrong.

Actually, there is a lot of meaning to life, but what that definition means will greatly depend on whose life it is that we're talking about. The meaning of life for Lady Margaret Thatcher was to change the course of the U.K.'s economic history. The meaning of life for Adolf Hitler was to kill jews and communists and expand the living space for Germany, while subjugating eastern Europeans and the Slavic race. For someone like Bill Gates, his destiny and meaning of life was to build Microsoft then spend his money on philanthropic causes he and his wife care about.

For someone like Warren Buffet, his life has been dedicated to building a fortune by taking advantage of the short-sightedness of the American investing professionals and investing public in general. The fact that there are so many money managers that cannot beat their respective indexes is also another indication that Americans can be had by razzle-dazzle and duped into believing marketing messages over reality.

As an aside, the vast majority of the money managers cannot add value above the S&P 500, because of several reasons: 1) By definition (not an opinion, but mathematical truth), if a portfolio is well diversified, it will mimic the S&P 500, which makes it very difficult to beat the S&P 500, but to reduce risk, portfolio managers have to diversify their portfolios, 2) because investors are impatient and want constant quarterly performance, money managers are forced to pursue short-term gains, thinking successive short-term gains will add up to a large long-term gain; however, this kind of strategy is no better than trying to figure out whether head or tail will be flipped next, and trying to build a successful portfolio based on guessing heads or tails, 3) because most money managers are motivated by short-term gains, they don't base their investment decisions necessarily on economic, sector and company fundamentals and basic research, but much of their decision to buy a certain investment vehicle is based on what they think the majority of the investors will do next and trading ahead of the herd, 4) money managers are more worried about not making losing bets than making winning bets, 5) they use obsolete and static analytical tools such as P/E (short-cut for DCF, and jast as much garbage-in, garbage-out as DCF), and other static metrics, and "all else being equal" analyses, 6) they rely far too much on historical performance and track-record, 7) don't know how to tell the difference between good and bad corporate managers, and 8) focus too much on whether a particular corporate strategy is good for the stock in the near-term or not versus the long-term. What this means is that a large portion of money managers are going to be ineffective in beating the markets as a whole.

Think about it; other than point 5), how are these money managers any different in the way they think than the average American? So, it's like the blind leading the blind. Therefore, this analysis should have some interesting consequences for how people manage their money. This means that the only money managers that have a shot at making money over a long period of time are value managers such as Warren Buffet. And, that is his destiny: To set the bench mark for other "professionals," not because he wants to do it intentionally, but jast because it is the result of his work. Regardless, the vast majority of Americans have not learned their lessons well. As an example, look at how many were fooled by Bernard Madoff! How can anyone believe in a profit and performance chart that goes straight up in a geometrically-precise linear fashion?

Anyway, getting back to the meaning of life, what is anyone's destiny and what is the meaning of life for any one person? Well, from a single person's personal perspective, I can pretty much assure any single person that their individual life will have absolutely no meaning, at least of any significance to anyone outside of their friends and family. However, this does not mean that an individual has to live a meaningless life for themselves or others. The meaning of life from any individual's perspective is what one makes of it. It really isn't that complicated.

Many people have told me that that's not what they're looking for; that what they're looking for is the reason behind why they exist: The big picture meaning to one's life. Let me end the suspense, there isn't any, which means that making up a dumb reason like the judeo/christian god putting everyone on earth to test them then send them to heaven or hell is still stupid. Such "imagination" only indicates how desperate people are to find meaning and will cling to anything or anyone who will provide them with some semblance of self-importance.

The reality of it is is that with a few, actually very few extreme exceptions, the vast majority of people as individuals are meaningless to the fortunes and history of mankind as a whole. However, as a group, all of the meaningless little people hold great significance. The concept is not all that different than voting. An individual vote has very little meaning, but as a group, the group's aggregate vote is all mighty and powerful. And, this should have great meaning to everyone.

Ultimately, every individual exists for one reason: As an indicator of the success and failure of the very extreme few and as an indicator of how society's philosophy is developing. So, the vast majority of people exist to show that Bill Gates is successful, because they buy his product and make him rich. People also illustrate the effects of policies and philosophies adopted by our leaders and reflect our philosophies in choosing our leaders. In this regard, the group as a whole has great meaning, but as single individuals no one has any meaning whatsoever, unless the individual happens to be someone like Bill Gates, Warren Buffet, Adolf Hitler, Margaret Thatcher, Napoleon, Alexander the Great, Julius Caesar, William Shakespeare, Abraham Lincoln, Vladimir Ilyich Ullianov, Galileo Galilei, Nicolaus Copernicus, Albert Einstein, Genghis Khan, Confucius, Buddha, Qin Shihuang Di, Sir Winston Churchill, Pope Urban 2, Deng Xiaoping, Ronald Reagan, Mikhail Gorbachev, among others. These people change or changed history and the effect of how they change or changed history is measured through the effect that it has on our lives, and that is the purpose of a single life in the greater scheme of human history. Individuals acting in a group and as a whole are the litmus test of changes in history. If the changes are positive and good then our lives will improve and people will prosper over a long period of time. However, if the changes are negative and poor then the effect on the masses will be bad and we will suffer over a long period of time.

As an aside, the effects of some of the changes cannot be measured for centuries like Pope Urban 2's decision to call for a holy crusade in the 11th century, known as the first crusade. This is the root of today's middle-east problems. What the pope thought was a great decision based on the bible's guidance turned out to be one of the most horrific decisions that humanity has to cope with almost a millennium later.

So, if anyone wants to know what they are doing on this planet, understand this: Every individual is the litmus test for the people that change the world and set the course of history. If one feels that this is not enough for them that they want to be the one that changes the world then they can try to do something about it: Invent something worthwhile, create a new company that does something better than existing companies. However, if these objectives are out of reach of any individual then at the very least they themselves can change. Any individual can start by thinking and acting differently than they used to, i.e., develop anew their Six Pillars based on the way I've outlined in this book. Then influence others to do the same. Be a part of the grassroots movement that will shake-up the world and change the course of history, like the patriots during the American revolution, like the defenders of democracy and the federation of the 1860s, like the industrial revolutionaries of the 1880s and beyond, like the veterans of WW 1, like the suffragettes of the 1910s, like the veterans of WW 2, like the patriots of the civil rights movement, and like the veterans of the Iraq and Afghanistan wars.

If anyone wants to change the world, they should start with themselves then rationally persuade others to join our cause, and never use force, coercion, extortion and blackmail to achieve these gains. If one cannot convince another of the rationality of my views then they are helpless and are no different than the people who committed suicide in Jonestown, in my opinion. What can be done about such mad blindness? Move on. But, if successful, and the word continues to spread, these people will become part of something truly great, perhaps as historic as what our ancestors did for us in WW 2 or what the constitutional framers did for individual freedom or what the civil rights movement did for human decency. If we succeed in changing the Six Pillars of the US and, ultimately, the world the way I've outlined, we will most likely be part of humanity that achieves world peace. Now that's something to fight for and be a part of, which would bring massive global significance and purpose to anyone's life.

What difference does it make if a few political extremists lose their rights?! What difference does it make if a few racial minorities lose their rights?! What difference does it make if we violate the rights of the few for the benefit of the masses?

As previously mentioned, Ernst Janning said these words or something like it. As a reminder, he was the head of the Nazi's "Justice" Department, and prior to the Nazis taking over was an extremely well respected legal scholar and wrote some great legal opinions, or so I read. So, his participation in the Nazi party lent it great credibility and cover, which is what made his participation even that much more despicable and vile.

As we all know, his excuse is inexcusable, and he should have known better. But this incident/affair deftly demonstrates how one's Six Pillars are completely independent of one's education-level, intelligence, wealth, ancestry or any other factor. An individual can be a blue collar worker or the Chairperson and CEO of a globally powerful company, a president or prime minister of a country, it doesn't matter what an individual does, their Six Pillars can be glorious or decrepit and what people do for a living, what their social position is, how much money they have, and what pedigree they have is irrelevant. So, judging and respecting a person for what they do for a living, how much money they have and what their social position is is offensive; i.e., judging a book by its cover is disgusting.

So for me, I have more respect for a prostitute who does what she does with honor and exceptional ability than an Ivy-League educated gold-digger; I have more respect for an efficient and courteous waitress than a mediocre portfolio manager; I have more respect for an honest plumber or electrician than doctors that look for ways to make money off of their patients illness or misery; I have more respect for a hard-working, efficient and diligent garbage collector than an arrogant self-absorbed athlete or entertainer; I have more respect for a hard working trader, analyst or investment banker making an honest living than any politician, who only looks for ways to get re-elected (are there any politicians that are left that really care about their constituents?) and sound good; I have more respect for hard-working non-labor union workers than lazy union protected workers, who rely on their union to gain more than they are worth; I have far more respect for our military than our labor unions. This is so because I believe that the people I respect have the right Six Pillars versus those I have no respect for who have rotten Six Pillars that they hide well. If people want to improve our country, they need to learn to penetrate the façade and identify that which really matters in issues as well as in people.

Anyway, going back to Ernst Janning, and the lesson that he unintentionally taught us, the key point is that he thought a little corruption would be justified by the greater good. However, as you may know, when one compromises core principles, one opens the way to ever more evil acts. This is the lesson that Ernst Janning taught us and one of the greatest lessons we could have learned from the Nazi years. This is also the same lesson that the US Supreme Court has enshrined when it comes to 1ˢᵗ Amendment rights. It is my fervent hope that the Supreme Court will apply such rigor to all of our rights and apply it to all of our citizens, including the inalienable and absolute right to our property at all times and under all circumstances.

Otherwise, as Ernst Janning said, what was supposed to be a passing phase that was meant to be for the greater good of the country will become a nightmare and a normal way of life. And, as Judge Dan Haywood said to Janning, "It came to that the first time you sentenced a man to death that you knew was innocent." or something like it. The first time that Americans were taught to think of stealing from the wealthy as justified for the "greater good," because politicians called it taxes, we opened the way to massive evil in the form of continued and uncontrolled congressional spending so the politicians could get re-elected. This resulted in more and more stealing of assets from the wealthy in the form of so called "progressive taxes." The initial violation of the rights of the wealthy has, in principle, not changed, but the magnitude of the violation has increased over the last 30 years. And, therein lies the crux of the violation. Once the principle is violated, increasing the magnitude is a mere matter of procedure. This is how all gross violations of core principles are achieved. People are convinced that a temporary violation of a core principle – especially when disguised as a necessity and given a different name – is absolutely imperative and for the benefit of all people. Then once people are used to the violation of a core principle, the excesses of the violation can continue to be increased with little fanfare, essentially nickel and diming the country to death.

This is how the Nazis did it, this is how the Russian communists did it, and this is how all dictators do it. This is always how all violations of core principles are executed, almost without exception – the magic formula, if you would. When core violations of principles are achieved, no matter how small initially, it becomes huge overtime – jast look at the state of our government's finances. If people need more evidence, all they have to do is look at the state that Greece finds itself in. Essentially, it may not seem like a big deal to give an inch, but before one knows it, they've taken a mile. This is why defending even a small violation of principle is so important, and why the Supreme Court will not allow even a minor violation of the 1ˢᵗ Amendment, as it should not.

Then, to restore the principle, it becomes not only a massive fight – political, economic, financial, and judicial, sometimes even war – but also a huge retraining effort to eviscerate the distorted paradigm and brain-washing imposed on the society. Don't forget, until the very end, there are going to be fanatics – Nazi Germany, Imperialist Japan, Communist China, current Greece and Spain, et cetera – that will not only fight to the bitter end, but also drag a lot of simple-minded, thoughtless, self-destructive or brainless people with them. The amount of effort, sweat, hardship and sometimes blood that is required is staggering, and typically very difficult to understand until many years after the "war" has been won. Inevitably, the long-term consequence of winning is well worth the effort, while the long-term consequence of losing or not doing anything is extremely devastating. Jast look at the price of appeasement that the UK and France – and eventually the US – had to pay for their neglect of German aggression in the 1930s.

The conclusion is that we would have been far better off today, if there were a handful of people that opposed the initial violation of the core principles, but now, we are left to fight the war that should never have taken place to begin with, and the price that we must pay to fight and win this war will be very, very high. However, it is something that we must pay, because the consequences will be that much more painful and horrifying, if we don't correct past mistakes as soon as possible. Think of it this way: There are no free lunches, which means that if we've been eating free lunches then the longer we eat these free lunches the larger the bill accumulates – plus compounding interest – that has to be paid. Otherwise, the result is complete devastation. Decades of socialist policies in Greece have bankrupted the country and now the bill that the Greeks have to pay is staggering, and the suffering that the Greeks will have to endure to restore long-term prosperity is unimaginable. What's worse is that if the Greeks don't go through the devastation now, the consequences will be even worse later, if that could even be imagined.

Also, think about the turmoil such a small country like Greece is bringing to the global economic scene. Now, imagine what would happen if we, the largest economy in the world (almost 25% of the global GDP), goes through what Greece is going through today. If Americans think that the Great Recession or even the Great Depression was bad, "they ain't seen nothing yet!" Those events could be described as taking a brisk walk through the park in summer clothes in the middle of a Norwegian winter, compared to what people will experience if the US goes through what Greece is going through today. That will make Americans feel like they're swimming across the Moscow River in the middle of the Russian winter buck naked with weights around their wrists and ankles after they've been beaten and cut with a razor blade all over their body.

This is what the typical, unthinking average American's shortsightedness, ignorance, greed and avarice has done to our country, and, ironically, the typical, unthinking average American will be the ones that suffer the most. So, stop voting for "social programs," force congress and the president to change the tax laws so that it is fair to everyone and only spend money on education, infrastructure and self-defense after the federal government debt is mostly repaid. Don't forget, when most of the government debt is repaid, we are creating optionality for the poor the next time (a matter of when not if) we run into systemic economic turmoil, as the government (actually Americans overall) will have the spare debt capacity to borrow money to help the struggling economy. And, when such a need arises, I'm sure that we, as a country, will be able to easily afford the temporary boost to our economy.

Everyone in America has to decide! We don't have much time left. If we don't fix the problems, we're going to find that economic turmoil will come more frequently, will be deeper and more painful, last longer and have more lasting negative effects. Until one day, we end up like Greece: We will not only be unable to fix our problems, but also have no control over how to fix them, if there even is a solution.

There are things in life more valuable than life itself

Most people can't think beyond their own life and the importance of it. Yet people believe in heroes and the concept of heroism. What is the connection? Who is a hero? In theory, a hero is someone that *voluntarily* does something great for others, sometimes for people that they don't even know. But is this reality? Can and do heroes exist?

Before I get to the point, let me ask two questions: 1) Ultimately, if people didn't have to worry about money then would they do what they want to do (I'm not talking about murder or acts of depravity)? 2) In the same vein, could we force someone to do anything that they don't want to do, if they are financially secure? Yes, con-artists do exist, and they do commit fraud, but if an individual is an honest person, conning someone would be very difficult.

Bottom-line is that heroes *voluntarily* do what they do because they *want* to, not because they don't want to or are forced to.

The reason why someone would *voluntarily* throw themselves on an enemy grenade, charge a machinegun nest, rush into a fire to save strangers, take a bullet for the president or do anything heroic is *simply* because they value saving others more than their own life. To be clear, what that means from a simple mathematically equivalent point of view is that these heroes believe that $1 million is more valuable than $1, and, therefore, taking $1 million is a better choice than taking $1. So, are these people truly heroes, given that they are jast making the more valuable choice to them? Yes they are!

But how can that be one may ask? Anyone would choose $1 million over $1, so if that is all that a hero is doing then that's not very heroic or so it would seem. The point is that the *voluntary* act is NOT what makes the hero a hero. What makes a hero a hero is the choice that the hero made a long time ago to put more value in saving another's life at the risk and peril of one's own life, and, most importantly, to give up one's life – if it comes down to that – to uphold the ideals and values that they chose, i.e., they have honor. That decision is what makes the hero a hero, not necessarily the *voluntary* act in and of itself. The *voluntary* act is "merely" the confirmation of the hero's ideals and values, and an exercise of the hero's honor. Based on this understanding of what a hero is, everyone could claim to be one, because they may *claim* that they too would *voluntarily* surrender their life – if it needs be – to save others. However, we all know that it is easier to think like a hero than act like one.

If one understands this concept: Basically, that the potential *voluntary* exchange of one's life for those of others can be – and is for a lot of people – a valid and justified exchange and value system then let's take this to a more *intangible* level. The *voluntary* exchange of one person's life for one or more lives seems like an equal exchange or better than equal exchange, but what about intangible concepts such as freedom, democracy, and Justice? These are some of the reasons why we went to war in 1774, 1812, 1861, 1917, 1941, 1950, 1991, and 2003 among others. Notice I did not include Vietnam, Spanish American, Indian or the Texas-Mexican wars.

Getting back to the point, is one's life worth *voluntarily* exchanging for ideals? That depends on what each individual defines as living. Should one rather live as a slave or die fighting for future freedom? If the answer is that it is better to live as slaves then what about for the children, grandchildren and all of the future generations of the slave to come? What about the freedom of future generations? I don't think that we should trade the freedom of future generations for our lives today. However, for purposes of completing the analysis, let's examine what someone's life would be like, if they were to trade their life for the freedom of future generations and see if it would be worth the exchange.

As an aside, one of the best lines in a movie that I ever heard – and which brings tears to my eyes – was from Braveheart when Mel Gibson's character says something to the effect of: "Yes, if you run you may live, but many years from now when you lie dying, what would you give to return to this day to stand and fight for freedom?!" This sent chills down my spine and tears to my eyes. Similarly, there was a line in another movie that I thought was priceless, and it goes something like this: Heroes die once, but cowards die many deaths.

Getting back to the point, if anyone answered that they'd rather trade their life for the lives of their future generations then they're saying that they're willing to inflict pain and torture on their future generations because they'd rather live a life mired in misery and leave the fight for freedom to future generations when it will be exponentially more difficult. So, what kind of a person is this? I'm not sure anyone would want to be their friend, let alone work with them or be their spouse.

On the other hand, if one doesn't have children then one could argue that it doesn't matter because they would be the last person to suffer in their lineage, and they're willing to live with the lack of freedom than risk losing their life fighting for something that they may or may not benefit from. If this is what someone wants to argue then they are truly saying that they'd pick their own life over anything else in the world, and to this choice I have nothing to add. However, I'd be happy to see such a "person" die a painful, drawn-out and agonizing death and spit on them as I walk by, because I think this is the kind of "person" that tries to have their cake and eat it too. If their mentality is truly known by others, this "person" would be hated, ostracized, and would have to live alone. And, should others win freedom for all, this "person's" life will truly not improve as they would not be welcomed into the new society. The quality of their "life" would be bad and, rightly so, and they would be looked upon as a coward, and, more importantly, immoral, i.e., a very bad "person."

If this is the kind of life that someone is willing to live with then by all means they should hold their life above all else, but then they shouldn't expect to be treated with respect or dignity. In reality, most people are afraid of risking their life for anything, even their loved ones, but hide it well, unless they're a mother, in which case, very few mothers wouldn't risk their lives for their children regardless of their own survivability. The negative aspect of a mother's protectionist nature is that some mothers take this concept to an extreme and won't think twice about hurting other children and their parents to allow their own children to get ahead or keep their own children from rightly being punished for what their children did wrong.

Anyway, I hope that people realize that there are things more important in life than life itself and, therefore, fighting for these ideals at the risk and peril of one's own life is well worth it. Specifically, concepts such as freedom, Justice, and inalienable rights are worth fighting for and those that lose their life in pursuit and protection of these immortal concepts are truly heroes.

Then what is the right philosophical construct? Think Justice and nothing but Justice

There are two perspectives that we need to consider: 1) From a societal point of view, and 2) from a personal point of view.

From a societal point of view, we've covered the tax aspect, but there is the issue of true equality. The US government must not discriminate against *any individual, in any manner, and under any circumstance* when it comes to people's rights. Treating one group the same, while treating another group differently is discrimination, no matter how one cuts it, dices it, or slices it; *Brown vs. the Board of Education* says so. This must be codified by law and through a constitutional amendment. The simple matter of fact is that if separate, but equal doesn't work then separate and unequal certainly shouldn't.

Again, let me be perfectly clear. Equality pertains to people's rights, including people's right to own their own assets (including their money), but does not apply to restrictions imposed by the government on its people. Such societally imposed restrictions as traffic laws that seek to hinder our ability to make our own decisions should not be allowed to exist at all, but if it is to exist then it must take into consideration our abilities.

The other objective that must be codified through a constitutional amendment is the supremacy of individual rights over "social rights." We must always keep in mind that every society starts with one individual. Therefore, we must never allow our government, our leadership, or any group in society to circumvent the rights of any individual, no matter what the reason for that circumvention may be.

In particular, in the US, property rights must be strictly observed. No one, our government or any individual, must be allowed to confiscate individual property under any circumstances, regardless of whether or not the majority voted for taking other people's asset and property.

This leads to the last point, and perhaps the most important point. There are certain rights that must not, cannot and should not be subject to a vote. Some of these rights that most people would understand as being inalienable are whether we should allow slavery or not, whether women should be allowed to vote or not, whether we should allow censorship of first amendment rights, whether we should abridge democratic processes, whether or not we should allow discrimination against any of our upstanding citizens, and whether we should support or favor one religion over another. Again, these rights must not, cannot and should not ever be subject to a vote and should be deemed inalienable. There ought to be one other inalienable right and that is the right to one's own property and assets and the freedom to dispose of it as the individual sees fit to do so.

In order for these rights to be absolutely inalienable, the US Supreme Court is the only institution in this country that can make it so. The congress and president would never let it happen because they would be afraid of losing the vote of the poor people. However, for the US Supreme Court to hear the case, it has to be brought in front of the Court, which would require an individual or group to spend the money to bring the case to court. If I had the money, I'd be the one to do it, but I don't have anywhere near the amount of money to make this happen. How sad is it that the Supreme Court is so inaccessible to an average citizen?

From an individual point of view, we have to look at morals, values, ethics, integrity, honor and honesty separately. So, let us tackle these one by one. Keep in mind that what I'm suggesting is exactly that and, therefore, subject to revisions, amendments, additions, and evolution as each individual sees fit, but always governed by Justice and logic. Regardless, I hope that the core principles that I'm outlining here will stay true with every individual.

- **Morals: That which is right vs. wrong.** One's morals must be based on Justice and ONLY Justice. This doesn't mean that concepts like compassion doesn't have a place in one's heart, but even compassion should be measured on the scale of Justice, i.e., everyone should ask themselves the following question: Does the person *deserve* my compassion? Personally, and typically, I don't cry for people who are homeless, but when I read the account of a Medal of Honor recipient, I shed tears. When I watch a particularly moving story on one of many Bud Greenspan's Olympic stories, I will be moved to tears. When I hear stories about how people go from living in railway freight cars to going to college and business school and reaching financial success, I shed tears of joy. Regardless, every individual must have some basic assumptions in order to apply Justice and rational thought to develop their morals. For me, the following are some of the basic assumptions that I make in determining that which I believe to be right versus wrong:
  - Justice must always triumph over all other considerations;
  - I believe that one should always think in terms of long-term benefits versus short-term gains; therefore, anything that perpetuates long-term benefits is right, good and moral, and anything that doesn't is wrong, bad and immoral;
  - Therefore, there are no shortcuts to or in life that are good for me in the long-run, no matter how enticing the shortcut may be in the short-run;
  - I believe that true selfishness is the right moral position for each individual and for the society as a whole;
  - I believe in respecting other people's position, only and as long as it is rational in both the assumptions and principles, not jast the logic;
  - Committing a crime is wrong; all crimes are a form of theft and all thefts are a crime;

- I always try to respect the rights of others and EXPECT others to respect mine; if my rights are violated first then I stand-up for myself, but more importantly, if the rights of others are initially violated I stand-up for their rights too;
- Everyone is born equal, but grow-up differently and die unequal; I try to judge and treat people based on who they are not what they are and what they have;
- Equality doesn't always mean Justice, but Justice is always fair, and should be equally applied;
- I believe that everyone **must** judge, make decisions and act upon those decisions; therefore, I make and act on my decisions, but, more importantly, if I am **proven** wrong, I am prepared to make amends;
- Mostly, it isn't about whether I always make right or wrong decisions, but what I learn from the outcomes of my decisions and how I apply those lessons going forward;
- Experience is meaningless unless it is interpreted correctly, and through the right principles and paradigms;
- I always strive and challenge myself to be at my best and do my best; if I am capable of becoming a noble laureate in physics, but settle for designing car engines, I am a loser relative to someone who is the best garbage collector, and who was meant to be a garbage collector;
- I **know** free lunches do not exist and "accepting a free lunch" is wrong;
- **Everything is black or white, right or wrong, good or bad**, but people try to make it gray, because it's easier to live in a so called gray world;
- Laws must be subject to rational assumptions and logical morality;

- **Values: That which one covets and places value or importance in.** Values should also reflect one's sense of Justice and one's morals. Here are some basics of what I value:
  - I believe there are priorities more valuable than my own life such as freedom, Justice and inalienable rights that I must defend and uphold;
  - I value people that have strong morals and values based on Justice;
  - I covet what I can afford and deserve and will reject that which I do not deserve and didn't earn;
  - I prize things that are of benefit to me, my loved ones and my friends in the long-term and don't give into the temptation of short-term gains;

- I value quality over quantity;
- I value truth and plain talk and dismiss with prejudice sugar coated bullshit and political correctness;
- I value reality over fantasy;
- I value substance over form; in fact, I pay little attention to form;
- I believe that white lies and political correctness are jast as evil if not more evil than any other forms of lies and deceit;
- I value intellect and the ability to apply that intellect over experience;
- I place value in history and perspectives of the elderly;
- I believe that "politics" of all kinds should be abolished and severely punished;
- I hate politically-oriented people, and view them lower than gang members, drug dealers, rapists, child molesters and murderers; of course, I'm the farthest from being political;
- I look at money as a form of reward for what one has accomplished and a tool, but not something that needs to be or should be coveted for its own sake;
- Most of all I value Justice over any other philosophical concept and absolutely reject any other philosophical concept that compromises Justice in any shape, way or form;
- I value earned loyalty, but not blind loyalty;
- I believe that both respect and loyalty have to be earned and never commanded;
- I have and value faith, but never blind faith;
- I value rational and logical arguments and prize new information;
- I value hard work and reaping *all* of the benefits of that work;

- **Ethics: It is the manifestation of one's morals and values through physical acts.** How one behaves should also be dictated by one's sense of Justice. Here are some basics that I abide by, or try to:
    - When I see injustice being perpetrated, I speak up, making sure that it is not a wasted effort;
    - I reward those that behave with honor and uphold strong moral standards and possess a strong value system;
    - I believe in acting for long-term benefits and reject acting for short-term gains;

- I reward people who work hard for the right reasons and behave with honor; in contrast, I deplore people who take short cuts through work, life and all other endeavors;
- I will never accept a free lunch without reason or cause in which case it doesn't make it a free lunch;
- I try not to offend, but when others offend, I will defend myself, my loved ones and my philosophy;
- I act on what I believe to be right versus wrong;
- When called for honesty, I will give it;
- When I'm asked to lie, I will decline;
- When I'm faced with a "moral dilemma," my position is that there are no such situations;
- When my job is threatened due to a "moral dilemma," I'm more likely to get fired;
- I don't believe in the "Kobayashi Maru" scenario that is depicted in Star Trek;
- I believe in fixing problems as soon as they are identified;
- I don't suffer fools, therefore, I like the fact that a vast majority of people don't like me, but I'm proud to say that I have a handful of very close friends;
- Relative logic, relative right and relative wrong do not exist, therefore, I'm not afraid to make decisions on an absolute basis and act on them;
- If I'm found to be wrong, I will change, but not before putting up a fight and making sure that the position I'm migrating to is flawless;
- When confronted with rules or laws that are stupid, and I can rationally prove it, I have no problems breaking laws and bending the rules – would you have abided by slavery laws or Jim Crow laws? Did the civil rights marchers? Should they have? Always think of rules, regulations and laws in this light: Rules and laws must be simple, make sense, be rational and **always be moral**;

- **Integrity: The consistency and preservation of one's morals, values and ethics.** There's really not much else to it, either an individual is going to have consistency throughout their morals, values and ethics or they're not and they are going to preserve their morals, values and ethics or they're not.

- **Honor: The pride of knowledge that one's morals, values, ethics and integrity is more valuable than one's own life and being ready to act on and defend one's Six Pillars at all cost.** Again, there really isn't much more that can be said about one's honor, people either have it or they don't. The vast majority of people don't even come close to knowing what honor is, let alone having any. The reason why few, if any, have honor is because the key to one's honor is Justice: People have to believe in Justice, have faith in Justice, think Justice, speak Justice and act on Justice for them to even attempt to have honor.

- **Honesty: Not jast thinking about it, but also telling it, most importantly to *oneself* and then to others.** This doesn't mean that we have to be ugly about it; we can be diplomatic about it, but be sure there is no mistake about what we are saying and why. This doesn't mean that everyone must always tell the truth. For example, if a soldier is captured by the enemy, this soldier must not tell the enemy anything, other than their name, rank and serial number. Anything else can and will be used to hurt the soldier's compatriots. So, is this a lie? No, it's an omission. But the use of omission is allowed only under such extreme circumstances, and the vast majority of us should never use it, if we are to have honor and integrity. The reason why a captured soldier is allowed this option is because the protection of the lives of their compatriots is more important than their own life; it becomes a matter of honor for the captive soldier. In all other circumstances, one must make an erstwhile (only word in the English language that *I know* has five consecutive consonants in the word) effort to speak the truth. And, for me, to uphold honesty, I don't believe in white lies, being humble, political correctness or any other misrepresentations of truth.

These are guidelines, my recommendations, and what I try to live by. Therefore, each person has to craft their own set of Six Pillars in order to make it work for them, but if one is honest with oneself and truly focused on the long-term benefits, I think every individual is going to come to very similar, if not exactly the same conclusions. Remember, I've had decades to think about this, so I have the advantage. Lastly, I'll point out that if one lives a truly solid life based on a strong set of Six Pillars, each person will find that their life volatility will be high in the beginning, but like many good things, if one works at it and stands by it, one will find that it has strong benefits over a longer period of time. And, once an individual gets there, they will not want to go back, because of not only how proud one becomes of oneself, but also because of how much the quality of one's life improves. Let me also sound a word of caution: The struggle to change will be difficult, and at the end of the day, not all will succeed, but this is where one's faith kicks in. I tell people who have judeo/christian religious faith that I have more faith than they do and it is stronger, because I truly know and believe in myself and my Six Pillars, my faith is tangible and I can rationally express my position and the merits and benefits of it, while they have to rely on *blind* faith to make their case. I call my version of faith, **real faith**, versus the judeo/christian faith, which is blind faith as acknowledged by all of the judeo/christian devotees that I've ever talked to – I make it impossible for them to deny it.

The change that one will have to go through will be more agonizing and drawn out then getting off of cocaine, heroin, crack, or other illicit drugs. However, like winning the battle against illicit drugs, the long-term benefits are immeasurable, and, like drug addition, one has to be very careful not to fall back into bad habits. This is what will be difficult, but if one has real faith versus blind faith, and when one perseveres, one will find that one's life gets better and better with time.

In reality, there is no such situation as a moral dilemma

As a related matter, a lot of people have asked me if there is the right time to lie. Yes, like most things in life, there is a time and a place to lie. When at war, obviously, deceiving one's enemy is a must. If an individual is under physical duress – kidnapping, potential assault or rape situation, or subject to other criminal duress – one has to say and do whatever one can to get out of the situation. If one's life or the life of one's family and friends are threatened, absolutely, do what one has to do to get them out of it.

The "gray" area that some people point out is when they are at work. It always comes up in the discussion. The scenario that inevitably comes up is the situation in which one has to do something immoral in order to save one's job or alternatively get fired. I've been in this situation, and I chose to get fired. I've also trusted rules, laws and my boss to protect me from unscrupulous and short-sighted people and have been burned. But, ultimately, some people argue that it depends on one's financial position, because if the person is wealthy, they absolutely can choose the high road, but if one is struggling to make ends meet then the decision isn't that easy. I would warn these folks that they are confusing short-term versus long-term, again. Also, if a person is wealthy then their financial independence necessitates that the situation that confronts them is by definition not a moral dilemma. So, a moral dilemma can only occur to those that face financial uncertainty.

Yes, in the short-run, one will benefit from making that short-term decision, but what is the price that one has to pay in the future, since there is no free lunch? Also, going to one's boss' boss or regulators and protest the perceived "no-win" situation will not change anything. However, if the boss knows that not only the first individual, but everyone else hesh tries to strong arm into doing something bad will protest that could be the difference. Also, perhaps the person facing the moral dilemma would never get a promotion or a raise and perhaps they'd never find another job, but acting morally with honor always has its benefits even though they may not be apparent the moment one has to make the decision. One jast has to find a way to turn lemons into lemonade.

The problem is that every time a person makes the short-term choice, it's like taking a shot of heroin to relieve the pain of withdrawal, making one's life that much more difficult in the long-run. Regardless, the solution to so called "moral dilemmas" is simple, but very difficult to execute: One must always act with honor. It may be painful in the short-term, but in the long-run, if everyone makes the right decision then it will be useless for the bad boss to even try to force the next person into making a bad decision. This is the fight that we all have to fight. Most importantly, this is part of our individual's responsibility to our society as a whole. We must all fight injustice, no matter where and when we find it. So, if everyone that the boss tries to bully fights back, sooner or later the asshole that is trying to force someone into a bad decision will get theirs; we all have to believe in that and act accordingly. Of course the dilemma is whether or not we should risk our job to teach the horrible boss a lesson that they deserve to get. The answer is always!

However, the fact of the matter is that most people cannot make the right choice, because they are too mired in gaining short-term benefits and living for the next paycheck. So, what most people do in this situation is to try to buy time. They drag their feet as long as possible to make the decision and in the meantime they look for another job. If they find one before having to make the decision, great, they move on. If not then they make the decision that buys them the most optionality, so that they can continue to look for another job. This isn't a bad strategy as long as they make the right decision, if and when the time comes.

The realistic situation is that people only really have two choices when confronted with a bad condition at work: Fight or flight. The problem is that fighting doesn't do anyone much good, because the vast majority of the people aren't that far removed in character from the bad boss, and most people don't give a shit about another person's "moral dilemma." And, I'll go so far as to say that most people don't even want to hear about another person's "moral dilemma" for fear that they may somehow be dragged into the same bad situation. Also, the boss' boss doesn't want to be embroiled in their subordinate's personnel issues in case they get blamed for something. So, if someone tries to draw their boss' boss' attention to what's going on, the boss' boss' reaction is most likely to be "talk to your boss." And, if the person says that they've tried that the boss' boss' typical reaction will be anger, because the boss' boss doesn't want to get involved, and getting dragged into a bad situation cannot possibly help their career. However, the boss' boss will hide their anger from the individual, because they don't want to seem careless and uncaring, because a senior manager is *supposed* to care for *all* of the people that work under them. Bottom-line is that the boss' boss will do whatever they can to protect their "reputation" and "image" regardless of whether it is well deserved or not and who may be screwed in the process. They'll justify this by saying to themselves, "it's them or me." If these people have any semblance of honesty, they'll never sleep well, but the vast majority doesn't seem to be losing any sleep. This obviously does not say many good things about corporate managers, but this should not be surprising. On rare occasions, there are honorable people, but they are far and few in between based on my travails through many companies.

Remember that in a vast majority of organizations, the people that succeed are the ones that are "politically" very astute and capable with an above average intelligence for the company they work for. This means that the higher one goes up in an organization the more political one has to be to survive and eventually the most successful politicians with a bit of luck and a bit of skill and intelligence ascend to leadership positions. This is why going to one's boss' boss is actually useless, if not downright counter-productive and dangerous for one's career. So, for most people, the answer is they leave as quickly as they can find another job that is appropriate.

For the very few conscientious managers that actually want to do a good job, a few words of advice: Study the people that your subordinates surround themselves with, it will tell you a lot about the people that are directly working for you. Then look at their retention rate and see who leaves and who stays. Also, when you have a companywide function see who comes, who doesn't, who enjoys themselves and who don't. You'll learn a lot more than you can imagine. Additionally, do real anonymous 360-degree surveys when possible that everyone knows is and can only be truly anonymous – doing the survey through a computer is out of the question; I would do the survey in a room with no windows, no audio-visual equipment, make everyone where latex gloves before entering the room and use a typewriter to take the survey, which is then sealed into an envelope using only water to do so then dropped into a locked-box that is only emptied after everyone has taken the survey. This will reveal a lot about what you are confronted with in terms of people. The trick is to know and understand what people are saying about each other, what's motivating them and what, if anything, you can do to reveal more clarity. Once you know the truth, you must act on the newly revealed information or all this work will be for naught and your credibility will be shot. However, results of such an anonymous survey could be extremely disruptive, because true honesty could be very eye-opening and, therefore, acting on the results could be very tumultuous. So, if you are going to do this, be prepared for shocks, and if there are no surprises, good for you and congratulations!

The bottom-line is that if people understand that the decision that leads to short-term gain is bad for them in the long-run, they will then start to realize that, in reality, there is no moral dilemma. The short-term choice is always wrong, but how could this be so, if making the right choice for the long-term cause people short-term financial pain? Because, otherwise, it may cost people something even more: Such things as one's reputation, honor, future earnings, and integrity is at risk.

Think of it this way, if one caves and makes the short-term choice, this may result in keeping one's job, but then the individual becomes an accomplice to their boss' immoral behavior. So, what will the individual do the next time they are asked to do the same thing? What happens if the "moral dilemma" becomes more and more painful, how does one avoid making these decisions? What if it results in the individual being blackmailed directly or indirectly? What can one do? Remember, there are no moral dilemmas, because there are no free lunches, so whether in the short-term or in the long-term, the price of making a bad decision has to be paid. It will only come down to when the individual **wants** to pay it, and, yes, the decision will be up to the individual. Lastly, remember that the longer one waits to pay the piper, the exponentially harder it will be to do so, and the more expensive it will be, too.

There are no sacrifices

People that we believe to be heroes will tell us that they are anything but heroes. These heroes will go on to tell us that what they did to earn the moniker of hero from all of us was nothing more than their job. For example, interview after interview with Medal of Honor recipients shows this to be the case. So, why is it that we believe that heroes exist and heroes think that they did nothing more than what they were supposed to do? Why is it that we view what the heroes did to be great sacrifices, while the heroes think that they only did what anyone else would have done in the same situation? How do we reconcile these two seemingly irreconcilable views?

The truth of the matter is that both views are correct, but in different ways. However, each view only tells us part of the story. Let's examine the viewpoint of the heroes first. Their view of what they did is absolutely correct, which means that they made no sacrifices. In fact, sacrifices cannot exist. What we think of as a sacrifice is either a correct execution of a value proposition, plain stupidity or something that we can't even imagine doing. Let me give a clear example of what I'm saying. When a soldier throws himself on a grenade, hesh is choosing to save the lives of many at the price of hes own life. This is "merely" a rational value proposition, at least in that soldier's mind: Trading one's life for the lives of many is a rational value proposition. Put it this way, everyone understands the value proposition that the hero made. The part that mere mortals can't easily come to grips with is that to be a hero one has to put one's life at risk of almost certain death, particularly in the above example. Because of this caveat, most people believe that heroes make sacrifices, which then earns the heroes their title. However, I would argue that heroism is not a physical act, but a metaphysical act. Again, the reason for this is that heroes make a value choice first before acting on their value choice later. Therefore, heroism is an extremely difficult but highly ethical act; it's either that or the person wanted to commit suicide, i.e., utter stupidity. As an aside, jast because I think suicide is stupid, it doesn't mean that every one of us shouldn't have the right to control one's own life and how and when to end it.

So, where's the sacrifice? Sacrifice, by definition, is the act of giving more for less. So, given the definition of sacrifice and the explanation of why heroes do what they do, sacrifices cannot exist, yet heroes do exist. What this means is that heroes exist, but they don't make sacrifices. What heroes do is they choose more for less. What they choose to do is to trade something less valuable for something more valuable, whether that be for many lives, an idea, an ideal, or a philosophy for their own life or something else that they possess of value, i.e., heroes consciously make a value choice. Nevertheless, jast because a hero's act is "merely" a value proposition, it doesn't mean that what they did is not heroic, because the value proposition involves a high probability of having to *voluntarily* give up something extremely valuable such as one's own life.

More importantly, heroes aren't born heroes, and they don't become heroes in a moment or an instant. Heroes are long in the making and training: Meaning that true heroes are groomed and molded over a long period of time. Put it another way, one cannot choose to be a hero at the moment of crisis when one hasn't been preparing to be a hero up to that point. Most heroes are heroes long before their act of heroism brings to light their true character to the public. The implication is that heroism is born of the mind, not of the body. Heroism is an act of the mind, which the body executes. So, again, heroism is not a physical act; heroism is a mindset, a belief, a life-style, a manifestation of a philosophical principle.

If one understands what makes a hero a hero then one understands why there cannot be a sacrifice. Then, by extension, every situation that one can think of as being a sacrifice isn't a sacrifice, but a choice, the choice to receive more than to give. A lot of people talk about the sacrifice mother Teresa made in her life. That's bull, in my opinion. What she did was to make a choice: In her mind, she chose to go to what she believed to be heaven after she died, i.e., eternal life in paradise that she imagined for hardship on earth for a relatively short time. That's a pretty smart trade if it were actually possible. Nevertheless, she made that choice believing that such a trade is possible.

If one understands why sacrifices don't/can't exist then one has to wonder what people are talking about when they talk about making sacrifices. For most people that are intellectually average, they are talking about the religious philosophy of giving to people at the cost to themselves and preaching the benevolence of blind giving. To those that are nefarious, it provides the "convenient" excuse for taking from others, whether that is money, time, intellectual property or other valuable assets. And, to those that are in power, the message of sacrifice is used to not only gain more power and political clout, but also to steal the productivity of others, while making the productive feel guilty about their own productivity, so the people in power can steal even more.

At the end of the day, the message is clear: Sacrifice, by definition, is giving more and taking less. And, there's nothing about giving more and taking less that is attractive. That means that if someone truly sacrifices, they are a moron. Otherwise, sacrifices cannot exist and, therefore, a "sacrificial" act is "nothing more" than putting one's own moral value system into practice. Of course, the difficult part is actually acquiring a strong, rational and moral value system that truly reflects Justice and then acting on it. Regardless, "sacrifices" don't/can't exist, it is an intensely moronic act or it is an act that we can't imagine doing that others have done like throwing one's self on a grenade to save the lives of others.

Only a coward will blame others for one's problems and issues

How many times has someone said to you something like this: "If you didn't do _____ then I wouldn't have suffered _____." For example, "if you didn't study so hard, I'd have been valedictorian!" or "why did you have to make that last shot? If you hadn't, I could have been the hero, damn it!" or "if you hadn't said anything, no one would know!"

Does the scenario and situation sound familiar? I'm pretty sure that many people have at one point thought these thoughts and likely actually said some like it. So, how many people have thought or said, "if it weren't for you _____, I could have _____." This type of thinking is one of the worst ideas anyone could practice in their lives: 1) It is incredibly indicative of how people jast don't know how to think, 2) demonstrates how much of an asshole the vast majority of people really are, 3) may be the reason why the saying "logic isn't everything" was invented, and how stupid that saying is, 4) how short-sighted people really are, 5) how massively lazy people really are, 6) how incredibly hard people search for a free lunch, and 7) how unbelievably insecure everyone really is.

Let me deal with 3) first. The grammatical logic of "if you hadn't _____, I could have _____," e.g., if you hadn't studied so hard, I could have been valedictorian!," is correct, but if one thinks about it from a moral, value, or ethics point of view, it makes little to no sense. Therefore, to most people, they conclude that the logic is incorrect. So, most people go around saying something as stupid as, "logic isn't everything." However, let me assure everyone that the grammatical logic is quite sound: If this then that. The problem isn't the logic; it's the assumption behind the logic. First, what makes people think the person who utters such nonsense deserve to be #1? If they didn't put in the work, weren't born with the talent or otherwise incapable of being #1, they should not covet something better than what they deserve, i.e., a free lunch. On the other hand, if they worked hard and still came in #2 or worse then people should behave honorably and sincerely congratulate those that did better than they did and either work harder for the next time, or if they know they've reached their limits then think about whether or not they should move on to something else. Regardless, they should be happy with what they achieved, if they truly gave it their all.

Because, if people's assumption is correct then why shouldn't they be happy about their rival getting hurt or even getting killed. For that matter, why not hurt or kill the rival themselves? For example, should Michelle Kwan, who was 5-times world champion and 9-times US champion, blame Tara Lapinski for skating better than she did at the 1998 Nagano Winter Olympics, and blame Tara for her silver medal performance? Should she have killed or have someone kill Sarah Hughes and Irina Slutskaya before the 2002 Salt Lake City Olympics, so she could finally win Olympic gold, instead of bronze? As much as all of us wanted Michelle Kwan to win Olympic gold in one, if not both Olympics, should one of us have killed any of the other three mentioned above? How absurd would that be? At the end of the day, the grace and poise with which Michelle handled her Olympic-misadventures makes her far more memorable than either Tara Lapinski or Sarah Hughes and more honorable for having suffered through those two defeats with such grace, poise and demureness. This is not to take anything away from Tara and Sarah who were both great Olympic champions in their own rights. However, how many people actually remember Tara or Sarah versus Michelle?

This example demonstrates not only how people jast don't know how to think, but also how people can compound the problem of poor thinking by distorting logic – based on faulty assumptions – and acting on it to one's own detriment. Staying with the same field of figure skating, does anyone remember the incident with Nancy Kerrigan and Tonya Harding, where Tonya Harding's ex-husband had someone club Nancy Kerrigan's knee with a collapsible police baton? This is the physical manifestation of the thought, "if it weren't for you, I could have _____." If one believes in that crazy saying, of course, it is logical to hire someone to hurt Nancy Kerrigan, assuming one got away with it. Of course, most people who think this way aren't too bright, which is why eventually the perpetrators get caught, as was the case in the Kerrigan/Harding incident. Unfortunately, this is not too far from the way most people think.

Right about now, many people are expressing outrage and saying something to the effect of, "I'd never think something like that, let alone do something like that!" How many people cheered when the opposing team's star player got hurt, or at least felt joy at the enhanced prospect of "their" team's chances of winning? How many people try to distract an opponent, while playing a sport or as a fan – like waving one of those stupid things behind the basket during an opponent team's free-throw at a basketball game? How many people have yelled out, "it's out of bounds" when the opposition player spikes the volleyball on the line at an Olympic match versus our US team? How many people have booed when the opposing team's baseball manager takes out the bad pitcher that their team was making minced meat out of? How many people have ever cried out "Foul, that was a foul!" when the opposing team's football player makes a great play? How many people have tried to cheat at sports – or anything for that matter – to try and gain an unearned advantage? How many people have ever tried to make someone else look bad in front of superiors or elders? How many people have tried to avoid fair competition? Has anyone felt joy in getting something for nothing? Has anyone ever enjoyed getting a so called "free lunch?" Has anyone ever stolen a boyfriend or girlfriend from someone? Has anyone ever deliberately cheated or lied to get what they want? How many people have ever coveted what someone else has? How many people have ever felt jealous? Has anyone ever resented someone else's success or wished that they had the other person's success without earning it? How many people have ever tried to blame someone else for something that went wrong? I doubt very many people, if any, said no to every single question in this paragraph. What this says is that more people are like Tonya Harding or her ex-husband than they think or know. To me, this is very scary.

People have to be very insecure to want something that they didn't earned or are very lazy. Yet, it's fascinating how happy so many people become when they think they got away with getting something for nothing. And, people don't seem to understand that it's all the same misplaced thinking: It's unjust to get something that one didn't earn. And, it's perverse to take something that which one has not properly worked for and justified. Most importantly, people don't seem to understand the magnitude of the negative impact of their bad behavior and how it destroys trust and faith in each other then they wonder why the world is so screwed up and are shocked when bad things happen to them. What people are missing is that when injustice is perpetrated, no matter how small, it destroys the quality of everyone's lives. Therefore, we must protect against even the smallest violations of Justice, quickly correct any injustices and keep faith with each other that others will do the same. This is the only social contract that we need. This is the only responsibility we have to each other and to society.

Understand that when someone says something like, "if it weren't for you, I'd be the winner," they're suggesting that the other person drop dead. This person is also coveting that which they didn't earn, and they desire that which they didn't either work hard enough for or weren't born with the talent to deserve or both. They are also saying that they are not only a bad loser, but a very jealous person that cannot look beyond their own hopes and dreams, and they'd rather trample the other person's achievements to gain their own glory, regardless of whether they deserve it or not. But most of all, the individual is saying that they will destroy to win, they will cheat and lie to get what they want that they view destruction as an equal to creation that pulling down someone on the ladder is the same as pulling oneself up the ladder. This is how ugly a lot of people are in this country, regardless of what comes out of their mouth. What's worse is that most people don't even know that this is how they are. This is what happens when people refuse to think. This is not how we should behave, and I know we can and should be better than this.

If people really want to know why the world is so screwed up all they have to do is to look in the mirror; we have no one else to blame, but ourselves. The good news is that we can still save ourselves; we jast have to start changing today. Start by taking small responsibilities building up to bigger ones and start becoming accountable for those responsibilities, first and foremost to oneself. People will find that they will not only shake off the insecurity about themselves, but also they will end up learning a lot more than they bargained for, and lastly, they will become a leader among their peers, co-workers, friend and family. But do it right, don't half-heartedly do it, don't jast pretend to change and only change the superficial or give up after a short while. Be persistent and persevere. If one has to, work with others and try to change together, helping each other and supporting each other to make the right changes, and most importantly, talking about and reviewing the progress and planning out the next steps. Over many months and years, anyone who makes the effort will be surprised at how much one changes for the better and how much better one's quality of life improves. Remember, one vote can't change the world, but a billion votes can and to get to a billion, we have to start at one; you!

Everything is black or white, good or bad, right or wrong; there are no relatives, no grays, no half-measures

Think about the statement, "everything is relative." The problem with this statement is that it is self-contradictory, because the statement, "everything is relative" is an absolute statement. Obviously, what makes it an absolute statement is the word "everything." The crux of the argument that people who utter such nonsense is trying to make is dead on arrival. Even before they can start to argue why everything is relative, their argument has been defeated by their own original statement. So, we know, everything cannot be relative. But does this necessitate that everything is black or white, good or bad, and right or wrong? Logic says jast because it isn't A, it doesn't mean that it's absolutely going to be B. However, it is my intention to prove that everything is black or white, good or bad, and right or wrong.

Let's start with your own life: When looking at your own life, you cannot predict the future. So, this means there is no certainty when it comes to the future and people use this as the reason to describe the world as being gray. However, looking back at anyone's life, decisions are judged by the harsh light of hindsight, truth and Justice. So, all that this means is that there was a right and a wrong decision at the time particular decisions were made, but no one has the ability or knowledge to predict the outcome ahead of time. So, again, based on future uncertainty, people argue that the world is gray.

No, it isn't, and the reason why future uncertainty doesn't mean that the world is gray is because people are confusing future uncertainty with the state of the world as it actually is, functions and is organized. Also, realize that if one makes a different decision, i.e., took another path the outcome is unlikely to be what one thought it would be or should be. Here's what I means. Let's say that someone is facing the choice of A or B and they chose A. Five years down the line, the individual discovers that the decision that they made (decision A) resulted in X. And, furthermore, looking at the results of their choice, they believe that had they chosen B instead of A, that they would have ended up with Y. Actually, in reality, had the person chosen B, it is unlikely to have resulted in Y, because choice B would have triggered a different set of circumstances and reactions from people around the individual that made the decision, and the outcome would have been very different then "all else being equal" and choosing B.

By the way, the "all-else-being-equal" analysis is by far one of the dumbest analytical tools that anyone can employ to do any kind of scenario analysis other than as an initial starting point. The core of the reason for why it is dumb is because **ALL ELSE CANNOT BE EQUAL.** If something changes this has a ripple effect that changes other things, which then changes even more things, et cetera, et cetera. Therefore, if the all-else-being-equal analysis does give someone the right answer, it is no different than a blind squirrel finding a nut: Occasionally, it can happen, and occasionally, one can draw to a one outer, get the straight flush and beat the four of a kind. It happens!

Moving on, what my example about choosing A or B illustrates is that decisions cannot be viewed in isolation of the result. Therefore, if one makes the best possible decision at the time that they have to make the decision based on and considering all of the information available to them then that is the right decision, no matter the outcome. As long as the future remains cloudy and there is no way to penetrate the effect of time, one cannot, must not and should not dwell on the uncertainty of the future. Otherwise, one will make the worst decision of their life, which is to say they will end up being indecisive. By the way, many indecisive people will pretend that they are being patient and act like they know it all and are under supreme control, when in reality they have NO BLOODY CLUE whatsoever. Do not be fooled by these people; learn to distinguish indecision from patience. Although telling the difference is very difficult to do, knowing how to distinguish indecision from patience will save people a lot of grief. The difference between patience and indecision is that when one is patient, one will still have time to execute on a chosen strategy. Another difference is that patience should result in additional information that will be useful in making a decision. Indecision will result in panicked decision making. Another difference is that if someone is patient, they should be able to tell you exactly what they are waiting for, why, what the probability of acquiring this information is, why they expect the additional information to shed clarity on the decision process, why it is worthwhile waiting for this new piece of information and what they would do if the information doesn't arrive on time.

Also, learn to distinguish between people who are building a consensus decision versus those that are looking for the best excuse when the decision that is made (typically not their decision) doesn't work out and looking for people to blame. Someone who is looking to build a consensus decision will ultimately take the responsibility for making the decision, those that are cowards will not and find very slick and sophisticated ways and reasons to blame others.

Enough diversions. The point is that there is a difference between not knowing and the world being gray. *If the world was truly gray, the outcome of any decision that one makes should never have clarity.* Think about it: If the world is truly gray and only gray, how can there be a conclusion to anything, or a final result of any action or decision? No endings would be possible, especially ones that are decisive, if the world was truly gray. The reality of the matter is that the world is black and white, we jast don't know which it is until we gets to the end. However, people use the lack of precognition (knowing events ahead of time) as an excuse or crutch, because it is far easier to make the excuse than take the responsibility of making bad decisions or being indecisive. Again, if the world is truly gray, we cannot have times of clarity in life. And, again, don't confuse not being able to see into the future or ignorance with how the world – or for that matter, the universe – actually functions and actually is.

Let me give a concrete example to reinforce what I've previously outlined: Let's say that Sally is confronted with two paths A and B, and either way, Sally doesn't know what will happen. Most people will say that this is a gray situation, because Sally doesn't know what will happen. That's wrong. The fact of the matter is that when Sally goes down A, it will result in something, and if Sally goes down B it will result in something else. Whichever path Sally chooses, the end result is black and white, it is clear. The fact that Sally doesn't know what that is ahead of time only means that Sally has no ability to tell what awaits her in the future or that she is ignorant, i.e., Sally has no precognition. However, this is not the same as the universe being gray.

Also, know this: The path that one came from and the path that one is about to take cannot be disjointed or inconsistent. Meaning – and to put it simply – if an individual always led a "bad" life that individual is unlikely to all of a sudden choose a "good" life going forward, and vice-a-versa. That means in essence, by the time one gets to a cross road, one's path has already been largely predetermined, and it is highly likely that the individual will favor one path versus another, whether they know it or not. It takes either an extraordinary person or an extraordinary set of circumstances for someone to abruptly change their path. So, in a way, even the decision of going down path A or path B isn't really a choice, but an illusion of choice, which suggests that even the decision itself is already set in stone, i.e., black or white. So, as we can see, there really is no gray; and gray is an excuse or often confused with ignorance or lack of precognition.

However, even the ability of precognition isn't outside the grasp of humans, because one cannot disconnect cause and effect, or the rational progression of each event or decision. Here's a simple example: On a sunny day one can't light a match and drop it on a forest floor that hasn't seen rain or snow in 12-months then expect rain to fall as soon as the lit match hits the forest floor. In fact, I'd guess that most people would say that the most highly likely outcome is that the forest will be ablaze shortly after the lit match is dropped. Another example, one can expect joy and happiness to emanate from a couple that love each other when they have their first baby after many years of trying.

Like these simple examples, there is a cause and effect that cannot be easily disconnected and a logical progression that cannot be easily disrupted. Every progression, and I mean every progression, has a cause and effect. The problem is that for most things that are important to predict, it is difficult to predict what will happen because it involves a lot of people and their history and Six Pillars or it involves predicting the course of natural phenomenon, which are influenced by extremely high number of factors and variables. However, if we could accurately track all these factors, we may be able to predict the future with a high degree of accuracy. Regardless, we are very far away from getting there, so it isn't worthwhile talking about it today.

So getting back to the point, the world is black and white, but people want to make it gray, because it's easier for people to live that way, since no absolutes mean that anything can be justified. Of course this means that one is also never wrong, and can do almost anything that they like and be justified in doing so. However, this is not reality and there are basic principles that we have to all abide by because that is the way the world actually works.

Some of the basic principles of how the world functions and how we should all think about the world doesn't ever change. Some of these resolute principles are:

1) Justice is the only fair pursuit for any intelligent entity, and, eventually, Justice will prevail,
2) therefore, there are no free lunches,
3) equality isn't always Just, but Justice, applied equally, is always fair,
4) for every action, there is an equal and opposite reaction,
5) logic is everything,
6) the universe is black and white,
7) blind faith is death, but real faith is life,
8) you cannot have your cake and eat it too,
9) a lie is a lie is a lie is a lie,
10) stealing is stealing is stealing is stealing,
11) intentions are only as good as the results,
12) the means and the ends must be consistent for any act to be Just,
13) the universe has a way of self-correcting, which means that karma is a real bitch,
14) time is a concept of man,
15) what is is,
16) beauty is really only skin deep,
17) most physically beautiful, superficial and pretentious people are like shit painted in gold,

18) it isn't what you are, how you look, what you own or what you do but who you are (your Six Pillars) that defines any individual and makes someone a winner or a loser,

19) jast because we all die in the long-run, it doesn't mean that we have to commit suicide in the short-run or plan only for the short-run,

20) when it comes to human endeavor and preference, very few things aren't "normal,"

21) history DOES repeat itself, but not exactly the same way,

22) there are absolute and inalienable rights that must not, cannot, and should not be abridged, negated, circumvented, taken away or voted on, ever,

23) majority vote and results aren't always right and there are certain rights that should not, cannot, and must not be subject to any kind of voting such as absolute and inalienable rights,

24) true respect cannot be bought, only earned; and it takes a life time to build and only a moment to destroy,

25) long-term, wealth cannot be generated from theft, it can only be created from ingenuity and hard work,

26) there are no short cuts in life that are good for anyone,

27) if one plays today, one will pay tomorrow,

28) the use of money and exercise of power is neither inherently good nor bad, but reflects the Six Pillars of the person who spends it or wields it,

29) in our country, we deserve the government that we have, because our government is of the people, by the people, for the people,

30) force should only be used in response to force,

31) in a democratic society, the forced imposition of ones beliefs on others is the ultimate evil,

32) honesty has a way of being rewarded; it may not be rewarded in the short-run and it may not come in the form that one expected, but it will be rewarded,

33) when righting the wrong, the longer one waits to do so, the more difficult it becomes to correct the wrong, and the more pain one will suffer to correct it,

34) when righting the wrong, the pain that must be endured is the reflection of how depraved the wrong really was,

35) if we solve for the short-term, we will find that we will continuously have to solve for the short-term,

36) beginnings and endings are also a man-made concept,

37) insanity is truly doing the same thing over and over again, and expecting a different result.

These principles may not always be obvious and may not always happen when one expects it to, but this is where faith has to come into play – real faith. One has to have real faith and believe in the basics, and never forget that time is a concept of man, not inherently part of the universe. And, don't succumb to the temptation of short-term gains, because one will have to pay for it later.

By living the virtuous life that I've outlined, I think people will find that it has a very strong positive long-term effect on one's life, but the short-term will be tumultuous. The most painful part will be coping with one's friends and loved ones. Because, what I've outlined here is not easy to implement, so one's friends and loved ones will be the most difficult to win over. In the long-run, one's friends will be more problematic to deal with than a person's loved ones. The good news is that people will find out who their real friends are, but the bad news (good news in the long-run) is that they'll lose a lot of their so called friends. However, if one truly makes the transformation and, they stick with it, one may find that the new friends that they make are well worth it. As one goes through this transformation, one will find that one's quality of life may sour quickly, dramatically and quite detrimentally in the near term, but then over time one will find that it improves steadily and the long-term effect will most likely greatly improve the quality of one's life.

Don't forget, the world will be against adopting my philosophy and people attempting to make the change will feel the temptation of taking the easy way out, but if one succumbs to this temptation, they will find that they will constantly have to fight the same fight over and over again. Ultimately, this is why solving for the short-term is so bad. However, for the moment, it is the easier way to live, there's no doubt about it. And, since the vast majority of Americans live for the short-term, one may find oneself thinking, "I'm normal," but in reality "normal" is meaningless. What matters is being right. But once again looking for good or bad, right or wrong, black or white is difficult and tiring, even though it is the right thing to do. So, what do most people do? Most people convince themselves that the world is gray, and they try to convince others the world is gray too.

Furthermore, if one succeeds and one does convince oneself and the rest of the world there is no good versus bad, right versus wrong, and black versus white, one can easily justify any act and do anything and not be wrong, immoral, bad or evil. This makes life a lot easier in everyone's mind. And, this is the primary reason why people **want the world to be gray**, because if the world is gray, it is a lot easier to live life. What people don't realize is that this may be good for them in the short-run, but in the long-run it is poison. This is no different than being addicted to tobacco or alcohol or taking illicit drugs like cocaine, heroin, angel dust, PCP, crack or some other illicit drugs; one may feel much better for a couple of hours when they take it, but in the long-run, it's a pretty good way of critically messing-up one's life or ultimately killing others or getting killed.

So, why is it so poisonous? It sounds good: One can never be wrong and everything one does can be justified. If one lives alone then that's fine, but the problem is that no one really lives by themselves. Think about why solving for the short-term is a problem when living in a society: If everyone sees what they do as being right, because anything can be justified, people will never come to agreement on anything. We cannot have a civil society if everyone believes what they believe-in, think and do are all moral, good and right, while everyone else's thinking and behavior is immoral, bad and wrong, and, most importantly, we cannot get to any conclusions, because there are no absolutes. The image of the gray society that I portrayed should feel familiar to everyone in the US, because it is the society that we are living in today. People always trying to assert their rights over everyone else's, people always trying to "win," people always acting from insecurity, people not respecting common courtesy (talking loud, drawing attention to themselves, acting boisterously, disrespecting each other, et cetera), people always trying to get the upper hand, people always trying to get one over on someone else, people trying to prove that they are better than others, people not knowing how to view the world other than through superficial and pretentious measures, people always looking to put down or belittle other people, et cetera. By now, we should all be sick to our stomachs and looking to change our country for the better. The fact that people talk about it, but that it hasn't happened is a negative testimony about our society. This makes me very sad and disappointed.

The thing is, even if the world is gray, we should all live life like it is black and white, but with an open mind and respect other people's opinions as long as they are rational and Just. If everyone does this it will lead to long-term harmony and civility, because we will all be able to understand what is truly right versus wrong, good versus bad and moral versus immoral. However, conflicts and turmoil may arise in the near-term, but this is the price that we, as a society, have to pay for the centuries of philosophical mismanagement in order to get to a more utopian society. Also, eventually, as bad opinions, immoral thoughts and actions, and evil is identified and rooted out of our society, we will achieve a far more consistent philosophical foundation that the vast, overwhelming majority can subscribe to which leads to a far more harmonious society and a better place to live in.

However, without the friendly, respectful and constructive conflicts that right versus wrong, good versus bad, moral versus evil and black versus white brings to our society, we can never reach the harmonious and utopian society that we all dream of. So, again, regardless of whether one thinks the world is black and white or gray, we must live like it's black and white, and convince others that they should too. As long as we all behave with civility, listen to rational and Just opinions, don't give even the semblance of credibility to arguments that are not rational and Just, and, most of all, continue to learn, people will find that the world that evolves from living a black and white life is far better than the one we are living in today.

What retarded jackass invented the saying, "Money is the root of all evil!?"

I really pity the idiots who go around saying that money is the root of all evil and have real doubts about those who actually believe in the saying in terms of both their psychological and intellectual capacities. These are probably the same idiots who likely think that guns should be abolished to prevent murders, like there were no murders before the invention of guns! Whether it is money or guns or any other inanimate object, inanimate objects cannot and do not have its own thoughts, do not talk, do not act alone and do not have any characteristics of humans, despite what people may have seen in the Disney movie the Beauty and the Beast!

Anyway, guns and other **inanimate objects are only tools** and, at best (and it's stretching the thought), they can only take on the moral characteristics of its owner. For example, if money is spent by morally upstanding humans then money will seem like it is taking on the characteristics of strong positive morals (e.g., charitable donations, helping victims of natural disasters, awarding diligent and productive workers, et cetera), while money spent by immoral people would seem like money takes on the characteristics of strong negative morals (e.g., blackmail money, payment for bribes, assassinations, funding illegal and immoral activities, et cetera). This is at best the only way to tie morality to money.

When explained this way, people can't disagree, but they still cannot get away from the thought that money is somehow evil. So, when I drill down on this issue, people don't really believe money is evil, but they believe that *money makes people do bad things to acquire it.* This is why people say that money is evil. But even if people think that money makes humans behave badly to acquire it, it is still clear to me that people are doing the evil, people are immoral and people are the ones who talk and act.

So, to make the phrase correct, we should say that people are the root of all evil – this seems so obvious. Then that begs the question: What makes people evil? As previously stated, what makes people who they are are their Six Pillars, i.e., their moral character, value system, ethics, integrity, sense of honor and honesty. So, what makes people evil are their reprehensive moral code, bankrupt value system, appalling ethics, woefully lacking integrity, and completely corrupt or lacking sense of honesty and honor. Then, the next question that has to be asked is where people get their Six Pillars from. It seems obvious that everyone gets it from parents, friends, teachers, relatives, politicians, and generally, from society. And, in our society, our Six Pillars stem from religious teachings; specifically, in North America and Europe, from judeo-christian (jc) philosophy. So, if the end result of jc philosophical teachings in our society is that the country's Six Pillars are extremely screwed up, this is a very serious rebuke and condemnation of the judeo-christian philosophy. More to the point, over a 5,000 year period the moral fiber of the world hasn't changed much, if any, and, if anything, it has gotten worse in many ways. And, given that most of the world's Six Pillars emanate from religious teachings, it doesn't paint a flattering picture of religion.

Some of the more clever (different from intelligent; jast to make it clear, when I say clever it's not a flattering or complimentary term) people have said to me that it's not the jc religious teachings that are evil, but the people who twist the teachings to fit what they want out of it, so ultimately, it is the people not the jc religious teachings that are evil. Like I said, it is a clever argument. But let me ask this question: How do people form the basis of their thoughts that eventually lead them to evil behavior? Because, the argument that these clever people are making is that the jc religious teachings are being manipulated by bad or evil people, and that the jc religious teachings are themselves being manipulated and are being abused by these bad people. So, if that's the case, how do these people become bad in the first place? Isn't it because of their Six Pillars? So, then where do people get their Six Pillars to start off with? Go back to the previous paragraph.

So, again, this example shows how decrepit jc religious teachings really are. So, to utter the absolute truth we should say that the root of all evil, at least in this country and Europe, is jc religious teachings and philosophy. I can see and hear the outrage and bitterness already. Some of the more clever people are arguing that even if evil people get their Six Pillars from jc religious philosophy, there are many aspects of the jc religious teachings that are benevolent and of the highest moral character and value, which should compel everyone to respect, if not adopt, its philosophy. Furthermore, these clever people will argue that such blanket statements about jc religion is not only an affront and insult to the respectability and dignity of the people that believe in the jc religious teachings, but also highly disrespectful of their god.

So, let's examine what people mean by the benevolence of the jc religious teachings. The core, the heart, the center, the bull's eye, the cream of the cream of the jc religious teachings comes down to one concept and one concept alone: Blind love or universal love. Ultimately, after hours and hours of arguments, most people hang their hat on universal love as the ultimate power, attraction, benevolence, and righteousness of the jc religious teachings. This is what makes the jc religious fanatics – actually lunatics in my view – adhere so fervently to the jc religious philosophy. They talk about how beautiful blind love is and how empowering it is and how wonderful it is to blindly love all, et cetera, et cetera.

However, oddly enough, my argument is that blind love or universal love is what makes the jc religious philosophy so dangerous, so offensive, so ridiculous and, ultimately, so evil. After a period of denial, shock and anger, ultimately, the final argument that is thrown in my face is: "You don't understand, because you don't have faith." Most people are nodding and applauding that someone finally put me in my place. Please, don't hold your breath!

judaism/christianity

Religion, specifically, the judeo/christian (jc) religion is the root of all evil, at least in the western world

Let me reiterate and reemphasize my previous paradigm in the open, upfront and in crystal clear language: *THE JC RELIGION IS A MANMADE CONCEPT, IT IS A FANTASY AND A FIGMENT OF SOME PEOPLE'S VERY GOOD IMAGINATION FROM SEVERAL THOUSANDS OF YEARS AGO, IS A DANGERIOUS AND ADDICTIVE DRUG BY DELIBERATE DESIGN, IS A DESTROYER OF MINDS AND SOCIETIES, AND POTENTIALLY THE #1 ROOT CAUSE OF HUMANITY'S FUTURE DESTRUCTION, AND, IN CASE THE MESSAGE ISN'T LOUD AND CLEAR, I ABHOR, DESPISE, AND HAVE NO RESPECT FOR IT, AND HAVE GREAT "SYMPATHIES" FOR THE PEOPLE THAT TRULY BELIEVE IN THE JC GOD.*

Here we go again! I can hear the hollering and howling, the death threats and the murderous intentions. Where do I start?! If one understands that the underpinnings of societal and national behavior is based on individual actions, at least in democracies, and that individual behaviors are controlled by their philosophical underpinnings then it's not difficult to say that for the last 15-20 or so centuries the main driver of western philosophical thinking and resultant behavior has been and continues to be judeo/christian moral philosophy. However, the truth of the matter is that we don't even need jc philosophical underpinnings in our thinking in any way shape or form to construct, support and live in a peaceful and harmonious society. In fact, we have a lot to gain if we drop all semblances of jc religious teachings and adopt a more Just, sane, ideal and rational philosophical underpinning such as the one I present in this book. The key and the important factor is that we would actually become far better people without jc philosophical underpinnings, if we replace it with my philosophical construct. I know it's hard for most people to believe, so let the arguments begin.

First, shall we talk about how many people have died throughout history in the name of christianity, because of christianity or due to christians? Due to a severe lack of historical perspective, people in this country fail to realize that the greatest threat to world peace that we face today – Middle-East conflicts – has roots in the christian crusades of the medieval times. Since then, countless have died due to conflicts in the Middle-East. In addition, numerous people have died through inquisitions, persecutions and poor guidance/leadership. If nothing else, the number of great scientific minds that have been killed, ostracized, censored or "exiled" because of their discoveries (Copernicus, Galileo, Darwin, etc.) that proved the bible wrong should be enough to convince people to finally turn away from christianity. People have tried to argue that these decrepit behaviors are acts of men, not of god, so I shouldn't condemn christiantiy. However, upon closer scrutiny, I think it will be obvious that this argument is really stupid. According to ALL christians everything that we do is the will of the jc god. So, if that's the case, how can evil acts be the act of anyone but the jc god? It seems that when it comes to bad results, jc faithfuls claim it may or may not be the jc god's will (this is contradictory), but if it is the jc god's will and we don't understand it, it means that there is a hidden agenda that the jc god doesn't deem necessary for us to know, so we mustn't blame the jc god, take its name in vain, blaspheme or otherwise judge, because we cannot divine the intent of the jc god. The first time I heard this argument I was stunned into silence because of the sheer fantasy, self-deceptive nature, stupidity and self-contradictory nature of the argument.   Since then I've learned to enjoy destroying this ridiculous argument.

What's really interesting is that such hypocrisy would not even pass muster with a logical and rational six year old, yet, jc faithful make ridiculous statements such as those mentioned in the previous paragraph as if those statements are indisputable logic and fact! If such self-deception and level of self-hypnosis wasn't so dangerous, it would be comical! Anyone with a semblance of reason would recognize how stupid jews/christians sound in this matter. How can anyone claim that all acts are the will of god then turn around and say that some acts aren't or actually are the will of satan, and do so with a straight face? Such statements should strike any half intelligent human being as being highly self-contradictory and highly nonsensical. To boot, if we are incapable of divining the jc god's will then we have no way of knowing what is the will of the jc god or an act of satan. If people used this kind of logic in business or scientific research their contemporaries would laugh and ridicule them into poverty. I'm sure words like stupid, idiotic, pathetic, retarded, or moronic would be freely voiced to describe these people. I would also venture to guess that most people would think that the people who voice such incomprehensible and irrational sentences are incapable of thinking.

What makes this contradiction so amusing is that jews/christians routinely contradict themselves without knowing that they are doing so and talk about the matter with exquisite sincerity. Think about it: On the one hand, jc believers are saying that all good things are the will of the jc god, but on the other hand all bad things are the will of satan. If that's the case then the jc god really can't be the master of the universe – the alpha and the omega – that they think it is. In fact, it is impossibility. The people that believe in the jc religion need to make up their minds: Is the jc god the master of the universe or isn't it?! If it is then it is making people do bad things, and therefore accountable for people's bad behavior and if it isn't then it is really not the master of the universe. And, if the jc god is truly not the master of the universe then there is absolutely no reason to justify following its teachings. And, if it is making people do bad things then, again, there is absolutely no reason to follow the evil that is the jc god. But that aside, I will show you that the fundamental teachings of the jc religious philosophy – their cornerstone – is very evil.

But let's start with why the jc god cannot exist, because this is where it all starts and begins to explain why the jc religion is the root of all evil, at least in the western world. The answer to the question of whether or not the jc god actually exists or doesn't exist is: *THE MASS OF THE UNIVERSE IS CONSTANT.* Let me repeat that. *THE MASS OF THE UNIVERSE IS CONSTANT.* Most are wondering what one has to do with the other.

Let's start with a basic scientific fact. If something has constant mass, it cannot be destroyed and could not have been created. This means that the universe has existed forever and will continue to exist forever, i.e., it absolutely could not have been created and cannot be ended. This means that the bible is not only wrong about the beginning of the earth, but also that of the universe. Don't forget, time is a concept of man. So, how do we explain the existence of the bible? Simple: Like any western religion, judaism/christianity is the creation of very smart men during their times and their need to explain how we came about and why we exist, so that they could use this "divine" insight as a basis to rule the populace. Also, why is it that all other religions are pagan and fantasy, while judaism/christianity is the word of a singular universal reality? Didn't all of the believers in these so called other pagan religions absolutely believe that their gods and their version of reality were absolutely true? So, why are the pagans wrong and the jews/christians right? There is absolutely no proof that pagans were wrong while the jews/christians are right, nor vice-versa. Yet, jews/christians laugh at the gullibility and stupidity of the pagans' beliefs. To me, this is one of the reasons why the jewish/christian religion and their believers are so puzzling. They use reasoning, scrutiny, logic, and *literal interpretations* of the pagan religions' beliefs to discredit those beliefs, while holding out faith, and figurative and subjective interpretations of the bible to defend the equally nonsensical, capricious and fairy-tale like (and not even benevolent or morally good) nature of their own religion!

Let me get down to some brass tacks, as they say. Take a look at the evolution of the interpretation of the bible. The bible's integrity, which was held as absolute truth for centuries, started to unravel in earnest as absolute truth with Nicolas Copernicus (of the fame that "earth is not the center of the universe") in 1543. This was followed-up by Galileo Galilei who confirmed Copernicus' discoveries through direct observations in 1610, further weakening the integrity of the bible in the literal sense. Since then, most of the assertions made by the bible about the creation of the universe and the past were proven to be dead wrong. So, what does the judeo/christian hierarchy come up with? "No, no, no, no, no, you can't take the bible literally, it is meant to be taken figuratively. The key point to note is that despite the fact that the earth is not the center of the universe, jast understand that whatever the composition of the universe, god is the creator, the all-knowing, the all-present and all-powerful and the most benevolent being." But, we know that this is delusional given that the universe was not created, not to mention the ridiculous contradiction of everything being the jc god's will.

Again, the "magic" of judaism/christianity is that every time that scientific evidence proved that the literal translation of the bible was dead wrong, jewish/christian hierarchy came up with excuses, the most conniving being that, "oh, no, no, no, the bible was never meant to be translated literally; it should be interpreted or taken figuratively!" This, despite the fact that for centuries the jewish/christian hierarchy preached the bible as being the only and absolute truth to be taken 100% literally. Well, of course, this is very convenient. What's very galling about this is that jewish/christian believers judge every other religion based on literal translation of the other religions' beliefs and utter such nonsense like "what you say is what you should be judged by," but not when it comes to the bible. Again, this is very hypocritical and very obnoxious, but very convenient for the jewish/christian construct, and a slick way to avoid the truth.

Don't forget, if everything is subject to interpretation with no final determination possible then anything can be interpreted any which way to be twisted to fit what one wants to say, which is exactly what the jewish/christian hierarchy does to make the excuse for their irrational beliefs and preaching. This is all fine and dandy – I couldn't care less about what they do or don't do, or believe-in or don't believe-in – but then the jews/christians use their religious philosophy to impose their Six Pillars on **everyone**. They do so by taking their jc religious beliefs and spawning political and social ideologies that they implement and force **everyone** to abide by whether it is right or wrong, good or bad, moral or immoral. Many of these ideologies involve stealing money from the wealthy to carry out what they believe is the right act for humanity without giving us any choice in the matter. The jc faithful then use the excuse that the majority voted for it so the wealthier people must be **forced to** spend their money the way the majority wants to spend it. Then, if the wealthy protest, the jc believers accuse the wealthy of being not only undemocratic and selfish – imagine that being accused of being selfish for wanting to spend our money our way – but then tell the wealthy, "if you don't like it, you should convince other people to vote against the socialist policies." Never mind the fact that there are rights that should not be subject to a vote, they know that the majority will never vote down what favors them in the short-term, so they can say with confidence that so called "social programs" should be put to a vote. It is because of such ridiculousness that judeo-christians espouse that I'm so insistent that everyone learn how to think for the long-term and behave more rationally. Anyway, the point is that the majority of the populations' behavior is bullying at best and, in reality, downright tyrannical – in this case, a tyranny of the masses.

The idea espoused by these jewish/christian faithful and liberals/socialists that is absolutely unforgiveable is that they accuse the wealthy of carrying out class warfare! This is extremely galling because I am the one trying to defend myself from thieves and pickpockets that are trying to forcibly separate me from my wealth and defend against the class warfare started by the jewish/christian faithful and liberals/socialists decades, if not, centuries ago. These people are trying to take away our freedom of choice and steal our money to perpetuate their ideology of "helping" the poor, and, yet, they accuse us of starting class warfare, when they have been waging class warfare for decades, if not, centuries! This is very twisted, repulsive and reprehensible. One would have to be very twisted, repulsive and reprehensible to accuse others of what they started.

Regardless, my thesis for how the bible came about and how judaism/christianity came about is simple. It was invented by some smart people – for their times – to try and impose law and order on the people that they governed. If one views it this way then the existence of the bible and this version of paganism makes preeminent sense. In fact, I propose that all western religions were invented by men to not only try to explain the existence of man, but also to allow the elite group of religious leaders that "know" the word of their version of god(s) to govern their community with authority of this alleged god(s). Not really all that difficult to understand the existence of any religion, if one jast calmly thinks about it.

In the particular case of judaism/christianity, the most evil and malicious aspect of the religion is the invention of god and the omnipresent, omnipotent and omniscient aspect of this invented character who, conveniently, is invisible and always absent. What makes this the most devious of inventions is that the will of god has to be interpreted, precisely because it (god) is invisible, but still omnipresent, omnipotent and omniscient, making it the single entity in the universe that controls everything, sometimes. So, who gets to interpret the will of the so called jc god? You got it: The priests – when I talk about priests, I include rabbis, friars, monks, padres, ministers, and all manners of preachers of the jewish/christian faith (actually, absolutely *blind faith*) – bishops, cardinals, and ultimately the pope. If people believe that absolute power corrupts absolutely then there is no question that these people were absolutely powerful and, history shows, often very corrupt. The vatican is one of the most wealthiest nations in the world, and the amount of art treasurers, historical artifacts and other priceless items are too numerous to count. And, we will never know how many children were sexually molested and abused by the clergy, and the vatican cover-up made it that much worse. The absence of condemnation during World War 2 in regards to the holocaust was also despicable. The religious persecutions of scientists for proving that the bible could not be reality is also reprehensible, not to mention the crusades, the inquisitions, the interventions in the course of history, condemnation of non-traditional sexual preferences, opposition to pro-choice, same sex marriages, among other acts were and are also despicable. If anyone wants to know how much absolute power can corrupt and what negative effects it has on society, jast study the history of christianity.

One of the most galling things about the christian hierarchy and leadership is the level of opulence that they possess, especially at the vatican. What's galling about this is that judging by the ever increasing opulence and wealth, apparently, not very much of the church's wealth has been given away; this despite their admonition for everyone else to give away their wealth, make sacrifices and be charitable. Also, given their preaching about the virtue of living a modest life, there sure are a lot of wealthy priests, preachers, etc. I've seen too many so called pious people driving around in expensive cars and living in very plush residences. Even more offensive is how they talk about the homeless and how we should all help, yet the amount of real estate the jewish/christian religion owns in each city in this country is staggering. If they took even half of all that real estate and used their wealth to build condominiums for the homeless then homelessness would end, at least in this country. Even then, the jewish/christian leadership would have enough wealth left over to continue to lead opulent life styles. So, instead of thinking about how to steal more from the wealthy, the jc religious hierarchy ought to think about how to use their own wealth to carry out their beliefs instead of imposing their will on everyone else and using everyone else's wealth to enrich themselves and be generous to the poor. Despite the obvious contradictory behavior of the church, it will never do the right thing. The reason why this will never happen is because it isn't about the poor, it's about controlling and moving the populace to do what the jc religious hierarchy wants the masses to do. In other words, it's about power and control, and power and control is wealth and wealth is power and control.

This aside, the other malevolent aspect pertaining to the invention of the jc god is that it helped a very few select men to control the general populace by taking independent thought away from the masses and forcing the people to abide by the will of the few that "know" how to "interpret the will" of the supposedly omnipresent, omnipotent and omniscient being. So, how did the few disarm the many, so effectively, and convincingly? Most don't have to be convinced too strenuously: A few fairy tales is enough. But there are some more rational minds that need a few more tricks than mere fairy tales. So, the evil minds came up with a trick to convince the rational mind that god must exist. The way they did this was to abuse logic and science. Here's how one of the more effective traps work that was invented in the 20th-century: Agree or disagree: Something cannot be created from nothing. Of course, a rational mind would agree. Next, they use evolution theory to deliver the coup-de-grace: If the big bang is the supposed start of the universe – the presumption is that there has to be a start and an end to everything, which obviously doesn't need to be the case, but almost everyone in the world instinctively believes that everything has to have a start and an end – and something cannot be created from nothing then where did the material for the big bang come from? The obvious answer, according to this evil deception, is that it must have come from the jc god. Therefore, even evolution is actually the work of god and the story of creation in the bible is jast a shortened and simplified version of this process. Therefore, to the perpetrators of this evil the connection between the bible and science goes this way: Given that the bible is interpretable, god is absolute, and the science is correct and rational, it must be that god started the big bang to create the universe. Pretty clever, isn't it?

Well, as I mentioned before, the science shows that the mass of the universe is constant. If that is the case then the universe couldn't have been created and cannot be destroyed. However, if that's the case then how does the big bang fit in? I haven't heard or read a good explanation of this, but my guess is that the *current form* of the universe started with the big bang and this one was one of an infinite number of big bangs that have occurred in the past and will continue to occur in the future, perhaps each bang occurring trillions of years apart. Then the next question that needs to be asked is how and why do these big bangs occur? In my theory, the science of how this cycle of big bangs occurs is more intricate. Apparently, the universe is in movement, specifically, accelerating or decelerating away from the center of the big bang. This means that at some point the universe will stop moving then do the opposite, which is to say that it should contract. What would cause the universe to stop moving then contracting isn't obvious, but my guess is gravity or some other force that we have not yet discovered. For argument sake, let's say that it is gravity for now. This means that gravity will eventually pull the universe inward and back towards the center where the big bang occurred. At some point thereafter, the mass concentrated at the center of the universe would be so large that it would start to repel each other and blow up, creating the next big bang, et cetera at infinitum. Bottom-line is that the big bang, as we know it, is only the beginning of this iteration of the universe, and is jast one of an infinite number to have occurred in the past and will occur in the future.

Please note that this theory is not originally mine but gotten second hand from a friend who got it second hand from someone else, and where that person got this theory is unknown. So, why do I call it *my* theory? Because now I own this knowledge, and I believe it, therefore it is my theory, the origins of which I don't know, and at this point, don't need to know.

If Adam and Eve were truly our sole ancestors then most people would be genetically very defective and mankind would not have survived

Think about how retarded the concept that one male and one female are the only two ancestors of ALL mankind. Do people realize that if Adam and Eve were the only two ancestors of mankind – of ALL mankind – by the time we got to the third generation of mankind, we'd all be retarded, genetically defective or otherwise handicapped? This means that the likely chance of mankind surviving by the time we got to the fourth generation would be very, very low. We would either be mentally incapable of surviving or physically impaired or both. Any species that tried to start their society with jast one male and one female of the species is doomed to extinction, yet man has survived and burgeoned. This likely points to the fact that mankind did not and could not have come from jast one male and one female.

Therefore, the concept that Adam and Eve were the only ancestors to mankind is ridiculously impossible. Yet the judeo/christian faithful continue to believe that we are ALL descended from jast one male and one female. This is one of the most retarded – excuse the pun – beliefs of the jc fairy tale.

The lunacy and the contradiction in the judeo/christian philosophical construct is laughable and so plainly obvious that even a reasonably intelligent grade school child should be able to point them out, if they haven't been previously brain-washed by the judeo/christian faithful. Yet most adults in America can't see how stupid they are in believing in the judeo/christian philosophy. What's more damaging to our future is that most Americans continue to preach – actually force – this highly poisonous philosophical construct to their children continually perpetuating the evil.

One of the main reasons for why people don't/can't think is because of this perpetual continuation of the judeo/christian philosophical construct from one generation to the next. Young minds tend to be and want to be logical and rational. But, given the self-contradictory and ludicrous nature of the philosophical construct combined with the forced preaching, it is no wonder that children stop trying to think. Essentially, parents "beat" the rationality and the logical mindset out of their children. Since parents can't explain the inconsistencies and ludicrous nature of the philosophy, they force the child to abandon reason and jast believe. And, children learn that to think is to suffer. So, they stop thinking. There is no mystery as to why our society is chock full of people who don't/can't/won't think. This is one of the main evils of the judeo/christian philosophical construct: The judeo/christian hierarchy want people who don't think, because it makes it easier for the jc hierarchy to rule common people's lives and get away with the contradictory nature of their philosophy. If people don't question and jast obey, it makes it very easy for the jc hierarchy to rule. This is what they ultimately want: Blind obedience. Evil, very, very evil.

This is exactly why we need people to learn how to think, so they can stand up to this type of assault on intellect, humanity and individual rights. The reader should now start to understand why judaism/christianity is the root of all evil in the western world.

The decay of morality in any western society is the inevitable result of judeo-christian (jc) religious teaching/preaching; it could not have resulted from anything else

I largely covered this before, but I want to expand on it and cover it in more detail, because I think it is a subject that is very important. When the bible was widely believed to be the actual word of the judeo/christian god, the bible was taken literally. The bible preached that god created the universe in six days and took the seventh day off. By logical inference, people assumed that since it took pretty much 5 days to create the earth and only 1 to create the rest of the universe, people assumed that the earth was the center of the universe. Furthermore, stars were jast small specks of lights in the sky. We now know better, because scientists – at great peril to their own lives due to religious persecution – have shown us reality.

Therefore, as genius and insightful scientists such as Galileo and Copernicus started to show that the bible could not be true, at first, the people in charge of the judeo/christian religion persecuted the scientists and tried to wipe out the knowledge that proved that the bible could not be reality. However, like any group that is discredited, to survive, it had to evolve and adapt to the changing realities. So, at some point, religious leaders started talking about the stories in the bible as figurative and interpretive and not literal. This was one of the cleverest tricks, confidence-jobs, deceptions, cover-ups, or smoke-and-mirror shows ever perpetrated on mankind.

This figurative interpretation of the bible actually made it a lot easier for the heads of the judeo/christian philosophy to assert more control and consolidate power than ever before. This was made possible by the fact that the need to interpret the bible gave birth to the notion that the average person needed interpreters. Who better than the clergy to interpret the bible? Or, so the sell job goes. This allowed the jc leadership to exert more control over the life of the people, because now people needed more guidance than ever before since the bible needed interpreting, which meant that the jc god's will also needed interpreting; very clever indeed.

The problem is that with interpretation comes the challenge of consistency. Meaning, the problem with lying isn't the act of lying itself, but keeping track of which lie was told to whom. And, as more and more people travel and hear different versions of the same story, it becomes impossible to maintain fealty to the church. Once again, the jc philosophy found itself at a crossroads. So, what was the solution? Further evolution of the lie, of course. This time it would be Martin Luther who comes to the rescue of the jc construct.

Since the inconsistencies of the catholic preaching became laughable, Martin Luther decided to create his own version of the jc god's will. This is how the jc construct survived yet another major crisis that would have otherwise destroyed the jc philosophy. In the beginning, the vatican was furious, because of the perceived usurpation of the catholic church's singular authority over the interpretation of the jc god's will. However, over time, as the so called protestant movement grew, eventually the catholic church slowly but surely began to accept the protestant movement; it didn't have much of a choice. And, today, we see the catholic church looking to align itself with the rest of the jc movements, including the jewish and protestant religions. What the historical progression of the judeo-christian construct illustrates is that if nothing else it is very adaptable and flexible. And, I think this is the best that anyone can say about the jc religious construct.

Over the centuries, to survive and continue to maintain a semblance of credibility of the fantasy that is the jc god, the jc complex has adapted to the scientific evidence that continues to prove that the existence of the jc god is impossible. And, the reason why we continue to have faithful servants and vassals of the jc philosophy is because of two main reasons: 1) people don't think, and 2) people don't care about perspective; meaning they have no historical knowledge or context. They are only taught that which is relevant to the jc organization today. They are not taught that the jc organization faced survival threatening crises over the centuries, which were overcome by usurping the truth and adapting itself to new realities.

Now, the latest usurpation of scientific fact is that even the Big Bang is not outside of the teachings of the jc beliefs. Remember the jc complex railed against evolution, railed against the Big Bang theory and railed against every new scientific discovery that was ever made when these discoveries first presented themselves to the world and absolutely and unequivocally destroyed the beliefs held as absolute truths by the jc complex. However, as the scientific evidence became overwhelming, the jc organization found ways to invent new deceptions to adapt to reality and maintain relevancy in the public's eye.

As an example, the original interpretation of the bible is that god created all the creatures that we see today. But when Darwin proved that the creatures we see today evolved from other creatures that were present from millions, if not billions of years ago the jc hierarchy first denied Darwin's absolutely factual scientific discoveries. Then, over time, realizing that their denials were going to look foolish to the greater public, and continued insistence on the validity of the bible's version of how animals came about in the world (including humans) was incontrovertibly retarded, the jc hierarchy came up with the next iteration of the fantasy. In this next iteration of the lie, the jc hierarchy tries to claim that even evolution is not incongruent to the biblical story that the jc god created all creatures on earth. This iteration of the fantasy claims that the jc god provided the materials for the Big Bang, which then started off the universe, including earth, and, like humans that were given free will, the universe was left alone by the jc god to grow and develop freely. Therefore, according to the new fantasy of the jc complex, the idea that the jc god created all creatures is not incongruent to the story in their book of genesis, because the jc god provided the materials necessary for the Big Bang. However, the problem with this new iteration of the jc-organization's fantasy is that it fails to explain how something can be created, if there could not have been anything to create to begin with.

The problem with the jc complex's fantasy that its god created the universe is that the universe could not have been created to begin with. This is ultimately why I say that the question to ask isn't whether the jc god does or does not exist, but whether it is even possible for the jc god to exist. Meaning, if the jc teachings is to have any credibility whatsoever, it has to be able to prove the following point:

- That its god created the universe.

The jc complex's entire credibility rests on this one singular point. Here's why. According to the hierarchy and leadership of the jc complex, since its god created the universe, it is the master of that universe. Therefore, if its god is the master of the universe then we, as its creation, must obey its will; much like children obeying their parents.

However, if it can be proven that the jc god could not have created the universe than the claim to its mastery falls to pieces and, therefore, the need to believe in its existence, let alone seek out its will and obey it, becomes laughable.

So, how do we, if at all, disprove that the jc god created the universe? Again, because the mass of the universe is constant, this means that the universe could not have been created. Said in a more simple and elegant manner: THERE IS NO BEGINNING AND NO END TO THE UNIVERSE. If the mass of the universe is constant, it can never be destroyed and it cannot have been created. Think about it from a much more simplified perspective. Take a cube of steel or even diamond. Left alone, it will eventually decompose and disappear. It may take a few billion years to do so, but it will decompose. However, if something doesn't decompose and stays constant then that means that it will last forever, i.e., exist into infinity. By definition, if it has an infinite life going forward then the life span of that object is infinite going back as well, and by definition infinity has no beginning or an end. Therefore, this means that the universe could not have been created and that its existence is infinite. However, this doesn't prohibit the universe from changing form, which it seems to do occasionally.

The other irrefutable conclusion to note about this fact is that if there is no end then there cannot be a judgment day either. Another reason for why we don't need to follow the jc god's will, even if it exists. If there is no judgment day then we don't need to be afraid of his judgment. A minor point since there isn't a jc god anyway.

Some people have asked me the following very interesting question: If the universe was not created and existed forever in time, how do we balance this fact with the Big Bang theory. This is where science comes into play. Scientific evidence indicates that the Big Bang is a certainty; meaning that it actually happened. Supposedly, scientists have tracked the origin of the Big Bang to within fractions of a second of the initial blast. Married to the fact that the universe is in accelerating or decelerating movement (it doesn't matter which way it's going), I believe that the Big Bang, as we know it, was the start of the *current form* of the universe, and that it is but one of an infinite number of Big Bangs that occurred throughout the infinite history of the universe.

Another interesting revelation about science is that it has established numerous irrefutable facts about the universe. One of these irrefutable facts is that both the universe and the earth is well more than 5,000 years old, yet I've met people who believe that the bible's timeline, which puts the earth and the universe at only 5,000 years old, is the undeniable truth. To these people, the science is wrong. How amazing is that?! I couldn't believe my ears!

Regardless, the universe could not have been created; this is an irrefutable scientific fact. This means that the heart of the jc philosophy is without a pulse, i.e., DOA. Therefore, the existence of the jc god can only be a fantasy and fable and should be treated as a mere tool of control like all other religions that were created by men in our past.

Think about it carefully. How is it that all other religions that have come and gone are thought to be creations of men, but the jc religion is thought to be fact, why? How? Moreover, numerous assertions in the bible that were once thought to be irrefutable fact have failed to meet scientific discovery and evidence, and has fallen by the wayside one by one, completely discredited and proven to be fictitious. Yet, because of the resiliency of the lies perpetrated by the jc leadership, the religion has managed to survive through these many centuries continuing to twist and distort the truth to its leadership's advantage and benefit.

The problem is that the dominance of the jc philosophy in the western culture has deeply ingrained all of the societies that adopted the jc philosophical construct with the Six Pillars of its philosophy. This means that all of these societies' citizens were taught to believe in and act according to the moral philosophy of the jc teachings. This is all fine and dandy, but for the fact that the jc teachings are rooted in the belief that its god reigns supreme and controls all. Therefore, any discrediting of the fundamental beliefs of the jc philosophical teaching starts to dismantle the invincibility of its god's image. People then start to doubt the teachings and the moral philosophy of the society that was once not only infallible but also ubiquitous and universal. And, without a replacement philosophy that presents itself as a better and truly absolute philosophy, the moral decay of the society not only gets worse and worse, but also accelerates.

This is where we find ourselves today. The moral philosophy of the society has decayed – no one truly believes in the moral fundamentals that were prevalent some 50-60 years ago – and no other philosophical construct has taken its place. The problem is that in the absence of something fundamental to believe in people will make up stuff, and it typically isn't philosophically deep or morally healthy.

Also, in the absence of true leadership and moral guidance, people have turned to that which is easy to determine superior versus inferior, good versus bad, and right versus wrong. People have turned to superficial and pretentious things: Money, notoriety, status, power, fashion, local sports teams' success, and other superficial and pretentious cues. Is there any doubt that our society is not living up to its full potential?

The problem with the jc religion is that it forces people to stop thinking, which is the root cause of our society's decay; this is one of the reasons why the jc religion IS the root of all evil

What do people do when they are confused and don't know what to do? They try to think. If they can't get an answer from thinking then what do they do? They ask people – but what makes anyone think that someone else knows better? By the way, when I say people ask others, I also mean that people perform research on the internet, read stuff, watch TV, listen to the radio or reference other communications medium, as well as physically asking people. Anyway, if people can't get an answer from some other source then what do they do? They stop thinking and do what is in their best short-term interest, because that is the only certainty anyone can have. This is very logical within the context of the sequence of events jast outlined. But the problem is that if people live their life this way, they end up in an even more confused state, which requires even more short-term decision making, which results in more confusion, etc. Please, make sure to remember this construct for how people think, while we go through this chapter.

The fact of the matter is that our society's Six Pillars are still being largely dictated by, heavily borrowed from and greatly influenced by the jc philosophical construct – look at issues involving contraception, abortion, taxes, social behavior (e.g., do unto others, love thy neighbor, to forgive is, et cetera.), criminal Justice system (specifically as it relates to the death penalty), homosexuality, morality laws (drug, prostitution, gambling, traffic, etc.) among others. However, over the centuries, the jc philosophical construct has been grossly discredited and continues to lack rational integrity, and is constantly scrambling to catch up to scientific realities and changing constituents' values. Therefore, as a society, the decay of our Six Pillars was not only inevitable, but also the resulting confusion – in the absence of another more rational and robust philosophical construct – has created a society that is focused on things that are completely useless, irrelevant, short-sighted and destructive to our society's future. Due to this decay, our society has lost its vision for the future and has turned its focus on things that are more immediately tangible like physical beauty, money, power, status/prestige, material goods and other superficial and pretentious concepts and materials. Compare this to 1950s America, when the jc philosophical construct was still very strong, held more validity and sway, and when people had not quite caught up with the science that would inevitably and irrefutably dismantle the jc philosophical construct. If people know anything about that period, they'd know that the uniformity of thinking in our culture along the jc philosophical construct was extremely high. Some of the more common beliefs were that:

- America always was and always will be on the side of good;
- Whites are superior to all other races;

- Communism should be completely rooted out of our society;
- Politicians, particularly the president, are to be trusted;
- Labor unions are great for the country;
- America only needs to pay attention to its own economy and markets;
- Taxing the wealthy at a marginal tax rate of 90% or more is thought to be Just and fair;
- Sex before marriage is an absolute no-no for girls;
- Smoking is cool;
- Censorship is thought to be absolutely necessary;
- The purpose of women getting an education is for them to attract the right husband;
- The rightful place for women is at home;
- The husband/father is strongly believed to be the family unit leader;
- That divorcing is a sin and something to be very ashamed of;
- Wives should overlook their husband's abuse;
- Wives should overlook their husband's infidelity;
- Wives and husbands should overlook and cover-up their spouse's alcohol or drug abuse;
- Wives and husbands should not bring to light their spouse's abuse of their children;
- Drinking and driving is quite normal and acceptable;
- Being the life of the party because of excessive drinking is good, fun and acceptable;
- Real Americans eat meat and potatoes at every meal, along with sweet deserts and no vegetables;
- Anything remotely regarding sex is not to be seriously discussed in public or even among family members;
- Abortion is an absolute sin;
- "Three strikes and you're out" laws are justified;
- Thinking about other races as being inferior is a matter of course, compared to the Caucasian race;
- Whites had the right to kill or round-up the savage Indians into concentration camps, take their lands and achieve the white people's manifest destiny;
- Spanking of both children and wives (watch reruns of *I Love Lucy* starring Lucille ball) by the father/husband is normal and justified;

- Women should vote the way their fathers or husbands vote;
- jesus christ, not only existed, but was white;
- The jews murdered/killed jesus;
- Use of corporal punishment is justified in schools;
- The use of the word nigger was taken for granted when talking about Americans from Africa;
- America was the best at everything; among others.

As one can see the list is quite expansive, but I'm sure that others could come up with a lot more. Regardless, if one looks at this list carefully, one will find that a vast majority, if not all of it can be tied back to one of two positions: 1) Religious doctrine, or 2) ignorance, scientific or otherwise. The other observation that I'll present is that the vast majority of people today would never subscribe to the vast majority of the beliefs held so dearly in the hearts and minds of 1950s Americans.

So, what happened in the 1960s? Rational thought by some individuals, which started to spread and catch on, and science started to shed light on the ignorance, stupidity and unjustified beliefs of the average American, which then led to rebellion and clashes, which continued the dismantling of the uniform philosophical construct of our society into the 1970s and beyond, among other developments. By my crude estimation, it wasn't until may be the mid-to-late-1980s or the early part of the 1990s, when the moral degradation of our society's core beliefs slowed-down dramatically, and when a substitute philosophical construct based on superficial and pretentious cues started to take over in earnest, e.g., the YUPPY movement may have been the start.

This decay was made possible, only by the fact that our core beliefs through the 1950s were based on highly flawed and deceitful construct of the jc philosophical theory. By definition, had the jc philosophical construct been rational, logical and true, there could not have been enlightenment, i.e., intelligent and rational people could not have challenged the jc philosophical constructs and won, and there wouldn't have been a dismantling of the society's core philosophical beliefs. The problem is that no one has come up with a substitute for the discredited jc philosophical construct that we can all gravitate towards to re-establish harmony and uniformity in our society and rid ourselves of the superficial and pretentious society that we live in today.

The problem is that we have to first understand specifics of how the jc philosophical construct has damaged our society before we can fix the problems. The true damage that the jc philosophical construct has reaped on our society is that it has forced people to abandon thinking, which in turn forces people to live for the moment. As an example, let's look at the issue of contraception, first from a societal point of view then from a single family point of view.

A recent study that I saw on TV suggested that the reason that the crime rate has declined over the last 3-4 decades is due to the proliferation and use of contraception and legalization of abortions. According to this study, the use of contraception and legalization of abortion have prevented many unwanted pregnancies, which prevented many children from being neglected or abused or both. This study believes that had it not been for the proliferation of contraception, and legalized abortions many of the unwanted children would have ended up becoming criminals. Therefore, this study concludes that the proliferation of contraception and legalized abortion is one of the primary causes for the decline in crime rates. However, despite this and other benefits, the catholic church continues to oppose the use of contraception and abortions. But more disturbing is that many jc religious faithful continue to oppose legal abortions and the use of contraceptives, and, in particularly, distributing condoms in high school as required and necessary. This is what the jc religion does to people: It makes people mindless and thoughtless automatons. We don't need the jc philosophical influence at the societal level. Furthermore, I strongly believe that at the family and individual level the conclusion is no different.

Again, religious leaders, particularly in the catholic faith, forbid or discourage the use of contraception. However, correct family planning is critical to the economic and mental well-being of any family anywhere in the world. So, what should a couple do: Obey religious doctrine and risk financial difficulties, or spurn religious doctrine and further pursue financial success before raising a family? If using a condom or an oral contraceptive is a sin against the jc god (assuming that one believes in the jc god) then obviously one shouldn't use them, but having a baby too early could make one's financial position more precarious, and more to the point, the child will have a lower probability of being successful due to a lack of resources. What can one do? Most people choose to go with contraception and ignore what the future brings, hoping that their god will forgive them their trespasses. This is living for the short-term at the expense of long-term (in the case of the jc construct, an eternity). No philosophical construct should force people to choose from two bad options, but that's what the jc religion forces people to do. So, no one should give the jc religious doctrine a second thought before completely rejecting the philosophy.

As an aside, if one confesses to their priest and asks for forgiveness, one is absolved of all sins in the catholic faith, assuming one truly repents. Obviously, this gives too much power to the clergy, assuming one believes in heaven and hell, and the jc deity. Also, given this amount of power, there should be no surprise that the clergy and, in particular, the vatican continues to amass an obscene amount of wealth.

Anyway, the point with contraception is twofold: 1) The choice people make when confused or conflicted is to choose for the benefit of the immediate, and 2) that deceit and lies – intentional or otherwise – of the jc hierarchy forces people to stop thinking. In addition, why can't the jc hierarchy say that if one choose to use contraception that one is obeying the will of the jc god or put it another way that the reason one chooses to use contraception is because the jc god put that thought into the user's head? Assuming that one believes in the jc god, given that everything is supposed to be the will of the jc god, it is the most rational reason for why someone chooses to use a contraceptive! This positioning would make it much easier for its constituents, while not changing the jc hierarchy's premise that everything is according to the will of its version of god. Also, since the jc god is supposedly omniscient, omnipotent and omnipresent, it should not matter if a couple uses contraception or not, because the jc deity should be able to make a woman pregnant at will, supposedly with or without a man's contribution! The hypocrisy and the self-contradiction are palpable! However, this hypocrisy and self-contradiction is not an accident, and cannot be avoided by the jc hierarchy. Think about it, if there is no sin then the jc hierarchy cannot make people feel guilty and, therefore, cannot make people seek counsel and eventually make people do their bidding, not to mention get money from their "constituents." Obviously, this is absolutely reprehensible. Again, at the end of the day, it is about power and control. If one sees the jc religion in this light, it is not difficult to understand why the jc hierarchy does what it does and why the jc philosophical construct exists the way it does. And, most of all, it helps the jc hierarchy, if people don't know how to think causing people to seek the clergy's advice.

Here's how it works: Let's say that no one has an immediate and absolute solution to one's problem, primarily because one priority contradicts another. One of the edicts that the jc faithful must follow as a servant of the jc god is to obey its words. The problem is that the jc faithful have no idea, which of its jc god's edicts they should follow. Going back to the contraception problem these are the issues that a jc faithful has to contend with:

1) According to jc religious leadership using any contraception is playing god, which one must not, should not and cannot do (supposedly, if one uses contraception then one is playing god because only god is supposed to determine when and if someone should get pregnant, not the individual) but by interfering with the natural process of fertilization contraception users are messing with the jc god's will – never mind the fact that if the jc god is truly omnipotent, omniscient and omnipresent, it can easily make any woman pregnant whenever it wants to make her pregnant, regardless of whether we mere mortals use contraception or not;

2) One must do one's absolute best to provide for one's children and take care of them;

3) If a couple uses the timing method, which, until recently, the catholic church saw as the only way to plan for a family, one cannot guarantee that the woman will not get pregnant – never mind the fact that this too is playing god because the couple is trying to determine when they will or will not have children, instead of the jc god;

4) If the couple uses contraception, they go to hell, but they reduce the chances that their child goes to hell – better financial resources allow the couple to better provide for their child, which reduces the chance that their child strays and does bad things;

5) And, according to most people, making sacrifices for others is an admirable trait, so the couple should "sacrifice" themselves for their child and go to hell to insure a better life for their child;

6) Also, the jc god is suppose to consider a person's intent before sending them to hell;

7) No one can really divine the jc god's intent; and

8) Therefore, how does one know what the best answer is?

There is no right answer. And, asking someone else doesn't get anyone anywhere either, because everyone else is as confused as every other person, and the clergy isn't looking out for people's best interest either. So, inevitably people give up and make the best (actually only) decision that they are capable of making, which is to do what is right for them in the very near-term. After repeated encounters of this nature from one's childhood and thereafter one learns fairly quickly that thinking doesn't do one much good and thinking can only get a person into trouble. The lesson that people learn is that when they think and come to an independent conclusion, and people who make the rules – parents, teachers, law makers, et cetera – don't agree with that conclusion then one gets punished for it, despite the fact that hesh thought that they made the best and most rational decision. So, again, people stop thinking.

But it doesn't stop there. People then figure out that the safest behavior is to not think and not make decisions, but to **blindly** obey rules, laws and regulations, while continuing to give people the impression that one thinks, because as an adult people are **supposed** to think. However, by pretending to think while really only obeying the rules, laws and regulations, in people's minds, they can't get into trouble and, therefore, can't be punished. I think this is why we have so many rules and regulations and why the proliferation of new rules and regulations seem unstoppable. This is also the reason why people continue to demand that the government "take care of things," so that people don't have to be responsible for their own actions, since they only want to follow laws, rules and regulations. As an aside, if we think about it, it makes perfect sense that people demand that the government take responsibility for the consequences of their actions. Why should someone be punished for following all of the laws, rules and regulations and doing what they are incented to do?

It should all makes sense to the reader now. If one is smart, one would have figured out that the teenage years is where the experiment with independent thinking kicks in, why teens do it, how they give up on it, why they end up succumbing to peer pressure and how and why they "grow out" of it. The conclusion isn't that people grow out of it, they give up; they surrender. And, as adults, to varying degrees, people become their parents. Again, this should all make sense to the reader now and shed more clarity to one's own life and the way people "mature" into an adult. If I haven't made people sufficiently depressed about how they've grown up and what they have become and why society is the way it is then I obviously haven't done a good job. So, let me give another example: Sex; a subject near and dear to almost everyone.

Who doesn't like sex?! Whether it is heterosexual, homosexual, transsexual, kinky sex, fetish sex, or sex of any and all color and flavor, who doesn't like sex? But, if the jc god exists, has anyone ever wondered why we start craving sex at the age of about 12-13 years old, but we aren't really ready for it until at least about 16-20 years old at the very earliest? Why did the jc god, if it exists and is our creator, give us the temptation, but not equip us to handle it mentally and financially until at a later age? If the jc god does exist and is our creator then I contend that the jc god is a cruel sadist and, therefore, a very ugly entity. How cruel does someone have to be to create such a fundamental desire then make it extremely difficult – actually almost impossible – to carry out the responsibility for acting on that fundamental desire, and at that without the benefit of contraception? Such sadistic torture alone should be enough to disavow the jc god, even if it exists, but the fact that the jc god tries to make it our fault is absolutely despicable. As the jc hierarchy argues, the temptation was put there to test us and to see if we take the right path. However, if the jc god is our creator and is truly omnipresent, omnipotent and omniscient then it should know what choices we're going to make and what results will occur. So, it has no reason to test us to begin with. Do you see the self-contradictory nature of the jc philosophy? Put it another way, if everything is the will of the jc god then there cannot be a test of any kind, and there is no free will. One can't contend that everything is the will of the jc god and have individual free will. This is a massive contradiction, and therefore it cannot be.

Therefore, for the feeble minded, the excuse that the jc hierarchy gives us for why the jc god gave us temptation is believable, but to the intelligent, rational and thoughtful minded person, it should be obviously very dumb. This is what the jc philosophical complex does; it preys on the weak, lazy, and feeble minded people to control society's philosophical construct. Unless one is capable of thinking on their own, people will continue to be vulnerable to not only the jc hierarchy's, but also other manipulators' (e.g., politicians) exploits and manipulations. What's worse is that I can't tell you how many so called intelligent people are brain-washed by the jc philosophical complex mostly due to brainwashing from early on and continued societal pressures and reinforcements. These people, even faced with incorruptible evidence, are so thoroughly brainwashed that they not only cannot overcome their prejudice and bias, but also will find all kinds of excuses and justifications – almost always very disjointed and discombobulated – to ignore the obvious and the self-evident. It's a wonder that these people are mostly very successful in their careers!

Essentially, based on my encounters with people from all over the world, I realized from when I was a child that even the smartest and most successful people don't think, particularly when it comes to religion. I also realized that, typically, thinking is physically or mentally beaten out of people from a young age and substituted with platitudes, clichés, rules, regulations, laws, programmed responses, and standardized socially-acceptable concepts. All this in an effort to normalize and indoctrinate people into a standardized society driven by the jc philosophical construct that began many centuries ago. And, those that do think don't necessarily think about that which is important, but think about clever ways to try and make sense of that which doesn't and won't ever make sense.

So the question becomes why? As stated before, when a society is standardized and "normalized" then it is not only very tranquil and peaceful, but also pliant, submissive and easy to control. However, unless the philosophical construct is timeless and immutable and new discoveries and knowledge doesn't impact the reality of the philosophy, it becomes poison to the very society it is trying to benefit.

To me, it is so obvious that the existence of the jc god is unquestionably impossible that it is as plain as the nose on my face. However, for those that are brainwashed into believing in the jc construct, no matter what, it is somehow obviously crystal clear to them that the jc god absolutely does exist. Regardless of their fervent beliefs, they present no evidence, no proof, not even a theoretical construct that makes sense, and yet they find a way to continue to believe. Seems ridiculous and insane, but there it is. In spirit, this is no different than the people at Jonestown who blindly followed their leader to their deaths. Many people have wondered how such atrocious behavior can occur, and they talk about the impossibility of themselves behaving that way. However, when people are so thoroughly brainwashed, anything can be possible; even suicide on command. There is very little difference between people who died at Jonestown and people who blindly believe in the jc philosophical construct after being presented with irrefutable evidence that the whole jc philosophy is bogus; the difference between these two groups of people may be one or two steps out of thousands. If people are brainwashed enough, they will spurn all logic and blindly follow. Look at history: Adolf Hitler's Germany for example. Why is it that even jews and christians acknowledge that blind faith in general is bad, but when it comes to their own religious beliefs they don't believe that their blind faith is bad? Even those that do agree that their faith is blind can't come to terms with the fact that their blind faith in judaism/christianity is bad. To me, this is very scary and damning!

The fact of the matter is that, in our society, the jc philosophical construct has deprived society of people who think and the resulting decay in the Six Pillars of our society is a direct result of the irrational and childish nature of the jc religious construct's success and subsequent long discredited decay. This resulted in other important issues from evolving despite the fact that when thought of purely on a rational basis they should have changed. But, religious mania and fervor keep important issues from evolving and remain unnecessarily controversial in our society. This is further evidence of how damaging and divisive the jc construct is to our society. These issues include the following:

1) Gays in the military: Thankfully, this is changing for the better, finally, but because jc religious followers believe that homosexuality is wrong, they try to keep gays out of the military; the jc faithful that continue to oppose and condemn homosexuality are absolutely horrible and disrespectful people.

2) Gay marriage: The fact that this is even being debated is a testament to how totally crazy and irrational jc doctrine really is. If two people want to get married and have the same legal, civil, and societal rights and privileges, who is anyone to say, "they can't have it and they can't be happy?" Jast because the jc faithful think it is evil and against their god's supposed will, these people have no problems causing misery and unhappiness among gays. People like these ought to be dragged out and shot in public for poisoning our children's minds and spreading evil among people. By the way, again, if everything is the jc god's will then homosexuality can only be the result of the jc god will, if one believes in the jc god. So, shouldn't it be embraced by the jc philosophy and allowed to flourish in the open?! Such hypocrisy and contradictions should not be allowed to exist. Ultimately, this type of behavior only serves to confirm that the jc construct is about power and controlling people, nothing more, nothing less.

3) Abortion: Due to the jc religious freaks, who think of abortion as murder, what should have been settled with Roe v. Wade is once again becoming a very controversial issue, and quite unnecessarily so. It should be left up to

each individual woman to decide her own fate. And, if she wants to consult a religious leader or follow religious doctrine that will also be her right and freedom to do so. Again, if the will of the jc god controls everything then the choice of the woman to get an abortion can only be attributed to the will of the jc god, if one believes in the jc deity. I can only laugh at the stupidity and self-contradiction of the jc believers.

4) Stem cell research: Stem cell research is one of the most important scientific breakthroughs in recent history, and holds out the promise for all kinds of innovative and revolutionary medical cures, including potential cures for such ailments as Alzheimer's disease, diabetes, Parkinson's disease, and heart disease among others. However, due to religious objections stem cell research has been set back and not likely to gain prominence or funding that it needs to save lives.

5) Assisted suicide: Again the opposition to assisted suicide is based on jc doctrine. But, again, if one rationally thinks this through, there shouldn't be any reason why people shouldn't have the *full choice* of what to do with their lives, including how and when to end it.

6) Separation of church and state: We absolutely should take out the word "god" from our pledge of allegiance, all military, judicial and civil swearing ceremonies and oaths, and from all currencies, if we are truly to have religious and philosophical freedom as guaranteed by the Constitution of the US. Why can't we say, "... one nation under Buddha, indivisible, with liberty and Justice for all."? Or, why can't we say, "I swear to tell the truth the whole truth and nothing but the truth so help me Bodhisattva."? Or, why can't our currency have, "In Allah, we trust."? Realistically, our pledge of allegiance should be changed to the way we had it until the jc religious freaks forced Congress and president to insert the words, "... under god ..." or change it to the following, which I prefer: "*I pledge allegiance to the flag of the United States of America, for which it stands, one nation, under the Constitution, indivisible with liberty and Justice for all.*" In courts, our swearing in should read, "*I swear to tell the truth, the whole truth and nothing but the truth on my honor and under penalty of perjury.*" And, all of our currencies should have the words, "*In the Constitution, we trust.*" The jc religious freaks should have absolutely no trouble with any of these changes, as the suggested changes are very American and universal to *ALL AMERICANS,* unlike the current versions, which prejudice against people who don't believe in their god or any form of god for that matter.

Historically, there were other issues that were "inspired" by jc religious fervor that have greatly negatively impacted our society and continue to impact us or had to change because of the irrational nature of the jc construct. Some of these historical issues that either remain and continue to negatively impact us or were changed because of the stupidity of jc religious fervor were:

1) The suffrage movement: Due to jc religious beliefs that a woman's place was in the home, women were not given the right to vote until 1919. All because jc religious practitioners objected and the jc construct opposed women voting. Disgusting.

2) Imperialism: This philosophy, like the Crusades of the Middle or Dark Ages, is greatly due to the belief that western supremacy, guided by its jc god, had the "right" to "civilize" the rest of the world. Whatever the hell it means to "civilize" the world. The vatican never objected to western imperialism, and many members of the jc hierarchy were at the vanguard of this movement, marching side by side with the military, and taking part in making the world more "civil." The jc hierarchy used the spread of imperialism to force the "gospel" of the jc philosophical construct on the conquered.

3) The Crusades: The one lunatic jc policy that has had the biggest impact on the world is the crusades of the Middle Ages or the Dark Ages. The ignorant jc religious leadership started a war almost a 1,000 years ago that still reverberates to today, and which continues to threaten world peace. This alone should be enough for everyone in this country to abandon the jc religion. Yes, jc religious servants are directly responsible for contributing to the maintenance of the number 1 threat to world peace.

4) Interracial marriage ban: Until 1967, 27 states had a ban on interracial marriage. The reasoning according to judge Bazile (judge in Virginia) in the landmark *Loving vs. Virginia* case "hinged" on the "fact" that the jc god put people of different colors on separate continents indicating that the jc god does not want racial mixing. This type of biblical "interpretation" is a great example of why the jc religion is the root of all evil. The ban on interracial marriage was permanently reversed based on constitutional law by the Supreme Court of the US in 1967. The prejudiced law was overturned at the US Supreme Court in an unanimous decision based on the 14th Amendment, which gives equal protection under the US Constitution and protects individuals from having their due process violated. What is

absolutely disgusting and a shameful blight on our society is that Alabama did not overturn its anti-miscegenation law until 2000; Alabama has one of the highest proportions of christians in the US!

Historical transgressions perpetrated on mankind in the name of the jc god is enough to disavow its philosophical construct, but the ongoing poison that it continues to spread in the name of their god, the poor or doing good is absolutely horrifying. And, for these transgressions, we should never forgive these evil, despicable, tortured, and thoughtless people that follow the jc philosophical construct, unless they repent and forever disavow their involvement with the jc philosophical construct.

For us to be able to regain a strong and vibrant philosophical construct that stands the test of time and forges the basis of a rational and constructive society, we must first learn how to think and get rid of all of the influences of the jc philosophical construct. Only then can we actually build the kind of philosophical system that makes sense and has the potential to deliver world peace.

More realistically, the jc philosophical construct was most likely a creation of some very clever people – for their times – some 20+ centuries ago

I can't say with absolute certainty what the exact timeline was, but the events described in the new testament of the bible dates back about 2,000 years and, including the old testament, could stretch back another 3,000 years or so – most jc experts say the bible's timeline is about 5,000 years old. Regardless, the creation of the jc philosophical construct can only be the invention of man like any other western religion that has ever come and gone.

Why is it so difficult for people to imagine that given that all other western religions are manmade, the highest probability for the origination of the jc philosophy is also man? The answer is that most are brainwashed into thinking that there is a jc god; it's that simple. The power of brainwashing is undeniable and potent, which is why, despite irrefutable evidence, denial is the order of the day for jc devotees. To me it is obvious that all other devotees of all other western religions went through the same thing when confronted with the reality of the fact that their religion wasn't real that their god(s) did not, cannot and will not exist, but it is infuriating how jc devotees can't live up to and face reality.

What about all the stories of how the universe was created? The story of the moon spewing out the stars and the sun creating the earth, that Zeus and his siblings controlling the universe from the heights of mount Olympus among other creation stories are jast as ridiculous as a single entity taking one day to create the universe and five days to create and "decorate" earth. When confronted with this inconvenient fact, the devotees of the jc philosophical construct will say something ridiculously insane like: "There is no timeline for god; one day could be less than a second to more than a trillion years and each "day" described in the bible may not be a day, but a chapter." How convenient of the devotees to forget that until science proved that the earth was not the center of the universe and is more than several billion years old that the bible was taken literally for hundreds, if not thousands of years! Therefore, this is evidence enough that the bible was written by those that believed in the fairy tale– in their minds knowing – that the earth is the center of the universe and that the moon, the sun and the stars were, in fact, nothing but simple globes and dots that the jc god put into the sky to shed light, measure time and help sustain all life on earth. Oh, by the way, has anyone discovered Eden? Or, evidence of Romulus and Remus? Or, other fabled sources of man's origins? Surprise, surprise, the answer is a defining HELL NO!

Anyway, getting back to the origins of the fairy tale in genesis, given that no real scientific knowledge was accessible by the human authors, it shouldn't surprise anyone that the authors believed that the center of the universe was earth. This is no different than if we told very young children that have no knowledge of science that earth was the center of the universe and they believe it. Yes, that's right; they'd have no problems believing that the earth was the center of the universe because simple observation would dictate that indeed the earth was the center of the universe. The observations that we make are as follows: When we stand still, we don't feel motion despite the fact that the earth is moving at great speeds, both around the sun and around the earth's central axis. Because we don't feel motion, without scientific knowledge, when we see the sun rise and set and the moon and the stars also come and go, it isn't difficult to believe that the sun, the moon and the stars rotate around the earth. By definition, this makes earth the center of the universe.

Imagine people observing the universe some 3,000-5,000 years ago. Without scientific instruments and knowledge, they could only conclude the same things that young children without scientific knowledge would conclude. In viewing the genesis chapter in the bible, if one understands primitive man's perspective, it isn't difficult to understand why genesis was written the way it was. If the bible is the word of the jc god then genesis would lead us to believe one of three conclusions: 1) The jc god lied to us about earth's position in the universe, 2) It was written by men who simply made up a story that fit their casual observations, or 3) the current scientific knowledge is dead wrong. Don't laugh about point number 3), I've met people who believe that earth is the center of the universe and the sun, the moon and the stars rotate around the earth. Seriously, no joke!

Anyway, what would one think is the most plausible explanation of genesis? That the jc god lied to us? What does that say about the jc god's respect for its creation? The explanation that the earth is in movement and this is what makes it appear that the sun, the moon and the stars rotate around the earth isn't something that is difficult to explain. This means that the jc god has absolutely no respect for man's ability to understand, despite the fact that it supposedly created us! So, if the bible is correct, then given that the jc god created us, it should have known that we would be able to understand. Yet another contradiction!

I know that some people probably are thinking that the jc god lied to us to test our ability to find the truth for ourselves. If that is so then given that our pursuit of the truth has led to the conclusion that the jc god cannot exist, what does that say about our mission to pursue the truth supposedly given to us by the jc god? What this is suggesting is that the jc god put us on the road to proving that it cannot exist. Obviously, the devotees aren't arguing this, but this type of argument is very typical of the way the jc faithful think. It is very discombobulated, disjointed, and isolationist and will argue what they want for the point, but then fail to extend and link the logic to other areas of their beliefs or take it to the end conclusion. This is another demonstration and example of how people aren't capable of or trained to think, and how people's innate ability to truly reason is wiped from their brain from an early age.

Regardless, look at the timeline of the bible; it implies that the earth is only some 5,000 years old. Again, this would fit the timeline that primitive man would have observed given how far back they could remember through word of mouth stories. Genesis also ignores the fact that evolution was what drove the presence of all of the animals and plants on earth. The bible states that the jc god "put" these animals on earth, and not put primitive forms of animals that grew into what we see today. Again, the version of the story that is in the bible of how all creatures and plants came to be on earth fits what primitive man would have observed, meaning in a period of 3,000-5,000 years, animal and plant forms would not have changed much and no other evidence would be visible to contradict this observation. So, to primitive man, it would appear that these animals and plants were put here at the same time man was put on earth. In a way this is true. We all came from single cell forms some 3-4 billion years ago, but all of the evidence would indicate that the bible isn't implying or suggesting this.

Another point that needs to be driven home is the time it took to create the universe. How is it that the jc god needs any time or needs to break down anything into parts? Meaning, if the jc god is truly omnipotent, omnipresent and omniscient (triple-o) then it should have no need to act in sequence. It would not need time, period. If it is truly triple-o then all that the jc god would have to do is to snap its finger, so to speak, and create everything all at once. So then why does the bible go through pains to describe the work that the jc god supposedly did to create the earth and the universe in 6 days and took the seventh day off? And, why so specifically 6 and 1? A supposedly omnipotent, omniscient, and omnipresent jc god wouldn't have needed to split time like this. However, if the authors of the bible were men and they wanted to have their people work six days and rest the seventh then it all of a sudden makes sense. The argument would go something like this: "If it's good enough for god, it's good enough for you." Funny though how the timeline that the bible wants people to function-in happens to fall into a seven day weekly routine that happens to best fit the amount of days in one year. Coincidence? No, I don't think so. I think it was very deliberate and calculated by the authors of the bible to make their society work six days and take one off.

What this implies is that the men (definitely not women) that wrote the bible lived in a society that functioned within a seven day weekly cycle. So, if we know which societies were the first to function in a seven day week, we may be able to pin down where the bible originated from. Meaning, who the authors were or at least where they originated from. I think it's an interesting thought to ponder.

Anyway, all evidence would indicate that the authors of the bible were human, so the question becomes why did these authors write the bible, if it isn't the word of a supposedly real omnipotent, omniscient, and omnipresent deity? Why did they create this fictitious character? I'll deal with this in another chapter.

So, the conclusion is that humans wrote the bible, but what about the existence of jesus christ? Rationally, given that the existence of the jc god is impossible and, ironically, the bible is the proof of that impossibility, it is likely that the existence of jesus christ is also impossible. However, if jesus christ did exist then the miracles are unlikely to have happened or greatly exaggerated, and if the miracles did occur then it is likely that jesus christ was an alien.

It is more likely that jesus christ was an alien than an actual being that the bible claims him to be, if he actually existed

I know; I've heard it all. But here's what I'm saying. The probability that jesus actually existed is so low that if he actually did exist, I believe that he was more likely an alien that took the form of a homosapien than actually physically a homosapien. Or, he was an android placed on earth by aliens. What I mean by "so low" is something like one in an infinity. The fact of the matter is that I don't think he actually existed or if he did he was not a single being but a conglomeration of multiple people combined into one to make the new testament of the bible more compelling. Regardless, assuming that jesus christ actually existed as a single being let me put forth some interesting observations:

1) Given the number of stars in the universe, the probability of intelligent life somewhere else in the universe is pretty damn high;
2) Of these intelligent life forms, the probability that some of them have vastly superior technology to ours is also extremely high;
3) If we rule out all that which is impossible then no matter how improbable, whatever choice remains has to be the correct answer;
4) Sufficiently advanced technology will look like magic or miracles to a primitive society; and
5) Any society 2,000 years ago would have looked upon the execution of even today's technology as a miracle, let alone that of a far more advanced

society. So, as an example, let's take the case of the miraculous conception of Mary. With today's technology, could we not make Mary look like she was miraculously impregnated without having intercourse? Hell yes! Ever heard of IVF?

All of the miracles that the character of jesus supposedly performed are all or almost all possible utilizing today's technology. Certainly, with jast a small stretch of the imagination, it would not be difficult to hypothesize how the rest of the so called miracles that jesus performed, if he even existed, could be done, if we had slightly better technology. Therefore, because the jc god's existence is absolutely impossible, in my opinion, the more plausible explanation is that jesus was an alien or an alien android – a robot – instead of an actual live human being.

Even with today's technology, many of the "miracles" performed by jesus would be possible with simple medicine in many cases. Walking on water is also not difficult as there are gadgets and toys that allow anyone to do so, which was invented not too long ago. So, the miraculous aspect of the so called jesus's work isn't too difficult to explain, if we believe that the so called jesus was an alien or alien creation. So then why would the aliens do this? Why would an advanced society mess with a society that is so primitive as not to matter to them?

There could be many reasons, including something as ridiculous as an alien prank or something more serious like testing of new technology, or something more sinister like controlling the evolution of humans or suppressing the development of humans. The sinister motive is one that is particularly unlikely given their advanced technology. If they thought we were somehow a threat to them, I'd have to assume they'd have a weapon that is so powerful that with one application it would wipeout the entire planet or completely disintegrate it. So, no, I don't think it is a sinister motive. So, then, what could it be? I think it has to be more benign in motive.

I believe that aliens that possess such advanced and miraculous technology cannot intend harm to our society and wouldn't need to do so. So, if the motive is more benign then what could it be? Honestly, I can't say for sure what that may be, but I do have a guess as to what it could be.

I strongly believe that if there is a society such as the one that I'm describing then I strongly believe that this society is very advanced and probably has a societal philosophy that is rational and completely grounded in scientific fact without appeal to paganism, religion, faith or any other irrational bias that takes away from a rational and thinking society. Furthermore, if they have the capability of inter-galactic travel that allows them movement from one galaxy to another as if we were flying from London to Paris then there is a very high probability that this society is not alone. Meaning, that it is very likely that this society is one of many in a federation like structure like we see in Star Trek. Who knows; Gene Roddenberry may have been their representative on earth!

Anyway, imagine this society that is so well structured, organized and advanced in its thinking. The introduction of a disorganized, chaotic, irrational group of people would disrupt the harmony and unity of such an universal federation (UF). Imagine all the preachers running around the UF trying to convert people to the jc philosophy. This would be a major pain in the ass for the UF to deal with! I don't think they'd want to deal with such nonsense.

So, before the UF reveals its presence to us, I think they'll want to know that humans are rational, thoughtful, considerate, and careful to consider the long-term effects of our decisions. So, perhaps what the aliens are doing is making sure that we are, that we can and that we will be able to fit into their federation. The only way this can happen is if they see that we are capable of making the right decisions by rejecting that which is obviously irrational and choosing the rational path for the long-term.

Think about it. If we were them, wouldn't we want to be absolutely certain that a new group wouldn't disrupt the harmony of our society? So, how does one go about doing that? One way to do this would be to give us a test. One test could be to introduce a character called jesus into our society who seemingly performs miracles in public to convince people that he is the promised resurrection of their god. Also, the aliens endow the character called jesus with characteristics that all living entities espouse like kindness, generosity, gentleness, and compassion. Finally, and this is the most important factor, after the aliens make sure that jesus has a following, they make sure that he preaches poison disguised as benevolence.

The poison being preached is universal love or more appropriately, blind love: That which espouses love without merit, that which preaches that Justice is irrelevant and, ironically, unjust, that which says we don't have to deserve something to have it, that which says that we don't have to work for something to own it, the concept that appeals without merit, the belief that is only skin deep, and most of all that which represents itself as good even though it is ultimately evil.

This then is the foundation of the jc philosophy, which has not only poisoned humanity's mind for over two millennia, but also is responsible for the greatest conflict humanity has ever known: The conflict with militant fundamentalist terrorists. Christian crusaders invading the Middle-East during the dark ages are the root cause of the deepest danger that humanity may have ever known or will know.

Regardless, the alien test is very simple: Can we recognize the hypocrisy of the jc construct and find the rational universal path? Can we save ourselves from death by slow poisoning and decay? Can we find peace amongst ourselves? If we proceed down our current path, I can easily imagine our own destruction: Financially from the burden of forced charity and physically from the threat of militant fundamentalists. Then, the aliens won't have to worry about keeping us away from the UF; we'd end our own lives and cause them no harm.

At least in America, I believe that it is only a matter of time before the blood-sucking politicians ruin our economy by continuing to steal from the wealthier segment of our society to secure the vote of the masses, while militant fundamentalists secure nuclear material, which they detonate on our soil, which leads to more and more broad and dangerous international conflicts.

However, if we can overcome these dangers through rational thought and establish a fundamental societal structure that is established on Justice then I think that the UF may reveal themselves to humanity, and help us overcome many physical problems such as illnesses, pestilence and hunger.

As kooky, loony and insane as the alien theory of jesus christ may sound, I believe that it is far more likely than the existence of jesus christ as written in the bible. And, I believe that the probability of the alien scenario being correct is in the trillions, if not quadrillions to one. That's how whacky I think jesus christ's existence was the way the bible suggests that it was.

But doesn't judaism/christianity represent good as well; what about its concept of universal love?! Universal love is evil!

Ah, yes, universal love. Let me put it very bluntly, not that I've held back so far. I stand for Justice and reason; universal love proposes to throw Justice and reason out the door. Not jast throw it out the door, but go further by rewarding the unjust and unreasonable. If I suggested to anyone that they reward slackers in their company, thieves that stole from them and murderers that killed one of their family members, everyone would say I was crazy. If I suggested that the gold medal for any Olympic event should go to the worst athlete or that it should go to everyone, any and all rational and intelligent human being would strongly object to my suggestion. Yet, when jews/christians (jc) preach universal love, the vast majority of the people in this country, if not, all of the people in this country dutifully nod their heads in agreement! I think there's something seriously wrong with that!

Perpetuating injustice, no matter how small, should not be tolerated. The problem with this is that most people are afraid of making a decision, taking a stance or exercising judgment. And, the jc religion continues to encourage people not to judge, not to take a stance and not to act on their judgment. This is not a coincidence. Like I said before, if people start to think and act for themselves then the importance of the leaders of the jc religion is greatly diminished, their control over the masses becomes tenuous and they lose control, power and wealth. So, it is not in the jc leadership's best interest for people to start thinking independently, making decisions, making judgments, and acting on these thoughts and conclusions. The other problem is that most people don't have the mental faculty or the tools to make judgment calls and decisions, because they were never trained to do so. In fact, they've been told all their life that they shouldn't judge others and that such behavior is arrogant and hubris. Statements like, "who are you to judge?," "he who casts the first stone ...," "only god has the right to judge," "your judgment too shall come soon enough," "leave it up to god," blah, blah, blah, are all designed to embarrass and humiliate people into stop judging and ultimately stop thinking and acting independently. This greatly benefits the jc hierarchy.

If people stop thinking and judging and stop acting on their independence then people need advice and guidance from the established moral leaders in their society. For most people, ultimately, it is their religious leaders. Therefore, the greatest beneficiary to the lack of independent thinking, judging and acting in our society is the leadership of the jc religion. This leaves much room for manipulation, abuse, corruption, and the continued erosion of people's mind by the jc leadership. So, to protect oneself from the invasion, capture and capitulation of one's mind, one needs to retrain one's mind to learn to think, judge, and, ultimately, act. However, this is not going to be easy. I know; I've been fighting people that tried to take away my independent thought, judgment and action away from me all my life. And, the fight to maintain my independence is still going on; I'm still fighting people who think that they know better jast because they have blind faith and I refuse to give into any form of blind faith.

But getting back to the issue of universal love; it is a terrible idea. Everyone should be judged and treated according to their attributes, character and qualities, i.e., by their Six Pillars. If people aren't judged according to their Six Pillars then it begs two questions that will lead to nothing but depravity and poverty: 1) By whose standard does one justify the exceptions, and 2) how much does one reward for the shortfall. Let me present a concrete example.

Let's use the Olympics again. We're at the 100 meter sprint and 8 runners are competing. How many should win the gold medal? I say only one person: The person who wins the race. Now, some people may want to reward the gold medal to both the 1st and 2nd place finishers, regardless of the time difference, some may want to do the same, but only if the time difference is less than 0.01 seconds. Some are going to justify this by proceeding to say that the wind conditions or track conditions were such that the 2nd place finisher may have had more head wind or a slower lane, which is unfair. Others are going to say that instead of doing gold, silver and bronze, the top three finishers should be given the gold and we should get rid of the silver and bronze medals. Others will then add to that and say, why not give the gold to the top 3 finishers, silver to the next 3 finishers and bronze to the last 2 since they are all winners, jast for making it to the Olympics. Carrying this logic further, others may argue that all of the athletes that made it to the finals should be given gold medals. Then, taking this stupidity to the ultimate, we should give a gold medal to everyone who makes their national Olympic team and don't even hold the Olympics. So, whose standard is right? And, so, how should we reward the athletes? Why bother even having races at all? Why don't we vote on it and whatever the majority votes for let's do that. Even then, who gets to vote: Everyone in the world, jast the professional athletes, the athletes and fans of the sport? Where do we stop the stupidity?

The standard is simple: In objectively determinable situations, one should only be given and one should only take that which they've earned. This is fair and Just and can be seen by all that it is fair and Just. Why is this important? Think about it from the race viewpoint again. Why should anyone strive to reach for gold, if coming in second entitles that athlete to the same awards, rights, privileges and honor of coming in first? If we extend this example to the economy and pay, why should anyone work hard to make more money, if they can get the same rewards, benefits, privileges and prestige of someone better than them, but not work as hard?

The problem is that the logic is easy to follow, but many people are saying that there are situations where there are no absolute standards to follow. For example, let's take children's art. Which art works get selected to be posted on the wall for student art exhibition day? Given that beauty is in the eye of the beholder, if it were left up to each parent, no doubt that each parent would select their child's work. This, obviously, would not work. So, how does the teacher or the school make the choices?

In this case, the selection of which art works will be shown was decided well before any of the art works were ever created, meaning the selection of the teacher predetermined the selection of the art works and everyone has to respect the teacher's decision. However, if the teacher is making repeatedly prejudiced decisions then there has to be a way to correct this mistake, too. But, otherwise, trust in the teacher's judgment must be respected.

To put it more abstractly, and in conclusion, for objective matters the result of the objective event must be allowed to determine the rewards, benefits, privileges, honor and prestige accorded to the people that participated in the objective event. For subjective events, we must make the choice of judges carefully based on the strength of their Six Pillars then largely leave the selected judges to do their jobs. Regardless of which situation, no rewards should be given to the undeserved and the basis of the rewards should be made as objectively as is humanly possible. Therefore, the concept of universal love, which completely flaunts Justice, is not only anathema to me – and should be to anyone who believes in fair play, fairness and Justice – but also very poisonous to the objective of living in a decent, harmonious, and, most importantly, a fair and Just society. Therefore, not only universal love, but also anything that flaunts Justice must be soundly, absolutely and forevermore finally rejected. Moreover, the people who support universal love or other unjust philosophies (including religions), standards, objectives, and competitions should be ostracized and cast out from society and social living. This is paramount to achieving a fair, Just and prosperous society.

The truth of the matter is that we don't need anything from the jc philosophy

Regardless, of the jc god's existence there is no redeeming quality to the jc philosophy. It is completely useless to the long-term prosperity of humanity, and, if anything, outright dangerous and very destructive to peaceful coexistence. The fact of the matter is that no one needs the jc philosophy to live, survive and thrive. In fact, everyone would benefit from disassociating one's self from the ridiculous, self-destructive philosophy that is the jc construct. The faster we, as a society, do this, the better it is for all of us.

First, the fact that the jc philosophy preaches universal love is absolutely horrible as it tells people to abandon Justice and give the same love to everyone; at the least not hate people no matter what they represent, say or do. Second, it requires people to abandon their own thoughts and abide by the will of some mysterious being that only a few are even allowed to attempt to divine. Third, it threatens people with eternal damnation for making a choice to not abide by and obey the jc construct, after being given the free will to choose otherwise; this is extremely hypocritical and absurd! No one among us would accept such edicts from anyone alive and breathing. To be given a choice and then told that the choice was wrong, so you're going to be punished is truly absurd, sadistic and cruel. No one would ever accept such guidance or choice from another human being, but many take it from something that we can't even see, hear or prove the existence of. It is puzzling at best. And, even if we knew that the jc god existed, no one should abide by such hypocritical, sadistic, cruel and self-contradictory edicts and commands. Finally, the self-contradictory and impossible events depicted in the bible, starting with the book of genesis, should be enough to convince people that the bible and the jc philosophical construct was created by man to control society and coerce people into abiding by the rules that the jc leadership set up or risk being punished (including execution).

So, what redeeming quality is there that someone would want to follow the jc philosophical construct? Faith? Actually, this is the most evil aspect of the jc philosophical construct. If it were real faith, I wouldn't think it was bad at all, but the fact is that the jc hierarchy wants people to have **BLIND FAITH, THE MOST EVIL CONCEPT EVER CREATED BY MAN.** Blind faith demands that we have no evidence, no rational argument, and no justification, and still trust and believe in the theory or concept presented. Very simply put, it demands that we commit self-hypnosis or self-brainwashing through prayers, rituals, mass, confession or other mechanisms to abandon independent thought and do as if the jc theory and philosophy as presented is absolute truth. So, blind faith not only largely makes people do the work for it, but once people convince themselves of the truth of the concept or theory presented to them, it demands that people continue to not only fool themselves, but also argue to death to support and defend that which is impossible to do so, no matter the cost.

This is very evil and history has shown humanity jast how evil blind faith can be. The most obvious example being Nazi Germany; however, other less impactful examples abound such as the mass suicides of Jonestown, the Manson cult, for that matter any cult, and cult behavior, Bernie Madoff, et cetera, et cetera. Yet, despite all this evidence that blind faith is hugely detrimental, the two cornerstones of the jc construct is universal love and blind faith. If the free choice argument doesn't convince people to abandon the jc construct then the requirement that people blindly have faith should.

If people are still not convinced then they are most likely not much different than all those people that committed suicide in Jonestown or Branch Davidians of Waco, Texas that chose to burn to death instead of surrendering to FBI agents or those that chose to follow Charles Manson; and I won't even go through examples in Nazi Germany. Who in their right mind would want to be like those evil and hapless people? Who wants to represent the epitome of evil? If people knew history, they'd know how damaging blind faith really is and would never agree to adhere by it.

Finally and most ominously, blind faith dictates that people stop thinking for themselves and jast believe. The jc construct also dictates that people not only have blind faith and stop thinking, but also to obey the leadership of the jc philosophical construct without hesitation and with absolute trust that the leadership best knows what the will of the jc god is and won't guide them in the wrong direction, deliberately or otherwise. Shall we talk about how many children were molested by the priesthood and clergy? How many children trusted the clergy to give them guidance and moral support only to be sexually molested?

By the way, one cannot kill that which was never alive or never existed. This means that I cannot kill the jc god or any other god, as some have accused me of trying to do or have done. That aside, people have argued that the jc philosophy means well, but the problem is that, ironically, the road to "hell" is paved with good intentions. At the end of the day, the jc philosophical construct isn't even good for everyday philosophical guidance. It is completely useless in every way imaginable. Yet many people still cling to these useless and antiquated beliefs. It is no wonder why our society is so messed up. Remember, society is made up of individuals, their "thinking" is dictated by their Six Pillars, and, in the western hemisphere, the vast majority of people's Six Pillars are based on and dictated – directly or indirectly – by the jc philosophical construct.

Therefore, the conclusion should be easy to understand: In order to change for the better and move beyond the current path of confusion, chaos and ruin, we need to first throw out the jc philosophical construct which is not only evil and immoral, but also a philosophical framework which doesn't work and has long been made obsolete. Next, and more importantly, we must adopt and embrace a new philosophical construct that is not only rational, logical, and moral, but also that which is timeless and fully based on Justice.

Why is Justice so important? Because it is the only standard by which human interaction should be measured

Justice is the supreme concept that should govern human interaction, perhaps the only concept that we need to live and thrive. So, what is Justice? Among other definitions, Dictionary.com defines Just as, "1) guided by truth, reason, and fairness: []; 2) done or made according to principle; equitable; proper: []; 3) based on right; rightful; lawful: []; 4) in keeping with truth or fact; true; correct: []; 5) given or awarded rightly; deserved, as a sentence, punishment, or reward: [].″ And, among other definitions, Dictionary.com defines Justice as, "1) the quality of being Just; righteousness, equitableness, or moral rightness: []; 2) rightfulness or lawfulness, as of a claim or title; justness of ground or reason: []; 3) the moral principle determining Just conduct; 4) conformity to this principle, as manifested in conduct; Just conduct, dealing, or treatment.″

What makes Just and Justice so important for humanity in dealing with each other is that they are something that everyone can identify with, relate to, believe in, and understand and do so on a common and uniform basis. Put it simply, it is something that **all of us** can relate to and have in common. However, there is a "trick" to having common Justice for all, and that is that we all have to agree on the **basis of Justice.**

In the past, the basis of Justice in the western world was the judeo/christian (jc) god and the teachings in the bible promulgated by the select and chosen few. As long as outside influences, such as science or a new paradigm isn't introduced then the common basis of the jc philosophical teaching can be maintained for a very long time, no matter how irrational or illogical, because of the construct of the jc philosophy, which keeps the power in the hands of the select few. However, anything that is illogical or irrational will inevitably and eventually beg the introduction of new thought, even without outside influences. And, this is what started to happen with the jc philosophy when people like Galileo and Copernicus started opening their minds to the pursuit of truth. And, once the road to the truth is paved, like Pandora's box being opened, it can never be taken back. Over time the truth has come out, but the blind-faith that was drilled into our society for centuries has prohibited the truth from fully taking hold. And, this has created mass confusion and chaos, leading to the society that we see today. So, the time has come for mankind to transition to a new paradigm and see the true enlightenment. And, this new enlightenment must be based on universal and inalienable rights, Justice, and logical reasoning.

Most people understand what inalienable and universal rights mean and, reading through my book, people should now know what they are, if they hadn't before, and people should all know what rational thought is. However, Justice may not be so obvious to many. So, again, why Justice? As the definition of Just above says, Justice is guided by truth, reason, and fairness and is made according to principles and based on right and rightfulness. And, most of all, it is in keeping with truth or fact. But what makes Justice the principle that should govern human interaction is that it is what governs giving or awarding based on that which is **rightly deserved** as either a reward or punishment, i.e., it governs fairness. And, because it governs fairness in a **transparent** way and it can be done so in a **universal** manner, it is what makes Justice the only principle that should govern human-to-human interaction.

However, there is one issue that needs to be settled before we can have universal Justice govern the affairs and interactions of all humans. And, that is a philosophical construct that is rational, based on universal and inalienable individual rights and that doesn't allow for nor require blind faith. It is my fervent belief that I have presented jast such a philosophical construct here in these pages.

The key to world peace is uniformity of thought and respect for other people

The key to world peace isn't rocket science. If everyone thinks the same way and believes in the same philosophy, we will have world peace. The problem is that religion has been dictating the way we think for millenniums, and each religious group has tried to impose their view of world order on each other, which has fractured the world, and even caused wars to be fought over religious idealism (e.g., the crusades in the Middle-Ages). This was then further exacerbated by economic and ethnic strife, which has made it almost impossible to achieve peace among all the different regions and areas of the world.

Note that throughout history, those that had similar philosophical thoughts and outlooks have always allied themselves with each other and against those that are thought to be diametrically opposed. Today, we find that we are once again confronted with the old religious conflict that was started by pope Urban 2 during the 11th century. This isn't the way that the western world views it, but it is the way that the Arab world sees it. So, it doesn't matter what our view is, if one of the two sides sees it that way then it is what we have to deal with, particularly given the fact that we are fighting on their home turf – so to speak.

So, centuries and millenniums of religious fervor and practice have led us to nothing but misery and danger. The only way for us to overcome the quagmire that we find ourselves in is to abandon the jc philosophical construct as the dominant influence in our thinking and adopt a new philosophical system based on rational thought and respect for each other's beliefs assuming these beliefs are based on logic and Justice. Furthermore, we need to not only abandon the jc philosophy, but also refuse to accept any other non-rational philosophical construct. However, we must learn to respect other people's view, even though we may not agree with them. Once we live a truly rational, non-threatening life and abide by a truly rational philosophical construct, we don't have to be in conflict with anyone else.

Then, we jast have to let our example lead the way, and others will follow, because we are rational, considerate, good people without contradiction, without espousing something that cannot be proven, without forcing others to believe what we believe or have the need to force other to believe what we do, and without disrespect or hatred of others. Remember that every human believes that they know that which is rational and that which is not, but what makes the difference between right and wrong are the assumptions in a vast majority of instances. In the case of our current societal philosophical construct, the jc philosophy holds the most sway by far, but the assumptions underlying the jc philosophy is irrational and decrepit and even outright dangerous. Therefore, there is nothing we need from the jc religion and jc religious fervor. Put it another way: Believing and trying to live by the jc philosophical architecture can and does hurt us, but abandoning the jc religion doesn't hurt us, and we can not only easily live without it, but also thrive and become better people for the absence of it.

Once we achieve a more rational and Just life-style, we don't have to fight to enforce our beliefs on others the way the jc hierarchy has done so for millenniums. The rational and straight-forward philosophical construct will make others convert voluntarily; however, if they don't, as long as they understand that we respect their views and life-style, have no intention of forcing our beliefs on them, we intend to live in peace, and will use force only in response to force, this will dramatically lower tension and potential for conflict.

On the other hand, if we win converts to my way of thinking all across the globe then we can have uniformity of the Six Pillars, which ought to lead to world peace and harmony. Every philosophy perpetrated on mankind must be able to stand on its own merit and be able to withstand rational and logical scrutiny. Finally, it must actually help develop a better society and help mankind thrive, economically, financially, culturally, and philosophically. This will then lead to world peace. I believe I have created jast such a philosophy and have presented it in this book.

The bottom-line is that there is nothing to lose by dropping our society's jc religious adherence from our thinking, but the trick is to find the right substitute; again, I believe that I have presented in this book more than jast a better substitute.

Many of you will say that I'm being arrogant and cocky and that I cannot possibly know what is good for all humanity or not. Moreover, many will disagree that my philosophy is even rational or Just and will argue that I am not only arrogant, but very dumb to boot. I've heard it all, and I acknowledge that I could be wrong and, therefore, very arrogant and stupid. However, be advised that in numerous conversations that I've had with many recognized intelligent people from all over the world, I have not been presented with any counter-arguments that negate my thesis and philosophy, yet. Regardless, there is the possibility that I have not thought of something; if so, I would love to hear it, and enjoy an on-line debate about it.

Persecution: The jews/christians' excuse for forcing others to their will

Let me be perfectly clear: There is no excuse for using the political system to execute religious doctrine nor is there a place for religious doctrine in developing and executing government policy. However, no one should be denied philosophical freedom (including religious freedom) in their individual lives and the right to this philosophical freedom must be protected at ALL cost – full stop, period, the end.

Now that I've made my position perfectly clear, I hope the many jews/christians that have accused me of persecuting them stop their nonsense. First of all, the vast majority of Americans are jews/christians. Second, the christians are and have been the instruments of persecution since the founding of this country, and, in the world stage, have been the instrument of persecution since the first crusades. Therefore, the idea that my book and my philosophy are aimed at persecuting jews/christians is jast about the most ridiculous argument that I've ever heard.

Again, let me make it perfectly clear, I will be the first one to defend the right of every American to believe in and practice philosophical freedom, including religious freedom, as long as it does not interfere with the rights of others to do the same. However, the problem with the current social and political construct is that the jews/christians ARE forcing the rest of us to do what they want us to do, and the rest of us are a vast numerical minority. Therefore, the ones that are truly being persecuted by the jews/christians are the rest of us. The jews/christians are forcing us to follow their philosophy and doctrine by pushing our country deeper into socialism. This is wrong and is at the crux of my argument.

However, many jews/christians have argued that I'm trying to persecute them and that my position is nothing but a repackaging of the "age-old" persecution of the jews/christians. And, these people have argued to me that this is the reason why the political system MUST be used to secure their philosophical freedom. It is truly a laughable argument; and I believe that I have already amply presented my thoughts as to why this is a ridiculous position, so I will not repeat it here.

The bottom-line is that EVERYONE is entitled to philosophical freedom – including religious freedom – not jast jews/christians. Yet, this is lost on many Americans and most deny that the US is following judeo-christian philosophical doctrine when developing and executing public policy for our country. Even those that do acknowledge that our government follows judeo-christian philosophical doctrine strongly believe that that is the way that it should be. They contend that the judeo-christian philosophical doctrine is good for everyone! When I point out that some of us don't believe in their philosophy, let alone their god, their response is that we should be FORCED to abide by judeo/christian doctrine, because we don't know what's good for us, but they do! So, who's persecuting whom?!

This is precisely the type of "thinking" that's made our current social and political construct obsolete and dangerous for our country, and one of the main reasons why I wrote this book. What I'm asking for is nothing short of full and complete philosophical freedom – including religious freedom – for **EVERYONE** guaranteed by the Constitution and exactly the same protection we are afforded for our 1st Amendment rights. I don't think that this is too much to ask for and should be considered fundamental to our lives as Americans, like our 1st

Amendment rights and all of the protections afforded us under the Constitution.

Pascal's theorem as to why we should believe in the jc god is clever, but wrong!

A lot of very bright people often cite Pascal's theorem to justify their belief in the jc god; it is a very clever argument, but extremely inadequate. A long time ago, one of my best friends, who I admire greatly, asked me this exact question: "Based on Pascal's theorem, what do we have to lose by believing in the jc god?" My answer: Because Pascal assumes that we cannot make a proper evaluation of the merits of the existence of the jc god.

As a reminder, here's Pascal's theorem:

- If we believe in the jc god and it exists then we can go to heaven;
- If we believe in the jc god and it doesn't exist then we lose nothing;
- If we don't believe in the jc god and it doesn't exist, again, we lose nothing; however,
- If we don't believe in the jc god and it does exist then we are going to eternal hell.
- The conclusion: Therefore, we have nothing to lose and everything to gain by believing in the jc god, because 3 out of 4 outcomes are favorable or neutral and one is absolutely horrible.

This is a very clever argument, but as mentioned before, Pascal's assumption is that we do not have the ability to assess whether or not the jc god exists. However, this is where I disagree with Pascal. As I've written in many chapters in this book, we *do* have the ability to assess whether or not the jc god exists, and I strongly believe that I have proven that the jc god cannot exist. Therefore, Pascal's theorem is a clever argument, but invalid.

In addition, regardless of whether or not the jc god exists or doesn't exist, I believe that I have demonstrated that by believing in the jc god and acting on behalf of the jc philosophy, we are greatly damaging our society. Therefore, this alone merits our condemnation of the jc god and its philosophy and strongly merits our adoption of a new and more rational and Just philosophy such as the one I've presented in this book.

Other

Listen carefully, there's no such thing as emotion and instinct versus rational behavior; they're all the same thing!

The short answer is compressed logic: Emotion and instinct are both compressed logic.

What is instinct? We all believe that it is a set of pre-programmed behavior that we execute without thinking or have to think about. OK, how did we get this instinct? Most people believe that we were born with it like the survival instinct. Then how did our ancestors get their instincts? From their ancestors, who got it from their ancestors, et cetera. But this train of thought doesn't answer how instincts originated.

My theory – yes, it is only a theory because no one can really prove the origination of instinct – is that it had to start from the very beginning. At the beginning of the earth's formation there must have been a vast number of single cell organisms each doing their own thing: Some may have had priority on eating, others on drinking, others on surviving, others on getting colors, some on getting fat, some on getting slim ... you get the picture. Simply put, almost an infinite number of behaviors were probably tried out by these single cell organisms, and, ultimately, those that survived and evolved are likely the ones that developed the right behavior patterns. These behavior patterns were probably initially very random and those that had the correct behaviors survived and those that didn't perished. The first of the successful behavior patterns likely developed into what we call the survival instinct, as it is the one that likely insured the greatest probability of long-term survival of the species.

Through millions and millions of years of evolutionary development these various creatures probably developed other behavior patterns and those that were successful survived, while those that weren't became extinct. Eventually, over millions of years, these successful traits were likely codified into what we now call genes through some coding process and the successful organisms passed these successful traits to their off springs. Regardless, I believe that these successful trial-and-error behaviors eventually became what we now define as instincts. So, the bottom-line is that instinct is compressed logical behavior that was passed down from generation to generation, which eventually became part of our genetic coding. The same can be said about emotion.

Don't think about other people when it comes to emotion, think about your own situation. Generally speaking, do you cry because you are sad or happy? Do you laugh because you are sad or happy? Do you get angry because you are being treated with respect or disrespect? An individual's emotional reaction is exactly that, a reaction. Typically, a reaction to an external cue, but it could be because of something internal like a memory. What this means is that what you typically think about as being an emotion abides by some sort of a rational cause and effect sequence: You are hurt so you cry; you heard or saw something funny so you laugh; you were wronged so you get angry, etc. This means that there is a logical/rational link between input (thought or action) and output (what you call emotional behavior, like crying, laughing, getting angry, etc.). Therefore, when emotion is boiled down to its essence, it too is a form of compressed logical behavior.

So, you see, LOGIC IS TRULY EVERYTHING.

So, why do people perceive some others as being crazy, irrational, emotional, smart, or rational? Simply put, those others that people agree with but do things better than them, people perceive as being smart or more rational. Those that people don't agree with or understand, people think of as being crazy, irrational, or emotional. Particularly with those whose behavior people do not understand, people label others as crazy, but really the difference isn't that one person is rational and the other is crazy, but that they believe in different assumptions, set of values or some other base level philosophical underpinning.

I'll make it easy to understand what it is that I'm stating with a saying: There is an old saying where I come from: Most people believe that anyone who drives faster than them is crazy and anyone who drives slower than them is stupid. But really is that true? No it isn't. How fast one person drives is a matter of THEIR perception of what is safe and what is not, almost regardless of the legal speed limit, what one desires and doesn't, what one thinks they can get away with or not, what their schedule looks like, what their priorities are at the time that they are driving and their level of patience.

Let's take a more complex example, the Middle-East quagmire. The simple truth from our perspective is that we, the Americans, are trying to help the Afghans and the Iraqis to be free and prosperous under democratic and capitalist ideals. Therefore, from our perspective, the Taliban and Al Qaida are terrorists trying to not only thwart our benevolent objectives for the Afghans and Iraqis, but also to "control" their own people under Sharia or Islamic law.

From the Taliban and Al Qaida's perspective, we are trying to steal oil from Iraq and expand our hegemony and imperialist boundaries, in effect enslaving the people of Iraq and Afghanistan, while from their perspective, all they are trying to do is bring law and order back to their home and liberate their people from the oppression of American imperialism and hegemony.

From our perspective, we are right, from their perspective, they are right, so which is it? We are right, and we can counter-argue everything that they are saying, but to simple, uneducated people in those countries that are going through the pain and agony of a war, which inevitably produces unintended civilian casualties, I understand why the Taliban and Al Qaida hold sway.

Ultimately, the proof will be in the pudding. Eventually, we will leave Afghanistan, Pakistan and Iraq. And, if we achieve our objectives, these countries will have functioning democracies and burgeoning capitalist economies that will create wealth for their people. And, ultimately, the creation of wealth for the masses is one key for global peace. But for this to happen we MUST stay the course and make sure the well-being of the Afghan and Iraqi people are taken care of. What if someone in Afghanistan or Iraq asks what guarantee is there that we will leave once peace is achieved in those countries? No guarantee; however, I note that we are the only superpower in history that has ever conquered a country, made it better and left it in peace to prosper, thrice that we know of and can historically prove: Germany, Japan and South Korea. No other superpower in the history of the world has done that, not the Egyptians, Turks, Greeks, Iraqis, Romans, Chinese, Japanese, Mongols, Russians, Spanish, Portuguese, Belgians, Dutch, British, Germans or the French.

The point is that perspective and assumptions are what make logic seem inconsistent and emotions appear to be a sign of psychological imbalance. However, neither logic nor emotions, for that matter even instinct, is that inconsistent from person to person; it is the assumptions that we make and our individual perspectives that dictate the outcome of our acts and thoughts. So, if one believes that there is nothing more evil than America and that one's life is but one small object to give for the cause of the destruction of the world's greatest evil then it isn't so difficult to be a suicide bomber and is actually very logical.

The logic is that if something is so evil as to threaten everyone in the world then it must be destroyed at all costs. If that evil is Adolf Hitler's Germany or Hideyoshi Tojo's Japan then who wouldn't agree? In fact many of our ancestors did act to destroy Hitler's Germany and Tojo's Japan, and many of them did give their lives willingly to do so. However, if that evil is the US then Americans have trouble accepting the argument that our country should be destroyed at all cost. The trouble isn't the logic, because the logic is sound, the trouble we have – as Americans – is the assumption that the US is the world's greatest evil. Why? Because we live in the US, and, generally, most of us believe that we are good people with good intentions though a vast majority of Americans don't know the first thing about foreign affairs, global economics, nor the Middle-East and its history. Actually, more to the point, most people don't care about foreign affairs and global economics because it doesn't touch their daily lives.

Regardless, the vast majority of Americans will never agree that the US is the greatest evil that mankind has ever witnessed and faced; however, for a very large portion of the Islamic world that is exactly what we – America and Americans – represent. Therefore, the logic that such evil should be destroyed is infallible and mustn't/can't be challenged. However, the assumption that the US is the most evil country in history absolutely can and must be challenged. So, again, logic is everything and logic is consistent between individuals no matter where they live; the difference is not the logic, but, again, the assumptions and perspectives.

Similarly, emotions are and can be viewed in the same way, because emotion is nothing but compressed logic. So, when one sees someone screaming and yelling in the middle of the street, without knowing why they are doing it, one may view them as crazy, especially if they are waving a gun in the air. But what if the person had jast lost their home? Some people would understand why someone may stand in the middle of the road screaming and yelling and waving a gun, but most people would say that that person is still crazy. What if the perceived crazy person lost their home because they were laid off and couldn't afford the mortgage? Now, a few more people would understand this deemed crazy person's behavior. Continuing with the example, let's say that this person had 2 years of living expenses saved up when they were laid-off, was 52 and was 20 years into paying down the mortgage. I'm guessing that this would drive anyone crazy and so the majority would begin to understand this person's behavior and may even sympathize – but not necessarily condone it. Finally, what if it was known that this person is now 54 years old has lost all of their savings because hes beloved spouse died of pancreatic cancer and they used up all of their savings to try to save hes spouse to no avail. And, because hesh was laid off, they had no medical insurance. Who among us wouldn't be highly sympathetic and understand this person's pain, especially if this person is waving the gun in the air threatening to commit suicide?

Who wouldn't understand this person's behavior now? With reasoning, it is rarely ever the logic that is at fault; it is almost always the assumptions and perspectives that cause differences in how we look at the world and act on it. With emotions, it is rarely, if ever, that emotions are irrational; it is that the circumstances of the emotional outburst is not known to the observers and the level of appropriate emotional intensity that is open for debate. Therefore, we do not need to differentiate among rational, instinctive and emotional behavior, because, really, they are all one in the same. But, the reason why we should continue to make the distinction has nothing to do with right and wrong nor good or bad, but to understand the root cause of the behavior and the appropriate approach to resolving any conflicts that arise.

Regardless, understand that emotions and instincts are nothing more than compressed logic and expressions of emotions aren't wrong, dangerous or foolish under a vast majority of circumstances. However, we are now forced to be guarded about our emotions because of the perspective on how our society interprets these emotional expressions and the insecurity of individuals to deal with these emotional expressions. Also, we are taught to control our emotions, because it inhibits our ability to think rationally, but what if we can think rationally while still being emotional? Regardless, there is nothing wrong with having emotions and being emotional; it is but another rational expression. However, our society still frowns upon such expressions – rightly or wrongly – and as long as it does, we are forced to curtail such acts, if we are to be successful in this society, even though there is nothing wrong with such expressions and are rationally based.

As an aside keep this in mind: The average American is afforded the luxury of not caring about foreign affairs because of the value system of our gallant military personnel. Their service (ethical behavior), which stems from the belief in their moral/value system, shields us from the threat of global animosities. Don't ever forget that. And to those that say we can live without the military or should dramatically cut back our military spending: Be aware that your stupidity and near-sightedness is permitted only because of the grace of our military. There is a threshold where our military strength can be reduced to so that we don't risk danger to our country and the world in the future. Then there is the threshold where our future will change and then there is the threshold where our future will no longer exist. But, what's laughable is that the vast majority of Americans doesn't care about foreign affairs and are in no position to judge that which is adequate for our military, yet they speak with authority about military spending, and they advocate for the wholesale mass reduction of military spending. The end result of their position is that they are inviting the potential destruction of the world, and certainly, asking to put the US at risk. Why is this so? Because, no one can be sure of what military readiness we need to insure the safety of our country. Therefore, we have to be safer rather than sorry, and have a stronger military than what may be perceived as being necessary today.

If you really think it's the guns then you should put a bullet through your brain and save humanity

"Get rid of guns and we'll have a safer society." This has to be one of the stupidest statements I've ever heard. Granted, the use of grammar is correct, but the statement is extremely irrational and this is where most people get confused. I'll illustrate a perfectly easy to understand example. If I said, "the color of the sky is electric lime-green," most people would say that I'm wrong, but wrong how? The grammatical construct of the sentence is completely accurate. So, if I substitute the word blue for electric lime-green, everyone would agree. Therefore, the original statement is wrong because the color of the sky is never electric lime-green.

Now apply this analysis to the statement "get rid of guns and we'll have a safer society." The grammatical construct of the statement is correct. So, if we substituted the words "the HIV virus" for "guns," the statement would be correct both grammatically and logically. However, as the sentence stands, it is highly illogical and quite stupid. It's saying that guns act independently of humans and is equivalent to saying that "money is the root of all evil." Whether it is guns or money, it needs humans to act with them to determine whether guns and money were used for good or for evil. This is then indicative of whether the person is good or bad, but neither guns nor money alone can be attributed with any moral or value principles. But when someone actually says something so stupid like "money is the root of all evil," and "get rid of guns and we'll have a safer society" they are saying that money and guns are capable of acting, talking and thinking independently of humans. Does anyone think this is jast about the dumbest idea that anyone could think let alone actually utter?!

But let me go further and illustrate how dumb it really is to think that getting rid of guns will make our society safer. Before the invention of firearms did we still have wars and murders? Jast in case anyone is wondering, the answer is yes, there were murders and wars prior to the invention of guns. Can we still have wars and murders after guns have all been dismantled? Yes. Can dictators, drug dealers, criminals, and evil people in general find other ways of killing? Yes. So what's changed: The ease at which murder can be committed? What do people think that drug dealers, for example, will do to kill their rivals? I'd say they'd use more bombs, poisoned darts and arrows. So, what's next? Wouldn't the next evolutionary development be to advocate for the abolition of explosives and poisons? Then, I'd suspect that these "people" will turn to advocating for the abolition of bows and arrows and knives. After that I suspect spears, clubs, and bats would be next, including baseball bats, golf clubs, croquette needles, forks, glass bottles, spray cans, nitrate fertilizers, ... What if criminals turn to using cars to run over their rivals? Shouldn't we abolish the use of all cars, trucks, trains, planes, and other moving vehicles? Could these people be really that dumb and myopic? Ultimately, shouldn't we cut off everyone's hands in case they use it to strangle people to death? What about feet and legs? Could I really be the only person in the world that thinks that one of the most retarded statements in the world is "get rid of guns and we'll have a safer society"!?

However, there is still one more point to make about the stupidity of abolishing guns in any society and that is simply the black market effect. When there is a natural demand for something and legal and legitimate sources don't provide the product then illegal and illegitimate sources will. We saw this with alcohol in the 1920s, we are seeing it with drugs today, and we will see it with guns, if we attempt to abolish guns. In fact, we'd likely increase violence, not decreased it, if we were to abolish gun manufacturing, trading, transport, and ownership. Why? Because, we'd have the mob or gun cartels (like drug cartels) fill the gap, which would create more gang violence making our society even more dangerous.

This is why I keep on advocating for people to truly think. The amount of stupidity that is circulating in our world and being passed-off as wisdom is staggering, and is causing our society to slowly decay. And, we need to put a stop to this nonsense. If people want to know what thoughts, concepts, priorities and philosophies need to be changed to improve our society, generally speaking, laws, regulations and rules that prohibit or censor an activity like making guns, selling drugs and prostitution is one aspect. And, principles that are self-contradictory, irrational or immoral including statements like "everything is relative," "money is the root of all evil," and "tax the rich more because they can afford it" are thoughts that we must abandon to better our society, country and world.

Another concrete example of mass stupidity is the argument that Hollywood is perpetuating violence by making violent movies. The morons that go around uttering such gibberish are the ones that we should throw in jail and throw away the keys, never to be heard from again. Another example of such stupidity comes from people who say pharmaceutical companies are ripping us off because they are selling drugs for $100 per pill when it only cost them $1 to make or music companies that are selling albums for $10-$30 per album when it only cost them pennies to make them.

Let me leave it to the reader to figure out why believing that Hollywood is perpetuating violence by making violent movies is such a moronic and retarded thought and statement. Please enjoy debating this with your friends.

How do you know you're an asshole? Because of road rage, which is completely justified, yes, completely!

Why do people have road rage? Most people can't even express why they have road rage and others think that people who do have road rage are crazy. But, if one thinks about it, road rage is actually quite justified in our society.

The reason why people have road rage is the perceived or real violation of one's rights. If it is imagined then it's wrong, but if it is real then it is justified to have road rage. Here's an example: Let's say that you are driving along and you are following the car in front of you at 70 miles per hour and have about three car lengths between you and the car in front of you. Not exactly safe driving distance, but not exactly reckless either. A car to your right changes lane into yours rather abruptly and without signaling and cuts you off. Should you be upset? Most people would say, let it go, it doesn't matter. But, really, what is the driver that cut you off doing or saying?

That person is saying that they don't give a flying fuck about your safety and that their right to be in your lane is more important than your safety. Furthermore, they are saying that they don't give a flying fuck about your right to be notified about the pending changing environment and feel absolutely no need to get your permission or notify you by signaling about the pending lane change, which will result in you being cut off. In essence, they are saying that you are trivial and inferior to them and therefore need no consideration of any kind and they have the right to do what they will do to you.

Some may think that the offending person is simply lazy and careless and therefore I'm exaggerating and that no person ever really thinks this way when they cut someone off, but most people fail to realize something very important. When someone is lazy or careless, this is exactly what they are doing whether they are consciously doing so or not. What the offending person is saying is that they don't have to think about other people's safety, let alone actually acting on it. They are also saying that they don't have to bother with being mindful and caring about others, so they don't have to learn such behavior. What could be more compelling than thinking about the safety of others on the road? What's even more exasperating is that these morons don't realize that the safety of others is their own safety!

The only question is does two wrongs make a right? No, it doesn't, but how else can one express one's outrage? Honking? Yes that's one way. And, if the person apologizes then most people will back off because the victim thinks that the offending person is at least aware of what they were doing and apologized or they have some pressing reason for what they did. But if the violator doesn't respond or even gives the victim the finger then what? Most rule followers say that people should put a camera into their car and film everything that goes on and report the incident to the police. However, who's going to pay for the camera and time needed to report the incident to the police? It could be argued that the person who's been violated, since they are the one who cares.

Though in theory this works, in reality, people are more likely to get a polite brush-off from the police, as I've experienced on more than a few occasions. Therefore, victims have little recourse. So, the only behavior that most victims can do is to teach the violator a lesson and make them pay for what they did by doing the same to them that the offender did to the victim. Realistically, given that the police will never act to punish offenders, revenge is the only way at least some Justice can be had and the only way to teach the offending driver how unsafe their behavior is. The problem, of course, is that one may have to risk one's own life to teach them a lesson, which seems to be an expensive price to pay. But what if everyone had road rage, and some acts did result in accidents or even deaths? How many people would risk cutting someone off? Does anyone remember the freeway shooting incidents in California and what happened to inappropriate road behavior soon thereafter, at least for a short while?

The point is that there are a lot of assholes on the road and judging by what I've seen, many may be the lazy types. Here's what makes people an asshole on the road:

1) People don't signal before changing lanes or turning;
2) People cut off other drivers;
3) After cutting drivers off people don't get out of the way of the driver that they cut off or don't accelerate or even slow down;
4) People go at whatever speeds they want in the left lane of a multi-lane road and, worst, they make others go around them;
5) People don't move from the left lane even when they are flashed or honked at;
6) People flash their lights or honk at other drivers to go faster in the furthest right lane of a multi-lane road;
7) People don't pay attention to what's going on around them;
8) People straddle lanes so others can't pass them;
9) People generally don't give a flying, leaping shit about other drivers' rights on the road and do as they please;
10) People cause an accident and then try to blame it on the other person, let alone apologizing for what they did;
11) When turning corners people get in the way of on-coming traffic making the other driver avoid them;
12) When parking people take up more than one space;

13) When parking people use any excuse to park in the handicap spot, despite the fact that they are not handicapped;

14) People don't think twice about double parking on a busy street because it's convenient for them;

15) When traffic is merging people ignore the inter-locking order of the merge (left side car merges into the mid-lane, then the right, then the left, then the right, et cetera or vice-versa);

16) When people arrive at an intersection, they ignore the first to arrive rule and if they arrive together, they ignore the fact that the person to their right-side has priority;

17) Busy talking on the phone – particularly without a head piece, Bluetooth connection or other car microphone – or texting while driving, causing people to not pay attention to their environment;

18) I reserve a special place in my heart for rubberneckers; it doesn't matter if people brake, take their foot off the accelerator or jast turn their head to look, rubberneckers are the biggest road-going assholes there are.

There are so many more behaviors that make people an asshole on the road, but I'm not sure this is the place for the complete list. Regardless, there are too many assholes on the road. But, one can make mistakes, and if one does happen to make an honest mistake, at least have the courtesy to acknowledge the mistake and give a sign acknowledging the mistake like lifting up one's hand and waving or turn the hazards on and let it blink a few times, so the victim knows that there was no disrespect intended. At least then others know there was no disrespect! Anyway, I suppose I owe the reader some clarity regarding some of the points in the above list. Let's talk about #3.

3) *After cutting drivers off people don't get out of the way of the drive that they cut off or don't accelerate or even slow down:* If one is at an intersection and is making a turn and the turn is made such that the person coming from a 90-degree angle has to slow down or brake, or worse, veer away to avoid the driver making the turn then the turning driver is cutting the other driver off. In another situation, if one is changing lanes and cuts someone off, at least have the courtesy to accelerate, so that the person that got cutoff can resume their travel speed and not get slowed down. Also, when moving into a lane on a multi-lane road, if one makes another driver brake or slow down then the one changing lanes is cutting the other driver off. Again, once this happens, have

the decency to at least accelerate and match the speed of the person in front, so that the inconvenience to other drivers is minimized.

4)-6) *People go at whatever speed they want in the left lane and, worst, they make people go around them:*   What kind of an insecure, screwed-up asshole/bitch is the person that has to inconvenience others and make it more dangerous to drive because of their stupid insecure behavior? This may be one of the most stupid acts I see on the road. Let me make it perfectly clear, no one should act like the police unless they are the police. If one is driving at 75 mph or even 95 mph in a 75-mph zone, this doesn't mean that they have the moral right to be in the furthest left lane. If the cars to the right are going at or even above the speed that they are traveling, they are an asshole/bitch. One is a bloody asshole/bitch, if they see cars building up behind them and they do nothing about it causing a traffic jam behind them. A driver is the biggest asshole on the road, if hesh is honked at or flashed at and they STILL DO NOTHING. Jast because a driver is traveling at the speed limit, it doesn't give hem the right to interfere with other people's right to pass hem. Certainly, an ordinary driver is not the police. The remedy is simple. If the cars are moving slower to one's right and someone approaches from behind, move to the right at the first opportunity that presents itself. Drivers approaching from behind must give the person in front an opportunity to clear the lane before honking or flashing then once the person clears the way, as one passes, one should either give the courteous driver a wave of thanks or flash the hazards three or four times to indicate gratitude for the other driver's cooperation. On the other hand, if one is the driver blocking the road in the farthest left lane and the cars to the right are going faster than the driver in the farthest left lane is a despicable asshole/bitch. In this situation, the driver approaching from behind should immediately flash or honk or both and the slow driver must clear the way as expeditiously as possible given that they are being an asshole/bitch. The proper way to clear the lane is to accelerate, signal then change lanes. So, why should one do this?

When one travels at speeds that are not commensurate to what others want to travel, one is inhibiting the right of others to travel at the speeds that they deem appropriate. Second, when a single driver blocks the way for other cars to pass, particularly if there is a lot of traffic on the road, the obstructing driver is further contributing to the congestion, because hesh is blocking the lane that could be used to decongest the road. This means that a lot of people become unnecessarily angry, which could cause these drivers to perform unnecessary and possibly dangerous maneuvers to get around the rude and inconsiderate driver, not to mention the wasted time. To remedy the situation, and get the traffic to flow more smoothly, all one has to do is to move one lane to the right so that the cars behind hem can pass, which gets the flow of traffic moving far faster and reduces congestion and traffic jams. This means that it is good for everyone as it reduces traffic jams all around, which reduces time on the road for everyone. It is also likely to save on gasoline consumption, which reduces money going to the Middle-East.

On the flipside, the lane on the right is where one absolutely has the right to go as slow as one pleases, regardless of the minimum speed limit. Here, the person honking or flashing to make another driver get out of the way is the bloody asshole/bitch. If one wants to get pass the vehicle in front of them in the farthest right lane, it is up to the passing driver to safely change lanes to their left and pass the car in front of them then merge back, if and as necessary.

If the freeway or road is a three lane road then the standard should be the same for the left lane and the right lane as a two lane road or freeway, but the middle lane is variable. It should travel at a speed faster than the right lane, but slower than the left. But, in any event the right lane should be traveling at or below the speed limit, the middle lane should travel at or above the speed limit up to 10 miles per hour above the speed limit, and the left lane should travel above 10 miles per hour above the speed limit. If there is a fourth lane, this should be for people who are willing to travel far faster than 20 miles above the speed limit, or used to pass people in the third lane (farthest right lane being lane 1). Keep in mind sometimes lane 1 or 4 are exit lanes, in which case it doesn't count as one of the travel lanes. By the way, if people travel to Europe and they don't abide by freeway courtesies, they're going to get honked and flashed at and hated to no end. Furthermore, if they find out that the driver is an American all that this will accomplish is to reinforce the image of ugly Americans. But people may not care if they're an asshole or a bitch.

The bottom-line is that road rage doesn't occur in isolation; it typically is triggered by some asshole/bitch doing something, which they're not supposed to do. This means that road rage is an indication of how much of an asshole/bitch people are and road rage is absolutely a justified reaction to what someone is doing to them. Wouldn't you get angry if someone pointed a gun at you, regardless of whether or not it's loaded, cocked or fired? If we are courteous to each other and act orderly then road rage should disappear. Apologize, if one commits a violation and rectify the situation as soon as it is practicable and safe. It's not rocket science. If people don't they'll be subject to road rage, which could lead to an accident they or their family may seriously come to regret.

Most importantly, courteous and respectful public conduct is one of a very few social obligations that we have to each other and it is a very important factor in building trust amongst us.

What are we doing as a country when we tax the money we pay our military personnel?! And, why aren't more people outraged?!

I couldn't believe it when I found out! The federal, state and local governments collect taxes from military personnel! Get this, the military gets paid with money collected as taxes from us then they get taxed on the tax dollars. How ridiculously messed-up is our society that we'd do this to the people that make our lives – at least in large part – possible?! If that were what we were going to do, we should jast pay them less and not collect taxes at all. This would save on administrative costs, which would save tax payers money. However, this is the second best solution. The best solution would be to pay them like we should and not tax them at all. If they are protecting us, they should be given the benefit of middle-class lifestyles. Meaning the starting salary of military personnel should be at least $25,000 per year, tax-free and in combat, it should be doubled, also tax-free.

We should also set aside money for the military personnel for their retirement, so that after serving their country, no solider is in the streets. For every year served, they should get half of their annual pay put aside in a savings account and released to the military personnel – tax free – at the same time they collect Social Security. However, if a military person is discharged honorably due to wounds received in combat or disability incurred while executing their military duties, their retirement account should be made immediately available to the person, if they so choose, also tax free. If the discharge occurs due to a combat wound then the retirement account should be doubled.

Any soldier who dies in combat or while performing their duty should know that their family will be taken care of. In this regard, the retirement account should be immediately made available to the family, 100% tax-free. In addition, the family should continue to receive the annual compensation – tax free – of the military personnel until the primary beneficiary passes away whether they are the parents, the husband, the wife or significant other. If the person that passed away was a decorated military person then the compensation to the family should be increased to reflect the courage. For example, a family of a deceased Medal of Honor recipient should be given $10 million tax free (adjusted for inflation) and double the last annual compensation of the deceased hero or heroine should also be awarded to the family on an on-going basis, again, until the primary beneficiary passes away. The family of the deceased military person who was awarded the Distinguished Service Cross, the Navy Cross or the Distinguished Flying Cross should be given $5 million tax free and 150% of the last annual compensation of the deceased hero or heroine on an on-going basis, again, until the primary beneficiary passes away. Each successive medal should increase the compensation by more than the base amount. So, if, on that extremely rare occasion, someone were to be awarded a second Medal of Honor then dies in combat, the family should receive not $10 million, not $20 million, but $40 million and 4x the person's last annual salary. I'm pretty sure there was no one who was awarded three, but if there were, the family should receive not $30 million, but $90 million and 9x the person's last annual salary.

Anyway, it is absolutely unforgivable that we tax the money that our military personnel earn. To use common language, these people "sacrifice" their lives to protect ours and allow us to do what we need to do to be happy. In short, they buy our prosperity and happiness with their lives. The least that we can do is to make sure that they are well taken care of and want for naught. I find it despicable that the politicians don't see anything wrong with paying our military less than minimum wage, while they collect multiples of the average income of Americans.

Also, what does it say about politicians who barter and bargain with our military personnel's lives? They trade favors and bargain for earmarks, so they can get re-elected, while withholding key equipment for our brave soldiers as a bargaining tool. How many soldiers died, because Congress dragged their feet allocating funds to supply armor protected Humvees to the military? Politicians disgust me.

Politicians should be made accountable too and should also be treated as guilty until proven innocent.

Truth be known, the slimy politicians that we see today are only a reflection of our country's philosophical state. If we, as a country, were smart, thoughtful, and really planned for the long-term well-being of our country then we wouldn't listen to politicians that lie about the benefits of "redistributing wealth," and how we need "social Justice" to cure the ills of our country. Also, "social Justice" is a made up phrase that has no meaning. What's the difference between "social Justice" and "normal Justice?" The phrase "social Justice" was made up so that politicians can justify stealing from the wealthy, pure and simple. How could anyone think that "social Justice" is something that can be separate from "normal Justice," whatever "social Justice" is versus "normal Justice!?" Instead we ought to throw all these bums out of office, starting with Obama and working our way down the chain.   This is not to say that Republicans are necessarily any better, but on a scale of -100% to +100% (for evil to good), if the Democrats are -95 then the Republicans are -90: Lesser of the two evils, but nevertheless very evil, either way.

So, why are Republicans slightly better than the Democrats? Look at the last budget/debt crisis negotiations. What did the Republicans want? The House passed $6 trillion in budget cuts, no increase in revenue and passed a balanced budget amendment; however, the Democrats wanted at least $1 trillion in additional theft through tax increases on the wealthy, reduction of mortgage interest deduction for the wealthy (another biased act against the wealthy), increase in capital gains tax and dividends (another biased act against the wealthy and the elderly), and paltry cuts in spending. This makes the Democrats more evil, because, they fail to recognize that the trouble that we are in is due to spending, not due to a lack of revenue. So, they are the ones that want to continue to perpetuate the evil and continue poisoning and killing our society. The Democrats are no different than the Greeks that are protesting in the streets to continue the high subsidies that they had been receiving, many of them not even realizing that they are asking to commit slow murder/suicide. I think Europe should let Greece continue with their subsidies and let them drown in debt. That should teach them a very good lesson. Of course that's not going to happen, but it's a fun thought.

Anyway, getting back to the US, what we need in this country is a new party that espouses real morals, values, ethics, and integrity that acts with honor and simple honesty; a party that really speaks the truth and nothing but the truth instead of telling people what they want to hear in the short-term so their members can get elected and repeatedly re-elected. The reason why the independent vote is getting larger and larger and larger is due to a combination of people losing their way and not knowing what's good or bad, and people trying to pick between the lesser of the two evils. If I were a multi-billionaire, say $20 billion+, one thing I'd do is to start up a third political-party called the Justice Party, have the bold eagle as the symbol of this new party with a donkey in one claw and an elephant in the other, a scale in the beak of the eagle, whose platform will be to run on the unvarnished truth and nothing but the truth and Justice. More on this later.

Anyway, the point that I'm trying to make is that who gets elected and what they do is a direct reflection of our country's Six Pillars. So, the sad state of affairs of our country is directly reflected by who we've elected into political office. And, given the human trash that are our politicians, we should all hang our heads in shame and reflect on how equally disgusting our Six Pillars are as a country to elect these human trash into political office. As sad as what I'm about to say is, I have to say it. The fundamentalist Muslim terrorist groups have one thing right: There are no innocent people in our country, because we elect our own politicians. The truth may not be that dramatic, but certainly, we are responsible for our political leaders, because we elect them. Therefore, out of every country in the world, if any country deserves the government that its people have, it is us.

Therefore, the problem is that until we elect politicians that are true leaders and visionaries, we have to change the way business is done in Washington, D.C. One of the priorities that we must achieve is to make Washington, D.C. politics transparent; very, very transparent. Politicians (mayors, city councils, state governors, representatives and senators, the president of the US, and federal representatives and senators) have passed laws that basically treat people on Wall Street and corporate officers as guilty until proven innocent. This is not only a massive violation of their rights accorded to them by the

Constitution, but also it sets an extremely bad precedent for other segments of our society.

Therefore, I propose that we treat politicians in exactly the same manner. All political meetings, all meetings between politicians and lobbyists, all meetings between and among politicians or their staff or aides should be recorded and monitored by independent watch groups, and made available to everyone through the internet. No politician should be allowed any gifts, travel, meals, or other benefit at all – no exceptions – and all politicians should pay for their own healthcare through the same group health insurance that the rest of the government personnel get and should be given last priority on all procedures, medicine allocations, and other medical benefits. And, they should not be allowed to use personal funds to acquire medical benefits, and if they want to use personal funds, they should be forced to resign, never to seek any public office ever again for the rest of their lives.

With regard to their pay, we should not only cut the salary of the politicians by half, 100% of the politicians' income and capital gains should be taxed at the highest marginal income tax rate in the federal, state and local taxes allowed, plus 10% more. Moreover, the higher the marginal rate goes the higher the penalty portion should increase for the politicians. Lastly, politicians' salary should fluctuate with the increase and decrease in the long-term unemployment rate. They should not be allowed to pass down any money to their children or others until they allow complete freedom of movement of money among the direct lineage in any American family. Also, upon their death and the death of their spouse, 100% of the money and assets they have left should be confiscated and donated to decrease the federal and state governments' debt unless they reduce federal or state debt by at least the same percentage amount as the number of years that they served in office. For example, if they served in congress for 10 years then they must have reduced the federal debt by 10% in order for their children, relatives or charities to receive any money from the dead politician's estate.

As for their retirement funds, it should also be cut in half and they should not be allowed to hold any stocks or bonds of private or public companies. Also, the money they earn in their retirement accounts should accrue in inverse proportion to inflation. If inflation exceeds 3.00%, they should earn no money in their retirement account. If inflation exceeds 5.00%, their retirement account should be deducted. Finally, if the government runs a budget deficit, the politicians that presided over the budget deficit should be given one year to fix the problem, meaning not only close the gap, but also make up for the deficit incurred in the previous year. If they can't/don't fix it, not only should they be forced to resign, but they should be arrested and thrown in jail, commensurate to the years that they served in government. Meaning, if they served 5-years as a congressperson, they should go to jail for five years and their retirement account and all assets should be confiscated to cover for the budget deficit.

If we do this, I wonder how long we'd run budget deficits, how quickly we'd fix the national debt problem, how much hanky-panky the politicians try to get away with, how long the high unemployment rates last and how high inflation rises in the future. The theory behind my thesis isn't complicated. If people want something done, provide the incentives to the people that are empowered to get it done. Typically, these incentives should be both positive and negative, but given the track records of congress, presidents, state legislatures, governors, mayors, and city councils, I think we should start with negative incentives first and see how they do. If they deliver results and make substantial progress then and only then we can look at instituting possible positive incentives.

Why is this justified? The politicians talk about serving, and how it's not about the money. OK, then let them prove it. Congress, state legislatures and city councils should have absolutely no problems passing these laws and the president, the governors and mayors should have no problems signing it into law. Anything short of passing and signing these measures into law would only be a reaffirmation of how corrupt our political system and politicians really are. It's really that simple.

Stimulus spending should be made as an exception, and that only as a remedy to a systemic problem and not as a matter of course

Given my vision of how politicians and legislators should be governed and how taxes should be spent, deficit spending would be difficult, even under trying economic situations like the one that we see today. But, when necessary, there has to be a mechanism by which deficit spending should be allowed.

First, an official declaration of a recession must be made by the National Bureau of Economic Research (NBER). Then either the Federal Reserve Bank or another independent third party must confirm. Second, the president (in the case of state governments the governor) will propose a stimulus spending package and the legislative branch must approve with at least a two-thirds majority by *both parties* in *both chambers* on an expedited basis. With the declaration of a recession, if the president does decide to propose a stimulus spending package then he must instruct the attorney general to appear before the Supreme Court and start the process for asking for a temporary exception to the constitution and explain to the Supreme Court how the money will be made available (e.g., taxes), what it will be used for (e.g., infrastructure, funds to charities for unemployment), how long it will last (my opinion is that no economic stimulus should last longer than 1 year), and, most importantly, how it will be repaid (i.e., how much tax money will be gathered from what source and over what period) and what benefits will be granted to the people that repay the stimulus spending, unless it is repaid by all tax payers equally. Then when the final stimulus package is passed, the Supreme Court will make a final deliberation as to the fair and Just nature of the stimulus package. If the Supreme Court decides to strike down the package then the president and the legislators must reconvene immediately and develop an alternative stimulus package to present to the Supreme Court and restart the process for gaining an exception.

In judging whether or not the stimulus package is fair and Just, the Supreme Court must consider who the stimulus package benefits and who ends up paying for the stimulus. If the benefits and the costs do not accrue to the same people, or there is no Just and fair compensation mechanism for the group that bears the costs but not the benefit of the stimulus spending, the Supreme Court must declare it unconstitutional and strike it down. Also, as the government argues the case for passing the stimulus, an opposition group must be formed to oppose the stimulus and argue the case against the government's in the Supreme Court. The selection of who should make the opposing argument is a difficult one and there is no obvious choice that I can think of. However, one suggestion would be for members of congress that opposed the stimulus package to appear before the Supreme Court to argue the case against the stimulus package. If the stimulus package passes with 100% of the members of congress voting for the stimulus then opposing members from state governments or representatives of independent third parties such as the NBER, federal reserve or professors from top academic institutions may be selected to argue the case opposing the stimulus in front of the Supreme Court.

If the recession is not over within the timeframe of the stimulus and the president wishes to renew the stimulus then the administration must reappear before the Supreme Court. Most importantly, each stimulus package must have an expiration date and no automatic renewal will be allowed under any circumstance. In addition, any and all stimulus packages will not be allowed to last beyond one year after the recession is declared as being over by the NBER and confirmed by an independent third party.

Never, ever listen to politically correct people; they will FUCK YOU UP and fuck up our society

Jast because people don't use the word stupid, retarded or moron – which, by the way were scientific terms – it doesn't mean that stupid, retarded or moronic people don't exist and that people don't view others as stupid, retarded or moronic. Despite this reality, some politically correct (PC) moron decided that the words retard, stupid and moron are offensive and decides to call these people "mentally challenged." "Mentally challenged?!" Does this change the fact that these people are stupid, retarded or morons, if they really are stupid, retarded or moronic? Of course not, but to the PC morons using the term "mentally challenged" somehow makes it less offensive or insulting than to say someone is stupid, retarded or a moron out loud. What these PC retards did not anticipate is that people now use the phrase "mentally challenged" to express derision instead of calling someone stupid, retarded or a moron. The PC morons *are* "mentally challenged" because they could not anticipate beyond the tip of their nose.

The concept that the PC police don't understand is that it isn't the word that matters, but the thought these words represent in people's minds, and with what intent people use these words. If people don't like a word, they're a moron, if people don't like the concept they are also a moron. However, if people don't like the derision then they are intelligent. Calling a moron, a moron, isn't an insult nor is it derision unless the person really is not a moron or didn't behave like one.

Regardless, let's take this to the ultimate level. Let's analyze the ultimate taboo word in our society: NIGGER. What is the origination of the word nigger? It's a derisive term for negro, which was a technical definition of dark-skinned people from Africa. However, some prejudiced, asshole bigot came up with the derisive term nigger, and used it to describe slaves then applied it to free black-Americans. After a while the term became the norm. Regardless, in the minds of the people that use the term, slaves and then black Americans were inferior, stupid, and in between human and ape. Therefore, it is very understandable why black Americans take such offense to the term, and rightly so.

Yet, in our society, niggers do exist. But from my perspective, niggers aren't required to be dark skinned. In my mind, drug dealers, rapists, child molesters, frauds, thieves, murderers, especially serial-killers are obvious niggers – they have the form of a human, but are worse than animals. But, I also believe that immoral, dishonorable, sinister, unethical, sneaky, short-sighted (including politically correct individuals) people and the vast majority of politicians are also niggers regardless of their skin color, because they don't know how to think and act worse than animals. And, these niggers should be treated as inferior, stupid and non-human, in my opinion. However, the realistic outcome is that some of these niggers are bosses, people with power, or others that could impact our life. So, each person has to decide for themselves how they want to deal with these niggers.

So, yes, the word nigger used in the historical context of the word is very offensive and should not be used as a derisive term to describe anyone, particularly those in our society that are dark skinned. However, there are appropriate uses of the word. When describing history and the environment that existed, it is very acceptable to use the word, such as I have here in the book. The other way to use the word is to use it in the way I've defined it and apply it more broadly to people that are less than human, *regardless of their skin color*. The other issue that one must realize is that almost any adjectives that can be used to describe human behavior or state can be used derisively. For example, take the word genius: "Aren't you a freaking genius!" So, again, it's not the word, but the intent behind the word, i.e., the person's morals, values and ethics that is the problem.

So, apply this to politically correct people. Essentially, these people believe that changing the name of a flower called rose to something else will make a rose have different characteristics. They would deny it, but think about it carefully: Jast because people say someone is mentally challenged does that mean that the person is not stupid, retarded or a moron? Jast because people say that a person is mentally challenged, does that mean that the people around them and the mentally challenged will not think that the mentally challenged person isn't stupid? Even if everyone all thought that the stupid person was truly jast mentally challenged – whatever that means – the people are still thinking that the IQ of the mentally challenged person is significantly below average. So, what's changed?

Again, ultimately what matters isn't necessarily the word that one uses but the attitude, thought, assumptions, and, most importantly, the intent behind the word that one chooses to use. If somebody says another person is a moron, and the person has an IQ of 50-69 that's fine or if somebody calls another person retarded and that person has an IQ of 70-85 that's fine too. Also, if someone calls their friend a moron or stupid to be funny or as a joke and they *both* appreciate the humor then that's fine too.

However, even if people don't use words like retard, moron, or stupid, if they don't think twice about using concepts that these words represent in an inappropriate fashion then that's what makes a person evil, not that they used a certain word. Anyone can say retard, moron or stupid all day long, as long as they don't use the words inappropriately and, most importantly, they don't use the words derogatorily or with malice. So, again, what's important isn't the word that someone uses, but the intent that they want to convey. This means that it's not important that people use politically correct language, but that they have good thoughts and convey those good thoughts appropriately.

So, what this means is that unless a word is created with deliberate malice, disrespect, humiliation, or harmful intent and meaning, it is people who make language ugly, because of their ugly minds and ugly thoughts. So, it doesn't matter that we, as a society, keep coming up with new ways to express concepts and situations, unless we, as a society, learn how to think and act properly people will always find a way to be ugly no matter the word used.

The fact that politically correct people don't know this, can't grasp this concept or think they are so much smarter than everyone else that they'd have the rest of us blindly abide by a rule that they set up, absolutely no one should listen to them, take their advice, consider their opinion or even give them the time of day. Politically correct people obviously don't know how to think, can't distinguish the meaningful from the superficial, reality from fantasy, and the important from the frivolous. Yet, many of these people are in position of respect, power and influence, because *they sound good*. This is absolutely ridiculous! Imagine these politically correct people leading our country; any country. What happens to a country led by politically correct people? The US government, that's what happens.

Finally, when I was growing up, I never heard kids calling each other "challenged," mentally or otherwise; stupid, moron, retard, idiot, numbnut, dingbat, yes, but never "challenged." Now, kids go around calling each other challenged, in addition to using all of the words that we used to say to each other. So, again, nothing has changed; children will be children. The only difference is that now there's one more word that children and adults have learned to distort and use derogatorily.

Political correctness is another way for people to pretend that they are thinking when all that they are doing is jast pretending. It is a clever short-term argument for why and how we should change ourselves, but it's no different than masking the symptoms and calling it a cure. It's jast another way to be short-sighted, so please stop and think before speaking or trying to speak politically correctly.

The best example of political correctness gone wild to the ultimate maximum and how it is the epitome of absolute stupidity that I've heard of is when a councilman in some city used the word niggardly in the proper fashion and had to apologize for using the word and being insensitive. ***ARE YOU KIDDING ME!?*** I couldn't believe my ears! The world has truly gone mad! If this example doesn't illustrate the absolute stupidity of political correctness, I think our country is beyond saving.

Age is NOT a good indicator of maturity

The vast majority of people equate age with maturity and adulthood. This is absurd in the most absurd way. As a younger adult, I was more mature than most that were in their 60s and older. More so now, I consider myself more mature, not to mention rational than the vast majority of people in this world. Before someone says something really immature let me jast say that I've lived in many countries across my life including countries in Europe, Asia, and the

Americas. And, I can tell the reader with unequivocal certainty that age has nothing to do with maturity.

In fact, most people really do not mature past early teen years and a very few mature through college. And, no one should confuse maturity with learning how to hide the immaturity better and better over time. There was a book written that implied that everything we need to know about life, we learn in kindergarten. In today's society that certainly seems true. However, this should not be the standard by which we live. I don't know about others but I don't think that we, as a society, should be satisfied with an overall maturity level of kindergarteners.

If people understand this and they believe that maturity cannot be measured by age, this means that there are a lot of issues that get thrown into the realm of uncertainty. Some concepts that get thrown into the maelstrom would include voting age, drinking age, age for sexual consent, including marriage, age for adult treatment in criminal cases, driving age, smoking age, gambling age and any other social rules based on age. Let's take drinking age as an example.

The first time I got drunk was when I was 12. My mother got me drunk, deliberately. I got hooked on the taste of Scotch and Cognac by my father when I was about 15. However, it may surprise the reader to know that since I was born, I've been drunk well less than 10 times in my life. The last time I was drunk, I was celebrating something with friends, did not drive, did not get into a car with someone who was drunk, and went to sleep straight after in a friend's home, all this according to plan. Lastly, I don't need more than 3 or 4 drinks to get drunk either. From an early age, my parents taught me that being drunk isn't a desirable condition because one loses control in more ways than one. Second, my parents taught me to appreciate fine alcoholic beverages, but taught me not to over indulge and certainly not to abuse alcohol. So, by the time I got to college, my curiosity for alcohol and drinking was none and potential abuse of alcohol was not even in the realm of possibility. I found it extremely intriguing and funny that my classmates constantly wanted to go drinking and get drunk and found drunken behavior funny. I still find it funny that people think getting drunk is fun and funny, no matter the circumstance and situation.

One of the best exposures that my parents gave me in regard to drinking was they allowed me and my siblings to indulge in small quantities of alcohol all through our teenage years, but always in a controlled environment with my parents. The other lesson that I learned from my parents is through example: My parents were never, ever drunk under any circumstances, ever! The final lesson is they always talked about how drunkenness is a mark of a complete loser and people who lack maturity and sophistication. There's no question that frequent drunkenness is a great indication of immaturity, in my opinion.

Let's contrast my behavior and history with those who get routinely drunk every week or almost every week. There is no comparison of maturity no matter the age. It is no different with people who blindly follow rules. These people are immeasurably immature compared to people who actually think. So, how can a society fairly adjudicate age-based rules and laws? The answer is it can't. Therefore, it shouldn't.

The point is that physical maturity does not equal mental maturity. But, because society needs to perceive that the laws and the government must be fair to ALL people, the assumption is made that ALL people are essentially the same and therefore must be treated ALL the same when it comes to social behavior. However, this is prejudiced and discriminatory in a different way. Despite this obvious discrimination, the need for superficial equality forces laws and rules to apply *equally* to everyone whether it is appropriate or not. However, the opposite problem is that unequal treatment of people under the same laws would raise concerns for subjectivity, favoritism and pleas for leniency and exceptions. These are legitimate concerns. The solution: Don't create laws that are unjust and forces unequal application of the laws.

Some people may be wondering why I'm advocating for the same treatment of everyone when I look for tax reform, but when it comes to age-based laws I don't want equal treatment for everyone. Sounds like it's a contradiction, doesn't it? It isn't. Here's why it's consistent and Just. Because both situations are giving everyone what they deserve and only what they deserve. The government service to everyone should be consistent and equal, so the payment for those services should also be equal. However, when it comes to age-based rules the government should treat people equally, based on their ability and maturity. Another way to look at it: The reason why the current tax laws are unfair is because the wealthy are paying for services that they don't receive, while current age-based laws are unfair because it is not only the wrong standard to use to regulate morality, but also that morality-based laws are inappropriate because it ignores each person's maturity level. In other words, taxes must not be about what one can afford to pay, but about the service that the government provides and what each individual in our society has to pay for those services. Therefore, given that the government must provide the same service to everyone, equally, the payment for those services must also be equal. In contrast, age-based laws are about determining when a human is capable of making mature decisions, independent of guidance. However, as I've demonstrated, age is no indication of maturity or ability to make good decisions, and that is why age-based laws are wrong.

Finally, from a personal relations point of view, individuals don't have restrictions that force them to treat everyone equally. So, make the distinction; treat people according to their true mental maturity, not their physical maturity. Most of all, don't respect people because of their position, but because of who they are. Don't envy those that are born with gifts (e.g., Tiger Woods, any supermodel, et cetera) or have wealth, but respect those that know how to use those gifts and wealth wisely and appropriately. And, always remember, jast because someone is physically mature, it doesn't make them mentally mature.

Avoid people who look for past experience as a good measure of potential future success; they don't know what they're thinking, saying or doing

Who's a better driver? A 30-year old responsible person who has been driving for 14 years or a 90-year old responsible person who has been driving for 74 years? Forget a 30-year old, what about a mature 17-year old that's been driving for only a year versus the 90-year old? No matter how responsible, mature and *experienced* the 90 year old person is, they're not going to be terribly good at driving, are they?

Well, if people understand this argument for why experience isn't a good measure for driving, why can't people understand this reasoning for a lot of other endeavors like for jobs and careers? When I interview and hire people, I don't look for experience in the field that I work in. On the contrary, given the way people are trained, I find it to be a negative if a candidate does have prior experience in the field of endeavor that I'm hiring for.

When hiring people, the first trait that I look for is intelligence, second, I look for ability to correctly apply one's intelligence – this includes the ability to think – third, I want a candidate that learns very quickly then applies that learning effectively and adaptively, fourth, I look for character, i.e., their Six Pillars, and lastly I look for personality and compatibility. If any one of these components are missing then the candidate is unqualified, in my opinion. Typically, a candidate either has all of these characteristics or none; very few have some, but not all of these traits.

One qualification that can be a dead giveaway for 1, 2, and 3 is where the candidate went to university. Typically, the better the school that a person graduated from the higher the probability that they have 1, 2, and 3, almost irrespective of their GPA. Even if a candidate was valedictorian at their university, if the school is mediocre then the candidate tends to be dull in 1, 2, and 3. This is not to say that a candidate doesn't have knowledge, but like I said, intelligence and knowledge should not be confused; they are clearly not substitutable. Raw intelligence with no knowledge is far better than a lot of knowledge with no intelligence, but typically, raw intelligence with no knowledge may indicate laziness, which is unacceptable, for it violates qualification #4. Also, if a person exemplifies themselves in one endeavor and the person wants to change their field of endeavor, typically they'll excel in their new chosen endeavor, particularly if there are some similarities or the person has some educational background in the new endeavor. Even if they don't, if the person is intelligent, there are very few fields of endeavors that require an educational background to excel in. The more important factors are: Does the candidate really want the job, do they know what they're getting into, do they have the raw materials and basic foundation to build on, are they capable of effectively applying what they learned, are they likeable? There are exceptions: Scientific and mathematical, medical, athletic, and technology-based endeavors that require specialized studying or training for many years. Virtually anything else does not require a lot of prior training or studying. If people hold out experience as an excuse to not hire someone then this is an indication that the person hiring is lazy, insecure, lacks judgment, is superficial and pretentious or jast plain dumb, in my opinion.

The reason why so many human resource people can't find a successful candidate to save their life is because they are more worried about keeping their job then doing it. What I mean by this is that the human resource person is typically more worried about the candidate failing and embarrassing them then they are exercising judgment to find the right candidate. In case the candidate fails, they want to be able to point to the resume and say, "but they looked so good based on the resume and such a nice person. Look at all of the experience they had … ." This way they can CTA – cover their ass! So, most human resource people can't find the right candidate to save their life, because they are worried about keeping their job. This is not to say that human resources people are bad people; not at all. A lot of them are very hard workers that try their best, but, regardless, because of their fear it inhibits them from doing their jobs properly. It's sad because many of them mean well. This situation isn't too different for recruiters either! They only know how to put a round peg into a round hole; they can't see beyond the immediate match. But they can't necessarily be blamed for their myopia, because their clients may be dictating what type of person they want to interview. Also, in many situations, the human resource person or the recruiter is recruiting for positions that they themselves typically never worked in, which makes it very difficult for them to exercise any judgment. Also, because the vast majority of clients want candidates with experience and there are typically a lot of potential candidates that do have experience, recruiters really don't need to go out of their way to do a more thorough search. Therefore, inevitably, I find that the best hires come from my own recruiting efforts.

Also, I find that a vast majority of people are taken in by smooth-talkers; people who know how to talk, but really have little or no substance. In fact, most people can't tell the difference between those that are genuinely intelligent and those that know how to talk a good game, and it doesn't matter who they are: Chairman, CEO and president of a company or the janitor. The only difference is that the Chairman, CEO and president thinks that hesh can tell the difference when in fact many of them cannot.

So, when it comes to hiring for most corporate jobs, don't look at experience; it's almost irrelevant. Look at the person's intellectual ability, adaptability, trainability and ability to apply well what they learned, the person's perspective and relevance to the company objective, style, character, personality-fit, but virtually ignore their experience. As long as their background or experiences are in the ballpark, it will work out well. The problem is that most people don't have the intellectual rigor and mind to be able to make these determinations, so they use experience as a proxy, and more importantly a crutch. What I mean by that last statement is that they think that if they hire someone with experience and the person doesn't work out, they have a defensible position, jast like the HR person noted above, "but they had prior experience, and everything else indicated that they are a good fit." Whereas if the person had no experience then they could be attacked on that front, "what were you thinking hiring someone that had no experience?!" The sickeningly funny aspect about relying on experience as a gauge of future success is the presumption that someone else's judgment about the candidate is more important – and perhaps more accurate – than one's own. This is jast plain crazy! Yet people continue to look at experience as the end all be all for judging whether or not a candidate is going to be successful or not in a particular endeavor! No wonder we can't get out of our own way where the economy is concerned!

This doesn't mean that experience isn't valuable, but experience is a relative matter. What I mean by this is that two people experiencing the same event could interpret their experiences very differently based on their Six Pillars. Let's say that there are two people of the same age living less than five miles apart, but in different towns that never met and will never meet for the rest of their lives. Let's say that both people grew up in a solid middle-class neighborhood and both fathers worked in white collar office jobs and their mothers were housewives. Let's say that about the same time, say in 8th grade, both fathers lose their jobs and for a year they struggle to make ends meet and both families end up declaring bankruptcy at the end of that year. Both families end up moving in with their grandparents that live in different states. A year after declaring bankruptcy both fathers find jobs and life goes on. Both families move out and achieve independence, but they never go back to where they were prior to their financial crisis, and they never again buy real estate. Is it possible that both children walk away with very different perspectives on life as they go forward? How different could they interpret their personal, but very similar experiences? Would it surprise you, if I told you that one turned out to be a very savvy and successful Wall Street trader and the other turned out to be a bum, an alcoholic and a drug addict? What if I told you that one is married, owns a great piece of property, has no mortgage and very little personal debt and a very robust investment account, while the other struggles to make ends meet, bouncing from job to job with long stretches of unemployment in between? What if I said that the successful person married late in life and have two children, while the other is divorced with one child that lives with the former spouse, would this surprise you? Neither story should surprise anyone. But, more importantly, there is an important lesson to be learned from this story.

So, one may be thinking well then I jast have to look for people who have experience and have interpreted their experiences through the right paradigm. However, in actuality, this is no different than looking for people with little to no direct experience but who have the right paradigm. Meaning, if a person has the right paradigm then experience is of little value. Because most smart people with the right set of tools don't have to experience things directly to learn; they are more than capable of drawing the right lessons from other people's experiences. This is no different than saying people don't need to experience death to know that they don't want to die. On the flip side, look at how many people didn't learn from prior economic turmoil. This current Great Recession should indicate to everyone reading my book the depth of people's depravity and how little people learn despite their experiences and watching other people's experiences from 2001, 1992, 1987, 1980-1982, et cetera.

The last point I'll make on this subject is this: Look at the success rate of CEOs. One will find that their success or failure is very largely independent of whether or not they've had experience in the field of their endeavor or not. That shouldn't be if experience is so important. If experience were critical in determining the success of a CEO then the ones with the most experience in the industry or company should make the best CEOs.

Let's take a look at an example from the auto industry. By my count, I'd say that the most successful CEO in the auto industry is Alan Mullally of Ford, who came from Boeing. Contrast him to Rick Wagoner, the former CEO of GM who'd been with GM since 1979 (he resigned at the request of the White House in March 2009). I challenge people to name two current or former CEOs that are perceived to be more far apart in their success in running their respective companies in the same industry than Mr. Mullally and Mr. Wagoner. I would guess very few people would be able to come up with a pair that are perceived to be – and probably are – the furthest apart in their success.

America's objective in Afghanistan is 100% clear: We must establish a democratic country based on a truly capitalist economy

Based on my view in this book, it may surprise you to know that I was absolutely against the war in both Afghanistan and Iraq, not because we couldn't win the war or it was going to cost too much, but because I have no confidence in the average American. And, my lack of confidence in the American public is well justified, given that the American public is proving my point.

What we need to achieve in both Iraq and Afghanistan is nothing short of establishing a clearly functioning democratic country, where transfer of power and control of the government is achieved through elections based on a rational constitution and a fair and anonymous voting process. In addition, we need to establish a strong capitalist-based economy in both countries with rational and fair rules. And, last but not least, we need to make sure that girls and women are treated with more respect and protected from unfair and unjust laws and rules, given the norms and mores of the respective societies.

To achieve these objectives, both countries must have a strong defense force, strong police force, strong and fair judicial system and due process, and a strong and Just constitution. To get all of this accomplished, it will take decades, and this is the challenge that I saw for our country: I have no faith that Americans will have the patience, understanding, knowledge nor vision to carry through these important missions. This is the main reason that I did not want our country to invade either Afghanistan or Iraq, not because the mission wasn't critically important.

Furthermore, it is better for us to have not invaded these countries at all than invade, do a half-assed job and leave. And, it appears that the American public is aptly proving my lack of faith in them by calling for the cessation and termination of our mission in Afghanistan, even before we've achieved any of the long-term objectives that need to be established to successfully end our mission in Afghanistan. So, my point of view begs two questions: 1) Why is the mission to overthrow the former governments and rebuild both Iraq and Afghanistan so important to us? And, 2) what's wrong with leaving the quagmire that is Afghanistan?

The missions in Iraq and Afghanistan are different. Regardless, in Iraq, our goals were largely and successfully met, which allowed our military forces to mostly withdraw with honor. Therefore, my discussion going forward will be largely limited to Afghanistan.

The following is a broad list of objectives that I believe that we should achieve before pulling out of Afghanistan:

- **Political:** Our political mission in Afghanistan is about removing the Taliban from power, driving Al Qaida out of Afghanistan, and bringing successive and lasting democratic and peaceful transfers of power well into the future. In addition, we must help in establishing permanent and fair political and societal institutions that will allow these peaceful transitions of power to not only occur, but also take strong roots.
- **Infrastructure:** These include a very strong, rational, and fair constitution that absolutely separates government and religion, and protects women from discrimination, being pushed down into a second-class citizenship and subservience, establishing some form of parliamentarian or congressional representation, creating a strong, fair, independent and respected judicial institution that is based on the constitution and not Islamic law, a fair, strong and politically independent police force that respects everyone's rights, the constitution and the judicial process, building and maintaining physical infrastructure, and last and most importantly building public but secular schools for all.
- **Economic:** From an economic point of view, it is our responsibility to make sure that Afghanistan's economy is based on capitalism with fair and Just rules of competition in place, including sensible and fair labor laws, but no unions. We must make sure that there is a strong, conservative and independent central bank, a solid banking system, and robust capital markets. All government owned businesses, if any, should be privatized and no subsidies should be allowed.
- **Societal:** From a societal point of view, we must make sure that socialism does not even have a toehold in Afghanistan's governmental institutions and in their policies. This is not to say that religion does not have a place in Afghan society or that charities should be banned; however, it must not be allowed to creep into government policies, institutions or organizations. We must also establish a strong medical data base and help build modern hospitals and medical facilities and make sure that they are well protected.

Lastly, we must ensure the establishment of independent media, including independent journalists and protection for these journalists, their editors and publishers.

- **Militarily:** We need to wipe out the Taliban and Al Qaida's presence in Afghanistan and help establish an independent, well-functioning military that is controlled by civilian leadership. We must also make sure that there are no divisiveness in the military or accidentally train subversives that are trying to undermine the newly established government. Although all US military forces should be governed by US law in military matters, in civil matters, US military forces should be subject to Afghan laws. Also, all courts martial must be conducted in Afghanistan in plain view of average Afghans. And, as part of this public display of judicial process, Afghans attending trials must be educated in both Afghan and US judicial due process and educated as to why these judicial processes are fair and necessary.

- **Religious:** We must ensure that religious freedom and right to religious belief is strongly established, but completely kept out of government institutions and policies. Every American that is in Afghanistan must be educated in Afghan religious beliefs and taught to respect and honor their beliefs, but not to kowtow or cater to it against the American's own beliefs. Most importantly, we must educate Afghans to the concept of religious freedom and separation of religion and government.

- **Education:** We must allow free and good education to be available to everyone, including all girls and women. The education system must neither preach for or against any religion and religious teaching must be left out of the curriculum. The educational system should be separated between academic and vocational tracks and students should have the option to constantly opt in and out of either program as long as they prove themselves in their previous program. Academic standards, curriculum and testing methods along with matters of school discipline and requirements for uniforms, if any, should be left up to the Afghans to decide. The only required curriculum for all grades should be civics – a course designed to educate Afghans on democracy and capitalism. Higher institutions of learning such as university, graduate and doctoral programs should also be made available to the top students in the country for free, regardless of wealth. Finally, teachers should be well paid, but held to the highest standards and scrutiny.

All of the above must be established before we pull out of Afghanistan or we risk consequences to us. In addition, the way we establish these objectives must be through partnership, education, respect, repetition, failure and tenacity. However, Americans should slowly, but surely, give more and more responsibilities to their Afghan counterparts to take over the responsibility for achieving these objectives as more and more Afghans become trained in their new constitution and ways of their new government.

So, why should "we" risk so much to "get it done" in Afghanistan? If we fail, Afghanistan is likely to fall into another chaotic civil war and the chance of a government remotely friendly to us is highly unlikely. Moreover, don't forget, winners write history: This means that our role in Afghanistan to date is likely to be very negatively spun, which breeds more hatred and more terrorists; terrorists that are highly protected by their own government. There is no doubt that these terrorists will target US interests all over the world and destabilize the world. This will create more and more instability, which would eventually necessitate our re-engaging our military forces in Afghanistan. This means that we would be fighting the same war twice and paying for it with Americans lives twice. This is not what we want, given that the reason why we invaded Afghanistan in the first place was to root out a government that not only protected terrorists, but also encouraged global terrorism. Therefore, we cannot fail in Afghanistan and the idiots calling for the premature withdrawal of US forces from Afghanistan must be ignored.

For those who have studied Afghan history, it is no surprise that few, if any, have successfully conquered Afghanistan, and some people are using this fact to argue that the US is doomed to fail and therefore we cannot withdraw early enough. However, keep in mind that we are not trying to conquer Afghanistan and subjugate their citizenry for the benefit of our own economy and people. Also, we are the only superpower in history to have conquered multiple countries and left them better than we found them: Germany, Japan and South Korea are jast three examples. Therefore, I believe that we can and will succeed in Afghanistan, especially if we stay long enough to win over the hearts and minds of average Afghans. In any case, we, as Americans, cannot afford anything short of complete success in Afghanistan. And, this is why we must stay, despite the costs, particularly in American lives.

The legacy of George W. Bush: The greatest president that ever lived, because he is the root cause of future world peace and harmony

Most Americans are not fond of George W. Bush (GWB), if not downright hateful of the man, but the dislike/hate is based on a whole lot of bull fed to the public by the liberal press and the Democrats, mixed-in with some facts, which are typically taken out of context. For example, according to Mr. Bush, the reason why he flew over New Orleans and not land in the city was because he wasn't given the authorization to land by the mayor of New Orleans. Also, the reason why federal help to Louisiana was so late in coming was because the state didn't request it, and the state has to request help from the federal government for the federal government to give help. Very few, if any, know this inconvenient fact. Most people are unaware of these distortions of truth, because the liberal press and the Democrats want to discredit Mr. Bush and make him hated by the public, so that the Democrats have a better chance at election/re-election.

Also, the real problem with the economy has virtually nothing to do with whether or not the so called rich got a tax break or not. People may think this is true, people may be told that it is true, and people may even be shown "data" that seemingly supports the argument. But let me assure everyone that the reason for our economic and financial mess has nothing to do with GWB's tax cuts; absolutely nothing. The reason for the economic mess has everything to do with the average American getting greedy and over-extending themselves and the financial mess is because the federal government has been spending above its means for 8 decades, period, full-stop, the end. And, I note, neither fact has to do with whether the Republicans or the Democrats were in control, per se, even though it started with a president from the ranks of Democrats (i.e., FDR; I believe FDR's presidency was the start of modern socialism in the US). Finally, one of the biggest reasons why – if not the single biggest reason by far – we can't get out of this economic mess is because the federal government so over spent that we (as a country) have no excess financial capacity left to give an effective boost to the economy. So, we find our economy in a situation where lowering spending will make the economy worse in the short-term, and raising taxes will make the economy worse in the short-term and long-term. And, cutting subsidies means that there is less money to be spent and more people may drop below the poverty line, and the worst of it will be borne by the least financially capable. On the other hand, raising taxes will choke off consumer spending in a broad fashion, which isn't good for the economy either. However, longer-term, the only policy that can help us to establish long-term prosperity is to cut federal spending and eliminate all "social programs."

Think about it from an individual's financial view point: If a person finds hem self in financial trouble, should hesh borrow more money, so hesh can maintain hes life-style, force someone into giving hem money against hes will, or should the individual cut spending and cut hes life style? I think the vast majority of Americans, at least those that are honest, would say that hesh should cut hes life style as much as hesh can to make ends meet, whether it is fair or unfair to do so in hes mind. So, why don't most people understand that this is the best solution for the country in the long-run as well? Regardless, the reason that the country is in such a mess has to do with people's greed and the federal government over spending. And, what caused the over-spending is the so called, "social programs," and these "social programs" continue to handcuff our country and drag us down into economic morass and oblivion. So, why pick on "social programs," why not military spending, which is also a huge part of the government budget? Can we live without any "social spending?" Yes, we can. We did so until FDR corrupted our country. Can we live without defense spending? No country has ever successfully existed without being able to defend itself. I challenge everyone to find one that has. But, no one will succeed, and if someone does come up with a seemingly good example, upon closer inspection one is likely to find some sort of extenuating circumstances, like the tribe is on a remote island that is inaccessible. There the self-defense is the water. In the case of Switzerland, the Alps are its defense. So, we can argue about how much defense spending we need, but not whether we need defense spending or not. With "social programs," we absolutely can live without it, and *must* live without it, given that it is a major corrupting force in the economy. The proof is Greece, Ireland, Italy, Spain, Soviet Union, UK pre-Thatcher, India-pre-1990s, China pre-Deng Xiaoping, et cetera. Enough said; I've beaten the dead horse enough.

So, what does this have to do with the legacy of George Walker Bush our 43rd president? A lot. Let me digress a little here – perhaps a little more than usual. I think most experts will agree that one of the major keys to world peace are to bring an end to the Israeli-Palestinian conflict, and put an end to Islamic fundamentalist terrorism. And, one of the primary root causes of these two issues is the crusades started by Pope Urban 2. Some may ask what the connection is. The connection is this: The invasion of Afghanistan in November 2001 and the invasion of Iraq in March 2003 could be the beginning of the road to world peace. IF I'm right and the two wars in Iraq and Afghanistan are pointed to as the beginning of the road to world peace then I think we could agree that George W. Bush was one of the greatest presidents we've ever had. I know that most people don't want to agree because of their visceral hatred of the man, but the hatred of the man has virtually nothing to do with the reality of the matter. So, again, if these wars prove to be the road to world peace then does that not make our 43rd president, one of the greatest man that ever lived, let alone one of the greatest American presidents?

The natural question that most people ask is how the Afghan and Iraqi wars lead to world peace. Let me paint a scenario. Imagine an Iraq and Afghanistan that are not only well-functioning democracies with equal and Just rights for all, but also successful capitalist economies. Further, let's imagine that the per capita income is in the $20,000/person level – the equivalent of Portugal today (32nd according to the IMF in 2010) – with growth levels in the 5%-7% and fairly low government debt to GDP versus Iraq's future per capita income of ~$20,000 (per capita GDP in Iraq sits at ~$2,600 and in Afghanistan it sits at ~$500 or 121st and 168th, respectively, according to the IMF in 2010). How would this be possible? Look at South Korea, China, and Brazil over the last 50, 30 and 20 years, respectively. For example, let's look at South Korea's per capita GDP: It was ~$100 in 1961, when the economic modernization program began under the then president and dictator Chung-hee Park. About 50 years later, Korea's per capita GDP is over $20,000, an increase of ~200 fold or ~20,000%. This was possible because the economy was turned towards capitalism and economic growth under a government led economic development program *without any "social programs" of any kind* to muddy the waters and priorities.

How would Iraq and Afghanistan get there? We only have to look at the recent histories of countries like South Korea, China, Brazil and India to know how Afghanistan may reach stronger economic footing. These countries are relying on the capitalist economic model – ironically their economies are more capitalist-oriented than ours in many ways – to grow their economies as rapidly as possible. So, it is very possible. Thus, if Iraq and Afghanistan become beacons of democracy and capitalism, it will apply a lot of pressure to its neighbors to adopt similar models. The success of Iraq and Afghanistan would make it all but impossible for Iraq and Afghanistan's neighbors to continue on their way as if nothing happened. If someone doesn't believe in the domino effect, jast look at what happened in Tunisia, which then spread to Egypt, Libya, Syria, Yemen and others in the region. Also, given the proliferation of the internet, it is quite possible that the liberalization of Iraq had a strong influence on Mohamed Wazizi's decision to self-immolate.

If Facebook was really as prevalent as news organizations claim it was in Tunisia and heavily and ultimately contributed to the over-throw of the Tunisian dictatorship then it is highly likely that Mr. Wazizi would have heard of the changes in Iraq, of the democratic voices that are being heard in Iraq, of the ever improving Justice system, and the opportunities that are blossoming. Of course, no one can say that he did or didn't with absolute certainty, but it would be a very strange coincidence that within months of Iraq going towards a more stable footing that Mr. Wazizi did what he did causing Tunisia's revolution. Perhaps, more to the point, after decades of silence, the youth of Tunisia decided to rise up and the people decided to join them in seeking Justice for their country soon after Iraq became more or less stable. Was this truly jast a coincidence? They are also looking to democratize their country, not turn it into an Islamic fundamentalist country. Again, I cannot believe that this is a mere coincidence. Same can be said about Egypt and Libya, and now Syria. Certainly, the people in Egypt saw what was going on in Tunisia and took heart and did what they did to overthrow their dictator and the Libyans succeeded as well, inspired by Tunisia to their west and Egypt to their east. Syria is also on the verge of over-throwing Assad, it seems. Again, it is very difficult to believe that all these events are jast mere coincidences after democracy and capitalism started to take irreversible hold in Iraq. I don't believe in coincidences. The point is that if Iraq and Afghanistan were to become economically successful then it should create a domino effect on countries like Iran, Pakistan, Syria, Jordan, Uzbekistan, Kazakhstan, and other dictatorial countries in the region. This may enable the region to become economically wealthier than they could possibly imagine today, like South Koreans couldn't imagine their world today, even 20-30-years ago, let alone 50 years ago. If such equivalent success is achieved in the Middle-East then it would have a dramatic transformative effect on the entire region and should propel the peace process.

Therefore, if the events in Iraq are already driving the Arab spring then what lies in store for the region in 10-, 20-, 30-, 40-, 50-, and 100-years from now? If the current trend in the Middle-East and North Africa continues, we should expect to see not only blossoming democracies (a republic, a constitutional monarchy, a direct democracy, and a federation are all possible forms of democracy that could take form in any of the Arab countries), but also very strong economies emerge that make their populace more and more affluent. And, affluence, combined with education, promotes more affluence, which is one of the keys to killing radicalism and hatred and promoting tolerance and peace. Notice that poverty and ignorance are often exploited to incite radicalism, so two vital keys to the cure against radicalism is affluence and education.

If this scenario plays out the way I think it may then how immense of an accomplishment will we, Americans, have achieved through our military endeavors? How great will this make George W. Bush and his vision as president and, ultimately, world-peace maker in the eyes of the world?

None of us – and for that matter I – can and will know the legacy of George W. Bush until all of the uncertainties surrounding Iraq and Afghanistan are properly settled. If my hope and vision comes true then GWB will be viewed with greatness and awe, but if Iraq and Afghanistan fall into chaos and mayhem then GWB will be viewed with great disdain and hatred, all over the world, and America, as a whole will suffer. This is why it is so imperative that we make sure we, as a country, finish what we started and make sure that both Iraq and Afghanistan succeed in becoming strong democracies with thriving, wealth-creating economies to back-up the democracies. In many respects, this may be more important to the ultimate survival of the world than what we do today to fix our economic and financial problems, because what happens in Iraq and Afghanistan may have long-term consequences that will change the course of world history like pope Urban 2's decision to launch the first crusade in the 11th century. This is the importance of foreign policy and, more importantly, American leadership of global political, economic, and military issues. This is why we – as responsible Americans – have to care about foreign policy and pay attention to what's going on. We don't have a choice because we are the only superpower left in the world, at least for now. Also, remember this with great pride: We are the only superpower in the history of the world that has invaded countries, only to leave it far better than when we first invaded and left a glowing legacy for the people that we conquered. As a reminder the three are Germany, Japan and South Korea.

It is super-imperative that we leave the same legacy in both Iraq and Afghanistan that we left in Germany, Japan and South Korea. And, if we do, we will not only be one step closer to world peace, but also George W. Bush, may become the greatest American president the world has ever known.

As an aside, two gentlemen at two different times told me something very disturbing. One of the reasons why it was so disturbing is that they both said the same thing. One gentleman was Indian from India, and the other gentleman was a citizen of a Middle-Eastern country, the origin of which was not revealed, I think by design rather than lack of effort to find out on my part. Anyway, both gentlemen said exactly the same thing: "In my country, democracy will never work." I asked why and, again, they both said the same thing. They said that democracy will not work in their country because the average man from his country – I presume they meant both men and women – are not intelligent enough, educated enough, nor care enough to make democracy work. Therefore, they also asserted that democracy will fail in Iraq and Afghanistan, which means that America is wasting its time. What is interesting is that India *is* a democracy. When I said this, the gentleman laughed and said that India does not have a *real* democracy, but he wouldn't elaborate beyond saying that the average Indian is too unintelligent and uneducated to truly and effectively participate in democracies. Both of them also mentioned that both countries did not have a history of democracy and so it would not work. When I countered that Japan and Germany didn't either until the 20th century, again, both of them said the same thing: It's because the Germans and the Japanese are both intelligent and educated.

I would dearly love to see both men proved wrong on the point about democracy failing in Iraq and Afghanistan, because the populace is unintelligent, uneducated, and uncaring. And, I fervently hope that the leadership in both Iraq and Afghanistan stand-up to this challenge and win. I believe it is vitally important that they succeed for the eternal greater good of **ALL** humankind.

The importance of history cannot be emphasized enough; in fact, no one should be allowed to vote unless they know at least the history of the US

I strongly believe that one of the reasons why most Americans keep voting for socialism and "social programs" is because most Americans have no clue as to what is true or not. It seems to me that the average American's ignorance is what compels them to continue to vote for socialism. If the average American had historical perspective, and they understood what socialism and communism have done to countries in the past (e.g., UK, Latin America, India, China, Russia, et cetera) and are doing in the present (e.g., North Korea, Greece, Italy, Spain, Portugal, Ireland, et cetera), they'd never, ever vote for increased "social spending" let alone support existing "social programs." Also, if the average American had historical knowledge and perspective, they'd know what dramatically reducing or eliminating socialism and communism has done for the financial and economic well-being of a country (e.g., China, Brazil, Mexico, India, and Russia, et cetera).

Even if the average American understood the history of the US and only the history of the US, they'd know that we not only existed without "social programs" before FDR, we actually thrived without it. They'd also know that "socialization" measures were supposed to be temporary when introduced by FDR and the income tax was also supposed to go away after funding WW 1 and WW 2. These were all supposed to be temporary measures. But because the average American has no historical perspective and understanding, they not only don't understand the issues and can't tell right from wrong, but also are doomed to repeat the same mistakes that have plagued other countries in the past and which continue to haunt them in the present. Of course, history doesn't always repeat itself in exactly the same way, but it's usually close enough for us to take historical lessons to heart.

If average Americans could understand jast five concepts – 1) Communism is not an ideal, in fact, it is not even valid enough to be considered a childish thought, 2) equality doesn't always stand for Justice, 3) short-term thinking is very bad, 4) Justice, rational thinking and communication are the only way to interact among humans, and 5) like pregnancies, there's no such thing as a little bit of corruption – remember the lesson taught to us by Ernst Janning – then we'd be at least half-way home to being rational thinkers and capable of making at least moderately rational decisions without necessarily repeating the same mistakes that other people in other countries have made in the past and continue to do so in the present.

In fact, I believe history to be so important that I would suggest that history teachers should be the highest paid in public schools, because they teach the most important lessons that every human must take to heart to have the correct perspective to be an upright and outstanding citizen of any country: They hold the knowledge to communicate lessons from history that could help people formulate the right Six Pillars that they and their future generation so sorely need. Of course, this is assuming that history teachers don't twist history lessons to suit their personal agenda.

The manipulation of selfishness: How organizations and governments get away with "murder"

A large part of the reason that people in such countries as North Korea haven't been able to overthrow the shackles of oppression has largely to do with the populace being afraid. Deception – through propaganda and brainwashing – by the government also plays a crucial role. However, if the entire population of North Korea were to revolt against the military and the government, they'd be nothing that the military and the government could do to stop the demise of the current government short of killing everyone. History has shown this to be absolutely true. Recently, look at Tunisia, Egypt, and Libya. Historically, look at America, Iran, Russia, China, and France among others.

The principle that these tyrannical governments are working on is that no individual will trade their life for the betterment of the society that they live in. Therefore, in most cases, the threat of death against any individual is enough to thwart any thought of rebellion against the tyrannical leadership. The principle at work here is no different than the concept of voting. No individual vote is important or significant, but all of the votes put together do become very significant and very meaningful. This is then very true of any tyrannical political government. One individual rebelling against the government is not only insignificant, but also very futile. Even a few rebellious people are insignificant, and can easily be stopped by force. Rebellion and protest are only significant if substantially all of the people group together to take action, but tyrannical governments know that bringing together substantially all of the people is highly difficult to almost impossible. Therefore, they work on placating or suppressing the few that could rally the people. The people that would need placating would be the fellow co-conspirators such as the military leadership or the political allies. The people that need to be suppressed would be grassroots leaders, average citizens that have been wronged and would become leaders of a rebellion, and, not infrequently, religious leaders and teachers.

This is not all that far from the strategy and tactics used by large corporations to mitigate their mistakes or cover-up product defects. They spend money to appease their political allies (congressional members, president of the US, legislators, governors, mayors, councilmembers, etc.) and suppress or get rid of objectors and protestors. Granted there are a lot of attention grabbing, lottery-mentality-minded, and self-serving assholes. But the fact of the matter is that many companies will obfuscate, deny, delay and blame everyone else for their product defects rather than owning up to the problems. Corporate America tries to make it as difficult as possible – within legal boundaries – for anyone to make complaints and try to get compensated for their grief and troubles. The corporations think that this is cheaper than correctly resolving problems on behalf of their customers for the long-run. And, in most cases, this is absolutely true, in the short-term.

Regardless, there are many ways companies can obfuscate, deny, deflect and otherwise make it very difficult for anyone to get Just compensation. However, in general, companies will try to make everyone's life very difficult by making the grievance process so painful it discourages anyone from not only making the complaint, but also having that complaint register with the various organizations that keep track of these events. Also, companies know that for individuals to go through the proper judicial channels to pursue Justice is not only expensive, but also very time consuming, which makes it very discouraging for individuals to take proper action. This is a huge comfort for companies, because short of a class action lawsuit, individual complaints can go largely ignored without company action and, more importantly, without cost.

The companies try to balance this obstruction strategy with how fast and far word of mouth could damage their reputations and limit sales. The number one tactic to prevent word of mouth destroying their reputation is to advertise and buy time while trying to find a solution to the problem. This is all being dictated by financial calculations that tell the leadership of a corporation what is the least cost way to manage the problem, again, in the short-term. If corporations were to really look out for their customers, they'd look at the best and timely solution for their customers, and not what the most cost effective solution is.

The problem is that if corporations acted properly by looking for the right solution instead of the most cost effective solution in the near-term, their stock price would take a hit in the near-term, because it is thought that the right solution will cost more than the most cost effective solution, by definition. However, by taking the short-term solution, the long-term effect is more costly to corporations, because it not only makes a lot of customers angry, but also reinforces the belief that getting new products into the market quicker is more important than bringing better products to market. This then makes more customers angry and eventually retribution can be a bitch! Ask Detroit!

The problem is that for most investors, it is very difficult for them to figure out what the long-term benefit of providing the right solution is, whereas the cost is immediately measurable. This is what causes stock prices to decline more than providing the most cost-effective short-term solution, which, by definition, has a lower measurable cost, regardless of the long-term efficacy of the solution. Therefore, most company managements – who by definition can't/don't think any differently than the average investor – will almost always opt to provide the most cost-effective short-term solution instead of the right solution. Some of the more clever managements will find a way to disguise the most cost-effective short-term solution as the right solution, which makes it even more difficult for investors to analyze the true costs and benefits for the long-term.

Companies like Microsoft Corporation and its Office Suite ©® is a great example of this phenomenon. For example, in my opinion, Excel©® is an inferior product to Lotus 1-2-3®©. But, Excel was able to beat Lotus 1-2-3 for reasons other than product quality. These include a stolen (my opinion, which the courts didn't agree with) interface from Apple, Inc. that is easier to use than what other products offered, a package of products that tied a spreadsheet, word processing, and presentation software in one, and domination of the operating system, which made it more difficult for competitors to innovate.

In contrast, the way Tylenol handled the recall back in the 1990s when some lunatic put poison into Tylenol bottles was not only admirable, but also very smart. Because the company adopted a long-term solution that regained the confidence of the public, the brand not only survived, but also regained its leadership position. Tylenol's handling of the situation should be a key management lesson that is taught in every business school and reviewed by every board and CEO of all major corporations.

Going back to Microsoft, as a demonstration of why I think Excel®© is inferior here are jast two factual and one subjective examples: 1) I can't tell you how many times that a computation that is supposed to result in zero, results in some number that is slightly different than zero and end up screwing up my computations and work. I never experienced this with Lotus 1-2-3; 2) Excel limits the conditional stack to seven deep, i.e., the "if-then" layers cannot go beyond seven, meaning the most Excel will allow is the following: If 1 then A, else if 2 then B, else if 3 then C, else if 4 then D, else if 5 then E, else if 6 then F, else if 7 then G, else H. I've gone well over 10 deep with Lotus 1-2-3, and simple tests will show that Lotus 1-2-3 has no limits as to how deep the stack can go. I also happen to think that the macro function is far superior on Lotus 1-2-3 than on Excel which uses Basic to execute macros. And, prior to about 2005, Excel could not deal with a spread sheet that was much greater than 40-megabytes, while Lotus 1-2-3 could do so easily. As a consequence, Excel would not only refuse to save a file that large, but also would crash the computer if one tried. They fixed this in the next iteration of the software, but the issue isn't that they fixed it, but that they put out such an inferior product to begin with.

Despite these short comings, Excel won the battle of the spreadsheets, while many of my complaints have gone unanswered. As one of my friends pointed out, Microsoft isn't going to address my problems because my issues are not common enough, i.e., it isn't cost effective. Eventually, I expect someone to put together a software package that is vastly superior to Microsoft Office©®, and destroy the market share of Office©. Until then, Microsoft will continue to put out a mediocre product – in my opinion – and make gobs of money taking advantage of the market's lack of competition. Unfortunately, and to the credit of Microsoft Corporation, the company was able to do this because of the ignorance of the general public and people's focus on the superficial. The general public was swayed by the easier interface, the superficial functioning, package offering of the Office© products and the relative ease of data transportability among the Office© software products. The fact of the matter is that the Microsoft Corporation saw the soft "underbelly" of the American public, struck it and bled it dry and continues to do so, in my opinion. But, ultimately, we cannot blame anyone else, but the general public for being ignorant and superficial.

Regardless, in my opinion, no company, including the Microsoft Corporation, will fix problems that are not cost effective despite the fact that it would be in their best interest to do so in the long-term. This behavior is nothing new to corporate America. The corporate playbook is very predictable when people detect something wrong with a product. When people call to complain, what is the first thing that the customer encounters: Multi-layers of computerized menu "options" followed by endless waiting. Then when one does get a live person, the first thing that the customer service representative (CSR) assumes is that the customer is at fault and makes the customer do stupid things, even though the customer tells them that they already did it. Then, once the problem is detected and sourced, the CSR tries to tell the customer that it's the customer's fault that something isn't working. Finally, the CSR will try to rush the customer off the phone by saying that the level of expertise needed to help the customer is a "higher pay-grade" than what they are capable of offering and will have someone call back. If the customer falls for this trick and hangs up then they're the sucker who never gets the call back. This discourages the customer from ever calling again and trying to fix the problems that they're having with the product. Sound familiar? I'm sure at one point or another that we all experienced such frustrating situations. But what does this say about corporate America?

Here are some interesting questions that I'd like to ask about corporate America, and I'd like the reader to think about them:

1) How long does it take to get to a customer service representative when you want to buy something versus when you want to talk to someone about a problem? In my experience it takes at least 5-10 times longer to register a complaint versus trying to buy a product. Test it out.
2) When you get a CSR that is selling something versus listening to your complaint and trying to "help," who is friendlier and more helpful?
3) When you are trying to buy something versus registering a problem, how quickly do the problems that you anticipate or are experiencing get resolved?

4) After you buy something, how much bargaining power do you have versus when you are trying to buy something?

5) How many times have you been told that it's your fault when in reality in turns out that it was a product defect or a design flaw?

6) How many times have you been asked to pay for something that you didn't order or were not aware of ordering?

7) How many times have you been charged a fee for something that you didn't do or have responsibility for?

8) In contrast, how many times have you been monetarily compensated for being inconvenienced? Personally, I can't remember the last time that I was monetarily compensated for anything that any company did that was wrong. In fact, I can't remember the last time I was compensated for anything that a company did wrong, let alone get compensated for something in cash.

9) In contrast how many late fees or penalties have you been charged over a life time?

10) When you are due a refund or a rebate has it ever taken less than six weeks? In my experience, refunds, rebates or other monies due me take between 8-12 weeks. In contrast, how many of your bills are due once every 6-to-12 weeks?

11) How many times does the CSR try to "upgrade" you or sell you an attachment or add-on when you call to register a complaint or a problem?

What the companies are relying on is the fact that to pursue the legal path, the effort, amount of money, and time needed to complete the pursuit of Justice is so much relative to the injustice that the corporations are willing to offend, insult and steal from their customers on a routine basis. Let me give you a great example of the case involving General Electric's subsidiary GE Money that I experienced. The following story is from my experience and perspective, but I'm sure that GE Money will argue differently.

Several years ago, I bought an item from a store and financed it for x-years without interest that the store offered. After several years of making close to minimum payment, starting in 2009, GE Money started playing games with due dates, changing it around so that it would appear that I had made late payments and charging me late fees. So, I protested and they said that they would fix my due date the way I wanted, but it happened again. All this time, I'm being forced to pay late fees by GE Money that were some $25 or more per occurrence. So, to avoid this trap, I made two consecutive payments about 2-weeks or so apart thinking that I'll make my next payment somewhat early to avoid the late payment for the following month. What do you think happened next? Yes, another late fee appeared on my next bill! I cannot tell you how surprised and angry I was. So, I called GE Money to find out what was going on. After much running around they told me that the second payment I made was applied to principal instead of the next month's payment. After arguing for 10 minutes, they agreed to apply the second payment I made to the following month's payment and correct the situation. So, I thought everything was fine. What do you think happened next month? What else? The same situation occurred: Another late fee. So, I called again and had the same conversation. They said they'd take care of the problem, but did they? No, they didn't. After several months of this, to add insult to injury, GE Money started charging me 24.99% interest on the remaining balance of the financing. When I asked what this was for, they said that it was for repeated late payment, when I explained what the situation is they kept on saying they couldn't do anything about it. Basically, GE Money hustled me, so that they could find a way to charge me interest on a financing that they couldn't make any money on or force me to pay it off, so that they didn't have to continue financing a 0% loan.

To accomplish this GE Money continued to lie to me about taking care of the timing of the payment then they used this as an excuse to charge de facto interest through late fees. To make sure that there was no paper trail, they verbally lied to me for six-months or so, while for legal documentation purposes, GE Money pretended that I was making late payments. So, by GE Money verbally lying about fixing the problem of the timing of the payments, I didn't do anything to nor could I do anything to fix the problem and GE Money used that as an excuse to charge me interest illegally. Also, given GE Money's verbal lies versus my documented payments, if someone were to legally track the sequence of events, they'd be no proof that GE Money did anything wrong, but they'd be a paper trail of something that I did. If audited, it would look like I made late payments and so they had no choice but to charge me interest. Pretty sneaky.

So, what would you do in this situation? If I continue to pay interest at 24.99%, I'm making them a lot of money and more than compensate GE Money for the free financing that they provided for the first several years. If I don't pay them then they can and will take legal action to recover their principal and in the process, I'd have my credit record damaged. If I pay them off then that's giving them what they want, so that they can stop funding me at 0% interest, which they must have realized was a mistake in the first place. The last choice would be to sue them, which I started to do. But, as my lawyer warned me, they'd be no assurance of winning, would cost a lot more money than what I've already paid them or could possibly recover. Therefore, he advised that the best course of action was to pay them off. Ultimately, this is what I ended up doing, not just because the financial calculation was worth it, but because I felt that the company I worked for would not be happy if they found out that I was suing General Electric's GE Money, since this may affect their business relationship with General Electric. So, I felt it wasn't worth risking my career to recover several hundred dollars. Regardless, in my opinion, GE Money concocted this con-job because they realized that 0% financing was a mistake, and instead of taking responsibility for it, GE Money hustled me into getting them off the hook. I'm sure that a vast number of people aren't surprised at this story, and probably can recant similar stories from their personal experiences. Sadly, this is the reality of the world that we live in.

The fact of the matter is that even with all of the late fees and the interest on the remaining principal balance, I got very, very cheap financing for several years, but that's not the point. They knowingly and creatively violated their part of the agreement and if it wasn't something that the higher-ups at GE Money was aware of then it was the line supervisors who did this to please the higher ups at GE Money from my perspective. Regardless, it was a despicable act, an act that they have gotten away with.

This is what corporate America has become, and mirrors what America has become: Small-minded, petty, self-destructive, insecure, highly near-sighted, disrespectful, inconsiderate and callous. If people ever wondered what small violations of morality and ethics do, I jast recanted one consequence involving GE Money. What are we, as a society, ready to do or are we going to let such petty, self-destructive, insecure, highly near-sighted, disrespectful, inconsiderate and callous behavior continue to happen to me, to others and, most importantly, to you and yours?

In some sense, I understand why there are so many frivolous lawsuits. If people continue to experience what I experienced with GE Money over and over again, I can imagine how much anger and frustration builds-up. I can see someone finally snapping and agreeing to participate in a frivolous lawsuit because they want some revenge for all those times that they were wronged. This doesn't justify frivolous lawsuits, but it does highlight one reason why many honest Americans may participate in one.

If what I contend about frivolous lawsuits is correct, corporations must take this to heart and learn from it. In effect, by trying to minimize the short-term effect of each lawsuit and problem, I am sure corporations are wasting more money in the long-run. This is very consistent with my hypothesis that Americans don't know how to think, let alone to do so for the long-term. Therefore, inadvertently or otherwise, Americans solve problems for the short-term, which only creates more problems in the long-term, which then necessitates solving more problems for the short-term, which then precipitates more long-term problems, et cetera.

Again, as a country, we must learn to think and do so for the long-term and stop shooting ourselves in the foot by acting on our short-term impulses. There is no more urgent priority than Americans learning to think and to do so on a rational and factual basis.

No more secrets: All judgments, settlements, and arbitration results from the past and in the future must be made public

Lawyers, judges, arbiters and corporations are going to have mass and massive coronaries and brain hemorrhages over this one, but for the greater good of the country, this information has to be made public. It will also shorten and greatly simplify all future legal disputes and awards. This means that the judicial backlog will be unclogged faster too.

Before we get to why this is good public policy to implement and why it is good for the country, let me spell out why the current system is good for lawyers, arbiters, judges and corporations then it'll be easier for people to understand why it is not good for the country. If the end results, settlements and awards are hidden then every time a new case comes up all negotiations have to start from scratch because no one but the attorneys, arbitrators and judges will know what the historical averages for settlements in similar situations look like. What this means is that it takes more time to get to a conclusion. This results in paying the lawyers and arbitrators more money, keeping judges more busy and more or less keeps everyone else in the dark, since no one else will have an idea of what are standard procedures, what are average settlements and generally what the steps are to getting to a conclusion.

Obviously, this logjam is good for everyone in the legal profession, including lawyers, arbitrators and judges and bad for everyone else. Therefore, lawyers, arbitrators and judges will tell anyone that will listen that the current system should not change, because it keeps the bias and consensus thinking to a minimum, which is the way it should be given that most cases are unique and should be treated as such. It sounds good, but it is baloney, and nothing but an excuse, a convenient/plausible excuse, a smoke screen, if you would; it's that simple. It's an excuse to allow the legal professional to control information. Also, lawyers, judges and arbitrators really don't treat each case as if they are unique. They talk so much about what is typical, what is usual, and what the probabilities are, it's sickening! So, again, keeping the current system only helps the legal profession, since it prevents people outside of the legal profession from knowing anything.

It isn't rocket science: When a small group of people are the only ones that know the truth, the rest of us have no choice but to rely on this small group of people to give us advice, and we really don't have much of a choice but to take their lead. However, if a lot of information was available to the general public then the general public can rely less on the legal professionals and would also have to pay them less. So, again, the current system is designed to keep information within the legal profession. It stands to reason given that information is king in the modern era, so whoever controls it stands to benefit. However, in the system that I am proposing, the general public will have way more control and access. This is good for everyone, but the legal professionals.

Also, by keeping judgments and awards sealed, it helps corporations, particularly public corporations, escape scrutiny by investors and hide information from the public. The second part is particularly useful to corporations, because if the settlement or awards are sealed, the next time the company is sued for a similar problem, the plaintiff won't know what to expect. This gives the corporations' lawyers a chance to lowball and divide and conquer, which potentially lowers the corporations' liabilities. This is obviously to the benefit of the legal profession and corporations. Also, by hiding the final judgment, corporations can bury a lot of other guilt that otherwise may have been brought to light in a manner that corporations would not have wanted to deal with. For example, let's say that a corporation is being sued for $1 billion, and investor expectations were for the company to settle for about $250 million. However, if the company settles for $200 million then they have $50 million of "play-room," which management could use to "fix" problems that they did not want to bring to light. To perpetrate this deception management would use their quarterly financials. This is how it could be done: Management would report a $275 million cash outflow from operations without getting into specifics about the break-down. To investors, this gives the impression that the settlement was for $250 million and that $25 million was for normal operations, when in reality the settlement was for $200 million, $50 million was for other problems that needed to be solved and $25 million was for normal operations. The reason why managements can get away with this type of deception is that they would cite the settlement agreement, which would stipulate that they cannot divulge the settlement amount.

It's pretty slick. However, I want to point out that the vast majority of managements are not scumbags and would never perpetrate such a deception, but all I'm pointing out is the fact that such deceptions can easily be perpetrated because of the secretive nature of legal settlements. Therefore, again, I propose that all legal settlements should be made public for the greater good of everyone.

Once a corporation is sued, if the company wants to make a settlement they should be obliged to admit guilt and enter a guilty plea, otherwise the corporation should be obligated to go to trial

If anyone gets a traffic ticket and goes to court to pay for the ticket, but not enter a plea, the municipal court judge typically will not allow that to happen and will force the driver to enter a guilty plea and pay the money or enter an innocent plea and go to trial. Once in a blue moon, if the municipality is really desperate for the money, the municipal court judge may allow such action to expedite cases, while still pulling in the revenue, but otherwise it never happens! Otherwise, typically, if an individual doesn't want to enter a guilty plea then not only does the person have to plead their case, if the individual loses, typically the penalty and fines are harsher.

However, when a corporation gets sued, they have the option of not admitting guilt while paying off the plaintiff. This may be good for the company in the short-term, but it is not good for the country in general and bad for corporations in the long-run as well. The reason for this is that by not adjudicating to an end result, it provides absolutely no clarity in future cases. So, again, the legal profession benefits from the uncertainty, companies can get away with bad behavior that is never publicly disclosed, and people who make a living off of frivolous law suits get paid off, unnecessarily draining money from, typically, public companies. None of this is good for our country.

If a company is sued, and they want to settle by paying, they must be forced to enter a guilty plea. If they don't want to enter a guilty plea then they must be forced to adjudicate to a publicly declared end result. This way, investors will also know whether or not management is guilty of any wrong-doing as well, which is vitally important.

In addition, if the company is innocent and is proven so, it will discourage other frivolous lawsuits, which saves corporations and investors a lot of money. On the other hand, if they are guilty then they should pay the full amount for their guilt, which discourages corporations from engaging in more bad behavior in the future. Either way, in the long-term, investors, not to mention the country as a whole, benefits greatly from this type of clarity.

Some donations that I'd make, if I were a multi-billionaire

For one, I would not give my money to organizations that dole out support to homeless and destitute people in a blanket fashion. I would not give it to most other charities either. Regardless of the financial well-being of an individual, I'd give my money to people who deserve it, and "earned" it according to the standards of my Six Pillars. Also, I may give some money to scientific research organizations like the Alzheimer's, some cancer, diabetes, and heart foundations and other scientific and technical research organizations. But, most of my charitable donations would be made to individuals that deserve it, in my opinion.

Some people – not in any particular order – that I'd like to reward, if I had the money, in increments of $1 million or more:

- **Sal Khan:** Sal is the founder of Khan Academy. Their mission statement is to provide world class education to anyone who wants it. They accomplish this through lessons that are scripted by Sal and posted on the internet for free. Their latest project encompasses designing lessons for all subjects at all levels of primary – and eventually, secondary – schools and providing a truly individualized comprehensive education for all students. His program is highly effective and helps teachers to be not only more effective, but also allow them to provide more personal and individualized attention when and where it's necessary. In my book, this man and his program is the bomb and should be handsomely rewarded for his ingenuity, sincerity, and caring. Therefore, this man should be given the Presidential Medal of Freedom and all people who are interested in furthering education should be generously donating to his program.

- **Jaime Escalante:** The high school math teacher that succeeded in helping students from a troubled neighborhood in LA pass the AP math test;

- **Erin Gruwell:** Another teacher that inspired at-risk students to go to college;

- **Joe Clark:** The principal who turned around troubled Eastside High School in Patterson, New Jersey;

- **Roberta Guaspari:** The music teacher that taught violin to inner city students in New York City;

- **Olympic medalists:** Not the high profile and highly paid athletes, but the ones that don't have any limelight, pay, or fame, but nevertheless train hard and do our country proud with honor;

- **Kim Rhode:** She won medals in FIVE CONSECUTIVE OLYMPICS; the last three was gold, including a world-record setting performance in the 2012 London Olympics – the event is irrelevant. Unbelievable!

- **Kerri Strug:** ARE YOU KIDDING ME?! I couldn't believe that she not only took that second vault, but she landed on ONE FOOT in pain, and still had the poise to raise her hands above her head to complete the vault and give the US a team gold at the 1996 Atlanta Games, the first ever! Unbelievable guts, determination and poise for a 19 year old, WOW!

- **Carly Patterson:** First all-around individual female gymnastics champion for the US in which there were no boycotts (Mary Lou Retton in 1984 was the first US female all-around individual gymnastics champion, but it was a boycotted Olympics).

- **Paul Hamm:** WOW! He fell in the vaults pushing him down to 12th place in the individual all-around competition for men's gymnastics at the 2004 Athens Olympics, but did two spectacular routines, one on the parallel bars and the other on the high bar to win all-around Olympic gold, the first ever for an American male.

- **Rulon Gardner:** At the 2000 Sydney Olympics, he defeated the "meanest man alive," Mr. Greco-Roman wrestling himself, the greatest of all-time, Alexander Karelin for Olympic Gold. An upset of epic proportions. In all fairness, Karelin had already won three successive Olympic Gold medals and was getting on in age at 33 years old, but regardless, he was still the heavy favorite. By the way, I am told that Alexander Karelin is a really nice guy in person, so the title of the "meanest man alive" is actually meant as a compliment not an insult.

- **Jennifer Moceanu**: Yes, Jennifer Moceanu, not Dominique. Jennifer is the biological sister of Dominique who has no legs and was given up for adoption upon birth in Romania. She is also the Illinois state tumbling champion and earns a living from acrobatics. She is inspiring and a true role model for everyone, handicapped or not. She is proof positive there is no such thing as can't.

- **Lolo Jones:** Not for her athletic achievements, but for her human and personal achievements.

- **Matt Long:** Again, not for his athletic achievements, but for his vision, grittiness and determination.

- **Mother of Mohamed Wazizi:** This man should be celebrated all over the world for his contribution to the global democratic movement; he's the fruit vendor in Tunisia that immolated himself because of corruption in his country, which then led to the toppling of the dictator, which led to the Arab spring, including the toppling of Egypt and Libya's dictators, and Yemen and Syria's democratic movements;

- **Anne Wolf:** The female boxing trainer that will give a chance to any young adult that will be willing to go through intensive training;

- **Elissa Montanti:** The woman who heads-up the Global Medical Relief Fund: On a shoe string budget, and shear will, this woman brings crippled children from around the world – from such places like Iraq, Pakistan, Nepal, Haiti, Indonesia, Bosnia, Ivory Coast and other desperately poor countries – and working with volunteer medical professionals, help to restore the lives of these innocent victims;

- **Leigh Anne and Sean Tuohy, and Michael Oher:** I would give a million per person. Leigh Anne and Sean because they did something great in terms of humanity and set a great example for all. And, Michael Oher because he led a "good" life, despite his "bad" environment and background, also setting a great example.
- **Mrs. Boswell:** The teacher who helped Michael Oher navigate through high school and getting the Wingate Christian School to help as well.
- **Jamie Leigh Jones:** Former Halliburton worker that was allegedly (I have to say this) drugged and gang raped by her co-workers while working in Iraq trying to help our military personnel, but because of a binding arbitration clause in her employment contract, cannot get her day in court. I'd like to give her money to help fight for her day in court.
- **Sergeant Dennis Weichel:** A soldier from Rhode Island, he died saving an Afghan girl from being run over by a runaway armored vehicle. Ironically and sadly, he leaves behind three children.
- **Any living Medal of Honor recipients,** like **Sergeant 1st Class Leroy Petry, Staff Sergeant Salvatore Giunta, and Sergeant Dakota Meyer;**
- **Any living Distinguished Service Cross, Navy Cross (like Sergeant Juan Rodriguez Chavez), Distinguished Flying Cross recipients;**
- **Any living Silver Star and Bronze Star recipients;**
- **Families of posthumously awarded Medal of Honor, Distinguished Service Cross, Navy Cross, Distinguished Flying Cross, Silver Star and Bronze Star** recipients.
- **Service Personnel's Wish-Come-True Foundation: A charity foundation for wounded and decorated service men and women and their families:** I would start this foundation dedicated to helping improve the lives of wounded and decorated service men and women by allowing them or their family members to realize a dream, a fantasy or a wish. Some projects that my foundation would work on would be allowing wounded and decorated service men and women or their families to spend time with the celebrity of their choice, or attend the biggest sporting events anywhere in the world (Olympics, Super Bowl, World Cup, World Series, The Open, US Open, any World Championships, NBA Finals, Stanley Cup, NASCAR events, et cetera).

The above is not the complete list by all means, but, in general, I would give my money to those that deserve to be rewarded, but never expect it, never got it, and was not motivated by the money. Also, don't even think about criticizing my choices: Because, IT WOULD BE MY MONEY, therefore, IT WOULD BE MY DECISION and ONLY MY DECISION. And, individuals can only advise me, if and only if I invite the guidance and advice, period, full stop, the end.

The Justice Party: The party for ALL Americans

I would also look to establish a new party called the Justice Party with the bold eagle as its symbol. The bold eagle would have a scale in its beak, a donkey in one claw and the elephant in the other. The objectives that this party would look to institute are the following:

➢ Seek out a constitutional amendment that prohibits the government from stealing from one group to benefit another in any way shape or form;
➢ Seek out a constitutional amendment to make it illegal for the government to treat different groups differently when it comes to rights, services provided or imposing restrictions on its citizens;
➢ Seek out a constitutional amendment to make privileges based on ability;
➢ Add a constitutional amendment to include inalienable property rights, including the right to one's own hard earned money;
➢ Add a constitutional amendment to make deficit spending illegal;
➢ Also, although implied, seek out a constitutional amendment to make explicit our freedom to choose not only a religious belief, but also freedom to choose political affiliation and philosophy without prejudice and interference from the government;
➢ Rewrite the IRS tax codes to vastly simplify and eliminate loop holes, subsidies, eliminate corporate taxes and other non-uniform applications of tax collection, and to introduce a flat tax to cover for only self-defense, education and infrastructure – the end result is that the tax code shouldn't be more than a few pages and tax returns shouldn't be more than 3-5 pages, including instructions;
➢ Look to immediately change the pledge of allegiance, swearing-in oaths in court and for the military and our currency to eliminate all religious references and references to any god;
➢ Drop all minority programs;
➢ Drop all subsidies;
➢ Eliminate all racial quotas;
➢ Change the tax codes so that there are no inheritance and gift taxes among direct family members;

- Eliminate taxes for members of the armed services;
- Change capital gains tax to 100% for holdings of less than 1 year, 80% for less than two years, 50% for less than 3-years, and 0% for greater than 3-years;
- Mirror the tax code for dividends and interest payments to match capital gain taxes;
- Make sure the federal government always runs a balanced budget or have the politicians arrested and thrown in jail according to the number of years served in congress with provision to allow for fixing the problem should spending increase above revenue without increasing taxes;
- Look to make stimulus spending an exception and force the administration to seek a Supreme Court ruling every time a stimulus spending program is proposed;
- Seek to monitor and record all conversations of all politicians and their staff or aides, anywhere in the world wherever and whenever they talk to each other, lobbyists, or their constituents with provisions for expulsion and jail time should they violate this law;
- Make congressional representative and senators, president, governors and state legislative members compensations correlate to long-term unemployment, interest rates, and inflation, while cutting overall compensation by half, drastically reducing the retirement package and withholding part of the compensation over a 5-year period so that it can be tied to long-term unemployment, interest rates, and inflation;
- Make congress, president, governors and state legislatures use the same healthcare plan as the ones that the rest of the federal or state government employees use;
- If no one runs for political office, a lottery will be convened to pick a random person from the populace to serve in the political office that is vacant; for this individual, the compensation will be quadrupled, retirement package will be far more generous, but their term will be limited to 12-years, and they still have to abide by the monitoring rules and balanced budget requirements;
- Restore the right to bear arms or eliminate the 2nd amendment completely;
- Either increase the voting age to 21 or drop the drinking age to 18 – it makes no sense that 18 year olds have the right to vote, but not the right to drink; I don't know about anyone else, but I think the right to vote requires

more maturity, intelligence and knowledge than drinking, so I think the current situation is ass-backwards;

➤ Largely abolish morality laws and make it illegal to have morality laws like prostitution, drug use, anti-abortion, DWI, anti-gambling among others;

➤ Eliminate conflicting or confusing business laws;

➤ Eliminate all business subsidies, unless it can be demonstrated that it is in the best interest of *every individual* in the US;

➤ Make it illegal to make laws that restrict consensual sexual behavior like sodomy and oral sex;

➤ Make it illegal to make laws that restrict gay marriages and other forms of marriage based on sexual orientation or preference;

➤ Allow gay marriages and accord them with the same rights and privileges of heterosexual marriages;

➤ Eliminate statutory rape laws if the sex is consensual, particularly among people of similar age;

➤ Look to privatize all charity functions that the tax payers currently support like Medicaid, Medicare, Social Security, Welfare, Food Stamps, Unemployment, Earned Income Tax Credit, et cetera;

➤ Eliminate civil laws and reduce criminal laws to one line: "Stealing or violation of other people's rights are punishable by jail terms or death," but providing sentencing guidelines;

➤ Immediate dismemberment of the male sexual organ for rape, sexual assault and sexual abuse of children, followed by the death penalty;

➤ Immediate elimination of the female sexual organ for rape, sexual assault and sexual abuse of children, followed by the death penalty;

➤ Eliminate all unnecessary cabinet positions, departments, congressional offices, aides and other government functions;

➤ Create a watch dog to monitor all corporate behavior and provide service and product reviews, independent of all political influence;

➤ Insure immigration of people that are smart or wealthy;

➤ Set up abortion as a legal right for all women, once and for all;

➤ Institute tort reform, so that punitive damages aren't restricted in the case where wrong-doing is found, but also allow juries to determine, if a lawsuit is frivolous and assess damages and punitive penalties to both the lawyers and their clients for bringing frivolous lawsuits;

- ➢ All judgments, settlements, and arbitration results to be made public and subject to review from independent and unaffiliated jurists to discern the fairness of the judgments, settlements, and arbitration results;
- ➢ Immediate withdrawal of all corporate involvement in every way from the judicial branch, whether it concerns the election of judges and attorneys general, selection and nomination process for judges and attorneys general, involvement in any court cases other than their own, unless called in as a witness;
- ➢ Turn all insurance businesses into not-for-profit or mutual insurance companies that work for the benefit of policy holders and no one but policy holders;
- ➢ Finally, seek a constitutional amendment that makes Justice the primary and sole motive of the US government, and requires all state and municipal governments to honor the same.

This list covers most of what the Justice Party would seek to do, but I'm sure objectives will be added and subtracted as necessary. Regardless, all objectives must adhere to the principles of Justice and only Justice.

Small-minded Americans still exist; these are the kinds of people we should root out of our society

I could not believe my ears when I heard that there was hate mail being sent to Elissa Montanti of the Global Medical Relief Fund (GMRF)! What small-minded jackass would do such a thing?! The argument that the haters make is that Ms. Montanti should be helping our children not those from countries that hate us. Some people are obviously sympathetic to such an argument, and some may have what seems like a good reason – perhaps those few that lost children, siblings or significant others to the Iraq and Afghan wars. However, keep in mind that what someone does with their time is their own business as long as they are not hurting anyone. Second, if someone is so worked up about Ms. Montanti helping children from other countries while not helping children in our own country, I say, first go out and achieve in the US what Ms. Montanti has accomplished globally then we can "talk," third, learn what America and Americans are about, fourth, the haters should lift their heads-up and see beyond the tip of their nose, and fifth, if people are so worked up about what Ms. Montanti is doing, donate money to organizations that help US children.

It's really not all that complicated. Ms. Montanti is correct. The children and their mothers and interpreters that get help from Ms. Montanti and the cadres of volunteers are and will continue to be volunteer "Ambassadors" for the US. And, talk is cheap, but a corroborating eye-witness whom one trusts is invaluable. Now, some people may argue that the people who get help from the GMRF will be brainwashed by the haters of the US in their country into thinking that all that the GMRF did was to partially restore that which was lost due to US involvement in their country. However, I would argue that that is not an argument that could be sustained as these children and their entourage make repeated visits for check-ups and replacements.

However, regardless of what ideology one argues for, all arguments should cease with the statement that one's own time should be used as one sees fit, not how others believe it should be used. Who is anyone to lecture about how someone should use their time? Some may argue – falsely – that I'm doing the same thing. The big difference – and it is the only argument that I need – is that I do not make people buy my book and force them to read it, which is essentially what those that are sending hate mail to Ms. Montanti are trying to do by telling her what she should and shouldn't do with her time.

We should all be thanking Ms. Montanti and donating money to her fund, which I have done, anonymously, let alone criticizing her. She is doing our country a great service and helping to achieve harmony and global peace. Thank you Ms. Montanti from the bottom of my heart and that of my family's. Please keep up the good work and don't let these detractors (retards really) get you down.

Stop making racial and ethnic distinctions; they are totally counter-productive, completely unnecessary and totally un-American

The more we insist on labeling, the more unnecessary differentiations that people can make, the more there is to categorize, and the more there is for people to group together, hate, ostracize, or otherwise compartmentalize. What is the big deal about being homosexual, heterosexual, bi-sexual, transsexual, white, black, Hispanic, Asian, a woman, a man, old, young, educated, uneducated, blue collar, white collar, rich, poor, CEO, janitor, handicapped, tall, short, fat, skinny, beautiful or ugly? People are people and the only point that matters is who they are, not what they are. Everything else is jast another way to allow for segregation, discrimination, exclusion or inclusion. So, we should stop labeling people; it is completely unnecessary, not to mention counter-productive. For example, labeling someone a black, Asian, white, or Hispanic doesn't mean anything. Either someone is or isn't an American and someone is or isn't a good person. If people want to label, let's start thinking about people in terms of whether they are a good person or a bad person, misguided or evil, moral or immoral, a thinker or tinkerer, smart or clever, ethical or unethical, honorable or dishonorable, honest or a liar, American or not. Let me illustrate with some concrete examples:

1. There are no such people as Hispanic Americans, Puerto Rican Americans, Latin Americans, African Americans, Black Americans, Chinese Americans, Japanese American, Korean Americans, Pakistani Americans, Indian (Asian) Americans, Vietnamese American, Italian Americans, Irish Americans, German Americans, Arab American, Jewish American, Catholic American, Mormon American or any other sub-Americans. People are either an American or they are not, because being American is about a philosophy and believing in a way of thinking, talking, and acting. It has nothing to do with what color one's skin is, how long one has lived in the territorial boundaries of America or where they or their ancestors were born. In fact, the only Chinese American is a Chinese person living in China that believes in the American philosophy and wants to live like an American and be an American. By this definition, there are a whole lot of people living in the territorial borders of America that really aren't Americans: Most people that support socialism, believes capitalism is a failure, socialists, communists, liberals, cheaters, criminals, bigots, religious nuts, et cetera. My beliefs have some strong implications for who should be deported, where to and who should be allowed to stay within the territorial borders of the United States of America.

2. Jast because someone is the president of the United States, a US senator, member of the house of representatives, governor, state legislator, Chairman and CEO of a US-based company, famous celebrity, accomplished athlete, millionaire, or billionaire, it does not make one a good, smart, wise, insightful, moral, ethical, honorable, honest, or useful person. In fact, many people in these positions are quite the opposite, as we all know all too well. So, what if someone is a black billionaire from Georgia? What the hell does

it matter to anyone? Who cares? And, more importantly, what does it mean?

3. In America and for Americans, labeling people by the color of their skin or by their ancestry is no different than classifying them under the color of their hair, by height, by body-mass index, by the color of their eyes, or some other random physical metric. It serves no other purpose than to divide and be divisive. So, as an example, if people want to call themselves an Italian American, they should go back to Italy, because that is the only place where someone can be Italian anything. And, the person certainly cannot be an American, if they think they have anything to do with Italy. A true American will be nothing like any other person in the world, because we are the only country in the world that was formed under a common philosophy, not based on a race, creed, ancestry or religion.

4. This also means that racial quotas should also be abolished, because they are not American nor for the benefit of America. This does not mean that we should not be vigilant against prejudice and bigotry, we absolutely must. And, everyone that wants admissions to something must meet that group's single and absolute admissions criteria. Also, people should be chosen because they are the best for the organization; not to further someone else's ideal of what is socially acceptable or not. Regardless, if an organization is truly American, matters of racial integrity will not be a problem. And we, as a country, unnecessarily spend way too much time on the "racial issue," which forces organizations to be sub-optimal. Enough already! For example, jast look at top California state colleges' and state universities' admissions policies. It's ridiculous and very un-American!

I cannot respect Martin Luther King, Mahomet Gandhi, nor Mother Teresa, but I respect Malcolm X

I can hear the howling already and visualize the offended looks, even murderous looks in people's eyes. I understand why people would be so offended: MLK, Gandhi and Ma T are some of the most respected people in the world for what they said, what they represented, what they did, and what they portrayed. In contrast Malcolm X is one of the most controversial, most divisive, most a lot of things, almost none of which would be viewed as positive by the vast majority of the people in this world.

The following is a direct quote from Dr. Martin Luther King's, "*I have a dream*" speech, one of the most profound, prophetic and inspiring speeches ever made by man: "I have a dream that my four little children will one day live in a nation where they will not be judge by the color of their skin, but **by the content of their character**."

So, how could I possibly feel this way about his words, but differently about the man? How could I feel negatively about MLK despite almost the entire world that feels the opposite way from the way I feel? Simple: MLK was an adulterer. According to his own words, we can infer that every person should be judged "by the content of their character." Well if MLK was an adulterer, what does that say about the content of his character? Yes, his words were unbelievably inspiring and Just, but how do we know that the motive was truly what he implied or if he said what he did to gain fame, fortune or prestige?

On the other hand, Malcolm X was true to himself and the world. What people saw was what they got, and he truly, not only believed in his cause, but also he sincerely wanted to help his constituents. But, most of all, when he realized that he was wrong, he changed course and tried to correct that which was wrong within him, twice. Judging by the content of his character, I'd say he's someone that is truly worthy of our respect and admiration, in all shape, way and form. To me, MLK is like Sammy Sosa or Mark McGuire: There has to be an asterisk next to his name to highlight the fact that there should be controversy to his accomplishments.

Now let's compare Malcolm X to MLK and Gandhi. Like Malcolm X, both MLK and Gandhi spoke beautiful words and performed some courageous acts, but could have been faking it, in my opinion. What they could have been faking was their moral high ground! Both men were unabashed, unapologetic and frequent adulterers. In my opinion, one cannot claim moral superiority and preach morality and yet betray one of the most core fundamentals of morality. This violation of basic moral trust is not something that should be memorialized, worshipped, and honored. If we do then we are saying that as long as one is perceived to have accomplished noteworthy goals and talk a good game, one can cheat all they want. And, when I say cheat, I don't necessarily mean stopping at adultery.

With adultery, it isn't the act of having sex with another person that makes it a big deal; it is that an individual is breaking their most sacred promise, their word, their integrity, **their honor**. That's what makes adultery such a despicable act, not necessarily the act itself. Moreover, if marriage is the cornerstone of family and family values and the family unit is the cornerstone of society then adulterers are violating one of the most sacred principles of any civilized society and they are not only betraying the trust of their spouse and family, but also showing utter disrespect for our society and the principles that our society holds sacred. If one really thinks about it, it's pretty despicable how adulterers trample on family values, reflecting the adulterer's Six Pillars. Therefore, if it were left up to me, I'd change all public memorials dedicated to MLK to Malcolm X.

So, what of Ma T? All that I've read about her is not very flattering. She was a terror to work for, and very sanctimonious. Also, I read that she walked around preaching about her christian god and acting holier than thou, while accepting all accommodations and luxuries offered. The bottom-line is that she was doing what she wanted and what she thought was the right behavior to get into her heaven, i.e., she was "selfish." So, why or how is that so noble? Long before she was well known, she made up her mind that she would "serve" her christian god, one of the most evil concepts developed by man. Knowingly or otherwise, Ma T is one of the symbols of the evils of the christian religion, and to boot, reputedly and ironically, not a good person. And, I don't like symbols that represent evil, in any way, shape or form.

Stop worrying and obsessing about China

I understand why so many people in the world are worried about China, and to a slightly lesser degree India. For the purposes of this discussion, I will focus on China only, but the discussion could be jast as applicable to India, but with about a 10-20 year delay.

Let's do the math. China has about 1.25 billion people and generates about $6.5 trillion in annual GDP that's growing at about 8%-10% per year – the per capita GDP is currently about $5,200. America has about 310 million people and generates about $15-$16 trillion in annual GDP that's growing at about 2%-4% per year – the per capita GDP is currently about $50,000. It doesn't take a rocket scientist to figure out that at these respective paces that China will surpass US per capita GDP by about 2050, but, more importantly, by about 2025

China's total GDP will be bigger than that of the US. To many, the "math" implies some very serious consequences. But let me make my point very plain and obvious: The reason why people are so worried is because they are using the overly simplistic "if all-else-being-equal analysis." Some conclude that if "all-else-remains-equal" then China will have more money than the US to spend on their military and thus present a geopolitical challenge that the US cannot meet. Second, the amount of pollution that China will create to achieve their economic prowess will be devastating to the environment and third – and most concerning for America – is that China's future economic might would make it the next superpower, relegating the US to #2. Sounds like a good analysis and something we should be afraid of, but it's total nonsense!

First of all, **all else cannot be equal**. Therefore, we must take into consideration changes that will occur. First of all, China's population is decreasing because of their "one family, one child" policy and for this trend to start reversing it will take a good 50 years or so according to experts. This means that China's dominance will be slower to come than scheduled. Second, and most importantly, China cannot grow at an average rate of ~9%/year at infinitum! If we take South Korea as a proxy, their high single digit to low double digits growth rate ended around 1997 during the Asian financial crisis and since then they have had trouble maintaining a mid-single digit growth rate of ~5%-7%. Third, like Japan and South Korea, China is going to have problems creating technological innovations. Fourth, the Chinese will take care of their environment on their own and in their own way. Again, let's take a page from South Korea. Until about the early 1990s, South Koreans didn't care about the environment, but this started to change about the time that South Korea's per capita GDP hit about $10,000. The connection between per capita GDP and the environment is that when people start to have disposable income, one of the ways in which people spend their money is to take vacations and enjoy their prosperity. But what happens when their vacations are ruined by smog, stench, pollution, sewage, garbage and other environmental disasters? What happens when people's food becomes poisoned and tainted due to negligent environmental management? What happens when people become more and more sick and unhealthy due to the environment? We don't have to do anything; the Chinese will fix their own environmental problems and soon enough at that. Until then, there is absolutely nothing the rest of the world can or should do about it. This doesn't mean that we shouldn't try to convince the

Chinese and others to be more conscientious; however, we must do so with the expectation that what we want isn't necessarily relevant to the Chinese, much like what they want isn't necessarily relevant to us either.

The other problem with the "all-else-being-equal" analysis is that it doesn't take into consideration the potential for political change. Like most countries that have gone from abject poverty to relative wealth, the Chinese are going to want political freedom as they become more and more wealthy. Again, take a look at South Korea's political history over the last 30 years. Therefore, even China will, at some point, become a democratic country, and most likely right around the time that the Chinese start to have substantial disposable income. For the South Koreans it was around the late 1980s to about the early 1990s with per capita GDP in 1988 (in 2005 dollars) at about $7,700 and in 1993 at about $10,400.

Once China becomes a democratic country then natural progress will force changes on the government and its people. Like all countries that transition to democracies from centrally controlled governments, they will have to contend with elections, which have a very negative influence on the economy via out of control regulations, need for consensus, and politics. These changes alone will create massive drag on the Chinese economy as it has done to the European and US economies. Next, there will be a major and massive financial crisis, probably rooted in real estate that will greatly and dramatically slow the Chinese economy. Lastly, but most importantly, like its major Asian economic brethren – the South Koreans and the Japanese – the Chinese economy will come to a point where copying other countries' technologies will no longer be enough to sustain the kinds of economic growth it had been enjoying prior to the democratization of its political system. This will be the coup de grace that, in combination with socialism, will ultimately derail the Chinese juggernaut that we see today.

Also, the democratization of China will greatly reduce Chinese military spending and greatly reduce tensions with the US, and may in fact create a very strong and cooperative working partnership as neither country wants to risk an outbreak of open hostilities anywhere in the world, as it will be bad for business, especially if the two countries involved were to be the US and China.

Regardless, the Chinese will eventually attain GDP numbers that are greater than that of the US, jast because their population is four-times that of the US, but it is unlikely to be as fast as projected and most likely after China has transitioned to a democratic country. However, on a per capita basis, it is dubious whether or not the Chinese will surpass the US, given that China does not have the ability to innovate, much like the Japanese and the South Koreans don't. Therefore, although China may have the most powerful economy in the world, it is unlikely to ever surpass our prosperity. In reality, my bet is that the Chinese will need at least the rest of this century to get close to our per capita GDP numbers and most likely will never get there. My feeling is that the Chinese will most likely have no problems getting to about half of our per capita GDP, but significantly beyond that (say 75%), I have my doubts. Nevertheless, at half of our per capita GDP, the Chinese economy would be double that of the US.

One would think that if the US GDP is $20 trillion, but the Chinese economy is $40 trillion then this would be a huge disadvantage to us, but I don't think that that is necessarily going to be true. It all depends on whether or not the Chinese economy is truly a free economy or still centrally controlled, how deep socialism stays rooted, especially after the country turns towards democracy, how many proprietary and profitable self-developed technologies the Chinese can create, if any, and how big their budget deficit and national debt will be in the future – there is no question, in my mind, that they will run a budget deficit in the future. To put a fine point to my theory, if the Chinese economy goes the route of the Japanese, Italian, Spanish, Portuguese, or Greek economies then, despite the scale of their economy, the Chinese will be relatively powerless and ineffective. However, if the Chinese can develop proprietary and profitable technologies and they can take leadership in several industrial and service sectors then we and the rest of the industrialized nations are toast: The Chinese WILL become the greatest economic power in the history of the world, by far.

However, let me be perfectly clear and straight. I don't think the Chinese will ever get there. In my opinion, I don't think they have the creativity, ingenuity – this is very different than cunning or cleverness – and long-term value system to be able to get there. Finally, and most importantly, I don't think they have the educational system to be economically successful in the long-term. Don't forget, there is only so much a country can do to improve their economic well-being when their economic wealth is controlled by foreign technology. China's development curve isn't too far removed from Japan's or South Korea's. And, from the 1960s through the 1980s, Japan did a lot of catching-up while South Korea did the same in the 1980s through the new millennium. But now, both economies are hopelessly mired in neutral, especially Japan's, and both economies are desperately searching for the next new technology that they can adapt. But this strategy has obvious limitations: Regardless of how good they master new technologies, they are still dependent on other countries' technologies. So, these two countries have found themselves in the unenviable position of being pressured from both the top and the bottom of the economic ladder. From the bottom, countries like China, India and Brazil are very quickly climbing up the low-to-middle end of the technology curve, while the technologically more advanced countries are more and more protective of their technological developments. So, how does Japan and South Korea escape this pressure cooker? The only way they can escape this conundrum is to develop their own successful and profitable proprietary technologies. To do this sustainably and successfully, they have to develop an educational system that is vastly different than what they have today, and this will be their challenge. In particular, they need to develop an educational system that fosters creativity, unusual thinking, and diversity. However, according to friends, it seems that this is in exact contrast to how all three countries educate their children today. In combination with socialist economies, they stand little to no chance of catching up to our prosperity – caveat to come later.

To date, China has done well by copying the Japanese and South Korean economic models. And, the good news for the Chinese is that they have a good 20-40 years before running into the brick wall currently facing the Japanese and the South Koreans. The bad news is that they'll need all of that time and then some to be able to change and remake their educational system to prepare themselves for the future. However, as I said before, I don't believe that the Chinese will be successful where the Japanese and the South Koreans have failed. Therefore, as long as we continue to pioneer new technologies, reduce the size of our government dramatically and truly let Justice prevail as a form of governance, the Chinese will not become a long-term problem for our economy to handle.

However, there is a caveat to my predictions: If the US continues to expand its socialism/communism policies then the Chinese won't have to step-up to take over the mantle of the most powerful economic country in the world, we will hand it over to the Chinese by debilitating our own economy, much like the Europeans have done over the last 50 years or so to theirs.

Real fight is more likely to be between China and India, not China and the US

India is the other superpower-in-waiting and will follow a similar course to the Chinese, but given that India is largely already a democratic and socialist country, they will encounter more of the problems earlier than China will eventually have to face. Regardless, due to the economic growth rates of both countries, tightness of resources around the world, competition for investments, competition for export markets, and weakened OECD economies, rivalry between China and India can only intensify. If this rivalry intensifies too quickly and antagonistically then a militarily-based conflict is not impossible, particularly at sea, where both countries will vie for dominance in the areas named the Bay of Bengal, Andaman Sea, the Gulf of Thailand and the South China Sea; key common trade shipping routes for both countries.

Also, both countries have developed their export machines to grow, and both countries are constantly and desperately searching for cheap resources to feed this export machine. Most importantly, both countries are searching for technological knowledge. This leaves both countries at critical odds with each other with the Chinese ahead of the curve by about 10-20 years versus the Indians. Chinese have per capita GDP of about $5,200 and the Indians are at about $1,500. The last time China saw $1,500 per capita GDP was in about 2004 or about 7-8 years ago. As a point of reference, the last time the South Koreans saw about $5,200 per capita GDP was in 1989 when they achieved $5,565 versus the latest estimate for 2011 of about $24,000; this represents a CAGR of some 6.8% per annum. This implies that China is unlikely to grow at the 8%-10% range for much longer, while the Indians have a lot longer leeway to grow at the 8%-10% range. The other critical difference is that India's population is still growing relatively very fast, which may be a double-edged sword. Therefore, the conclusion that we can reach is that China, though economically ahead of India, will likely face more challenges in the near-term, including the transition to a democracy, while the Indians though economically behind the Chinese will have more running room to grow, but potentially debilitated by its myriad of "social programs." Regardless, both countries will grow far faster than the rest of the world which puts them at odds with each other, particularly at the scale that they have the potential to grow given their respective populations of about 1.25 billion in China and about 1.1 billion in India – combined about one-third of the world's population. This makes potential military conflicts, particularly at sea, more and more likely as trade becomes a larger and more important part of both countries' economies.

However, despite having a substantial length of common border between the two countries, a land war is not likely as the border region is extremely mountainous and very difficult to navigate. Furthermore, a land war would greatly favor India as the Chinese would have to supply its army across a vast desert region and its supply-line would be greatly stretched from its coastal industrial base. This is not the case for India as the capital, New Delhi, is only about 250 miles from the border with China. Therefore, the Chinese would not start a land war and would only have to maintain a strong defensive position to deter India from instigating one.

On the oceans and the seas, the Chinese have the distinct advantage as they already deploy nuclear and brown-water attack submarines, and are on the verge of building its first aircraft carrier. However, it would be very difficult for the Chinese to instigate aggression against the Indian navy as the US would not sit idly by and jast watch. And, despite their advances, the Chinese navy will be no match for the US navy for a very long time to come. On the other hand, the Indians don't have the capability to mount any kind of effective attack on the Chinese navy. Therefore, a seaborne conflict is also unlikely. However, in international waters, constant contact between the two navies will be inevitable and India will come to the realization that a strong naval presence will be integral to their economic success, forcing the Indians to build-up their naval presence, increasing the potential for conflict with China.

The real frightening scenario is the potential for exchanging nuclear attacks on each other. Although the Indians do not yet have intercontinental ballistic missiles and the Chinese are on the verge of developing their own, sooner or later both countries will have this capability, as both countries have developed space rockets capable of launching satellites. We can only hope that both countries exercise the restraint and common sense shown by the US and the former USSR during the cold war when it comes to the potential for nuclear weapons use.

The bottom line is that China and India are the two countries whose rivalry needs to be watched and monitored extremely carefully. There really is no significant rivalry between China and the US that we need to worry about. And, more importantly, there is nothing that we need to fear from the Chinese or the Indians. Ultimately, we are not the rivals for China and India, it is the two that are rivals to each other, and we jast have to make sure that the rivalry doesn't turn into conflict.

Again, the one caveat that I will leave the reader with is that we don't go down the path of socialism/communism, and we revert back to true capitalism and we continue to be the technological leader of the world. If we can achieve these objectives then we have absolutely nothing to fear from the Chinese, the Indians, nor the rest of the world.

Two other goals that I think are important to achieve: Conversion to the metric system and 220-240-volt electric grid

The second to last goal I'll advocate for is the conversion to the metric system. People need to realize how much money this will save our country in the long-run, and how much this will help our companies be more competitive overseas. Americans really have no idea. This is something that we **MUST DO** with all haste.

And, the last goal that I will advocate for is the conversion of our electric grid to 220-240-volts. I strongly believe that this is not only a necessary cost saving measure in that it will save us a lot of money due to less line loss, more energy efficiency, less equipment maintenance and creation of a more robust grid, but also, it is vital to allowing penetration of electric vehicles into our society. With 220-240-volts, charging times can be cut by more than half, which makes it more of a viable alternative to gasoline vehicles.

By the way, in case anyone was wondering, the solution to short-ranges of electric vehicles is to convert or add electric charging stations to every gasoline station. The way this would work isn't that we'd drive up to a gas station and plug in our car to charge, but we would pull into a gas station to *exchange* our depleted battery for a fully charged one. This should take well less than 10 minutes to do, which should be about equivalent to filling-up any gasoline engine car at a gas station today. It would then be incumbent on the gasoline station owner to clean and re-charge the empty batteries. Of course, there are technical issues to overcome and pricing issues to be worked out, but I strongly believe that this is the best way to fast track electric vehicle sales in the US.

Let's get one thing straight, if Robin Hood or Zorro existed today, they'd be taking from the poor and giving to the rich

Most people are taught and strongly believe that Robin Hood and Zorro's mission was to take from the rich and give to the poor. Actually, this is as far from the truth as it gets. It's only coincidence of history that the oppressors were the rich and their only choice of victims was the poor. The real mission of Zorro and Robin Hood wasn't about wealth and who it belonged to, it was about correcting an injustice. The injustice was about the rich taking what did not belong to them because they could; mainly through military force. And, what they stole wasn't jast wealth through "taxes," fees or levies. It was also other oppressive behaviors like slavery or forced indentured service, not allowing the poor to control their own destiny or have a say in it, primae noctis, and other forms of injustice and oppression. Money was a way to keep score: The sum total of how much injustice was perpetrated on the victims.

Today, the victims of injustice are the wealthy, productive and intelligent and the oppressors are the liberals and socialists with their unwitting allies, the poor, and the tool of oppression is the democratic process. The liberals and the socialists justify anything and everything through voting, regardless of whether or not a particular subject matter should be put to a vote or not. They justify this view by talking about how there are no other fair ways of settling matters. However, they conveniently neglect to tell people that there are certain principles that should never be put to a vote and must be protected as inalienable and irrevocable rights. Such issues as slavery, voting rights, free speech, freedom of philosophy (which includes religion) and property rights should never be subject to a vote.

The reason why the liberals and socialists try to justify everything through the voting process is because they will win 100 out of 100 times if they do. Think about this: Who wouldn't want to get something for no effort, in particular, if they are told that there will be no consequences? Who wouldn't pocket a $100 bill, If they found it on the street? It is this expectation that a free lunch is possible – literally in this example – which the liberals and socialists exploit. By promising the poorer segments of society that they can have all the free lunches that they want – and to get them, all they have to do is vote the liberals and socialist into power – the liberals and socialists have not only controlled the politics and the agenda around the politics for the last 80-or-so years, they are slowly but surely pushing the country towards the proverbial financial cliff. What's more astounding is that most of the common liberals and socialists are sincere in the pursuit of their agenda and believe that they are doing good for our country. However, there are a select group of liberals and socialist who are pursuing their agenda because they want to get ahead in life without thought to the others in our society. These people are typically politicians who want to get ahead, knowing that what they are doing is devastating for our country. Either that or they are very, very stupid, blind and very, very short-sighted.

Regardless, if Zorro and Robin Hood were alive today, I strongly believe that they'd be taking back what was stolen from the wealthy, productive and intelligent and giving it back to them. Think about it: Do the rich have a choice? By definition, they (the 1-percenters) are outnumbered 100-to-1. Even if they were outnumbered jast 10-to-1, the rich don't have a voice even though people pretend that the rich have a voice. But, clearly, it's a false sense of control as long as people get to vote on how they get to spend other people's money. Next, what happens if the rich don't pay the extortion money? They lose everything or almost everything, i.e., they go to jail. Even after they die, they have virtually no say in the use of the majority of their money, because estate taxes (could be as high as 70% when federal and state taxes are combined) take it away from them and their loved ones. This means that the rich are ultimately working for other people and not for themselves nor their children and relatives. This means that the ultimate beneficiaries of the wealth created by the wealthy are total strangers. This is not right! So, the rich not only don't get to keep a very large chunk of what they earned, they are forced to labor under the false pretense that the money that they earn is theirs when in reality when they die the vast majority of it is taken away from them and given to total strangers. So, it shouldn't surprise anyone that the rich keep on trying to create loop holes in the tax system. Under the circumstances that the rich toil under, anyone would try to stop getting extorted or at the very least reduce the extortion payment. Bottom-line, the rich are the victims in today's society; this is why Robin Hood and Zorro would be working for the benefit of the rich in today's society, not the poor, if they are truly angels of Justice. So, abandon the quaint and child-like notion that Robin Hood and Zorro stole from the rich and gave to the poor. That's not what they did; ultimately, what they did was to correct an injustice. This is a very subtle, but very important distinction that must be emphasized and remembered.

The perfect illustration of how little people actually think

Let me illustrate how little people actually think and when they do try to think how short-sighted they are. The following is based on a story featured on 60 Minutes on CBS, one of our favorite shows.

On one 60 Minutes episode, they featured a story on what I'll call African deer. These African deer are extinct in Africa, but are thriving in a US state. The reason for the deer's initial success in the US was due to a visionary philanthropist that saw the threat to the species and wanted to rescue the species from its eventual fate in Africa and imported them starting in the 1970s. Later, as the species started to thrive in the US, the philanthropist started selling the deer to ranchers that charge a fee to hunters to shoot the deer for trophies. All throughout this process, the African deer population had been growing in the US, so much so that a country in Africa has been re-importing the species into a reserve.

So, who would object to helping the African deer grow in population to the point where they number in the hundreds, if not the thousands, and have the opportunity to repopulate their homeland? How about a so called conservationist? Much to my surprise, a so called conservationist wants all hunting of these animals to cease in this country, and this person has successfully sued to highly restrict the hunting of these animals. The success of this conservationist is very surprising in the sense that the courts have agreed with this person, so far. The reason why it is surprising is because the ranchers are very judicious about how they dispense licenses to hunters – typically the ranchers do not allow more than 10% of the herd to be culled. In addition, the herd has been growing in numbers, albeit slowly, but nevertheless growing. Also, the ranchers are able to maintain the herd precisely because they offer hunting permits at such a price as to afford to maintain the herd. And, this is the key point that seems to be lost on this so called conservationist.

Without the hunters and hunting, the ranchers cannot afford to maintain the herd and slowly, but surely the numbers would dwindle and eventually they'd be extinct in this country too. And, if there are any problems in Africa, the new herd there could also be quickly extinct, and the world would lose yet another species of animal that we did not have to. All because a so called conservationist didn't want these animals hunted on US soil. Now how dumb is that?! So, when the reporter asked: "Wouldn't the chance of the species surviving increase, if they were allowed to thrive in both continents? And, if the price that has to be paid to allow that to happen is that a small group of the species is hunted in the US, isn't that ultimately for the benefit of the species?" The so called conservationist's answer: "I jast don't want them to be hunted in the US." Now what kind of a stupid answer is that?

Even in the wild, any species of what I would call deer have predators and a number of the deer would be hunted and killed by these predators. This obvious point must have somehow eluded this so called conservationist. Moreover, the answer to the question that the reporter asked is obviously yes, but because the so called conservationist didn't want to admit hes stupidity hesh dodged the question completely. This tells me that the so called conservationist is stupid or short-sighted or both, or hesh didn't understand the question or didn't know what to say. How could this so called conservationist possibly go around calling hemself that? It's absolutely ridiculous! This type of "thinking" is too typical of too many so called Americans.

Other injustices that need to be fixed (not necessarily the same magnitude of offense, per se)

➢ Did any of those self-righteous and arrogant journalists that criticized Venus and Serena Williams' father for claiming that his daughters would be number 1 in the world apologize to Mr. Williams?

➢ Did any of the popes apologize for pope Urban 2's decision to start the first crusade?

➢ Did any of the popes apologize for the acts of pedophilia by its priesthood and attendant cover-up?

➢ The Japanese must apologies for the atrocities committed in China and other countries from 1910-1945, especially for the Rape of Nanjing, and imperialist colonization of Manchuria and Korea.

➢ The Japanese school curriculum must be amended to tell the truth and the whole truth about all of the atrocities their ancestors committed during World War 2.

➤ The people who tricked Caster Semenya into taking a gender test must be stripped of their livelihood, have all of their assets awarded to Caster, and should be thrown into the streets after being forced to issue a public apology to Ms. Semenya and going through a publicly conducted gender test.

➤ We must compensate the American Indian tribes for the way they were treated by our ancestors.

➤ Adam Lambert, Crystal Bowersox, and Joshua Ledet or Jessica Sanchez should have won American Idol in their respective seasons; this is not to say that Chris Allen, Lee DeWyze or Philip Phillips weren't good, but based on pure singing talent, the first four are much better, in my opinion.

Other off the wall remarks and opinions, and tidbits

• **The perfect sunny-side up egg**: Recently, I read an article talking about how to cook the perfect sunny-side up egg, and I can tell you that no one got it right. Before going on, let me describe the perfect sunny-side up egg: To me, the perfect sunny-side up egg has a fully cooked egg white with a warm yoke and no trace of the fully-cooked pale yellow pasty yoke. With that in mind as the definition of a perfect sunny-side up egg, let me give the reader the story behind how I found out the secret of the perfect sunny-side up egg and what that secret is. I've been searching for the perfect way to cook a sunny-side up egg for almost my entire adult life. Then, a couple of years ago, my friend, who is a sous chef at a casino-hotel in Las Vegas, told me that a customer revealed the secret to cooking the perfect sunny-side up egg: Separate the yoke and the egg white, being very careful not to burst the yoke. First, heat the frying pan on the lowest setting possible and coat the surface with the preferred non-stick ingredient such as olive oil, butter, or bacon lard – I use an oil mister to spray the pan with olive oil. After separating the egg, put the egg white and only the egg white into the pan. Then season the egg white with one's preferred seasoning – I like to use salt and pepper and either, chopped rosemary, cilantro or dill. Then, when the egg white is cooked about ~80%, add the yoke on top of the egg white and season it the same way that the egg white was seasoned – the reason for cooking the egg white ~80% only is to make sure that the egg yolk binds with the white. After seasoning the yoke, cover the frying pan with the lid made for the frying pan – this is very important as it will allow the yoke to warm quicker without creating the fully-cooked pasty yoke.

After about one-to-three minutes (depending on the heat of the stove, the temperature of the yoke and how warm the yoke needs to be served) serve the egg. After the technique is perfected, I think everyone will agree with me that this is probably the best way to cook a sunny-side up egg. This way of cooking the sunny-side up egg also appeals a lot to the over-easy crowd as it allows the egg white to fully cook, while warming the yoke.

- **In my opinion, anyone who thinks or says that the height of sophistication in food is French cuisine is a pretentious and superficial jackass, doesn't know squat about food, has a simple palette, or sells or promotes French cuisine:** When it comes to the height of sophistication, no cuisine beats Chinese food. Whether one looks at it from the number of ingredients, cooking methods, combinations of ingredients, taste variations, or jast the sheer number of dishes, nothing comes close to Chinese cuisine. I would say that Indian cuisine would be second, and I would even put Italian ahead of French food in terms of sophistication and Spanish would vie for third, fourth or fifth place. On the other hand, if one is talking about simple sophistication then I would put Japanese cuisine at the top of the list, and it could be argued that French or German cuisine comes second – many may not consider French food simple, and I wouldn't argue against this. Regardless, I have not had extensive experience with many cuisines, so I may be missing something, but certainly, based on the foods that I have had a lot of experience with, I stand by my position.

- **When it comes to wine, I would call it a tie between California and French wines:** Some may argue that Italian or Spanish wine could compete for second place and may even argue that one or the other should be on top, and I couldn't argue against this opinion. However, getting back to my opinion, some of the best wines that I've ever consumed came from French vineyards, but some of the worst – especially for the price – have also come from French vineyards. On the other hand, California wines are far more consistent – I am told that this is so because the Californian vintners apply more scientific and technologically-savvy processes to create their products. In my opinion, not only are California wines far more consistent than French wines, but also California wines are very, very good, have gotten a lot better over the last 30 years, and continue to improve. Over the next 20 or 30 years, I expect that California vintners will produce not only consistent products, but also the best in the world. Then and only then, I would expect the French vintners to react to the threat of California wines in earnest.

- **Dress codes; it's time to get rid of suits and formalwear at work:** There is absolutely no reason for any company to enforce a formal dress code on their employees in this modern day and age. Many research papers have been published indicating that dressing down at work helps with productivity and idea generation, not to mention that if companies truly care about their people then they should listen to them. And, any company that makes the excuse that their clients want their employees to dress formally is truly saying that they care more about their clients' "feelings" than their own employees' comfort and productivity. These companies should stop telling their employees that the management cares about their employees and that the employees are the company's most important asset because that is BULLSHIT! Some clever people have argued that if we take the logic to the extreme then we should not prohibit nudity at work. Like I said, clever, but not valid. The reason why we should allow dressing down, but not nudity is because our society's norms and morays have accepted dressing down as a valid form of business dress, but nudity has not been accepted as a norm or moray for any place else other than the privacy of one's home and, in particular, one's own bedroom. In my opinion, formal business wear is jast another way to discriminate and categorize and we should stop this practice. Also, for the vast majority of jobs there is no reason to wear anything other than comfortable clothes. However, dirty clothes are a completely separate issue. Dirty clothes go to health concerns and, therefore, should not be allowed anywhere.

- **It wasn't easier to make money in the past, it jast seems that way because of hindsight:** Every time I've asked people whether they think it was easier to make money in the past or in the present, I don't think I've ever gotten an answer other than that it was easier to make money in the past. I would contend that the reason why everyone thinks so is because people have the benefit of hindsight. What I mean by this is that many people, at present, are trying to figure out if there are better and more lucrative ways to make money and are coming up short. However, when these same people reflect on past innovations, they know exactly what succeeded and could imagine themselves doing what the pioneers did to create new industries and businesses. Also, no one hears many stories of failures in the past, while we witness failures in the present, including our own sometimes. Moreover, we have more knowledge than our ancestors, so many of the past innovations and technologies seem simple and easy to develop versus trying to create something today. However, while it is true that on an absolute basis, past innovations were simpler and easier to develop, I would suggest that the relative knowledge among our peers versus our ancestors' peers would be about the same, which gives neither group an advantage in trying to innovate. Therefore, I would conclude that it was neither easier nor more difficult (relatively or otherwise) to make money in the past.

- **There are certain golf rules that should be changed:**
  1) If a golfer drives the ball in the fairway and the ball stops in a divot, the player should be allowed a free drop. The fairway is supposed to be fair and a divot is not. Therefore, the golfer should be allowed a free drop out of the divot. Also, a golfer should be tested for how well they hit a golf ball, not how lucky they do or don't get.
  2) If a ball is on the green and obstructed by a ball mark, a golfer should be allowed to at least fix the ball mark, if not allowed to move the ball so the ball mark is no longer obstructing the path of the putt. The green should be well kept and pristine. Also, a golfer should be tested for how well they putt a golf ball, not how lucky they do or don't get.
  3) This is more controversial, but I think it should be allowed. If a player finds hes ball in a bunker that was not perfectly raked, I think the player should be allowed to rake the bunker smoothly and place the ball back on the bunker; the only exception would be a fried-egg situation.
  4) If the player did not touch the ball, but it moves because of gravity, wind, or the player walking around the green, the player should not be charged a penalty.
  5) If the ball is on the cart path or the player's foot/feet are on the cart path, the player should be allowed to drop on either side of the cart path within one club length, instead of the cumbersome rules that we have today.
- **The perfect golf score is 36:** Assuming that the course is a standard par-72 with a reasonable total yardage and with 4 par-3s, 4 par-5s and 10 par 4s, the perfect golf score is 36. If the par-5s are reachable in two then the perfect golf score is a 32. On every hole, a player can eagle the hole. This means that a perfect round of golf would be a score of minus-36 for the 18. The perfect score would be lower by one for every par-5 that is reachable in 2 and for every par-4 that is reachable in 1.

Conclusion and Wrap-Up: Justice is the Only Fairness

Justice is the only measure of fairness when dealing with others and for governments the only right public policy

"Equality isn't always Just, but Justice, applied equally, is always fair."

Think about this: If the US government were to impose catholicism as the universal religion for the US and made illegal the worship of another god or religion, who amongst us would agree to that? If the US government were to require everyone to donate 10% of their income to charities that are designated as the "right" charities, no one would agree to that either. Why not?

Part of the reason why people wouldn't agree to either would be because people not only want the freedom to choose, but also, and more importantly, people want to control their own destiny and their own property. In other words, people want to be able to make the decisions for what to believe-in and how to spend their money for themselves. People don't want the government telling them what to believe in and how to spend their money. And, it does not matter that the greatest majority of the country decided to vote for the worship of catholicism or that the overwhelming majority decided which charities are worthy and which are not. Finally, one could cite the Constitution's guarantee of freedom of religion as the reason why someone would oppose mandatory worship of the catholic version of god and their interpretation of its will as the main reason for why someone would oppose mandatory religious worship. However, has anyone ever asked why the Constitution was written to not allow mandatory worship of a single religion?

Most people who have studied the Constitution tell me that religious persecution was the main reason why some people fled Europe and that is why the Constitution was written to ensure that religious freedom was preserved in the US. Then one may ask why is religious freedom so important that the Constitution was written to guarantee it? I never got a good answer to this question from anyone. But, I do have an opinion – surprise, surprise – as to why religious freedom is so important.

Look at the history of religion: How many wars, how many conflicts, how many lives were destroyed by religious strife? However, if there was a country that could guarantee the rights of every human to worship whichever god they wanted, would that not promote peace? How many religious-based wars or conflicts have we had in the US? It should be no surprise that we've never had any religious-based wars in the US. So, what is the difference between religious freedom and philosophical freedom?

If we strip out the deity factor, religion is jast another philosophy. Think about it carefully. Religion promotes a way of life. I'll let individuals figure out the how and the whys, but if one wants to figure it out, start with the ten commandments in the bible. If people think about it, the judeo-christian framework is about obeying its version of god and living the life that its god wants people to live. And, the reason why people are told to obey its god is to become a better person and because it is supposedly our creator that is benevolent, omniscient, omnipotent and omnipresent or so the fairytale goes. And, because it is triple-O, we are told that if we do wrong by their version of god, we will go to hell for eternity and if we do well, we will go to heaven for eternity. Bottom-line, we are told to follow the word of the jc god to become a better person and be a benevolent factor on earth.

Moving on to philosophy, it is about how to live one's life with the expectation that if we do live the life spelled out in a particular philosophy that we become a better person and we are rewarded with good feelings and good things in life. Many philosophies also attempt to explain how the universe functions and why it functions that way. So, then, what's the difference between philosophy and religion? The only difference is the deity factor, that's all. But, from a practical day-to-day living perspective, there is hardly any difference between what religion is trying to promote and what philosophy is trying to promote. And, if we take into consideration that we cannot even come close to proving (or disproving in some people's mind, which I don't agree with) the existence of any god or gods then there really is absolutely no difference between religion and philosophy.

Therefore, the freedom of religion in the Constitution should be equally applied to freedom of philosophy. In other words, the freedom to worship what and who one wants, which then translates into the freedom to live the way one wants to should be no different than the freedom to believe in whichever philosophy one wants to, which then leads to the freedom to live the way one wants to. Either way, we end up exactly in the same place: Everyone believes in something, whether it's religion or philosophy; we believe in what it is that either is trying to teach us how to be and how it is that we should want to live in order to have a richer, fuller and better life. So, the US government should want and, more precisely, every American should want the freedom of philosophy as much as the freedom of religion.

The problem with today's laws and rules in the western hemisphere is that they are based on the judeo-christian moral philosophy and the rules and laws do not allow anyone the freedom of philosophy and imposes the judeo-christian philosophy on everyone. This has resulted in socialization of our country: Forced charity. This is wrong, not only because it violates the Constitutional rights to freedom of religion (including philosophy), but also because it deprives us of the right to our own assets and property against our will and more importantly against our philosophy.

From the tax aspect, which is what I started with, this means that current government policy forces everyone that is deemed "wealthy," which is very arbitrarily determined by majority vote, to subsidies the less affluent. This means that the "wealthy" do not have the right to their own property and assets, because the majority, who is substantially less "wealthy," will always vote to take from the "rich." This will be particularly true if the less fortunate are told that the right to steal from others is justified, whether it is called taxes, redistribution of wealth, social justice or fluberguble. In the prelude, I stated that I will show that most people believe in the following seven premises:

1) People believe that two wrongs do make a right,
2) People believe that stealing is righteous,
3) People believe that thinking is wrong and that they shouldn't do it,
4) Rules and laws are always right,
5) It is justified to have slaves in society,
6) That equality is Justice, i.e., people are largely strong believers in communism, and
7) That dictatorship is perfectly fine as a form of government in the US.

The fact that people continue to vote for socialization of wealth and forced charity proves that people believe 1) and 2). People believe that poverty in and of itself is something that must be rectified and that it is wrong to have poverty when the country as a whole is so wealthy. So, people believe that poverty should be eradicated and so they support "social programs" in the name of "social justice" and vote for taxing the "wealthy" more than the poor on both a relative and on an absolute basis. This is what proves that people believe in 2).

Then people believe that because these higher "taxes" are law that they must be enforced, regardless of the morality of these laws, which is why I say people believe in 4). The problem is that when people decide that so called "progressive taxes" are fair, not only are they justifying the immoral seizure of property and assets, people are also saying that it is moral for one group of society to be enslaved by the other, because stealing from one group to support another is moral and that forcing one group to partly pay for another's life style is also morally justified. This is why I said that most Americans believe in 5). Now, the thing is that people do all of this with the righteous indignation of the moral and the heroic, because they believe that equality in wealth is absolutely correct and, therefore, moral, no matter how the poor became poor and the wealthy became wealthy. People do all of this without realizing that they are actually supporting and justifying immorality and communism, and ignoring the fact that equality isn't always Just and Justice isn't always equal. So, this is why I say most Americans believe in 6). Also, people believe that equality is always Just and that Justice must always mean equality. No, actually, there is a relationship between equality and Justice, but it isn't what people may think:

❖ *Equality isn't always Just, and Justice doesn't always mean equality, but Justice applied correctly is always fair and must be applied equally*, or put another way,
❖ *Equality isn't always Just, but Justice applied equally is always fair*.

Then people believe that because the US tax system is voted on by the masses and approved by the masses that it is fair and Just. However, in reality, like freedom of speech, like the right to vote and like the issue of slavery, there are certain rights that cannot, must not and should not be put to a vote, i.e., they should be inalienable, unabridged, and interminable rights. The right to one's property and the right to do with it as one pleases should be one of those inalienable, unabridged, and interminable rights. Regardless, people believe that one's property shouldn't be in one's control and that the disposition of it should be prioritized by people other than the owner of the property, and that properties should be forcibly removed from the owners, if the owners don't succumb to the extortion racket. This is why I say that people believe in 7), because people believe that the masses have the right to vote on how wealthier people must spend their hard earned money. So, people believe in the dictatorship of the masses.

Lastly and finally, people believe that I'm nuts and even refuse to rationally consider my position and argument, mostly because it is so contrary to what they've been taught, know and what other people agree with, but also because they cannot think the issues through. Many people are lost and can't even follow the logic and those that can have visceral reactions and display strong emotional attachments that won't allow them to think and be rational. This is what makes me believe that people don't, won't and can't think, which goes to show why point 3) above is true. However, even among the rare ones that do get it, they talk about how my position is ideal, but impractical. And, they say this with such pride – and sometimes condescension – as if they already knew everything that I've said, but didn't take it any further because of the impractical aspects of my plan, which makes it useless to contemplate.

So, even those that have the rudimentary ability to think, can't think beyond the tip of their nose, and believe that it is wrong to be ideal due to short-term concerns when in fact the ideal is the only practical solution in the long-term. Jast look at the slavery issue. Many well-intentioned people objected to the end of slavery because of what they conceived of being as the impractical aspects of not knowing what to do with or expect from freed slaves. Does anybody think there are impractical issues in dealing with freed slaves today?

"Practical" arguments for why something should not be done are jast another excuse to not behavior properly from people that are clever in knowing how to disguise their objections to do the right thing. Alternatively, some who raise practical issues as objections to doing the right thing could be lazy or weak minded. If one looks back at history, there have been a lot of objections to why something should not be done due to practical reasons; however, over the long-run these arguments are forgotten and nullified. Another example of this can be clearly discernible from the civil rights movement. How many arguments were made about how impractical it would be to integrate schools, public facilities, and private businesses? Another example can be seen with the integration of the military. Regardless, I don't think there are more than a handful of people left that still believe that there are integration problems in the US. All that the arguments of practicality amount to are excuses not to chase after the ideal objective. Period, full-stop, the end. The problem is that most people are heavily swayed by these short-term arguments of practicality, which again goes to prove that most people don't know how to think. Don't forget, throughout our history, when **tasked to do the right thing**, we –

Americans – have found ways to make sure that the right-thing happens. Look at what we have accomplished since before the Revolutionary War: We over-threw the yoke of tyranny, held together a country through multiple external and internal threats, including the Civil War, we ended slavery in the US, we gave equal voting rights to women in the US, we helped save Europe twice from destroying itself, we ended tyranny in Germany and Japan, we saved at least the southern portion of Korea from disintegrating into oblivion, we largely ended discrimination in the US, and we are helping the Iraqis and Afghans find freedom and have a real chance at raising their standard of living.

Our last great challenge should not be to end poverty, because no matter what we do, poverty will always be with us, and if we are to have a healthy society, there's no avoiding it, nor should we try to. Instead, what we need to focus on as a country are three important objectives: 1) Continued technological leadership and innovation, 2) an end to property rights discrimination and philosophical discrimination, but most of all 3) we must learn to think rationally for the long-term. Don't forget that the current tax system is jast postponing the inevitable and is jast not the right public policy. If we continue on this path, we will end up like Greece. It may take 50 more years or even a 100 more years to get there, but it is inevitable. This is not a matter of conjecture, speculation or wishful (or hateful?) thinking, this is an absolute fact proven by history in many countries.

Also, the most important point that must be remembered is that my plan gives **EVERYONE** the right to live their life the way they want to. The current tax plan and social philosophy does not. If we cut everyone's taxes to support only self-defense, infrastructure and education there would be a lot of money left over for everyone to spend as they wish. If individuals want to spend all of their excess money on charitable contributions then they can do so. If people want to invest 100% of it then they can do that instead. If Americans want to keep it all in their bank account then they can do that too. Each American has the choice and the freedom to do with *their money what they will* under my plan.

And, for the last time, please stop talking about how poor people will rebel, because they are poor, and, therefore, how everyone else's charitable contributions to the poor are helping me for free. Absolutely not! When people make charitable contributions, all that they are doing is they are helping to extend poverty, prolonging and extending not only the feeling of entitlement, but also the right to entitlements, especially if it comes through government programs. What's worse, if people allow government "social programs" to make these charitable contributions then we will **ALL DROWN IN DEBT**, and **ALL OF US** will get dragged into financial hell. If people continue to allow government theft of the wealthy, they'll come to realize that the Great Recession was only a taste of what's to come, and only the tip of the iceberg. And, note that this burden of debt will affect our children and grandchildren far worse than it would us.

So, it has now come down to everyone needing to make a choice. Our current path may help resolve short-term issues, but by definition, the problems will come back – and comeback far worse overtime – because all that is currently being done is helping to soothe short-term problems and not addressing the long-term fundamental issues. My plan will exacerbate the short-term problems, I guarantee it, but the extent of the pain is only reflective of how corrupt and decrepit our policies have been, particularly over the last 80 years, and how much we have to change to get back to true long-term and sustainable prosperity. But, I will also guarantee that the pain will end and after this painful period, we will be on a path to long-term and sustainable prosperity. Does this mean that we will have no more recessions or depressions? No. Does this mean that we will end poverty? No. Does this mean that we will end unemployment? No. So, what am I promising to deliver?

I'm promising to deliver long-term prosperity in the sense that recessions will become shorter and shorter, less intense and far easier to work out of over time. I'm promising that poverty will not end, but that there'll be far fewer poor people and our standard of living will increase faster and go higher. I'm not promising the end of unemployment, but lower and more sustainable overall unemployment. But most of all, I'm promising that under my plan technology and innovation will be faster in coming and more of it will be available at a cheaper price. And, more importantly, I promise that more and more capital and intelligent labor will flow to the US to fuel this innovation and technological development, which in turn will help sustain our economic growth, keep unemployment low, and reduce poverty, which then attracts more capital and more intelligent labor, which then fuels the virtuous cycle.

Ultimately, it comes down to two things and two things only when it comes to taxes: 1) Who owns the money that is being collected for taxes, and 2) Is the tax money being collected directly benefitting the tax payer? If the answer is anything but 1) the person who earned the money, and 2) yes, then we have a very immoral situation that must be corrected immediately. As a society, we must never forget these two questions and answers. Moreover, if these two principles are violated, we, as a society, must rectify the situation with all due haste and urgency, because there is no moral violation that is irrelevant or meaningless. Morality by its very nature is based on principles, which are thoughts resident in your mind and are typically only enforced by inner determination to preserve it. Therefore, violations of moral principles are easy and, in many cases, unnoticeable. But it is this very fragile and tenuous nature of morality that makes it incredibly important to not allow even minor violations, because, as easy as it is to violate moral principles, it is incredibly difficult to correct the violations.

Ultimately, everyone has to choose, but keep in mind that we don't have much time left to decide. And, the longer we wait to solve the long-term problems, the exponentially more painful and more difficult they will become to fix.

Legality is meaningless, if it isn't moral

The vast majority of Americans believes and thinks that laws are absolute. Absolute in the sense that laws are to be absolutely obeyed, absolute in the sense that laws are absolutely right, and absolute in the sense that laws are absolutely moral. However, laws aren't always absolute, nor always right, and certainly not always moral. Look at slavery laws, voting laws (or more accurately, laws to limit voting rights), segregation laws and Jim Crow laws. These laws once held great sway and support in our country, but none of them exist in our society today. Once laws, they were deemed to be so immoral and decrepit that we even fought wars to end some of them, not jast in the US, but all over the world. So, what is the meaning of laws?

Bear in mind that laws in and of themselves are meaningless. Laws should only have meaning and bear obeying because of the moral weight that it reflects. So, when thinking about what is right or wrong, don't think about what is legal or illegal think about what is moral or immoral. The rest of it is a distraction. So, don't be afraid to break rules and laws, if you know them to be antiquated, irrelevant, immoral, wrong or evil. But, most of all, don't be afraid to fight for a change in law when you know it to be immoral, wrong or evil, remembering that certain laws, while in the context of one action is moral, but in the context of another is immoral. For example, while the white supremacists and bigots only saw that civil rights protesters were breaking the law by demonstrating without proper permits, the right to protest injustice can never be immoral. So, while protesting without proper permits was illegal and should be illegal, the act of protest to stand-up for the rights of the oppressed in the face of authorities who would not issue permits to civil rights protestors is absolutely the right behavior.

So, remember that legal is wrong when it is immoral and no matter how illegal, if it is moral then it is right. Slavery though legal was wrong because it is immoral, and this immorality was the reason that many people fought for the overturn of slavery. Therefore, while smuggling slaves out of the south to freedom in the north was illegal, it was supremely moral to do so. In today's context, while the so called "progressive tax" is legal, it is immoral, because it supports theft and promotes biased treatment of a minority of our citizens by our government and the majority. Therefore, it should be overturned and a new tax system that treats every citizen the same way and for the same benefits should be developed and executed.

Always remember: Legal isn't always right and moral, while many moral acts and behaviors can be illegal.-What everyone must focus on is that which is moral, and not on that which is legal. Most importantly, fight for that which is moral and Just, even if it means engaging in behaviors that are deemed illegal, like protesting without proper permits.

So, for example, some of the most decrepit laws that we should fight to abolish in our society today other than the so called "progressive tax" system are: Laws opposing gay marriage, laws curbing the right of women to abortions, and anti-suicide laws. There are also so called "morality laws" that are highly immoral: Anti-prostitution laws, anti-gambling laws, and anti-drug laws, among others. Any true American must fight to abolish these immoral and unjust laws and any other immoral and unjust laws, rules, and regulations in our country.

Biography and Other

A great time to lie

For those that are wondering, "who the hell is this arrogant person that is telling us, 'you screwed up the world, so fix it!'" I will say this: I am a true American, and true Americans focus on Justice and nothing but Justice. I am not an Islamist, and my name is not Alex Hussein Ahmedinejahd (Aha!). I picked this name to drive home the point that the superficial is irrelevant and anyone who focuses on the superficial and are pretentious should be ostracized from our society. Also, I have nothing to do with any sort of organized or other forms of religion. In case people are wondering, let me make it perfectly clear, I'm not an atheist, I'm not an agnostic; I don't define myself in terms of any religious terminology; I'm a believer in Justice, a faithful practitioner of Justicism and consider myself a Justisopher. I've made up two words and will make-up another: 1) I'm a Justicist – a person that believes in, stands for and acts on behalf of Justice, 2) I believe in and am a practitioner of Justicism – the belief that there is no more noble cause and honorable pursuit than Justice for all mankind, and 3) I am a Justisopher – a lover of Justice, and a thought leader, practitioner and student of Justice. And, again, I did not write this book in anger, and I am not an angry person! I am passionate, emotional, outspoken, speak my mind and proudly exercise my judgment, but I'm not an angry person.

The most important concept in this book and the world is Justice. Therefore, from now on Justice should be spelt with a capital "J" to represent the primary importance of this concept and philosophy above all else. Has anyone ever noticed that the diminutive application of the word "just," as in "don't pay him any mind, he's just retarded" has the same spelling as the most important concept to man called Justice as in "we have to have the same flat tax amount for every individual to make the tax system Just for all." If I were a conspiracy nut, I'd think that this was deliberate by the people who controlled the development of language, having been very heavily influenced by the jc hierarchy.

Regardless, I propose some changes to the way we spell words to de-emphasize the irrelevant and highlight that which is more important:

- Most importantly change the reference to the jc god to "god" from "God."
- In fact, we should get rid of all references to and use of the word god and replace it with the universal word that refers to people's imagined super-

being, which is referred to typically as a "deity," since all gods are creation of man.

- Unify all religious importance to what it is: That which is no different than any paganism beliefs by changing the capitalization of judaism/jews/christianity/christians/catholicism/catholics, et cetera.

- In contrast, as previously stated, we should change the convention for the spelling of just/justice to Just/Justice, given the supreme importance to humanity and humanity's future.

- To distinguish between the diminutive application of "just" and the all-important Just, the diminutive spelling should be changed to jast from "just."

Moving on; most people probably already figured out that I'm not a writer. And, I apologize now and forever more for my long prose and repetitiveness. So, anyway, who am I? The following is a description/biography of who and what I am. However, because I want to remain anonymous, I'm not going to reveal my gender, race, physical characteristics, location of my childhood, my profession, my area of residence, and age, and some "facts" I list here will be outright lies. Yes, it is OK to lie in this instance, because I'm pursuing a higher value to me: Me and my family's privacy and safety. Besides, I'm warning my audience that not everything is true ahead of time. So, here goes.

➢ I was born in Europe, but grew up most of my life in the US.
➢ I was born a US citizen, and live somewhere in the 50 states, but travel a lot.
➢ I have multiple advance degrees in engineering, business, finance, and economics, but no philosophy degree.
➢ I am married to the love of my life and soul mate.
➢ I have two children.
➢ I hate injustice with a passion, no matter what form it comes in.
➢ I'm not a millionaire, but I am better off than most and have a source of income.
➢ I've lived in many countries including some in Europe and the Americas, and a little in Asia.
➢ I enjoy playing some sports, but the sporting event that I like to watch most is the Olympics.
➢ I like romance and get emotional when watching Bud Greenspan's Olympic series – I am very sorry to see him pass and hope that someone else will follow his work – and shed tears for people who overcome injustice or

struggle to succeed, but couldn't care less about homeless people in general.

➤ I hate people that are blindly religious, superficial, pretentious, politically correct, short-sighted, sugar-coat words and ideas, indecisive, careless, foolish, don't respect people for who they are, but respect people for what they are, and I don't like people that treat others with disrespect and disdain, because they can and can get away with it. Most of all, I hate the vast majority of politicians, all stripes and colors of the jc clergy, sexists, bigots, socialists, communists, terrorists, rapists, child molesters, and powerful and wealthy people that abuse their power and wealth to get what they don't deserve.

➤ I find that a lot of physically beautiful people are like a beautiful sculpture made from shit and spray painted in gold.

➤ I respect, admire and reward our military personnel and have done so long before it was popular to do so.

➤ I don't have a lot of friends, but a handful of close friends.

➤ I'm afraid of being murdered by some religious nut job or some freak that wants to gain fame for the sake of it, if I do become influential and famous, which is one of the reasons why I choose to be anonymous. By the way, I want to be influential, but I don't want to be famous, and this is because I want to guard my privacy and my family's privacy, and my security and my family's security. In this regard, the Supreme Court got it wrong, there is no reason that because someone makes a living from getting paid by and seeking wealth from the public (actors, athletes, famous people in general) that that is an automatic license for the paparazzi or others to invade the famous person's privacy.

➤ I enjoy managing my own money and will only trust a very small handful of people to give me advice in financial matters or give them my money to manage.

➤ I am not physically handicapped, blind, deaf or retarded (at least by most standards).

➤ My IQ is about 130-145 depending on who measures it and how it's measured, i.e., I'm not a genius.

➤ My favorite colors are primary colors, and black and white depending on the purpose and reason.

➤ I don't have a favorite car, or dream about a particular home.

- I enjoy going to Las Vegas and indulge in low stakes gaming, but go for mostly golf, food and shows.
- I've never employed an escort, male or female, nor have I ever visited a bordello or "stud ranch."
- I occasionally enjoy an alcohol-based drink, but don't smoke, and I'm proud that I've never, ever taken any form of illicit drugs.
- I'm generally fairly quiet and easy going, but when someone touches my nerve or I get going on a particular subject that I'm interested in, I am very passionate; however, many people are intimidated by my passion or think I'm "out of control." This should not surprise anyone since most people aren't passionate about anything significant, are insecure, think showing others any kind of emotion is wrong, regardless of circumstances and situations, don't understand passionate behavior and can't tell the difference between passion, emotion, and plain-old craziness.
- I'm blunt to a fault, and don't mince words, but I don't mean to offend, insult or disrespect, unless I'm provoked then try stopping me; I'll give the offending person a piece of my mind and then some.
- I'm not a smooth talker, and certainly far removed from being politically correct as they come.
- I love dogs, but I'm not a big cat fan, and I'm not thrilled about insects, rodents and reptiles.
- Hawaii is one of our favorite places to go, and my entire family loves to snorkel in Hawaii.
- I like to visit Europe for certain cultural and culinary activities and believe that the main reason that they don't like us is because we are obnoxiously loud and too self-righteous and self-indulgent.
- I speak a little bit of French and Spanish to be dangerous, and believe that all Americans should be at least bilingual, and live in a third-world country for at least three years of their lives.
- I believe that there is a time and a place for almost everything, even profanity.
- I believe in capital punishment, corporal punishment and real deterrence.
- I have been told that I make Ronald Reagan look like a communist and that Genghis Khan is on the political left compared to me.
- I'm writing this book in the hopes of changing the world for the better, starting with the US.

- ➤ Fox TV show *Glee* rules; favorite characters are Rachel (Lea Michelle), Brittney (Heather Morris), Coach Sylvester (Jane Lynch), Kurt (Chris Colfer), and Finn (Cory Monteith) in our family.
- ➤ We also enjoy *American Idol* and *So You Think You Can Dance*.
- ➤ We think Lea Michelle is probably one of the top 10 best non-operatic singers alive today in the US, if not the world. The others that make up the top 10 may include some of the following, in our opinion, Josh Groban, Jennifer Hudson, Beyonce, Adam Lambert, Crystal Bowersox, Jessica Sanchez, Amber Riley, Joshua Ledet, Barbara Streisand, Maria Carey, Idina Menzel, Kristin Chenoweth, Celine Dion, and Charice.

I hope you enjoyed reading my book and, at the least, I helped stimulate your mind and provided endless topics for conversation among your friends, co-workers, relatives and family. Furthermore, I hope to convert you to a Justicist and a believer in Justicism for I truly believe that Justice is the only means of dealing with people, and rational thoughts and assumptions based on inalienable and universal rights are the only basis for communication and Justice. If anything, I hope you understand that we – Americans – are headed in a bad direction and that we don't have much time to fix our problems. Socialism, not capitalism, has had 80 years of time to do right for our country and has failed miserably and repeatedly. So, I believe it is time for a change. We must eradicate all traces of socialism and communism in our country and go back to the roots of our country, which are true individual rights, true capitalism and true Justice. And, I strongly believe that my book puts us on the right path, if adopted. However, there still needs to be much discussion to work out the details on how to execute my vision. Most importantly, I am not going to be 100% right about everything and would welcome debate and criticism, but I ask people to do so in a rational manner without appeal to religious doctrine, discussion of any god's will – whichever god that may be – nor on an "emotional" basis or based on a plea for humanity – whatever that means.

If you've enjoyed reading my book, please find ways to **BUY** multiple copies and distribute them to your friends and family, and also recommend my book to your friends, family, relatives, colleagues and co-workers for **PURCHASE**. In general, please recommend my book, but discourage everyone from copying, downloading and otherwise obtaining the book without proper payment. Thank you for your ownership of my book, and mostly, thank you for reading it.

And, I wish Justice always prevails for you and your family, and that you and your family always pursue Justice.

One last thing: If you know who I am or even if you think you may know who I am, please don't discuss with anyone or tell anyone or approach me or ask me. Thank you.

Please feel free to visit my website for discussions of all the issues in my book and more at www.undertheconstitutionwithlibertyandjusticeforall.com. I can also be reached at alexahmedinejahd@yahoo.com. Thank you.

www.ingramcontent.com/pod-product-compliance
Lightning Source LLC
Chambersburg PA
CBHW070539270326
41926CB00013B/2149